Ordnance Survey Ireland

National M
ww

G000292707

SPECIAL THANKS TO FÁILTE IRELAND, DUBLIN CITY COUNCIL,
DÚN - LAOGHAIRE RATHDOWN COUNTY COUNCIL,
FINGAL COUNTY COUNCIL AND SOUTH DUBLIN COUNTY COUNCIL.

Map data reprinted with amendments 2015.

11th Edition Published December 2015

10th Edition Published 2013
9th Edition Published 2010   8th Edition Published 2009   7th Edition Published 2007
6th Edition Published 2005   5th Edition Published 2004   4th Edition Published 2002
3rd Edition Published 1999   2nd Edition Published 1997   1st Edition Published 1995

Route Planner	
M50 Map	II
OSI Publications and Tourist Information	III-IV
Dublin Public Transport Frequent Services	V-VI
Dublin City Council Information	VII-VIII
Dublin City and District Maps	1-68
City Centre Maps	69-76
Town Maps	77-92

Town Maps

77	Ashbourne	86	Dunshaughlin
79	Balbriggan	87	Kilcock
81	Blessington	88	Lusk
82	Clane	89	Rush
83	Delgany/Greystones	91	Ratoath
85	Donabate	92	Skerries

Garda Road Safety Information	93-94
Embassies	95
List of Hospitals	96
Industrial Estates and Business Parks	97-98
Street Index	99

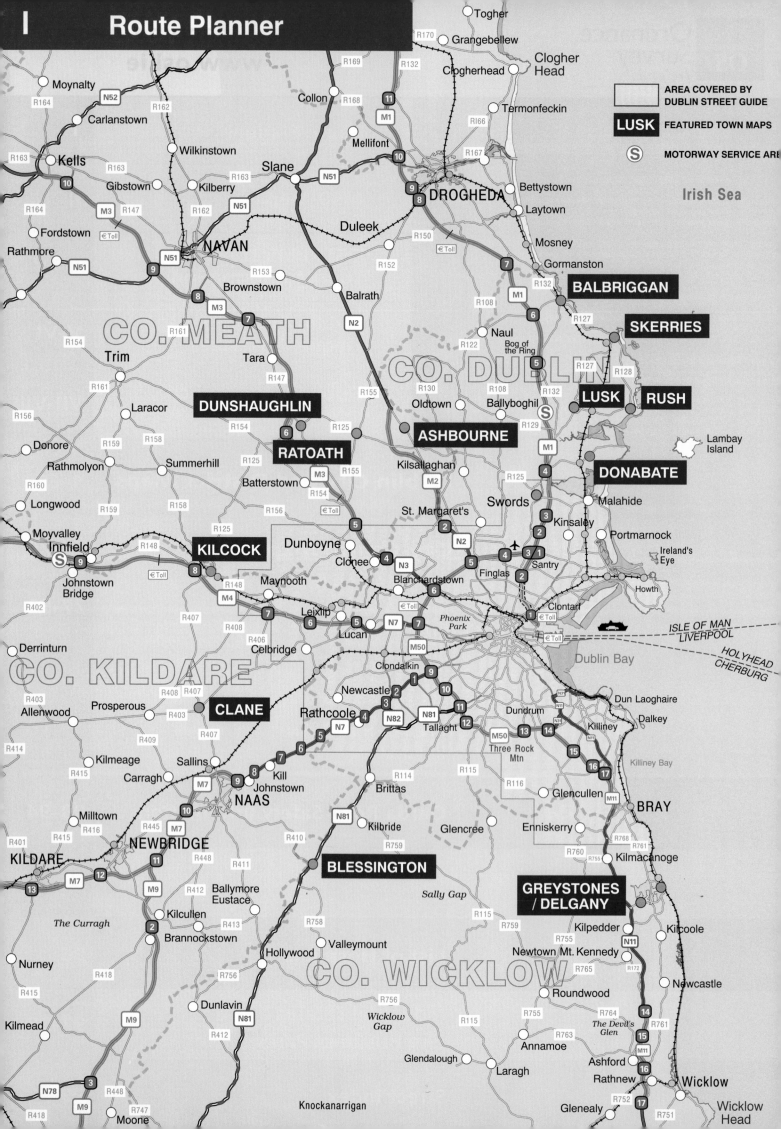

Route Planner

Bray to Ballymount

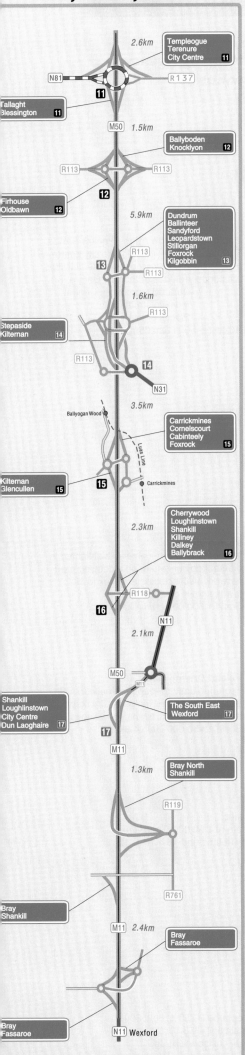

Ballymount to East Wall

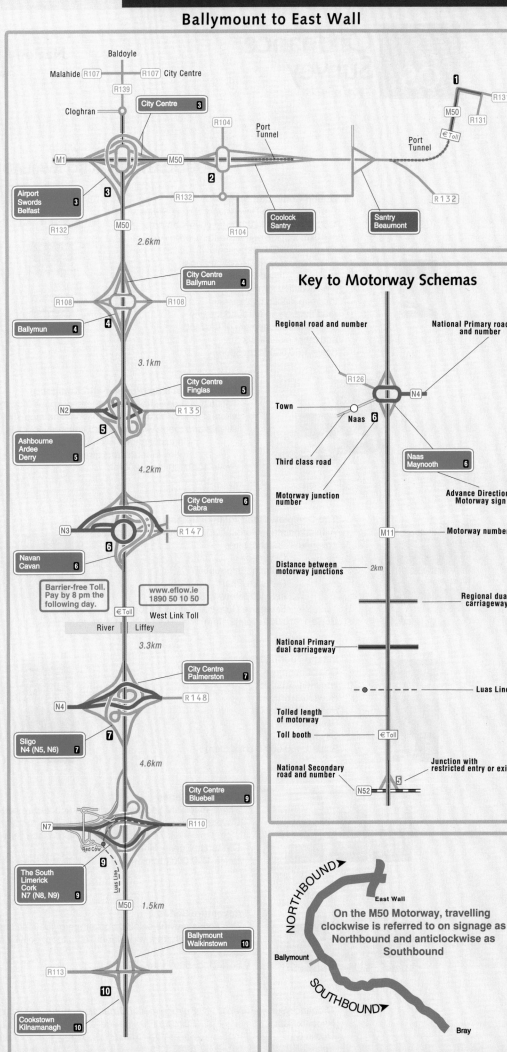

Key to Motorway Schemas

- Regional road and number — R126
- Town
- Naas
- Third class road
- Motorway junction number
- National Primary road and number — N4
- Naas Maynooth 6 — Advance Direction Motorway sign
- M11 — Motorway number
- Distance between motorway junctions — 2km
- Regional dual carriageway
- National Primary dual carriageway
- Luas Line
- Tolled length of motorway
- Toll booth — €Toll
- National Secondary road and number — N52
- Junction with restricted entry or exit — 5

On the M50 Motorway, travelling clockwise is referred to on signage as Northbound and anticlockwise as Southbound

NORTHBOUND
East Wall
Ballymount
SOUTHBOUND
Bray

Barrier-free Toll. Pay by 8 pm the following day.
€Toll

www.eflow.ie
1890 50 10 50
West Link Toll

River | Liffey

National Mapping Agency
www.osi.ie

PUBLICATIONS ALSO AVAILABLE

Dublin Commuter Map
Derived from the Discovovery Series Series
1:50,000 mapping,this map covers an area
of 40km x 30km of the greater Dublin Area.
·HGV restrictions
·Speed Detection Zones
·Tolled Roads
Ideally suited for the motorist,
this map highlights the main
road through and around the city
and detailed schemata of the M50
and other motorways.
Scale 1:50,000 (1cm:500m)

Dublin City Centre Atlas - Pocket Series
This handy pocket guide of the city centre
area is invaluable for those whose activities
are concentrated near the City Centre:
·Detailed Map of city Centre
·Index to streets
·Places of Interest
Scale 1:6 500 (1cm:65m)

Dublin Street Map (Popular and Compact)
This easy-to-use street and general purpose map includes
a street index and tourist information. The map shows
streets and roads with additional features including
·Tourist features and public buildings
·Index to roads and streets
Scale 1:20 000 (1cm:200m)

The Complete Road Atlas of Ireland
A spiral-bound motoring guide, containing road maps
covering all ireland, plus:
·City maps
·Motoring Information
·Distance Chart
·Ireland Moterway Schema
·Extensive Gazetteer (index to Town)
Scale 1:210 000 (1cm:2.1km)

Ireland Map
Map of Ireland with counties highlighted in
different colours featuring a detailed road
network also including an index to all
towns shown on the map.
Scale 1:600 000 (1cm:6km)

Ireland Touring Map
One of our most popular maps,
featuring detailed
Road network
Holiday information
Scenic routes
City maps
Scale 1:450 000 (1cm:4.5km)

Ireland Driving Map
Featuring easy-to-read road network with
distance indicators. Includes City Maps
and index to cities, towns and villages.
Scale 1:450 000 (1cm:4.5km)

Discovery Series
These maps are designed for tourist and leisure activities.
Covers an area approximately 40km x 30km at the scale of 1:50 000. There are
92 in the series; 74 are published by Ordnance Survey Ireland and 18 by
Ordnance Survey Northern Ireland.
Scale 1:50 000 (1cm:500m)

Adventure Series
This series provide selective coverage of the Irish landscape will focus on
those areas where a wide variety of outdoor activity or adventure tourism
takes place.
Scale 1:25 000 (1cm:250m)

Ordnance Survey Ireland
Phoenix Park
Dublin 8
Ireland

Suirbhéireacht Ordanáis Éireann
Páirc an Fhionnuisce
Baile Átha Cliath 8
Éire

Telephone [+353 1] 8025300
Facsimile [+353 1] 8204156
email custserv@osi.ie

Connect with us today on #LOVEDUBLIN

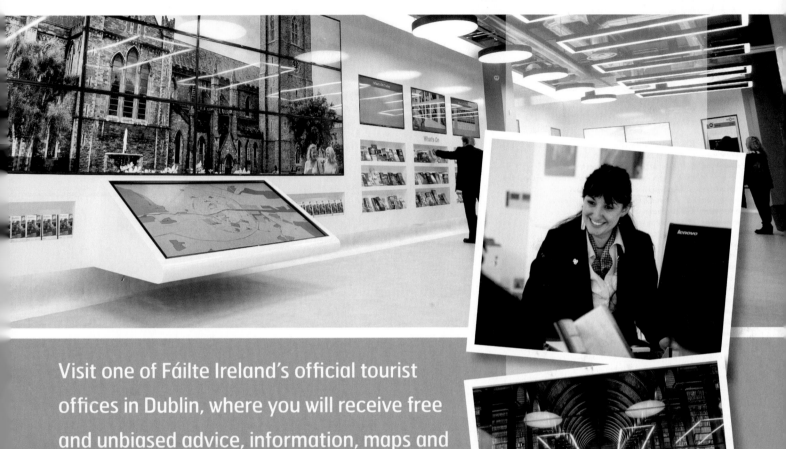

Visit one of Fáilte Ireland's official tourist offices in Dublin, where you will receive free and unbiased advice, information, maps and literature from the people who know the city best. You can also book accommodation, attractions, events, festivals, tickets and tours.

>> **Visit Dublin Centre**,
25 Suffolk Street, Dublin 2

>> **Discover Ireland Centre**,
14 Upper O'Connell Street, Dublin 1

>> **Discover Ireland Centre**,
Arrivals Hall, Terminal 1, Dublin Airport

>> **Discover Ireland Centre**,
Arrivals Hall, Terminal 2, Dublin Airport

National Tourist Information Line: **1850 230 330**

DISCOVERIRELAND.IE

visit **Dublin** .com

Dublin Public Transport Frequent Services

V

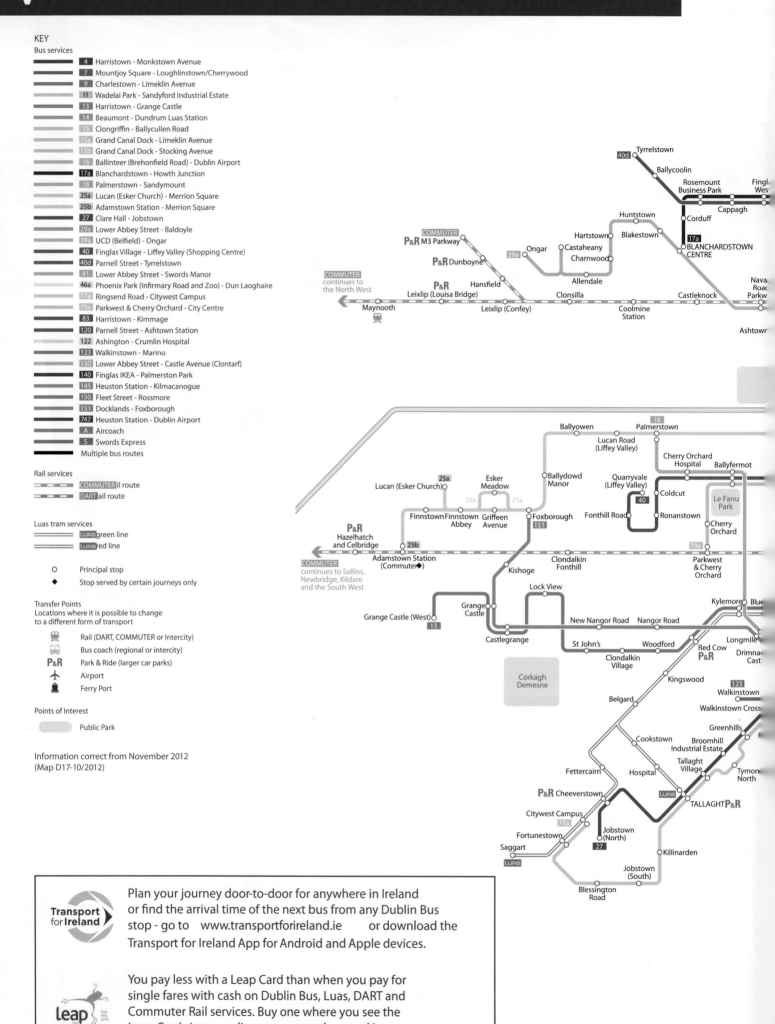

KEY

Bus services

4	Harristown - Monkstown Avenue
7	Mountjoy Square - Loughlinstown/Cherrywood
9	Charlestown - Limeklin Avenue
11	Wadelai Park - Sandyford Industrial Estate
13	Harristown - Grange Castle
14	Beaumont - Dundrum Luas Station
15	Clongriffin - Ballycullen Road
15a	Grand Canal Dock - Limeklin Avenue
15b	Grand Canal Dock - Stocking Avenue
16	Ballinteer (Brehonfield Road) - Dublin Airport
17a	Blanchardstown - Howth Junction
18	Palmerstown - Sandymount
25a	Lucan (Esker Church) - Merrion Square
25b	Adamstown Station - Merrion Square
27	Clare Hall - Jobstown
29a	Lower Abbey Street - Baldoyle
39a	UCD (Belfield) - Ongar
40	Finglas Village - Liffey Valley (Shopping Centre)
40d	Parnell Street - Tyrrelstown
41	Lower Abbey Street - Swords Manor
46a	Phoenix Park (Infirmary Road and Zoo) - Dun Laoghaire
77a	Ringsend Road - Citywest Campus
79a	Parkwest & Cherry Orchard - City Centre
83	Harristown - Kimmage
120	Parnell Street - Ashtown Station
122	Ashington - Crumlin Hospital
123	Walkinstown - Marino
130	Lower Abbey Street - Castle Avenue (Clontarf)
140	Finglas IKEA - Palmerston Park
145	Heuston Station - Kilmacanogue
150	Fleet Street - Rossmore
151	Docklands - Foxborough
747	Heuston Station - Dublin Airport
A	Aircoach
S	Swords Express
	Multiple bus routes

Rail services

COMMUTER rail route
DART rail route

Luas tram services

LUAS green line
LUAS red line

○ Principal stop
◆ Stop served by certain journeys only

Transfer Points
Locations where it is possible to change
to a different form of transport

🚉 Rail (DART, COMMUTER or Intercity)
🚌 Bus coach (regional or intercity)
P&R Park & Ride (larger car parks)
✈ Airport
⚓ Ferry Port

Points of Interest

Public Park

Information correct from November 2012
(Map D17-10/2012)

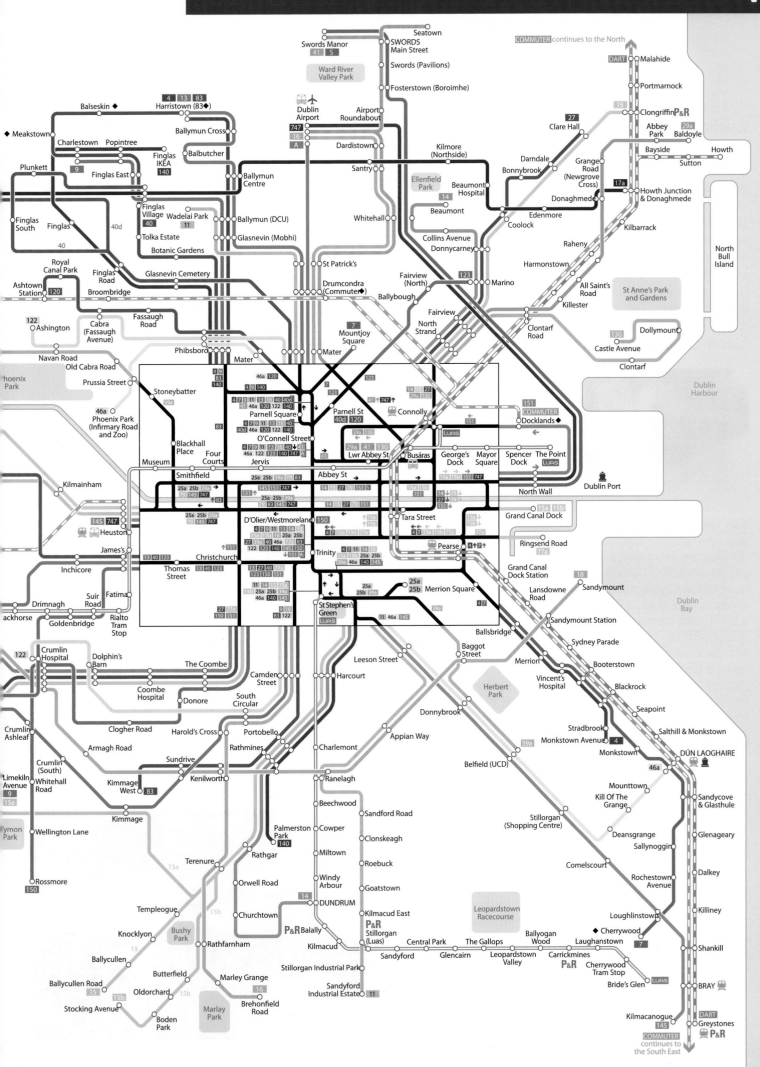

Cycling in Dublin

Dublin City Council has played a leading role in the growth of cycling within the City. Council initiatives such as Coca-Cola Zero Dublin bikes, which has seen over 10 million journeys taken since its launch in 2009, awareness raising events like Dublin Bike week and better cycling facilities have contributed to this growth. For information on cycling in Dublin, safety tips, maps of family-friendly cycling trails in Dublin city parks and much more see **www.cycledublin.ie**

Coca-Cola Zero dublinbike

This is one of the world's most successful bicycle rental schemes. There are over 55,000 annual subscribers and this number is continuing to grow. Members have taken taken over ten million Coca-Cola Zero dublinbikes journeys since the scheme was launched in 2009. The first 30 minutes are free and it's a great way to get around the city. There are 1,500 bicycles based at 101 stations in the heart of the city. Annual membership via **www.dublinbikes.ie** costs just €20. You can also join as a short-term member for three days at credit card enabled stations for €5. The scheme is open from 5:30am until 12:30am, seven days a week and you can return a bike 24 hours a day so day trippers or night owls are easily catered for. Bicycle docking stations are located in close proximity to key attractions in the city so all of Dublin's major cultural attractions are within easy reach.

Canal Way Cycle Route pp 72, 75, 76

The Canal Way Cycle Route is very popular with cyclists and has increased the amenity value of the Grand Canal. The mainly off road cycle route is approx. 3.6km long and runs along the Grand Canal from Rathmines Road Lower to Sheriff Street at Spencer Dock, Royal Canal. The route features a 3.5 metre wide 2-way cycle track along the northern bank of the Grand Canal and redesigned junctions at a number of locations featuring dedicated cyclist signals. It includes a 100 metre long boardwalk on the western approach to Leeson Street Bridge, which provides additional space for pedestrians and cyclists. It is the first phase of dedicated cycling facilities along the Grand Canal within the city in addition to other planned cycle routes including the Royal Canal.

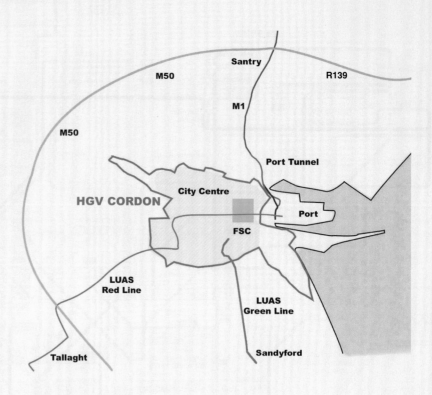

Secure bike parking at Drury Street 75 B1

The ground floor of **Drury Street Car Park** features a free indoor, dedicated bike park area. An entire floor of car parking spaces was removed to provide space for bikes. The facility is designed for short-term use so this means anyone from commuters, to tourists, to shoppers can use it. It's conveniently located near shops, bars, restaurants and cafe's, right in the heart of the city. The cycle parking area is under constant CCTV surveillance and is free to use to the public. It is open Monday to Saturday between 7.30am and 1am and on Sunday between 11am and 7pm.

5+ Axle HGV Ban

A 5+ HGV ban operates in certain areas of Dublin City at certain time periods. A limited permit scheme is in operation for those that need to load/unload during the restricted time period.

HGVs CANNOT enter the restricted zone without a valid permit during the hours of 07:00-19:00, seven days a week.

HGVs CAN enter the restricted zone during the hours 19:00-07:00, seven days a week.

HGVs with 4 axles or less are allowed to enter the restricted zone at any time, day or night. For more details see **www.dublincity.ie**

College Green Bus Corridor

The College Green Bus Corridor was introduced in May 2009 by Dublin City Councillors and it diverts private motor traffic away from College Green during specific times. As of August 2015 only public transport is currently allowed to travel through the area between 7am and 7pm Monday to Friday. This is to facilitate the Luas Cross City works, which pass through the College Green area. The Bus Corridor reduces congestion in the area and improvres conditions for pedestrians, cyclists and public transport. The scheme significantly reduces journey times for cross city public transport and allows increased reliability and frequency.

On Street Real Time Displays

Real Time Passenger Information, RTPI, will show you when your bus is due to arrive at your bus stop . The National Transport Authority and Dublin City Council are currently providing a RTPI service for bus passengers in the Greater Dublin area. RTPI is displayed on signs at bus stops and shelters . This allows you to plan your journey more accurately. As at the end of September 2015 there are over 600 RTPI signs in operation. Sign locations are based on where they will provide information to the greatest number of bus passengers and to include as many main routes as possible.

Park with Parking Tag

Parking Tag is Dublin City Council's cashless, mobile phone-based parking system which allows you to pay and top up by your mobile. Parking Tag is a Pay by Phone solution provided in the Dublin City Council area. Once registered, you simply text or call to pay for parking. All it takes is another quick SMS to extend parking for an additional period of time and no more rushing out to top-up the meter! You even get a reminder by SMS 10 minutes before your parking time expires. Registration is free on **www.parkingtag.ie** or T. 0818 300 161.

Walk Dublin – Dublin City Council's free app to get you around the city

Walk Dublin enables people to orientate themselves and obtain walking directions to all of the city's key cultural destinations. Discover what places of cultural significance are closest to you at any time, find out a little more about them and get walking. Walk Dublin is available on the App Store and is free to download.

Recycling in Dublin City

Dublin City Council operates a range of recycling facilities, which include Recycling Centre, WEE Collection, Bring Centres and over 100 Bottle Banks. For further information see **www.dublinwaste.ie**

Sports and Leisure Facilities

Dublin City Council operates 20 sports and leisure facilities. All offer excellent facilities and many contain pools, gyms etc. Gyms offer pay-as-you-go facilities. For information on opening times, locations, costs and facilities see **www.dublincity.ie**

Corballis Golf Links

▼18

Strand

1

IRISH SEA

2

COAST ROAD

Castle
Robbswall

The
Lighthouse
ROBSWALL
WALK PATH
THE
CRESCENT
The Anchorage
The Spinnaker
Sports
Ground

R106

THE
CRESCENT

3

MONKS
MEADOW

LIME TREE AVENUE

ELMER
COURT

CONNOR LANE

ASHLEY RISE

HEATHER
GARDENS

FIELD
OVE

WHEATFIELD
ROAD

BRIAR WALK

BRACKEN DRIVE

KELVIN CLOSE

BLACKTHORN
CLOSE

DEWBERRY
PARK

HEATHER WALK

Martello
Tower

4

WENDELL AVENUE

Alder
Court

WENDELL AVE

TELLO COURT

CARRICKHILL
RISE

ICKHILL
LOSE

PORTMARNOCK

PARK WALK

CARRICKHILL
WALK

GROVE

CRESCENT

STRAND ROAD

The
Quarry

PARKVIEW

RISE

PORTMARNOCK
DRIVE

FITZHARROCK
AVE

CARRICKHILL HTS

BURTON CT

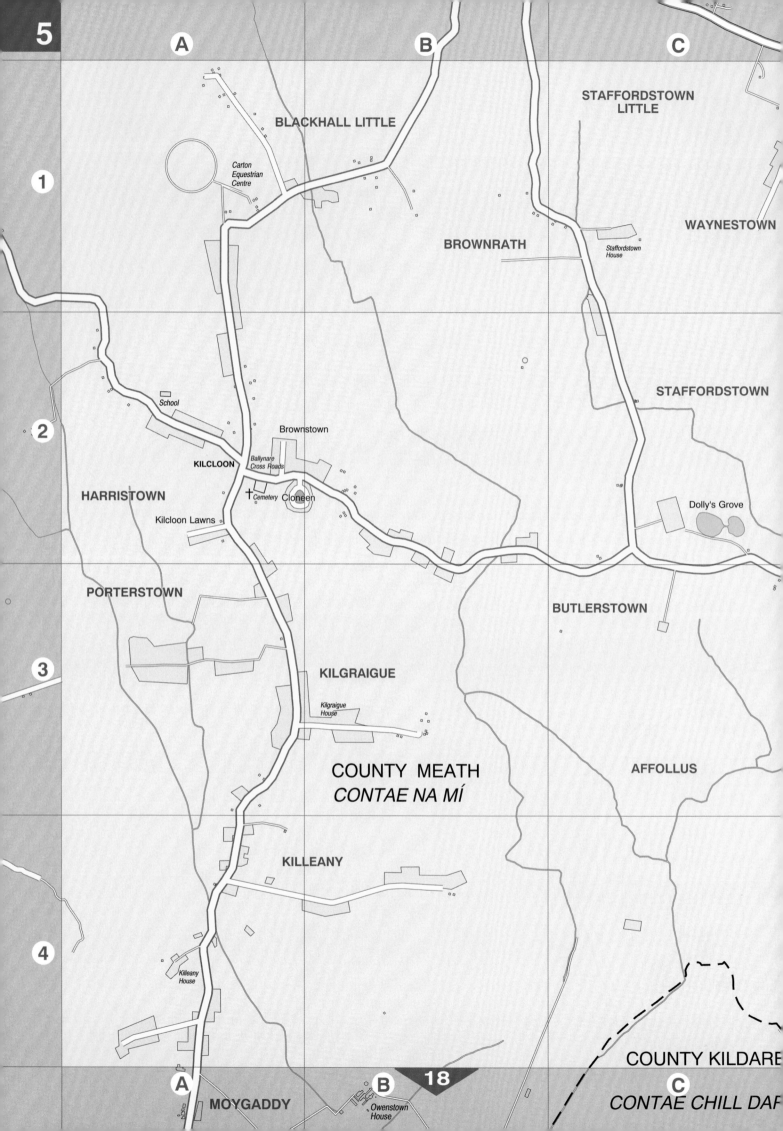

STAFFORDSTOWN
LITTLE

BLACKHALL LITTLE

Carton
Equestrian
Centre

BROWNRATH

Staffordstown
House

WAYNESTOWN

STAFFORDSTOWN

School

Brownstown

KILCLOON

Ballynare
Cross Roads

HARRISTOWN

✝ Cemetery Cloneen

Dolly's Grove

Kilcloon Lawns

PORTERSTOWN

BUTLERSTOWN

KILGRAIGUE

Kilgraigue
House

COUNTY MEATH
CONTAE NA MÍ

AFFOLLUS

KILLEANY

Killeany
House

MOYGADDY

Owenstown
House

COUNTY KILDARE

CONTAE CHILL DARA

Warrenstown

R156

BAYTOWNPARK

CUSHINSTOWN

Brookville
Stud Farm

R156

CORNELSTOWN

307

Cornelstown
House

SARNEY

COLLIERSLAND

Ballymacoll
Stud

HAMWOOD

BALLYMACOLL

R157

Cast

R157

Hamwood
House and
Gardens

Killarkin House

rave Yard

SALESTOWN

R157

18

Club House

Dungrange
Golf
Course

GRANGE

MILESTOWN

Castle
(in

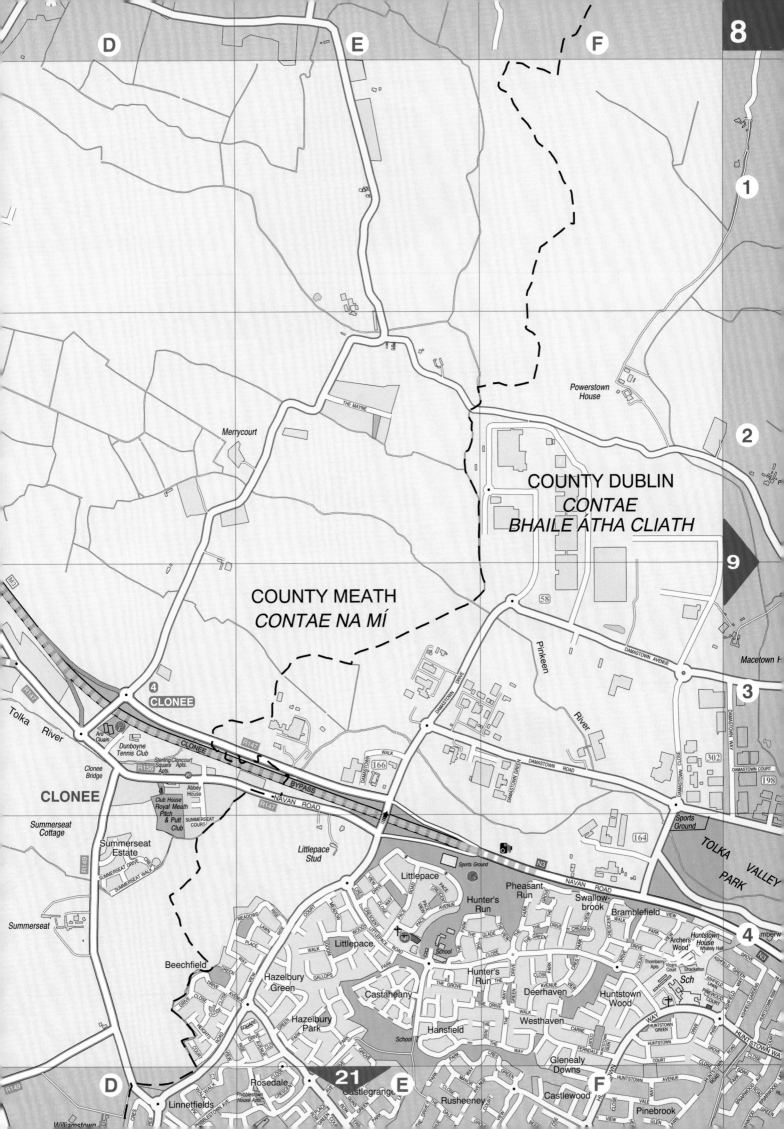

1

D E F

COUNTY DUBLIN
*CONTAE
BHAILE ÁTHA CLIATH*

2

Powerstown
House

9

COUNTY MEATH
CONTAE NA MÍ

Macetown H

3

Merrycourt

THE MAYNE

Pinkeen

River

DAMASTOWN AVENUE

Damastown Way

302

198

DAMASTOWN CLOSE

DAMASTOWN COURT

M3

R147

Tolka   River

Ard Cluain

Dunboyne
Tennis Club

CLONEE

R156

Clonee Bridge

4
CLONEE

CLONEE

R147

BYPASS

NAVAN   ROAD

DAMASTOWN DRIVE

DAMASTOWN   WALK

166

DAMASTOWN GREEN

DAMASTOWN ROAD

58

164

Sports
Ground

TOLKA

CLONEE

Summerseat
Cottage

Sterling Clioncourt
Square Apts.

Abbey
House

Club House
Royal Meath
Pitch
& Putt Club

SUMMERSEAT
COURT

R147

NAVAN   ROAD

N3

Sports Ground

Littlepace
Stud

Littlepace

Pheasant
Run

Swallow-
brook

Bramblefield   VIEW

VALLEY

Summerseat
Estate

R149

SUMMERSEAT DRIVE

SUMMERSEAT WALK

Littlepace

Hunter's
Run

THE GLADE

THE GREEN

Archers
Wood

Huntstown
House   Whately Hall

PARK

4

N3

Summerseat

Beechfield

Hazelbury
Green

LITTLEPACE   ROAD

School

Hunter's Run   THE

Deerhaven

Thornberry
Apts   Vicars
Court   Shackelton

Sch

Huntstown
Wood

HUNTSTOWN WA

Hazelbury
Park

Castaheany

Hansfield

School

Westhaven

Gleneaily
Downs

HUNTSTOWN

21

D E F

Rosedale

Phibblestown
House Apts.

Castlegrange

Rusheeney

Castlewood

Pinebrook

R149

Linnetfields

Williamstown

D E F

1

Broghan New Br.

Broghan House

Pitch and Putt

Dunsoghly Castle

Newtown C

KILSHANE

Cement Works

Kilmore House

Woodlands

Kilshane House

Kilshane Cross

2

Barrier

Kilshane Avenue

Stable Campus

Mitchelstown

Old Quarry

Old Quarry Campus

Kilshane View

Kilshane Park

Sports Ground

Primeside Park

Kilshane Drive

Kilshane Road

Sand & Gravel Pit

11

Kilshane Way

Burial Gd

201

Cloghran House

202

13

203

Rosemount Park Road

133

Ballycoolin Road

Rosemount Park Drive

Cappagh Road

Kildonan House

Electricity Station

4

28

CAPPOGE

Cappoge Cottages

Premier Business

Sp Gro

SEA

The Steer

Martello
Tower

Ireland's
Eye

Carrigeen Bay

Rowan Rocks

Thulla Rocks

Thulla

Lighthouse

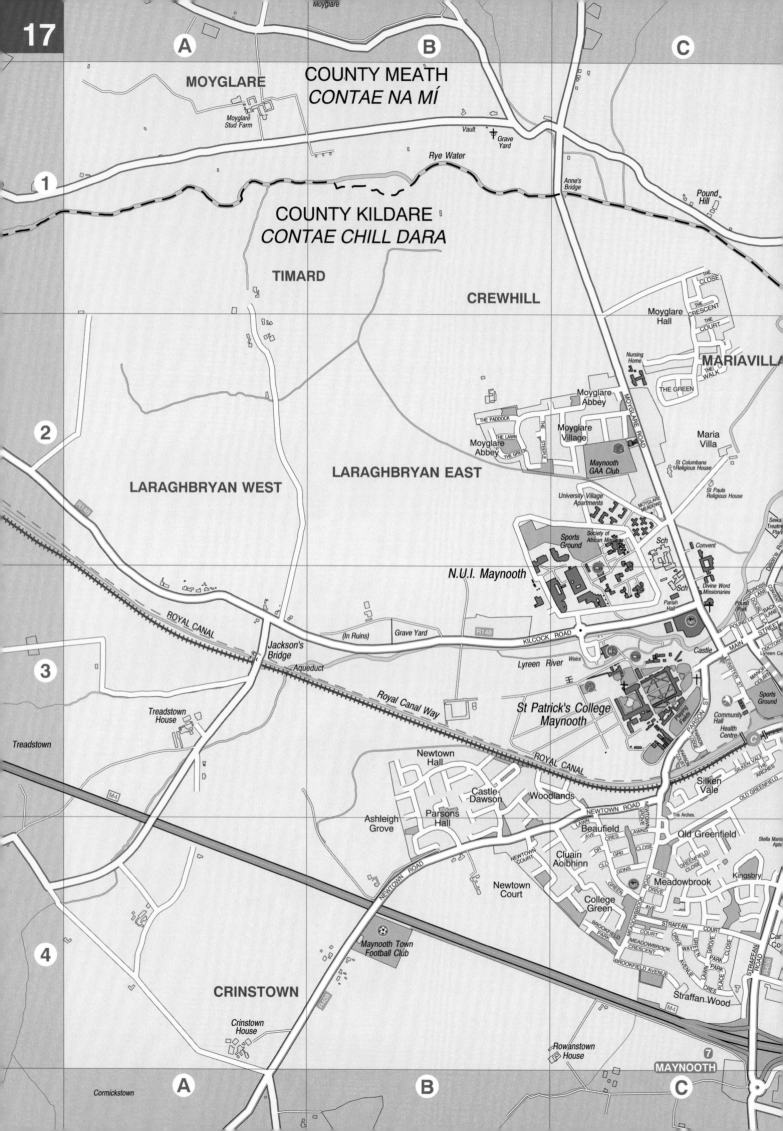

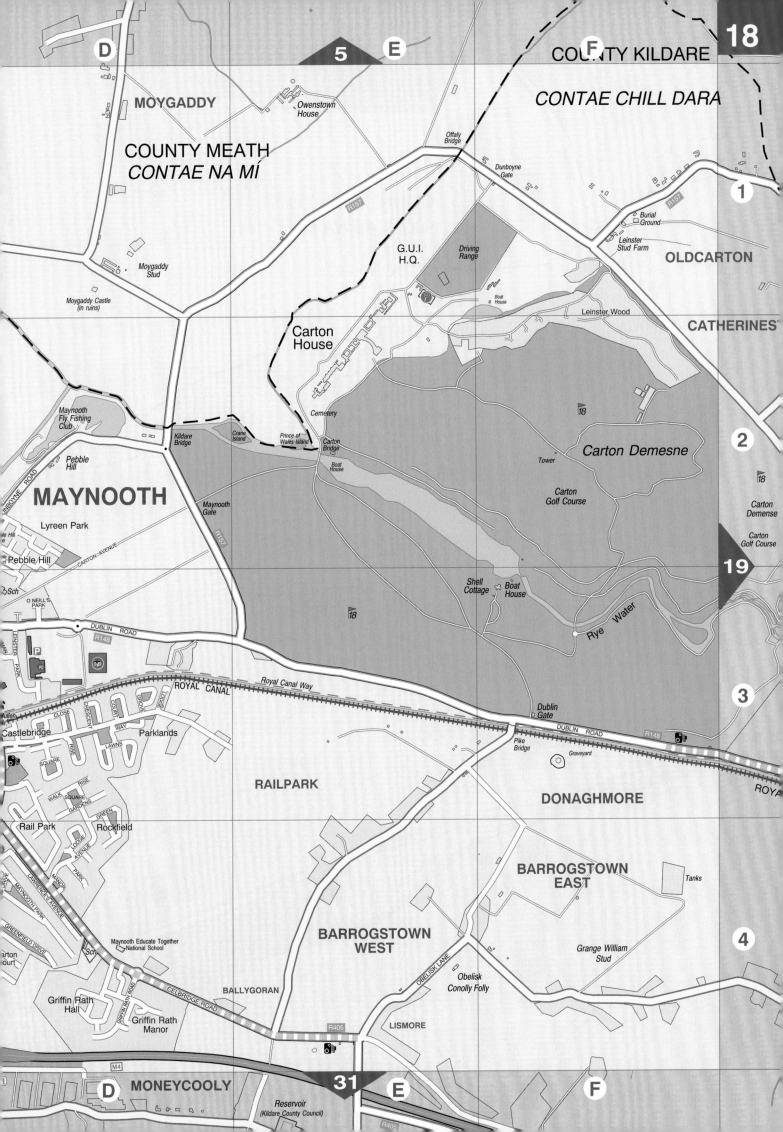

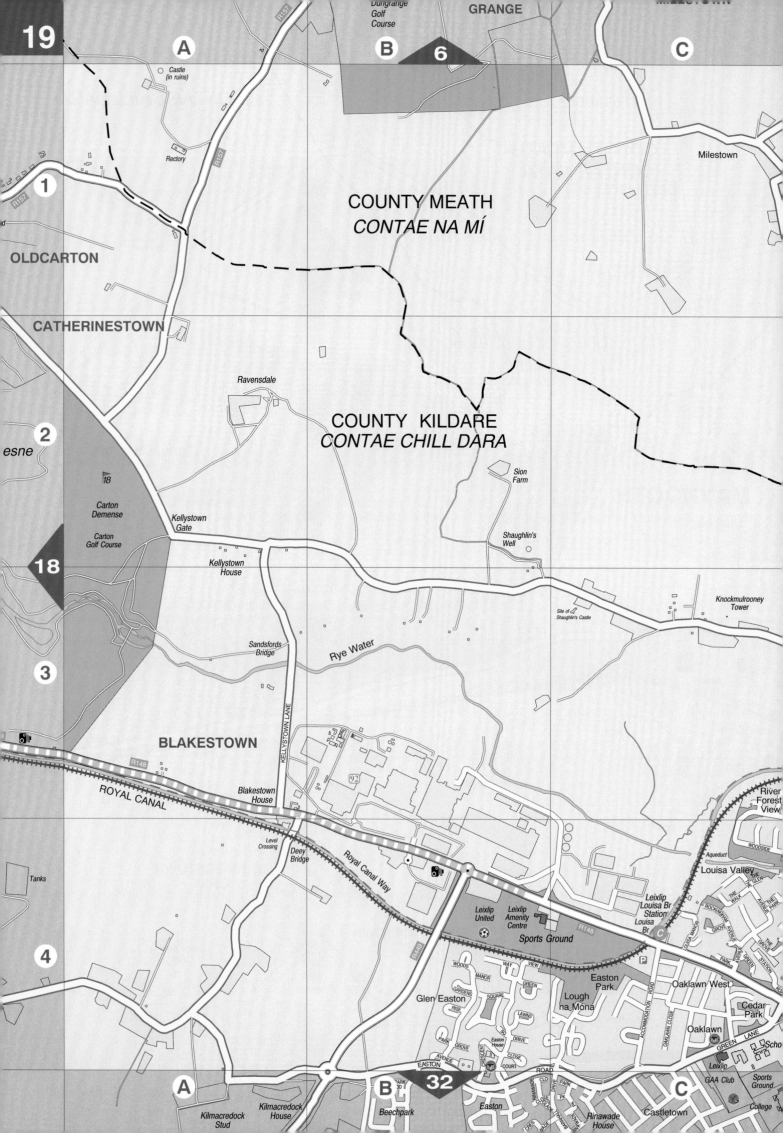

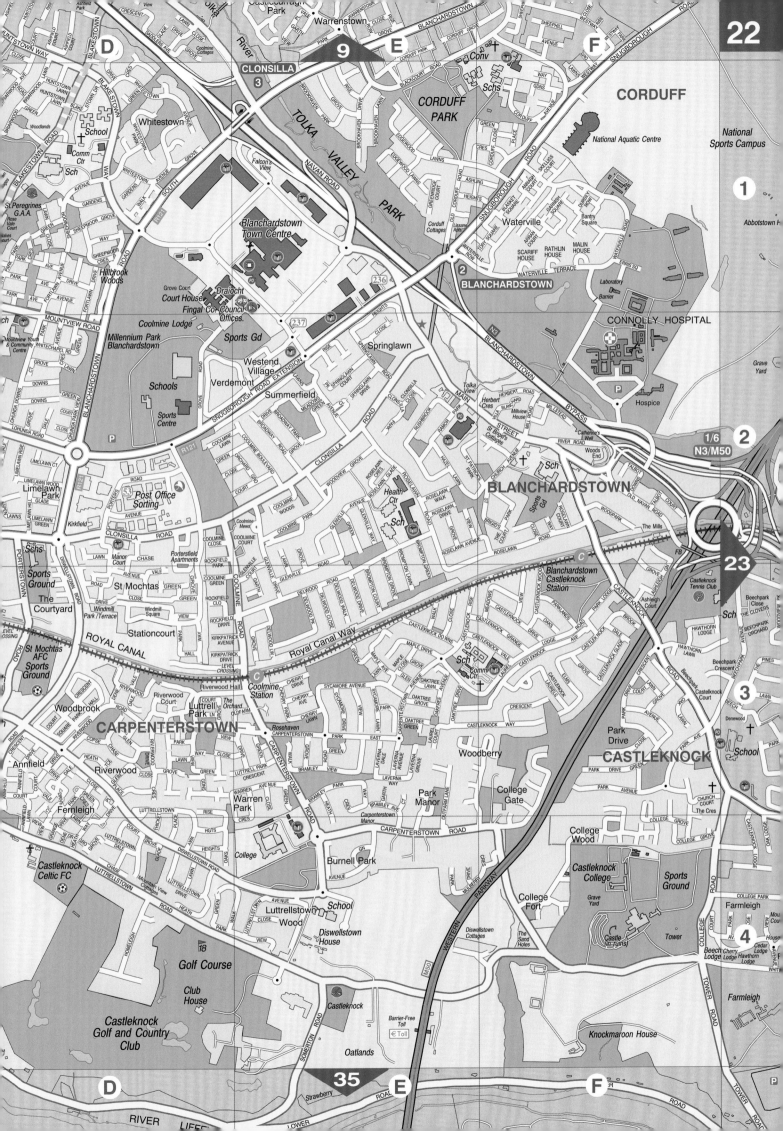

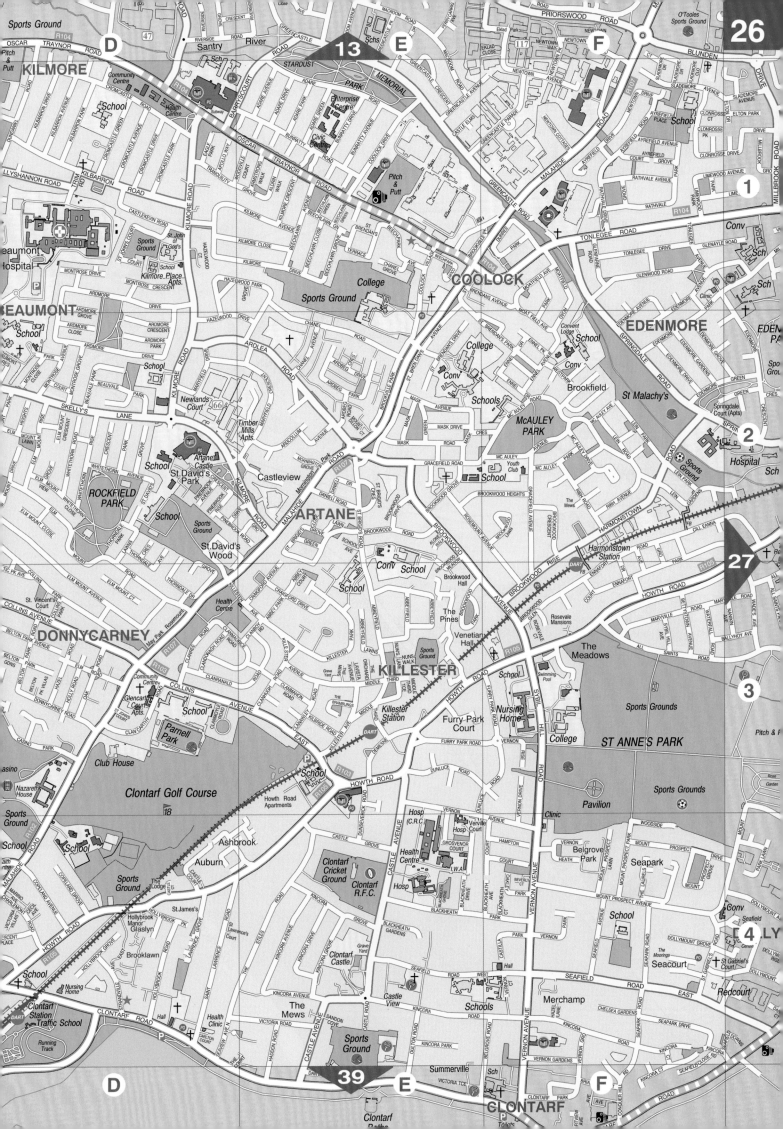

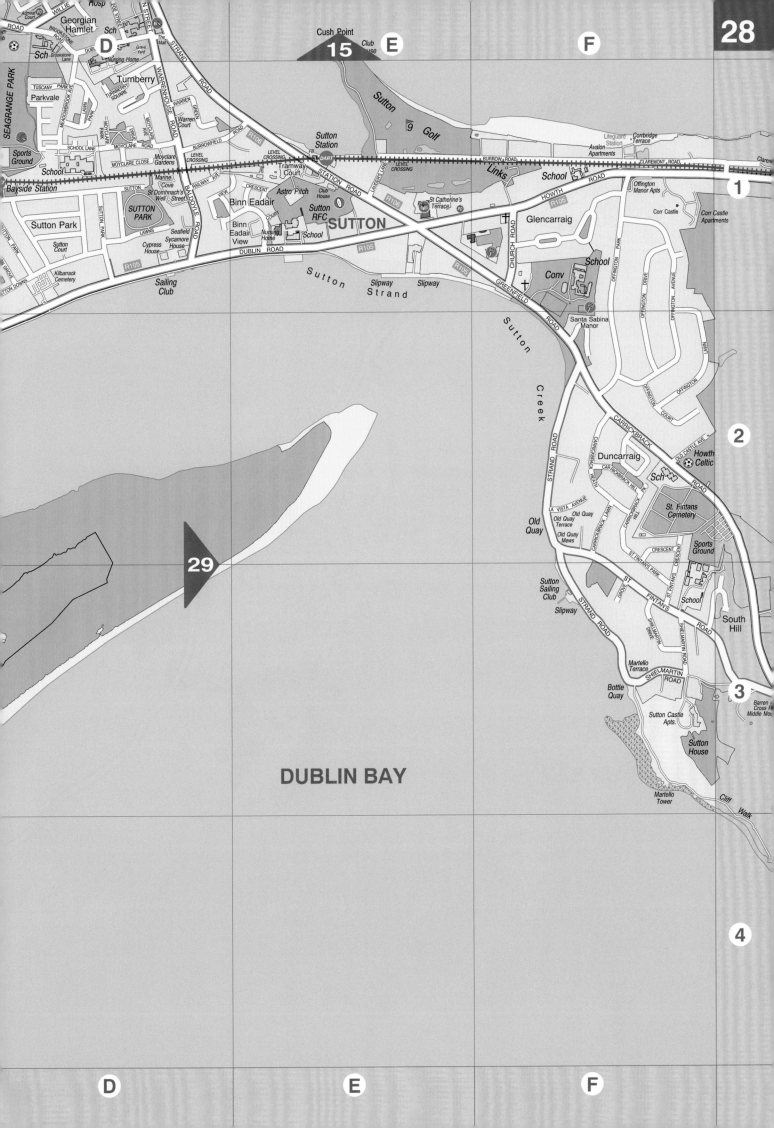

DUBLIN BAY

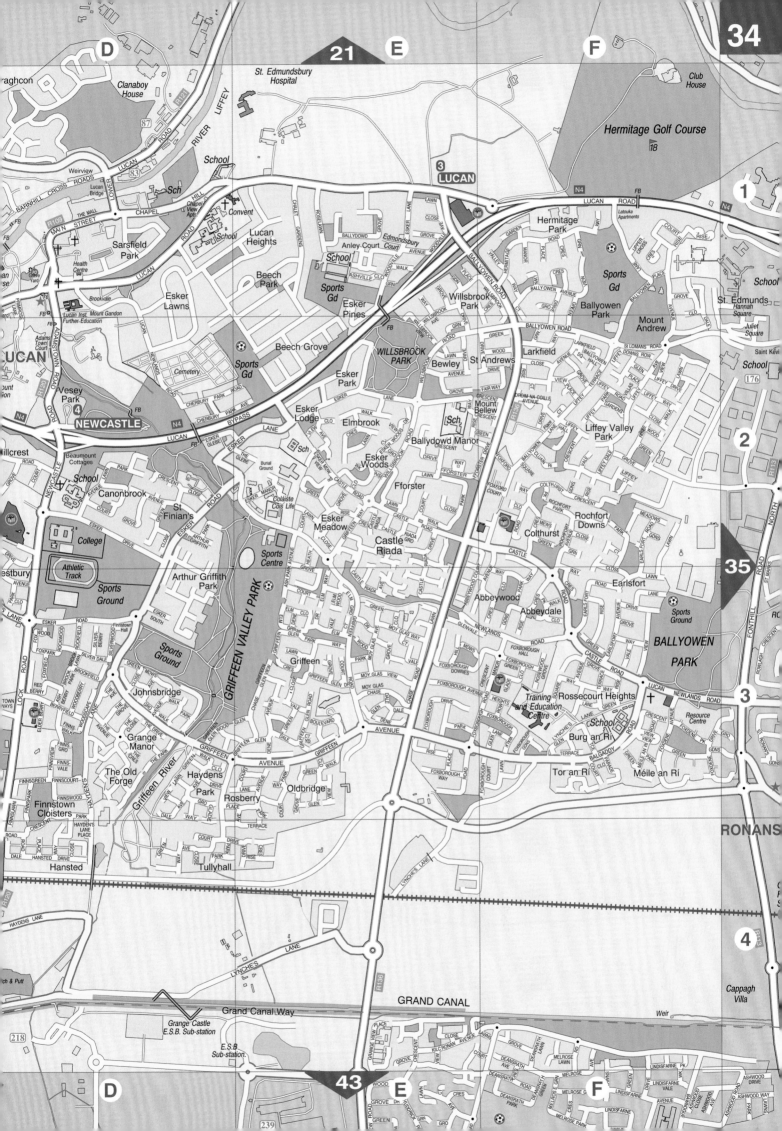

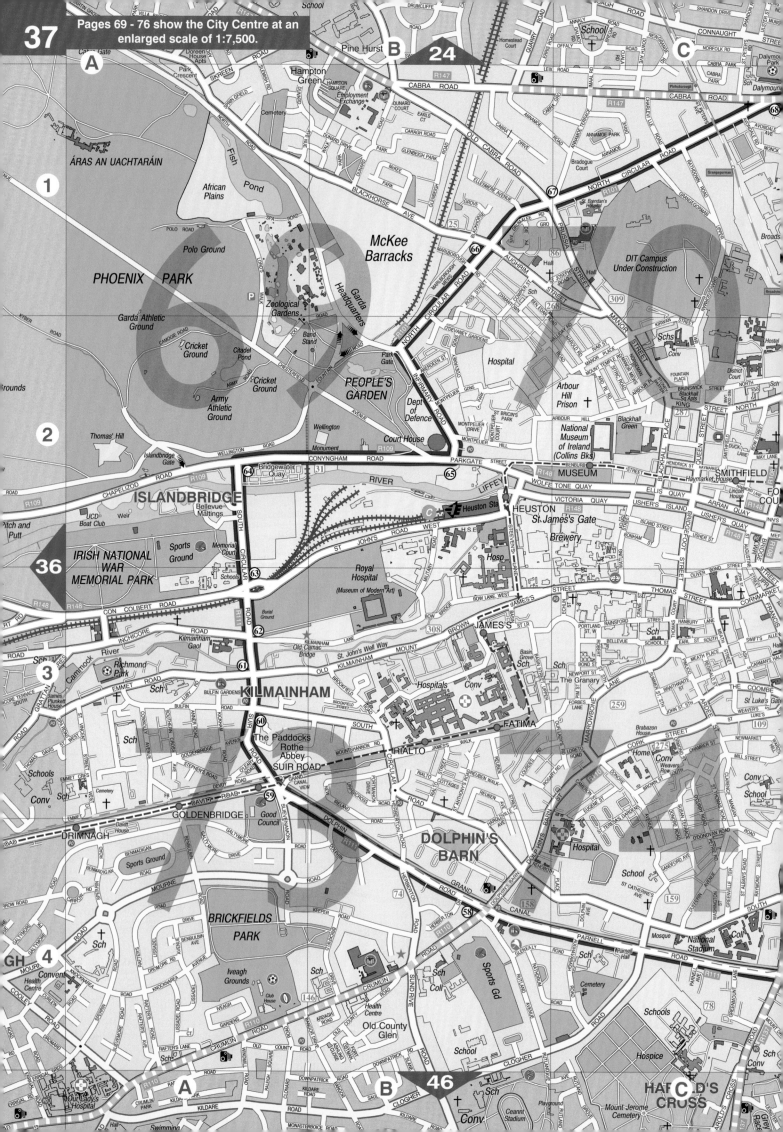

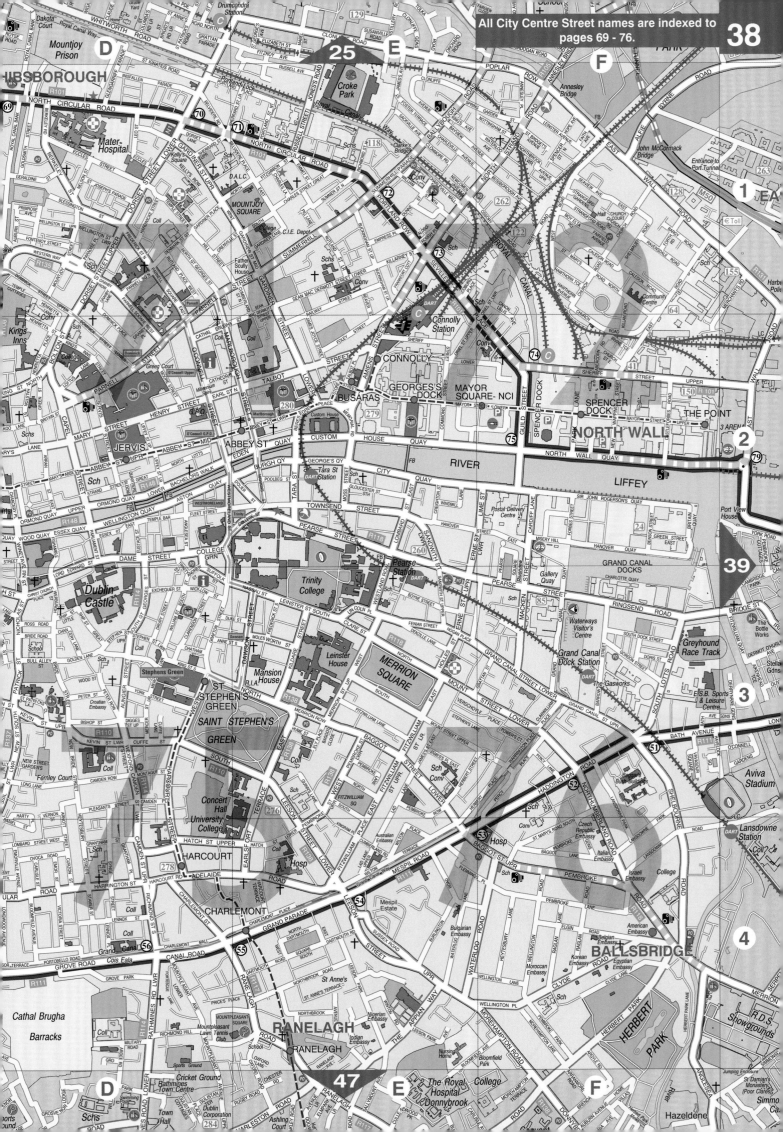

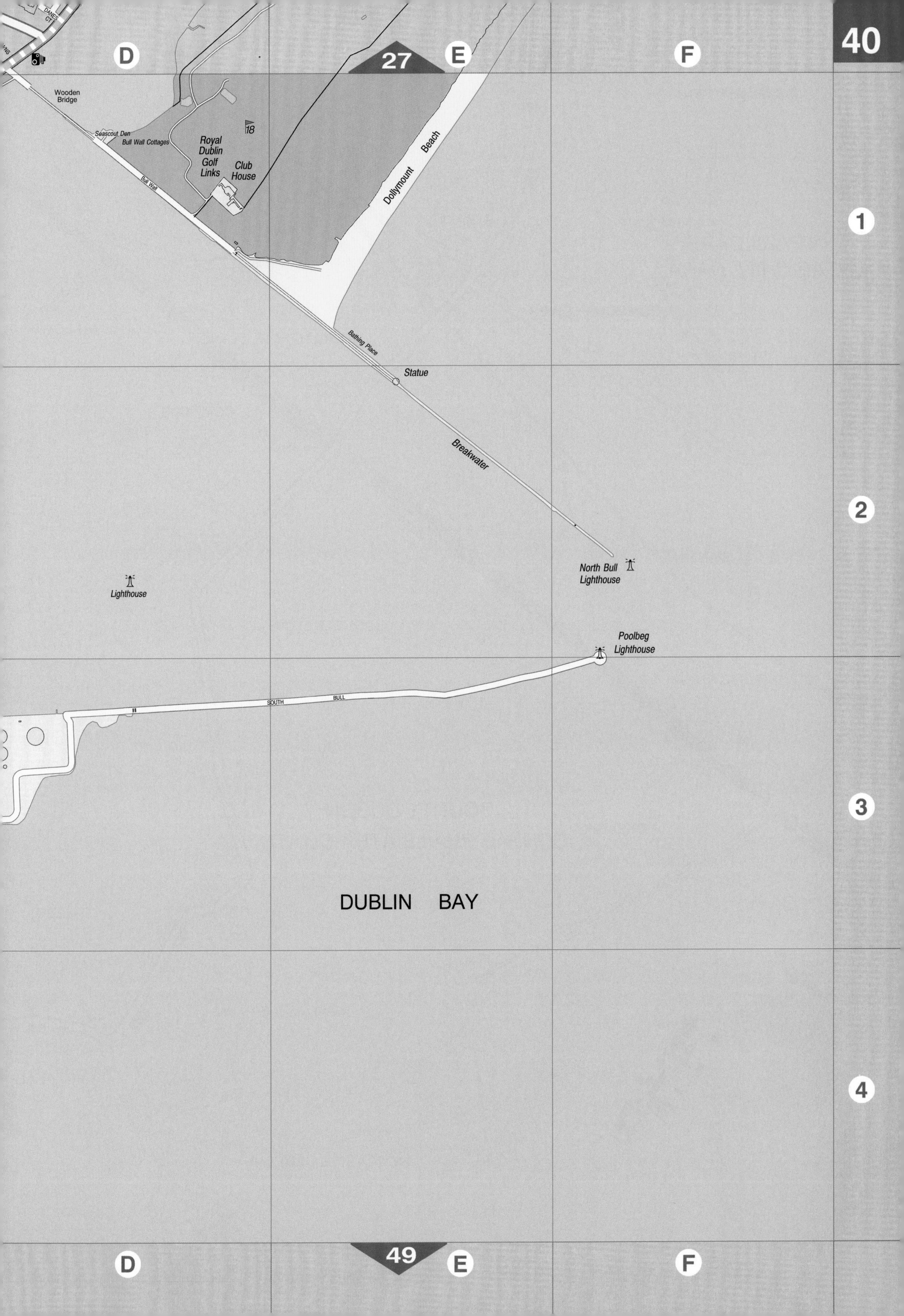
D
27
E
F
DANES CT
Wooden Bridge
Seascout Den
Bull Wall Cottages
Royal Dublin Golf Links
18
Club House
Bull Wall
Dollymount Beach
Bathing Place
Statue
Breakwater
1
2
North Bull Lighthouse
Lighthouse
Poolbeg Lighthouse
SOUTH
BULL
3
DUBLIN BAY
4
49
D
E
F

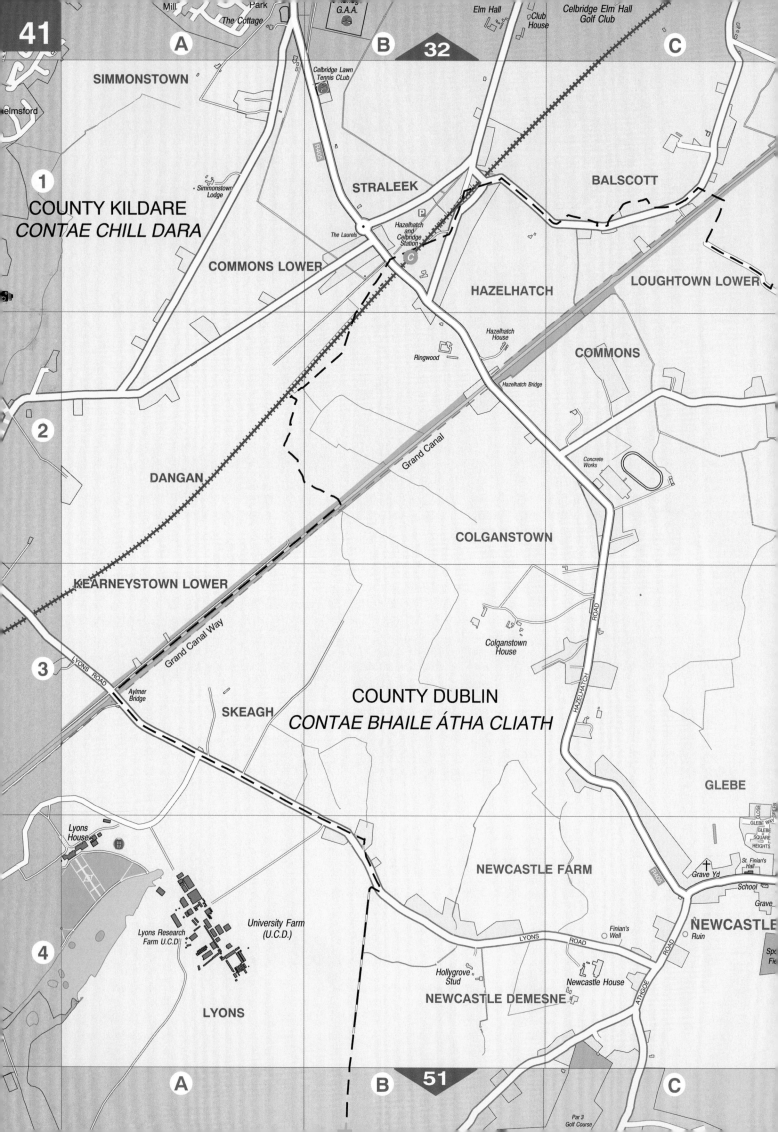

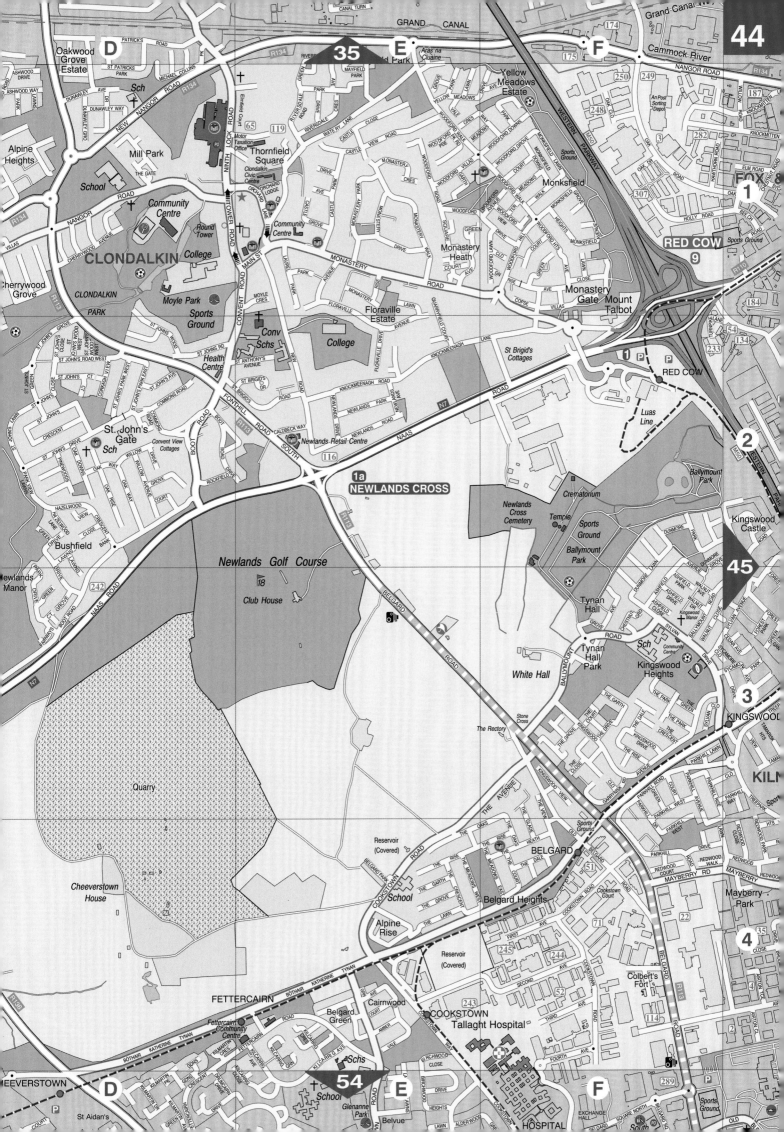

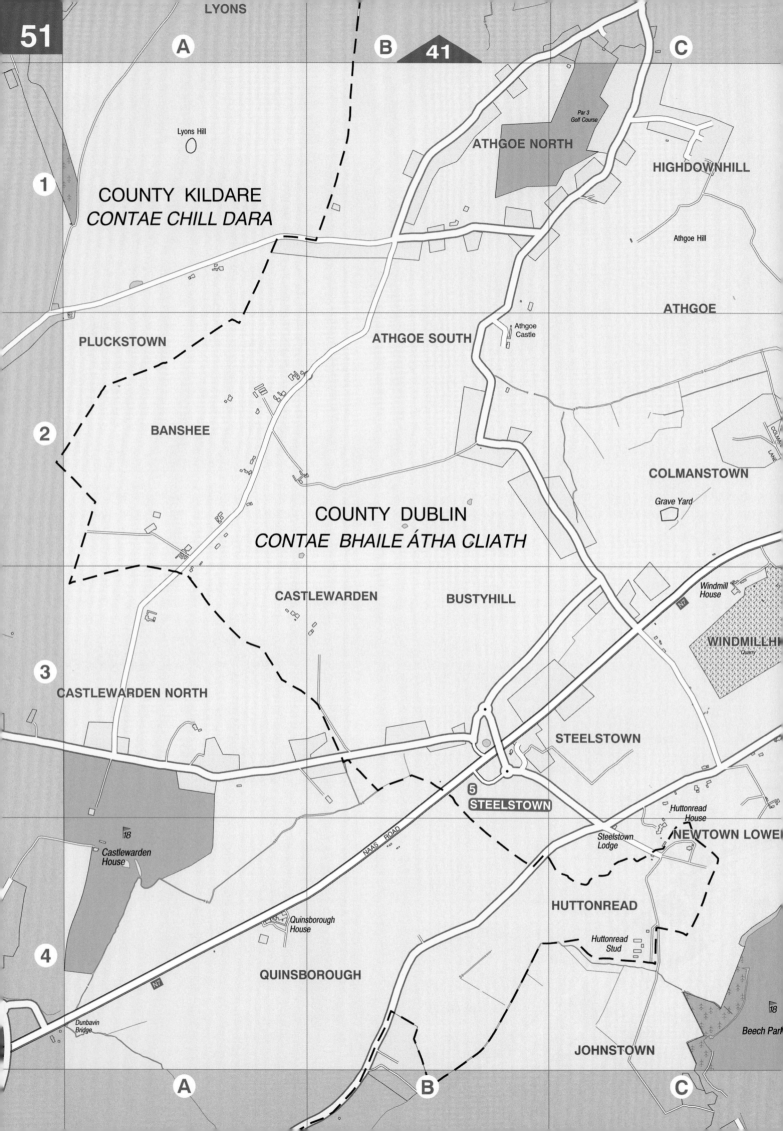

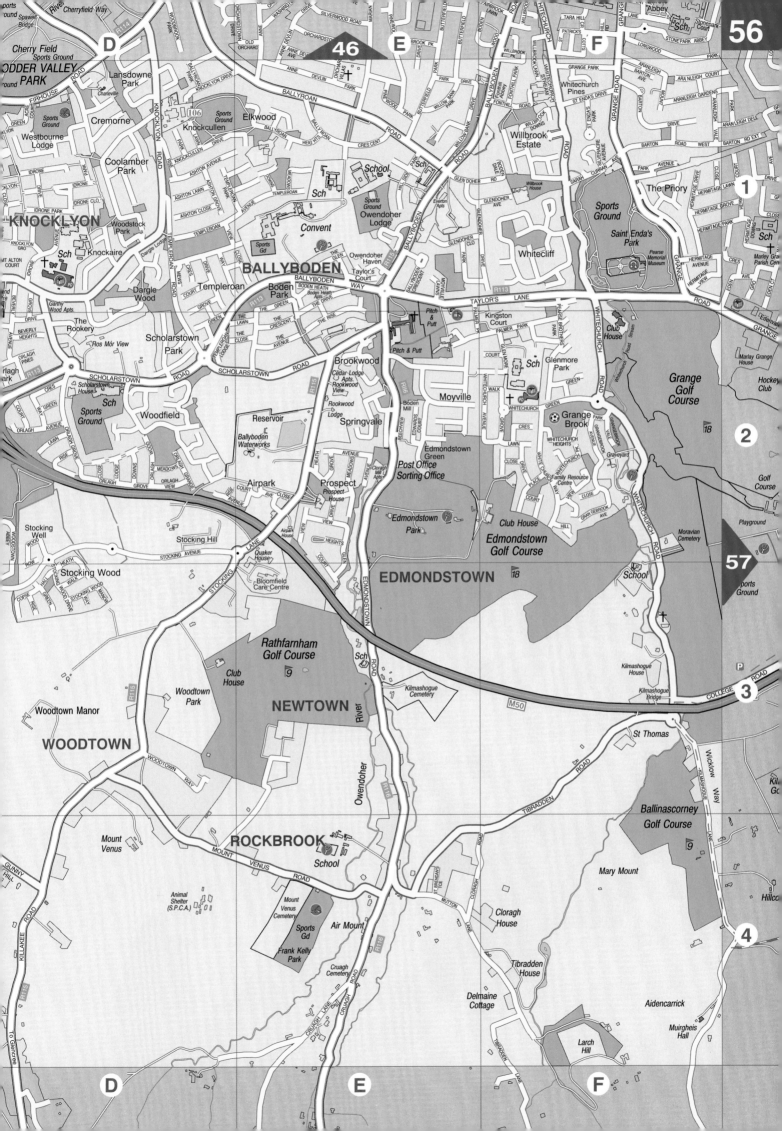

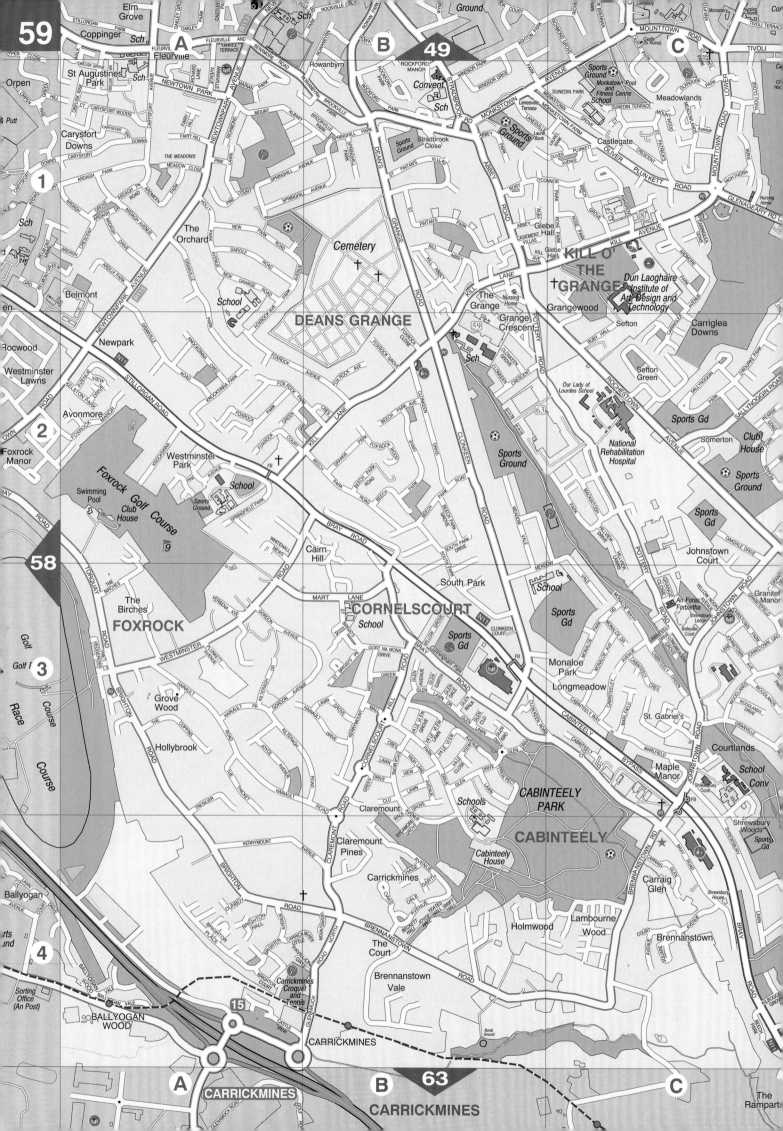

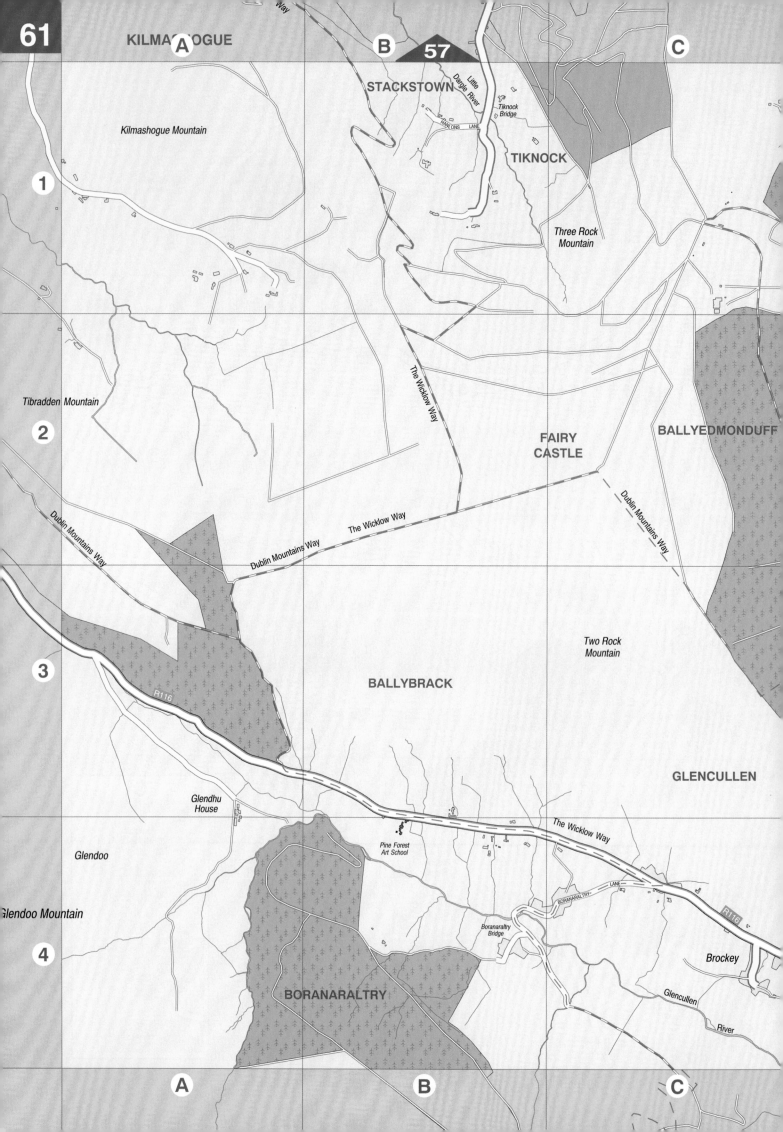

KILMASHOGUE   **A**   **B**   **57**   **C**

STACKSTOWN

Little Dargle River

Tiknock Bridge

HANLONS LANE

TIKNOCK

Kilmashogue Mountain

1

Three Rock Mountain

Tibradden Mountain

2

The Wicklow Way

FAIRY CASTLE

BALLYEDMONDUFF

Dublin Mountains Way

The Wicklow Way

Dublin Mountains Way

Dublin Mountains Way

Two Rock Mountain

3

R116

BALLYBRACK

GLENCULLEN

Glendhu House

The Wicklow Way

Glendoo

Pine Forest Art School

Glendoo Mountain

BORANARALTRY LANE

R116

Boranaraltry Bridge

4

Brockey

Glencullen River

BORANARALTRY

A   **B**   **C**

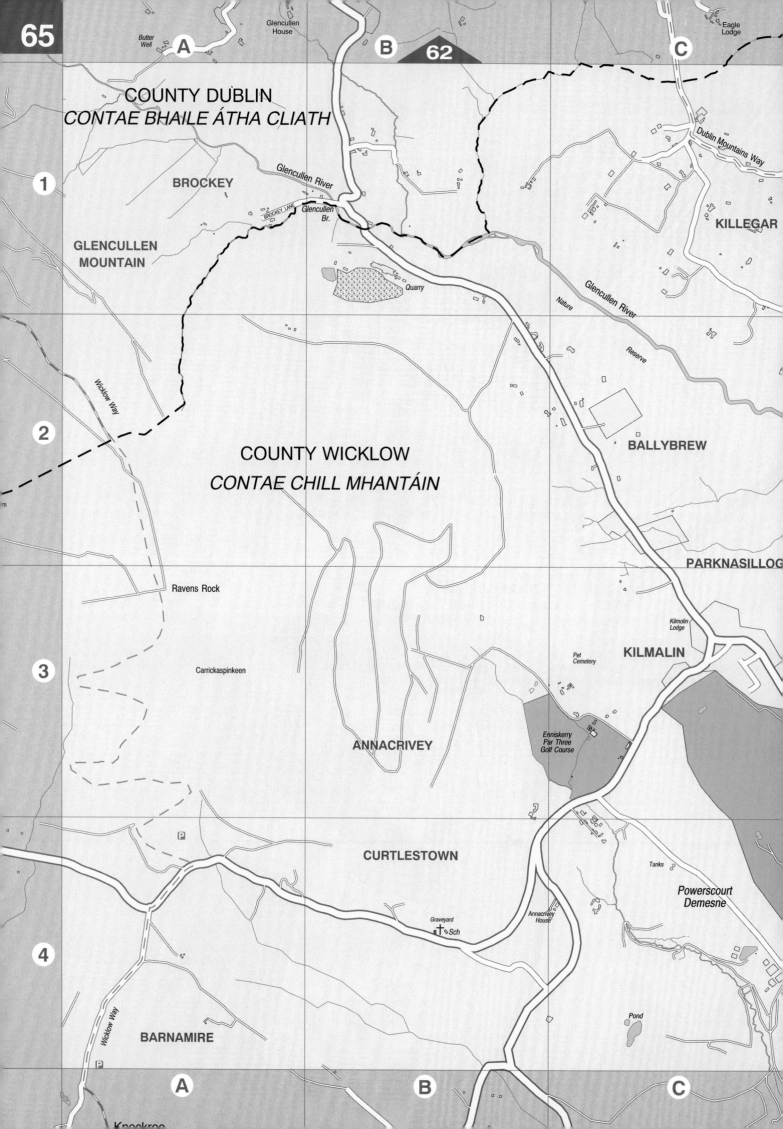

D   E   F

1

BRAY

National Sea Life Aquarium

IRISH   SEA

2

Naylor's Cove

Fontenoy Terrace

RAHEEN PARK

RAHEEN PARK AVENUE

Raheenacluig Church (in Ruins)

Golf Course

Eagle's Nest

3

Briar Wood

Bray Head

Tunnel

NEWCOURT

COUNTY WICKLOW

4

Bray Golf Club

18

CONTAE CHILL MHANTÁIN

Tunnel

Tunnel

Tunnel

Tunnel

D   E   F

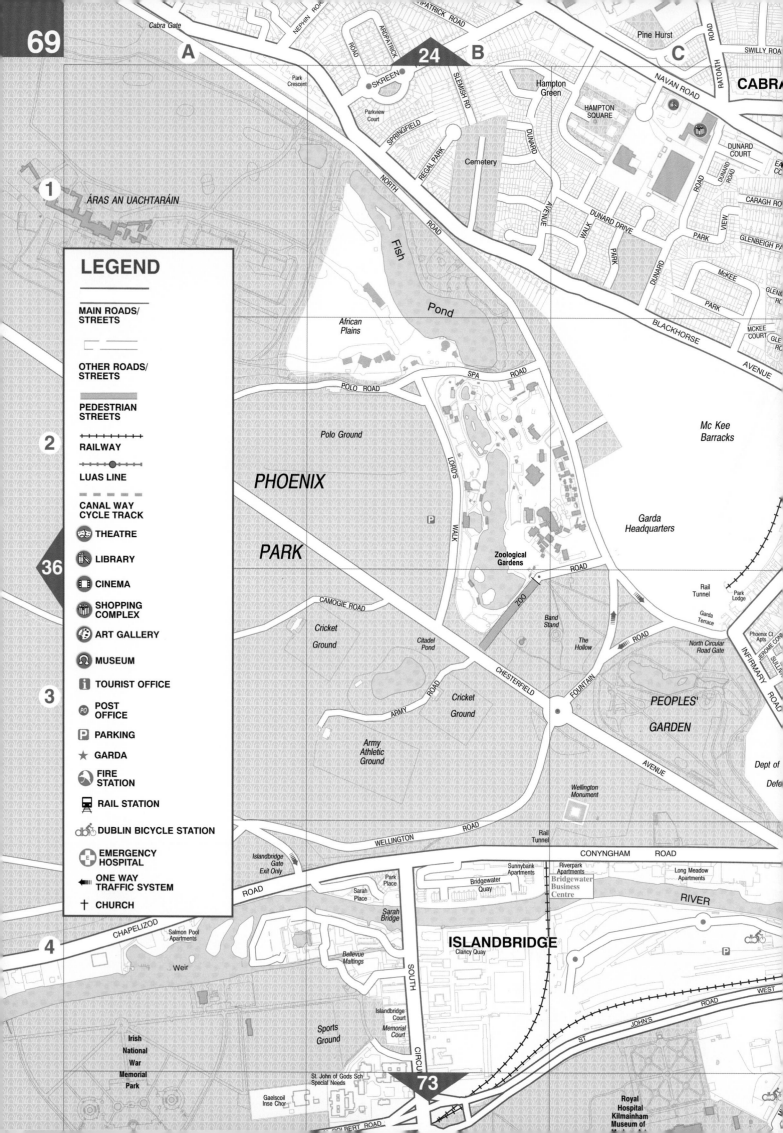

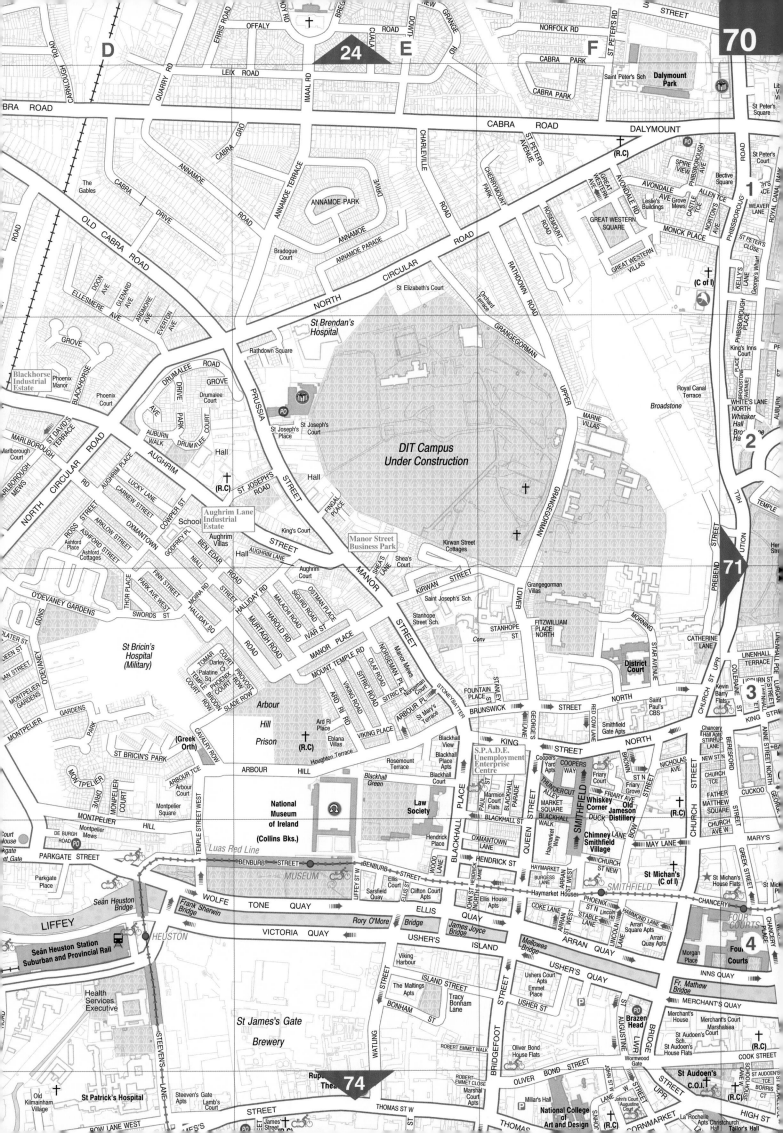

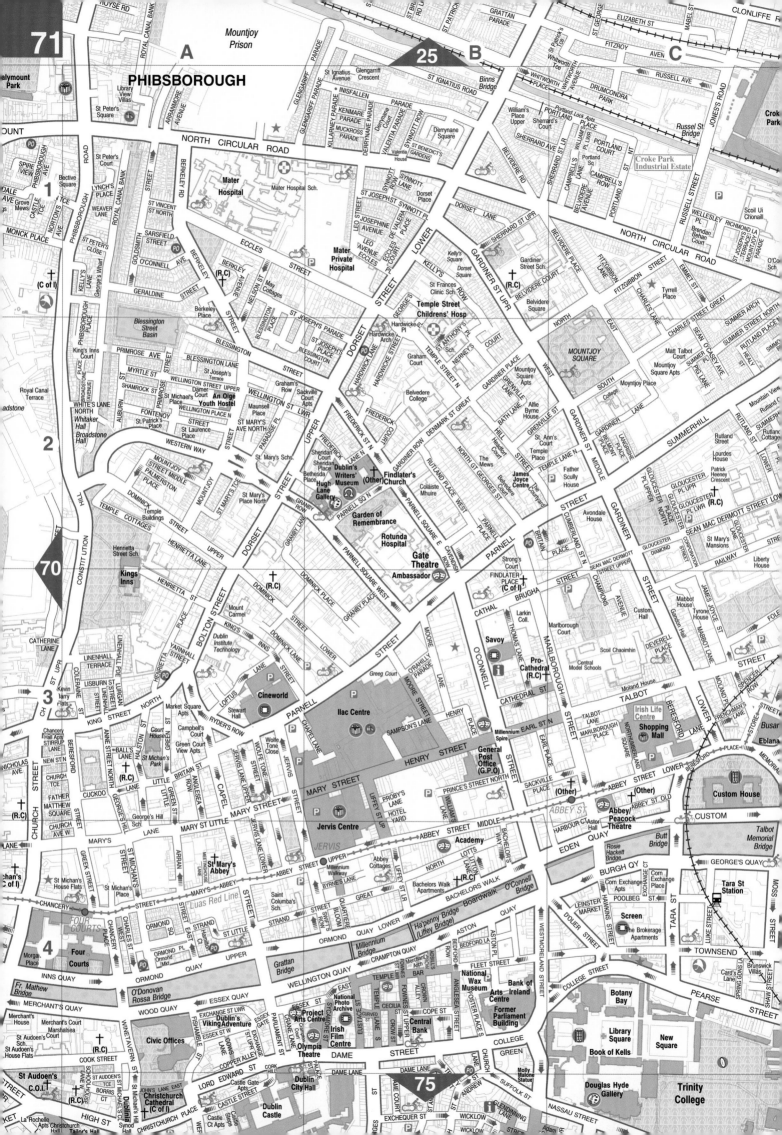

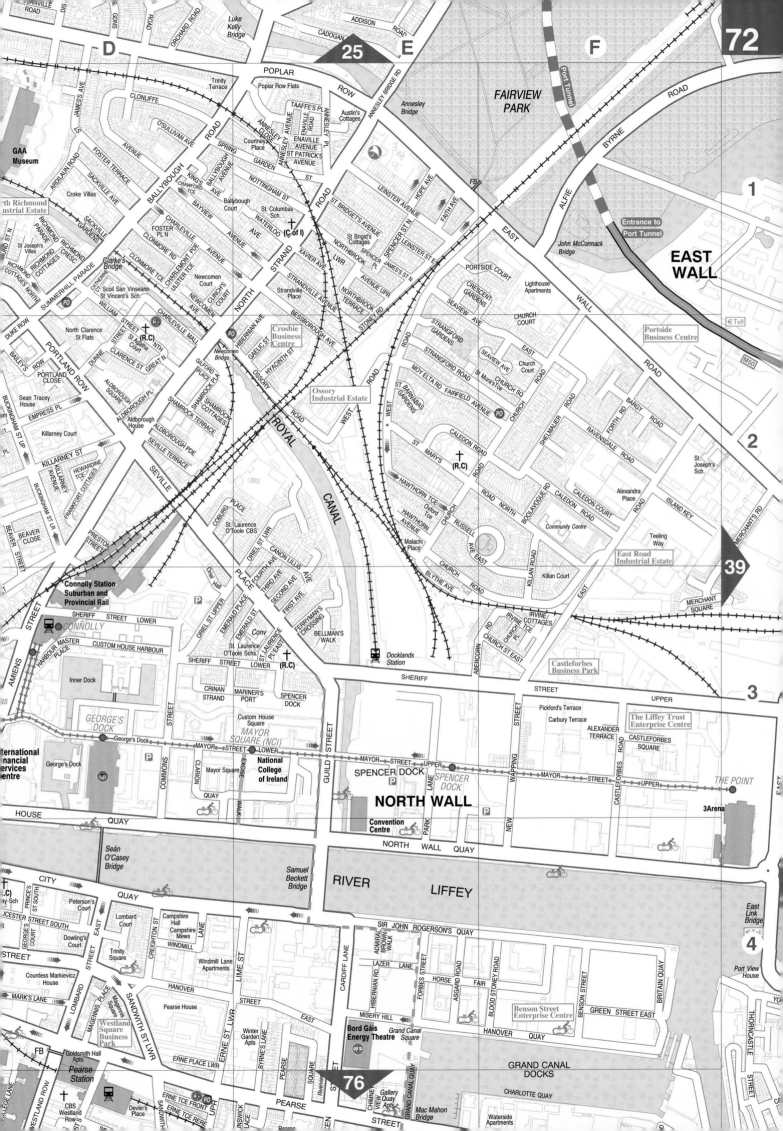

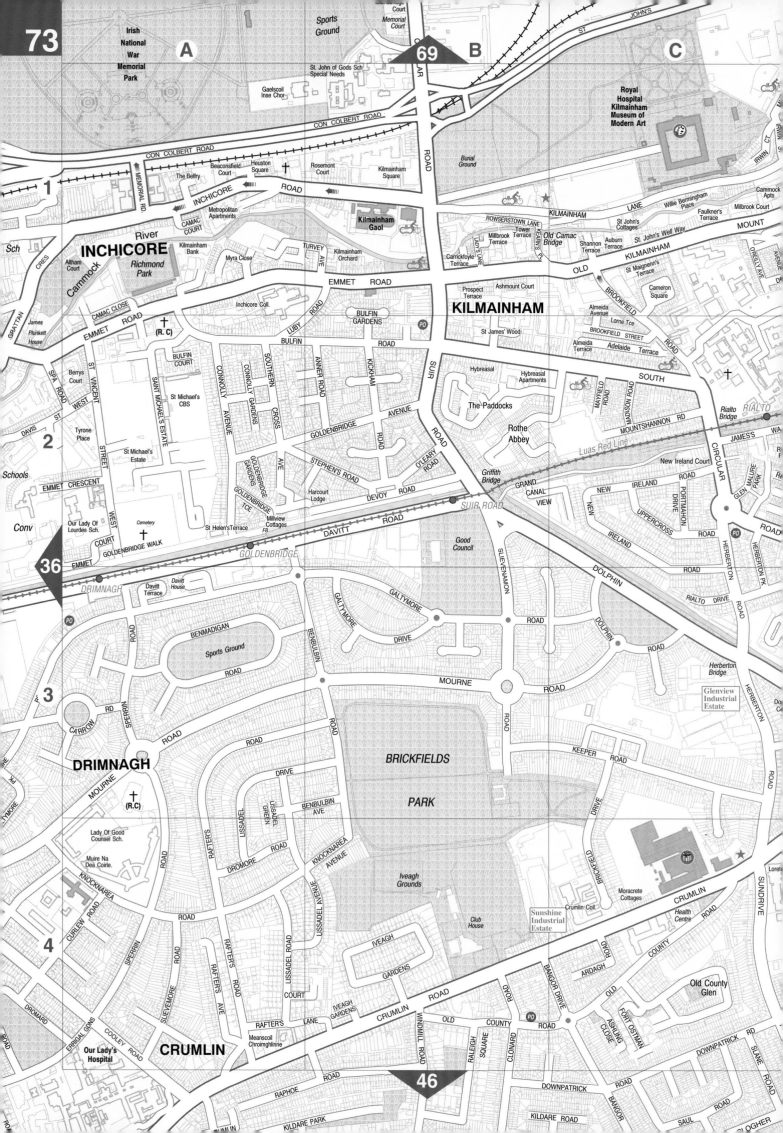

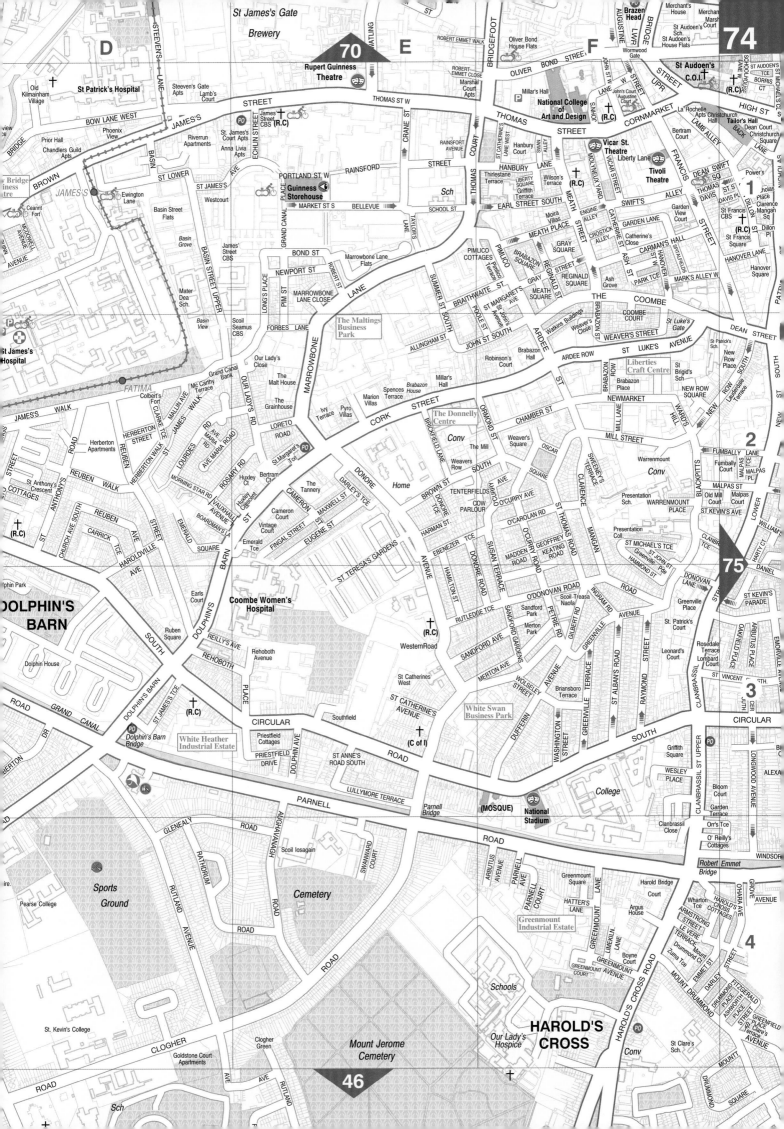

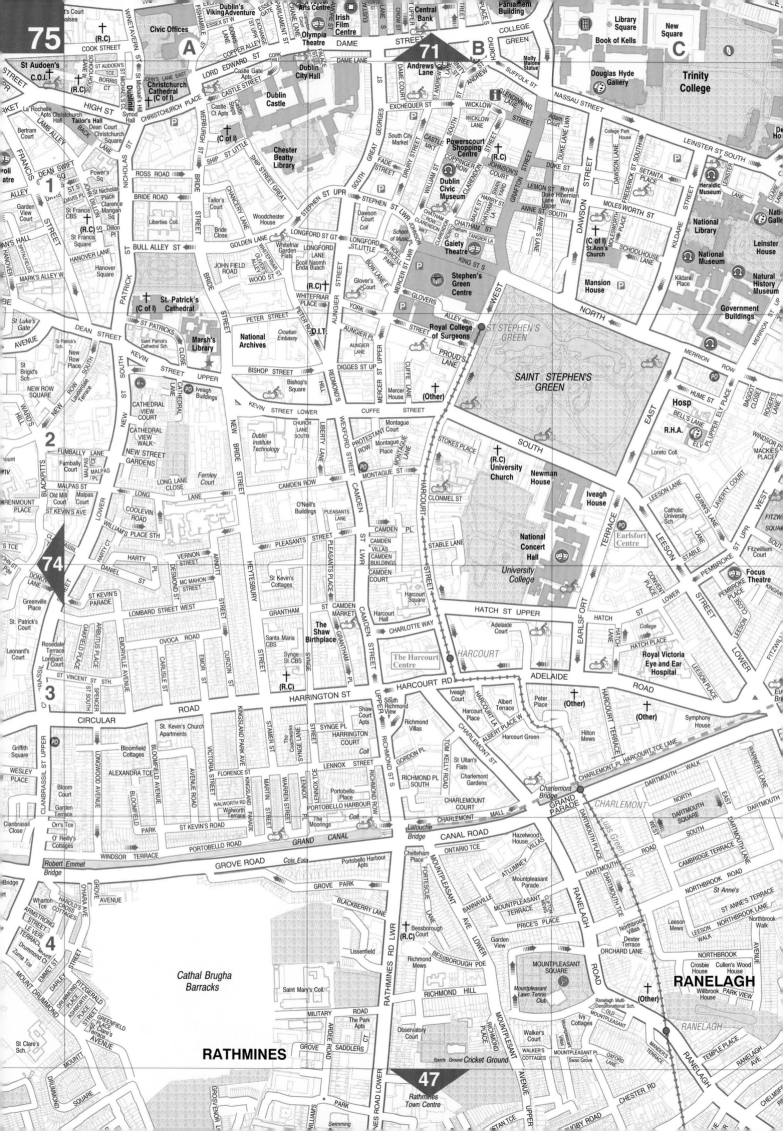

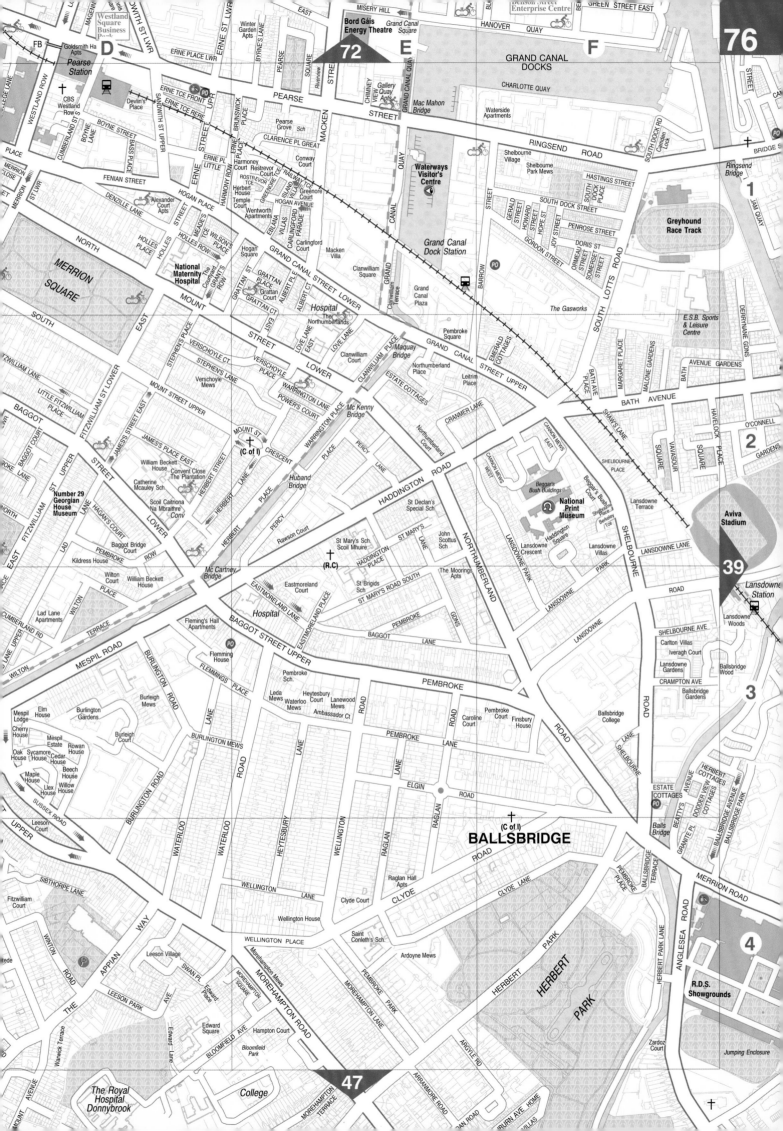

ASHBOURNE

LEGEND

M1	MOTORWAY
N9	NATIONAL PRIMARY ROAD
N81	NATIONAL SECONDARY ROAD
R683	REGIONAL ROAD
	MAIN ROADS/ STREETS
	OTHER ROADS STREETS
	NARROW STREET/ PRIVATE ROADS
	ROAD UNDER CONSTRUCTION
	PEDESTRIAN STREETS
	GREEN AREA
	WOODED AREA
	COMMERCIAL/ INDUSTRIAL
	HOSPITAL/ SCHOOL
	WATER
✚	HOSPITAL
	FIRE STATION
★	GARDA
P	PARKING
PO	POST OFFICE
✝	CHURCH
■	MONUMENT/ STATUE
	LIGHTHOUSE
	ONE WAY STREETS
	MAINLINE RAIL STATION
	ART GALLERY
	SAMPLE LANDMARK BUILDING
	CINEMA
	GAELIC GROUND
	LIBRARY
	MUSEUM
	RUGBY GROUND
i	TOURIST OFFICE
	SHOPPING COMPLEX
	SCHOOL/ COLLEGE
	SOCCER GROUND
	THEATRE
	VISITOR CENTRE
⚑	GOLF COURSE
⛺	CAMPING SITE
	CARAVAN SITE
	RAIL LINE

L C
(Level Crossing)

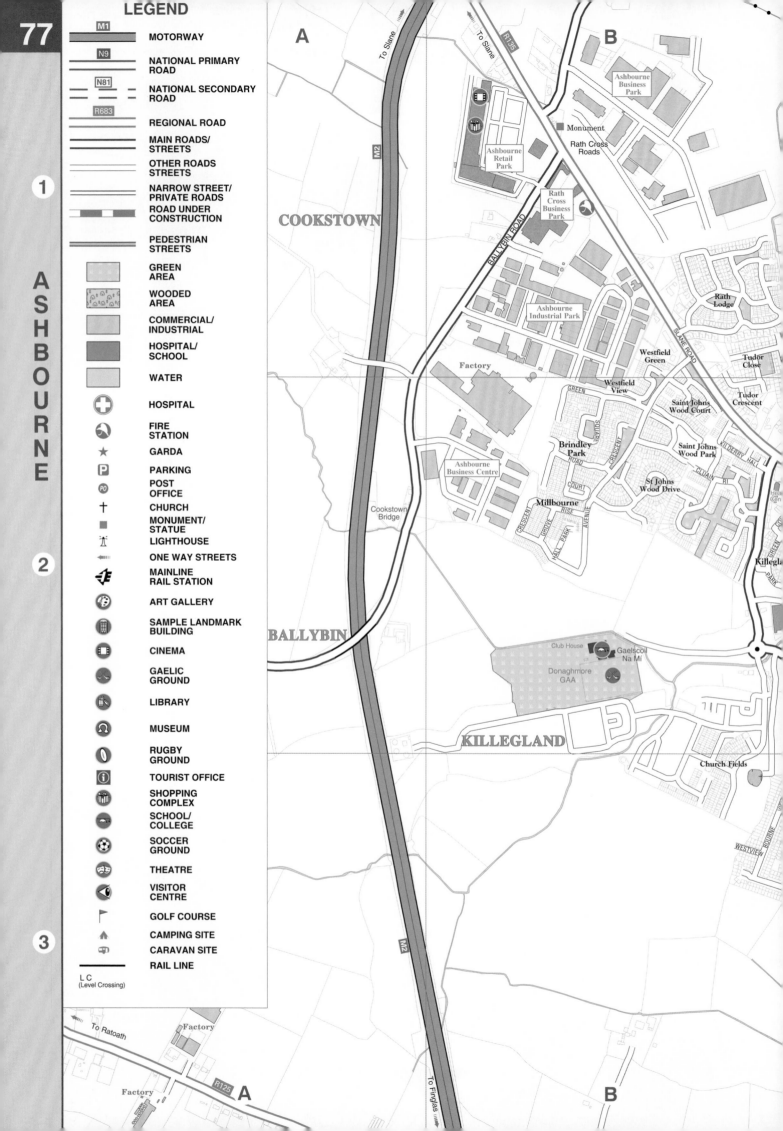

A

B

COOKSTOWN

BALLYBIN

KILLEGLAND

To Slane

To Slane

R135

M2

Ashbourne Business Park

Monument

Rath Cross Roads

Ashbourne Retail Park

Rath Cross Business Park

BALLYBIN ROAD

Ashbourne Industrial Park

Rath Lodge

SLANE ROAD

Factory

Westfield Green

Westfield View

Tudor Close

Tudor Crescent

GREEN SQUARE

Saint Johns Wood Court

WILDERRY HALL

Brindley Park

ROAD

CRESCENT

Saint Johns Wood Park

CLUAIN RI

St Johns Wood Drive

COURT

Millbourne

RISE

AVENUE

Killegla

Killegla PARK

CRESCENT

GROVE

HALL PARK

Ashbourne Business Centre

Cookstown Bridge

Club House

Gaelscoil Na Mí

Donaghmore GAA

Church Fields

WESTVIEW

BOURNE

To Ratoath

Factory

Factory

R125

A

To Finglas

B

ASHBOURNE

Alderbrook Downs	C3	Broadmeadow Castle	C2	Lindsay Mews	C3
Alderbrook Glen	C3	Broadmeadow Green	C3	Maple Avenue	D2
Alderbrook Heath	C3	Broadmeadow Road	C3	Maple Close	D2
Alderbrook Park	C3	Brookville	C2	Maple Drive	D2
Alderbrook Rise	C3	Brookville Apts	C2	Maple Grove	C2
Alderbrook Road	C3	Castle Close	C3	Meadow Brook Court	C2
Alderbrook Vale	C3	Castle Crescent	C2	Millbourne	B2
Archerstown Road	D2	Castle Park	C2	Millbourne Avenue	B2
Archerstown Wood	C2	Castle Street	C2	Millbourne Crescent	B2
Arkle Hill	C3	Castle Way	C3	Millbourne Grove	B2
Asbourne Bridge	C2	Castle Park	C2	Millbourne Hall	B2
Ashbourne Business Ct.	B2	Cedar Road	C2	Millbourne Park	B2
Ashbourne Business Pk.	B1	Cherry Court	C3	Millbourne Rise	B2
Ashbourne Industrial Pk.	B1	Cherry Fields	C3	Milltown Bridge	D3
Ashbourne Retail Park	B1	Cherry Lane	C3	Milltown Estate	C2
Ashdale Crescent	C2	Church Fields	B3	Milltown Road	C2
Ashewood	C2	Cluain Rí	B2	Pinewood Court	C2
Ashewood Close	C2	Cookstown Bridge	A2	Racehill Lodge	C1
Ashewood Court	C2	Crestwood	C2	Race Lane	C1
Ashewood Drive	C2	Crestwood Avenue	C2	Racehill Manor	C1
Ashewood Glen	C2	Crestwood Green	C2	Racehill Manor Close	C1
Ashewood Green	C2	Crestwood Park	C3	Racehill Manor Court	C1
Ashewood Grove	C2	Crestwood Road	C2	Racehill Manor Crescent	C1
Ashewood Heath	C2	Deerpark	C3	Racehill Manor Park	C1
Ashewood Lawn	C2	Dublin Road	C3	Racehill Manor View	C1
Ashewood Meadow	C2	Frederick Street	C2	Racehill Road	C1
Ashewood Place	C2	Frederick Court	C2	Rath Cross Business Pk.	B1
Ashewood Walk	C2	Greenfield Grove	C3	Rath Cross Roads	B1
Bachelors Walk	C2	Hickey's Lane	C3	Rath Lodge	B1
Baldara Court	D3	Hunters Lane	C2	Regents Hall	C2
Ballybin Road	B1	Huntsgrove	C2	Saint Anthonys	C2
Bourne Avenue	C3	Kilderry Hall	B2	Saint Johns Wood Court	B2
Bourne Court	C3	Killegland	B2	Saint Johns Wood Drive	B2
Bourne View	B3	Killegland Court	B2	Saint Johns Wood Park	B2
Bridge Street	C2	Killegland Crescent	B2	Slane Road	B1
Brindley Park	B2	Killegland Green	B2	Sycamore Drive	C2
Brindley Park Court	B2	Killegland Hall	C2	Tara Close	C3
Brindley Park Crescent	B2	Killegland Park	B2	Tara Court	C3
Brindley Park Green	B2	Killegland Rise	C3	Tara Lawns	C3
Brindley Park Road	B2	Killegland Road	C3	Tara Place	C3
Brindley Park Square	B2	Killegland Street	C2	The Bailey	C3
The Briars	C3				
The Courtyard	C2				
The Crescent	C2				
The Green	C3				
The Hawthorns	C2				
Tudor Close	B1				
Tudor Crescent	B2				
Tudor Grove	C2				
Tudor Heights	C1				
Westfield Green	B1				
Westfield View	B2				
Westview	B3				
White Ash Park	D2				

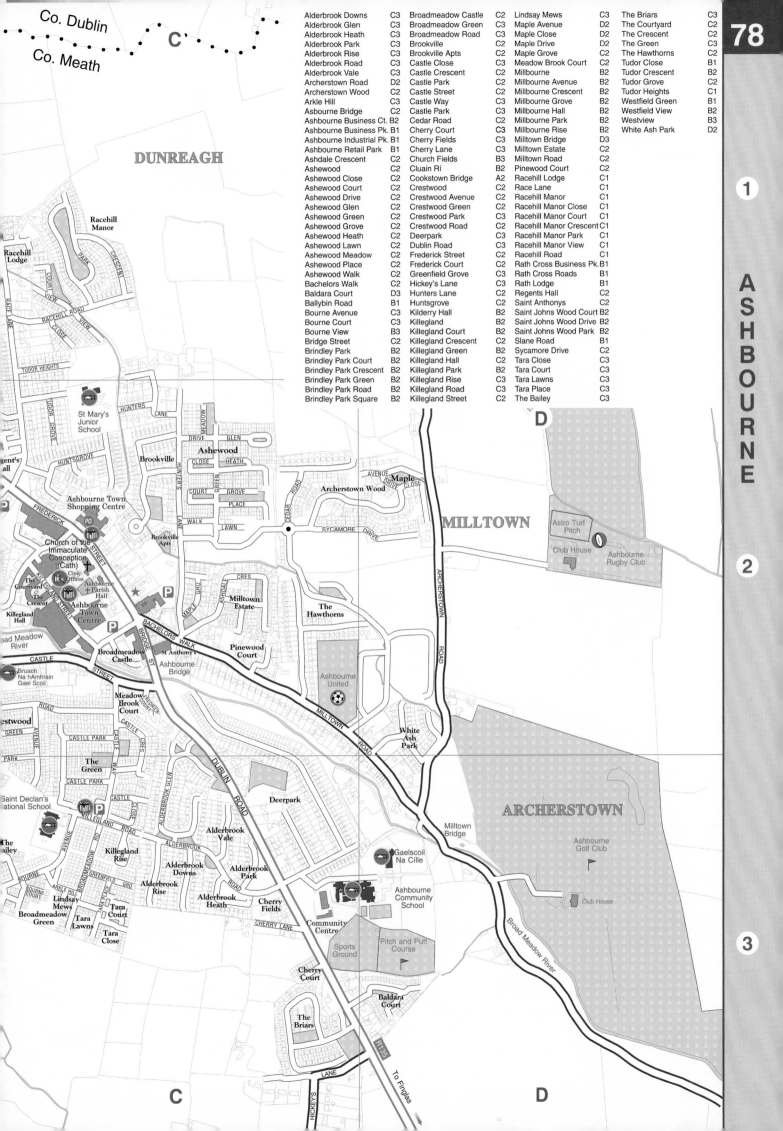

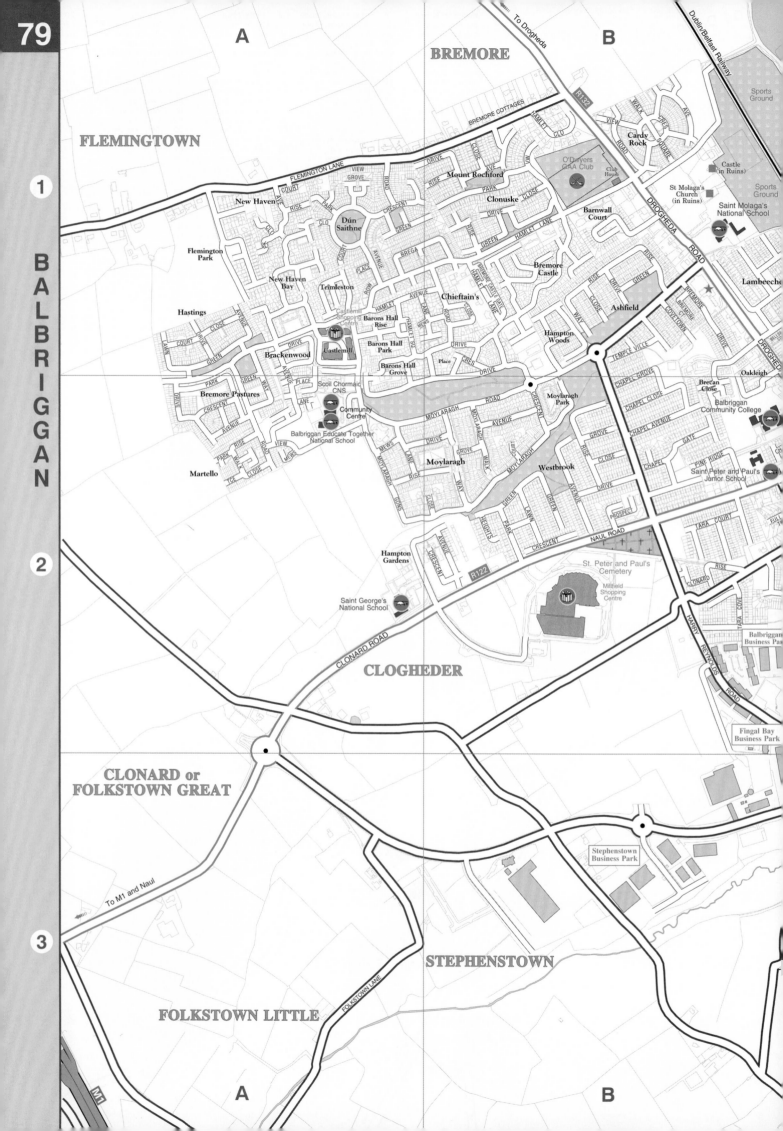

BALBRIGGAN

A

B

BREMORE

FLEMINGTOWN

1

To Drogheda

Dublin/Belfast Railway

Sports Ground

R132

FLEMINGTON LANE

VIEW GROVE

New Haven

Mount Rochford

Cardy Rock

Castle (in Ruins)

O'Dwyers GAA Club

Club House

St Molaga's Church (in Ruins)

Saint Molaga's National School

Sports Ground

Dún Saithne

Clonuske

Flemington Park

New Haven Bay

Trimleston

Barnwall Court

DROGHEDA ROAD

Lambeeche

Bremore Castle

Hastings

Chieftain's

Ashfield

BREMORE COTTAGES

Castlemill Shopping Centre

Barons Hall Rise

Hampton Woods

Brackenwood

Castlemill

Barons Hall Park

Temple Ville

Oakleigh

Place

Brecan Close

Scoil Chormaic CNS

Barons Hall Grove

Moylaragh Park

Balbriggan Community College

Bremore Pastures

Community Centre

Moylaragh

Westbrook

Chapel Grove

Chapel Close

Chapel Avenue

Pine Ridge

Saint Peter and Paul's Junior School

Balbriggan Educate Together National School

Martello

2

Hampton Gardens

R122

Saint George's National School

St. Peter and Paul's Cemetery

Millfield Shopping Centre

NAUL ROAD

Clonard

Tara Court

Balbriggan Business Park

Fingal Bay Business Park

CLONARD ROAD

CLOGHEDER

HARRY REYNOLDS ROAD

CLONARD or FOLKSTOWN GREAT

Stephenstown Business Park

To M1 and Naul

3

STEPHENSTOWN

FOLKSTOWN LITTLE

FOLKSTOWN LANE

M1

A

B

Street	Grid
Ardgillen Close	C3
Ardgillen Drive	C3
Ardgillen Lawn	C3
Ardgillen Road	C3
Ashfield Close	B1
Ashfield Drive	B1
Ashfield Green	B1
Ashfield Rise	B1
Ashfield Way	B1
Balbriggan Business Park	B2
Balbriggan Retail Park	C3
Barnwall Court	B1
Baron's Hall Grove	A1
Baron's Hall Park	A1
Baron's Hall Rise	A1
Baths Road	C1
Bellsfield Court	B1
Brackenwood Avenue	A1
Brackenwood Drive	A1
Brackenwood Lane	A2
Brackenwood Place	A2
Brecan Close	B2
Brega	A1
Bremore Castle	B1
Bremore Castle Gate	B1
Bremore Cottages	B1
Bremore Court	B1
Bremore Drive	B1
Bremore Pastures Ave.	A2
Bremore Pastures Cres.	A2
Bremore Pastures Drive	A2
Bremore Pastures Green	A2
Bremore Pastures Park	A2
Bremore Pastures Way	A2
Brick Lane	C2
Bridge Street	C2
Cardy Rock Avenue	B1
Cardy Rock Crescent	B1
Cardy Rock Road	B1
Cardy Rock Square	B1
Cardy Rock View	B1
Cardy Rock Walk	B1
Castleland Court	C2
Castleland Park View	C3
Castlelands	C3
Castlemill	A1
Chapel Avenue	B2
Chapel Close	B2
Chapel Court	C2
Chapel Gate	B2
Chapel Grove	B2
Chapel Street	C2
Chapel Street Crescent	B2
Chieftain's Close	B1
Chieftain's Crescent	B1
Chieftain's Drive	B1
Chieftain's Lane	B1
Chieftain's Mews	B1
Chieftain's Place	B1
Chieftain's Road	B1
Church Street	C2
Clonard Court	C2
Clonard Rise	B2
Clonard Road	A2
Clonard Street	C2
Clonuske Close	B1
Clonuske Drive	B1
Clonuske Green	B1
Clonuske Park	B1
Clonuske Rise	B1
Clonuske View	B1
Convent Lane	C2
Cornmill Apartments	C2
Covetown	B1
Craobhin Close	C2
Craobhin Park	C2
Curran Park	C2
Derham Park	D2
Drogheda Road	B1
Drogheda Street	B1
Dublin Street	C2
Dún Saithne Avenue	A1
Dún Saithne Close	A1
Dún Saithne Court	A1
Dún Saithne Crescent	A1
Dún Saithne Green	A1
Dún Saithne Grove	A1
Dún Saithne Park	A1
Dún Saithne Place	A1
Dún Saithne Road	A1
Dún Saithne Row	A1
Dún Saithne View	A1
Fancourt Heights	D2
Fancourt Road	C2
Fingal Bay Business Pk.	B2
Flemington Lane	A1
Flemington Park	A1
Folkstown Lane	A3
Fullam Street	B2
Fullam Terrace	B2
George's Court	C2
George's Hill	C2
Gibbons Terrace	C2
Glover Court	C2
Hamilton Avenue	C3
Hamilton Terrace	C3
Hamilton Walk	C3
Hamilton Way	C3
Hamlet Avenue	A1
Hamlet Close	B1
Hamlet Lane	B1
Hamlet Square	A1
Hampton Court	C2
Hampton Cove	D2
Hampton Gardens Av.	C2
Hampton Gardens Cres.	B2
Hampton Green	C2
Hampton Place	C2
Hampton Street	C2
Hampton Woods	B1
Harbour Road	C2
Harry Reynolds Road	B2
Hastings Avenue	A1
Hastings Close	A1
Hastings Court	A1
Hastings Drive	A1
Hastings Green	A1
Hastings Lawn	A1
High Street	C2
Lambeecher	B1
Laragh	C2
Lawless Terrace	C2
Linnen Hall	C2[1]
Martello Close	A2
Martello Mews	A2
Martello Park	A2
Martello Rise	A2
Martello Road	A2
Martello Terrace	A2
Martello View	A2
Martello Walk	A2
McNeill Hall	C2[2]
Mill Race	C2
Mill Street	C2
Mill Walk	C2
Mount Rochford Avenue	B1
Mount Rochford Close	B1
Mount Rochford Drive	B1
Mount Rochford Rise	B1
Moylaragh Avenue	B2
Moylaragh Close	B2
Moylaragh Court	B2
Moylaragh Crescent	B2
Moylaragh Drive	B2
Moylaragh Gardens	A2
Moylaragh Grove	A2
Moylaragh Lane	A2
Moylaragh Mews	A2
Moylaragh Park	B2
Moylaragh Rise	A2
Moylaragh Road	B2
Moylaragh Walk	B2
Moylaragh Way	B2
Naul Road	B2
New Haven Avenue	A1
New Haven Bay	A1
New Haven Close	A1
New Haven Court	A1
New Haven Park	A1
New Haven Rise	A1
New Market Green	C2
Oakleigh	B2
Old Market Green	C2
Papworth Hall	C2[3]
Pine Ridge	B2
Pinewood Green Avenue	D3
Pinewood Green Close	C3
Pinewood Green Court	C3
Pinewood Green Hill	D2
Pinewood Green Lawn	C2[1]
Pinewood Green Lawn	C3
Pinewood Green Road	D3
Prospect	B2
Pump Lane	C2
Quay Street	C2
Railway Street	C2
Seapoint	C2
Seapoint Lane	C2
Skerries Road	C2
St. Molagha's Terrace	C2
St. Paul's Crescent	C2
St. Peter's Terrace	C2
Stephenstown Bus. Pk.	B3
Tanners Water Lane	C3
Tara Court	B2
Tara Cove	B2
Templeville	B1
The Bower	D2
The Chantries	C3
The Square	C2
Trimelston	A1
Vauxhall Street	C2
Westbrook Avenue	B2
Westbrook Close	B2
Westbrook Crescent	B2
Westbrook Drive	B2
Westbrook Green	B2
Westbrook Grove	B2
Westbrook Heights	B2
Westbrook Lawn	B2
Westbrook Park	B2
Westbrook Rise	B2

Streets not named but shown as small numbers:

C2	1	Linnen Hall
	2	McNeill Hall
	3	Papworth Hall

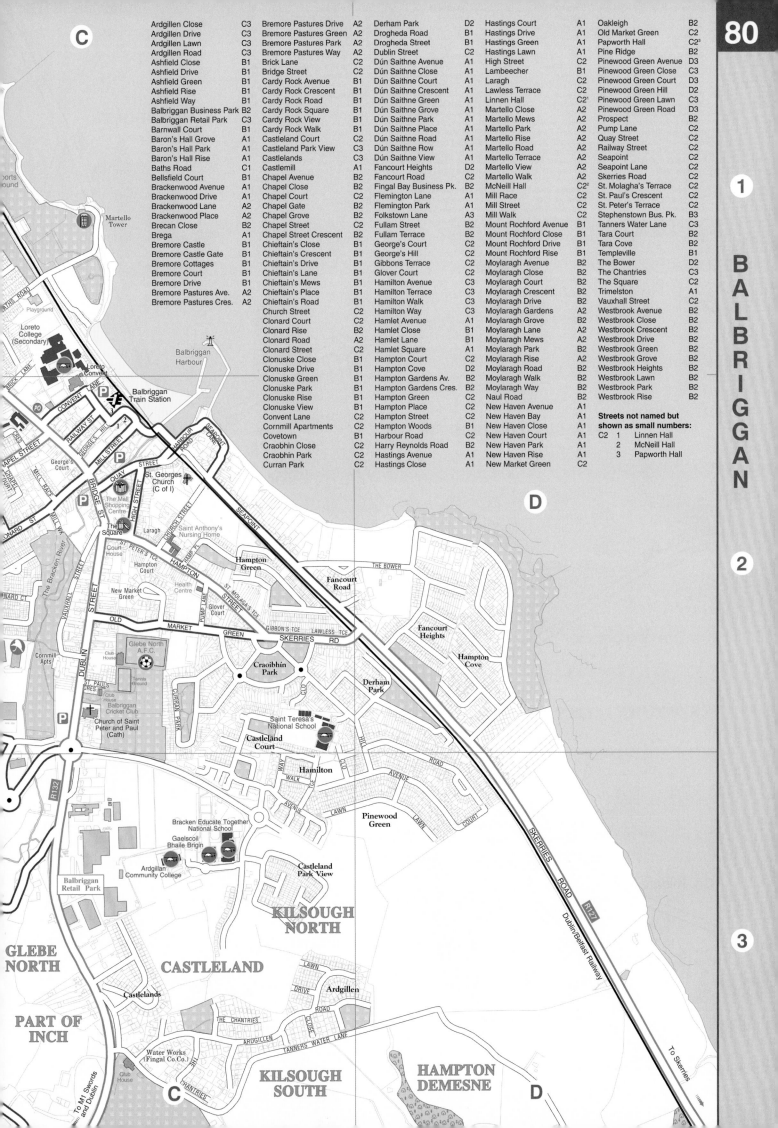

BALBRIGGAN

1

2

3

Map labels: Martello Tower; Loreto College (Secondary); Loreto Convent; Balbriggan Harbour; Balbriggan Train Station; St. Georges Church (C of I); The Mall Shopping Centre; The Square; Laragh; Saint Anthony's Nursing Home; Court House; Hampton Court; Health Centre; New Market Green; Glover Court; Glebe North A.F.C.; Craoibhín Park; Saint Teresa's National School; Castleland Court; Hamilton; Balbriggan Cricket Club; Church of Saint Peter and Paul (Cath); Bracken Educate Together National School; Gaelscoil Bhaile Brigín; Ardgillan Community College; Balbriggan Retail Park; Castleland Park View; Fancourt Road; Fancourt Heights; Hampton Cove; Derham Park; Pinewood Green; KILSOUGH NORTH; CASTLELAND; Ardgillen; Castlelands; GLEBE NORTH; PART OF INCH; Water Works (Fingal Co.Co.); KILSOUGH SOUTH; HAMPTON DEMESNE; Cornmill Apts; Skerries Rd; The Bower; Dublin/Belfast Railway; Skerries Road; To M1 Swords and Dublin; To Skerries; R132; R127

Ashton	A2	Deerpark Drive	A2	Lakeside Downs	B2	The Green	B2
Avon Rí	B3	Deerpark Green	A2	Lakeview	B3	The Green B.Abbey	A3
Baltinglass Road	A3	Deerpark Road	A2	Main Street	B2	The Green D. Park	A2
Beechdale	A2	Deerpark View	A2	Milltown Gate	A3	The Grove D. Park	A2
Beechdale Close	A2	Deerpark Walk	A2	Mountain View	B3	The Park B.Abbey	A3
Beechdale Green	A2	Downshire Park	A2	Naas Road	A2	The Walk D. Park	A2
Beechdale Grove	A2	Dublin Road	B2	Oak Drive	B2	The Way D. Park	A2
Beechdale Lawn	A2	Glenview	A2	Old Ballymore Road	A3	Tramway	B2
Beechdale View	A2	Glenview Court	A2	Old Lakeview	B2	Troopersfield	A3
Beechdale Way	A2	Haywood	A2	Park View Villas	A3	Westpark	A2
Blessington Abbey	A3	Kilbride Road	B2	Pipers Stones	A2	Woodleigh	B1
Blessington Business Park	B1	Kilmalum	A3	Rocky Pool Crescent	B3	Woodleigh Avenue	B1
Blessington Ind. Estate	A3	Kilmalum Avenue	A3	Rocky Pool Gardens	A3	Woodleigh Close	B1
Blessington Manor	A3	Kilmalum Close	A3	Rocky Pool Villas	B2	Woodleigh Grove	B1
Blessington Orchard	A3	Kilmalum Crescent	A3	Saint Joseph's Road	A3	Woodleigh Park	B2
Blessington Retail Park	A3	Kilmalum Drive	A3	The Avenue D. Park	A2	Woodleigh Way	B1
Burgage Business Park	A3	Kilmalum Green	A3	The Close B. Abbey	A3		
Burgage Manor	A3	Kilmalum Grove	A3	The Close D. Park	A2		
Carrig Glen	B3	Kilmalum Road	A3	The Dale D. Park	A2		
Deerpark	A2	Kilmalum View	A3	The Drive B. Abbey	A3		
Deerpark Close	A2	Kilmalum Way	A3	The Gate Lodge	A2		
Deerpark Court	A2	Lakeshore Holiday Village	B3	The Glen B.Abbey	A3		

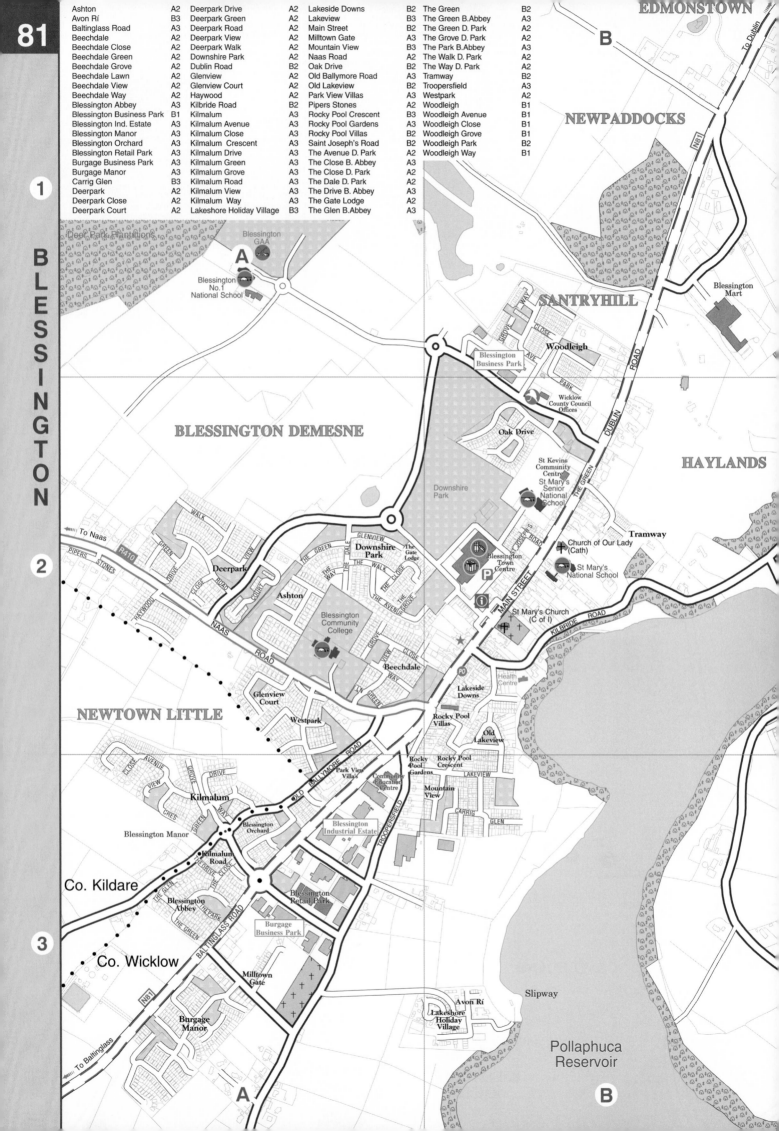

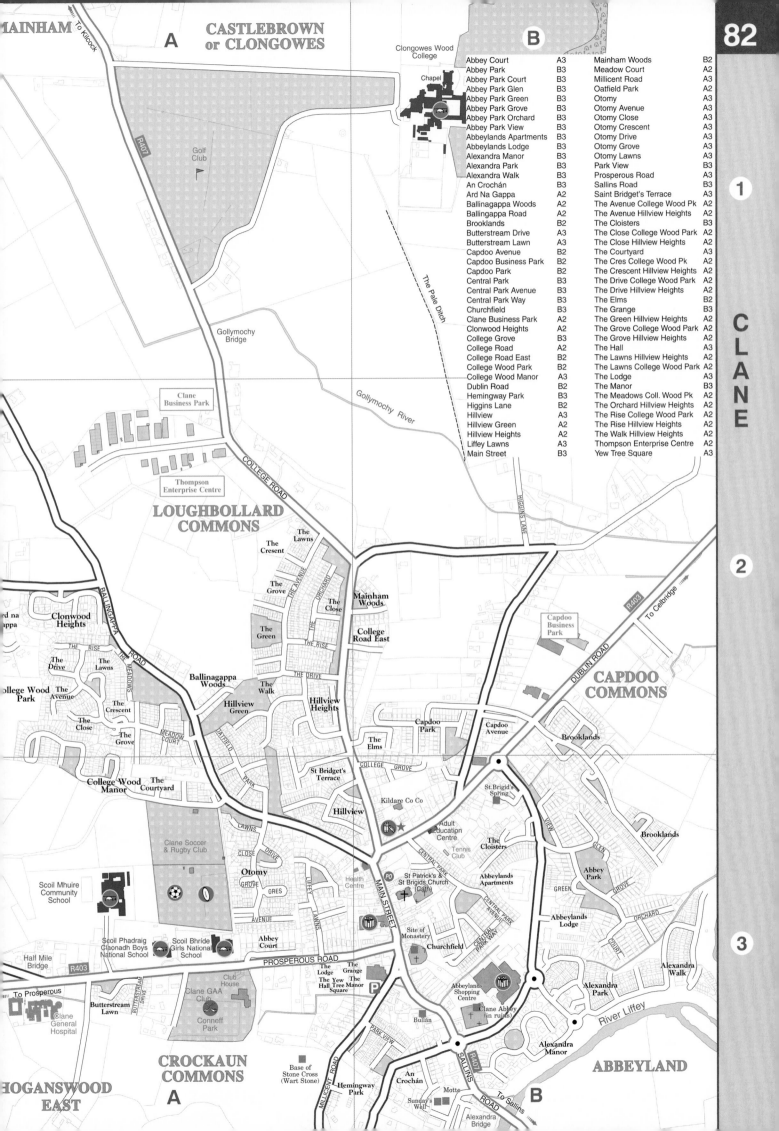

MAINHAM

To Kilcock

CASTLEBROWN or CLONGOWES

A

B

Clongowes Wood College

Chapel

Abbey Court	A3	Mainham Woods	B2
Abbey Park	B3	Meadow Court	A2
Abbey Park Court	B3	Millicent Road	A3
Abbey Park Glen	B3	Oatfield Park	A2
Abbey Park Green	B3	Otomy	A3
Abbey Park Grove	B3	Otomy Avenue	A3
Abbey Park Orchard	B3	Otomy Close	A3
Abbey Park View	B3	Otomy Crescent	A3
Abbeylands Apartments	B3	Otomy Drive	A3
Abbeylands Lodge	B3	Otomy Grove	A3
Alexandra Manor	B3	Otomy Lawns	A3
Alexandra Park	B3	Park View	B3
Alexandra Walk	B3	Prosperous Road	A3
An Crochán	B3	Sallins Road	B3
Ard Na Gappa	A2	Saint Bridget's Terrace	A3
Ballinagappa Woods	A2	The Avenue College Wood Pk	A2
Ballinagappa Road	A2	The Avenue Hillview Heights	A2
Brooklands	B2	The Cloisters	B3
Butterstream Drive	A3	The Close College Wood Park	A2
Butterstream Lawn	A3	The Close Hillview Heights	A2
Capdoo Avenue	B2	The Courtyard	A3
Capdoo Business Park	B2	The Cres College Wood Pk	A2
Capdoo Park	B2	The Crescent Hillview Heights	A2
Central Park	B3	The Drive College Wood Park	A2
Central Park Avenue	B3	The Drive Hillview Heights	A2
Central Park Way	B3	The Elms	B2
Churchfield	B3	The Grange	B3
Clane Business Park	A2	The Green Hillview Heights	A2
Clonwood Heights	A2	The Grove College Wood Park	A2
College Grove	B3	The Grove Hillview Heights	A2
College Road	A2	The Hall	A3
College Road East	B2	The Lawns Hillview Heights	A2
College Wood Park	B2	The Lawns College Wood Park	A2
College Wood Manor	A3	The Lodge	A3
Dublin Road	B2	The Manor	B3
Hemingway Park	A3	The Meadows Coll. Wood Pk	A2
Higgins Lane	B2	The Orchard Hillview Heights	A2
Hillview	A3	The Rise College Wood Park	A2
Hillview Green	A2	The Rise Hillview Heights	A2
Hillview Heights	A2	The Walk Hillview Heights	A2
Liffey Lawns	A3	Thompson Enterprise Centre	A2
Main Street	B3	Yew Tree Square	A3

Golf Club

R407

Gollymochy Bridge

Clane Business Park

Gollymochy River

The Pale Ditch

Thompson Enterprise Centre

LOUGHBOLLARD COMMONS

Higgins Lane

R403

To Celbridge

The Lawns
The Cresent
The Grove
THE AVENUE
THE ORCHARD
The Close
Mainham Woods
College Road East

Capdoo Business Park

Clonwood Heights
BALLINAGAPPA ROAD
THE RISE
The Drive
The Lawns
THE MEADOWS
The Green
THE RISE
Ballinagappa Woods
The Walk
THE DRIVE
Hillview Green
Hillview Heights
College Wood Park
The Avenue
The Crescent
The Close
MEADOW COURT
OATFIELD
The Grove
PARK

CAPDOO COMMONS

Capdoo Park
Capdoo Avenue
Brooklands

The Elms
College Wood Manor
The Courtyard
St Bridget's Terrace
COLLEGE GROVE
Kildare Co Co
St.Brigid's Spring
Brooklands

Hillview
VIEW
Abbey Park
GREEN
GROVE
ORCHARD

Adult Education Centre
Tennis Club
The Cloisters

Scoil Mhuire Community School
Otomy
GROVE
GRES
CLOSE DRIVE
LIFFEY LAWNS
AVENUE
Health Centre
PO
St Patrick's & St Brigids Church (Cath)
Abbeylands Apartments
CENTRAL PARK AVENUE
GREEN

Abbeylands Lodge

Scoil Phadraig Claonadh Boys National School
Scoil Bhríde Girls National School
Abbey Court
Churchfield
Site of Monastery
CENTRAL PARK WAY

Half Mile Bridge
R403
To Prosperous
Butterstream Lawn
BUTTERSTREAM DRIVE
Clane Soccer & Rugby Club
The Lodge
The Grange
The Yew Hall Tree Manor Square
PROSPEROUS ROAD
MILLICENT ROAD
P
Abbeylands Shopping Centre
Clane Abbey (in ruins)
Alexandra Park
Alexandra Walk

Clane General Hospital
Clane GAA Club
Conneff Park
P
Bullán
PARK VIEW
SALLINS ROAD
River Liffey
Alexandra Manor

CROCKAUN COMMONS

A

Base of Stone Cross (Wart Stone)

HOGANSWOOD EAST

Hemingway Park
An Crochán
Motte
Sunday's Well
Alexandra Bridge

To Sallins

B

ABBEYLAND

1

2

3

DELGANY

GREYSTONES

Adare Close	C2	Cherry Court	C2	Hawkins Lane	D2	Old Mill Road	D2	The Poplars	C2
Applewood Drive	C1	Cherry Drive	C2	Heathervue	D1	Orchard View	C2	Thornbury	C3
Applewood Heights	C1	Cherry Gardens	C2	Hillcrest Avenue	C2	Park Lane	D2	Trafalgar Court	D1
Bayswater Terrace	D1	Cherry Glade	C2	Hillside	D1	Pavilion Road	D2	Trafalgar Road	D1
Beach Road	D1	Cherry Glen	C2	Hillside Road	D1	Portland Place	D2	Turn Pike Lane	D1
Beechbrook Park	C2	Cherry Grove	C2	Hunter's Brook	B3	Portland Road	D2	Upper Grattan Park	C1
Belleview Demesne	C1	Cherry Lane Nurseries	C2	Kendalstown Rise	B1	Portland Road North	D2	Valley View	B3
Bellevue Cottages	B2	Cherry Orchard	C2	Kenmare Heights	C2	Priory Drive	C3	Victoria Road	D1
Bellevue Court	B3	Cherry Rise	C2	Kilcoole Road	C3	Priory Gate	B3	Wendon Brook	C3
Bellevue Heights	C2	Church Gate	D1	Killincarrig Road	D1	Priory Rise	C2	Wendon Drive	C3
Bellevue Lawns	B2	Church Lane	C1	Killincarrig Village	C2	Priory Road	B3	Wendon Park	C3
Bellevue Park	D1	Church Road	C3	Kimberley Court	D1	Priory Way	C2	Whitshed Road	D2
Bellevue Road	D1	Church Road	D1	Kimberley Road	D1	Quarry Road	D2	Willow Bank	C1
Blackberry Lane	B3	Church View	C3	Kindlestown Heights	B2	Rathdown Close	D1	Willow Park	C2
Blacklion Manor	C1	Churchfields	C2	Kindlestown Lower	C2	Rathdown Court	C1	Willowmere	INSET
Bow Lane	D1	Cliff Road	D1	Kindlestown Park	C2	Rathdown Lawn	C1	Woodlands	D2
Burnaby Avenue	D3	Convent Court	B3	Kinlen Road	D2	Rathdown Park	C1		
Burnaby Court	D3	Convent Road	B2	La Touche Close	D1	Rathdown Road	INSET		
Burnaby Heights	C2	Delgany Gate	C3	La Touche Park	C1	Rathdown Road	INSET		
Burnaby Lawns	D3	Delgany Glen	C2	La Touche Place	D1	Redford	INSET		
Burnaby Manor	D1	Delgany Hills	C3	La Touche Road	D1	Redford Court	INSET		
Burnaby Mews	D1	Delgany Park	C3	Lower Grattan Park	C1	Redford Park	INSET		
Burnaby Mill	D3	Delgany Wood	C2	Manor Avenue	C1	Redford Rise	INSET		
Burnaby Park	D2	Dromont	B2	Marine Road	D1	Rivendell Grove	C2		
Burnaby Road	D2	Drummin Rise	C3	Marine Terrace	D1	Riverfield	C2		
Burnaby Woods	D2	Easton	B2	Meadow Court	C3	Saint Crispins	INSET		
Carrig Meadow	C3	Eden Road	D1	Mill Bank	D1	Saint Vincent Road	D2		
Carrig Orchard	C2	Elsinore	D1	Mill Road	D2	Sea View	INSET		
Carrig Villas	C2	Ennis Lane	INSET	Mill Road	D3	Seabourne View Apts.	D3		
Castle Villas	C2	Erskine Avenue	D2	Millbrook	D3	Sidmonton Road	D1		
Castlefield Terrace	C2	Fair Green	A3	Millgrove	C3	Somerby Road	D2		
Chapel Road	C1	Fairfield Park	D1	Millgrove Close	C3	South Place	D2		
Chapel Road	C2	Farm Lane	D2	Mount Haven	INSET	Southern Relief Road	D3		
Chapel View	C1	Glen of the Downs	A3	Mountain View Park	C1	St. Bridget's Park	C1		
Charlesland Court	D3	Glen Road	B3	New Road	C3	The Arch	D1		
Charlesland Grove	D3	Glenair Manor	C3	New Road	D1	The Bawn	D1		
Charlesland Park	D3	Glenbrook Park	C3	Oaklands	C1	The Manor	D1		
Charlesland Wood	D3	Harbour Court	D1	Oaklands Court	C1	The Nurseries	C2		

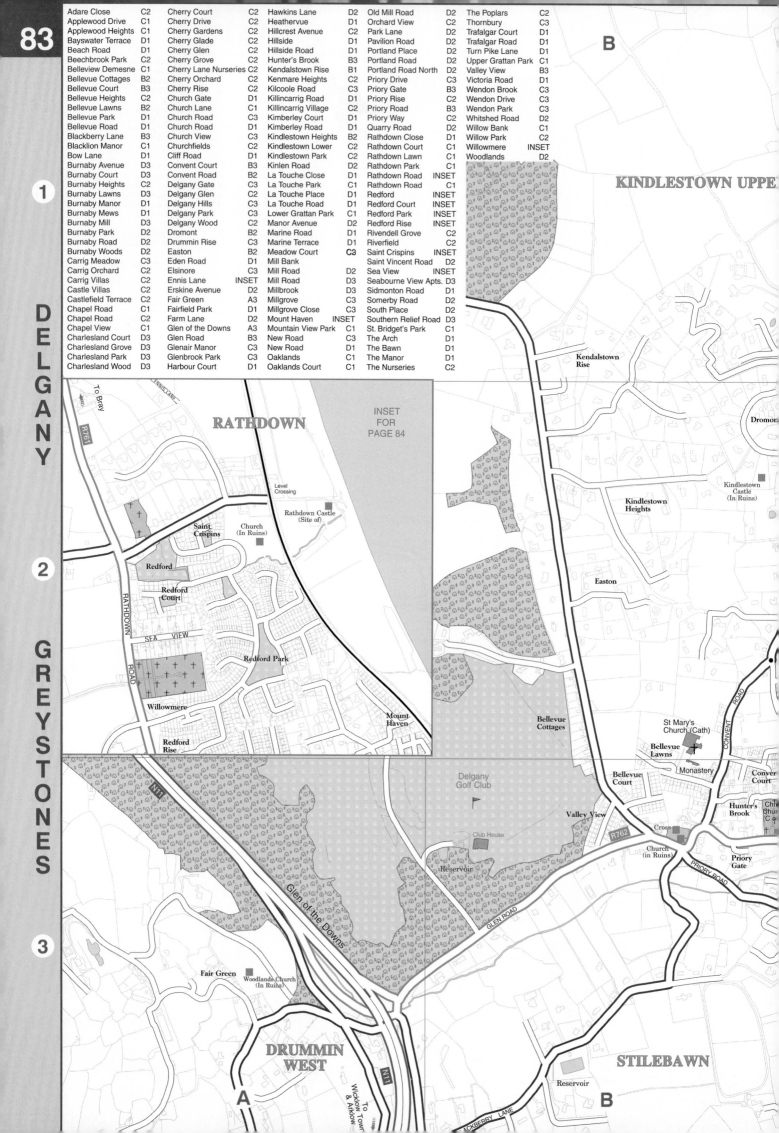

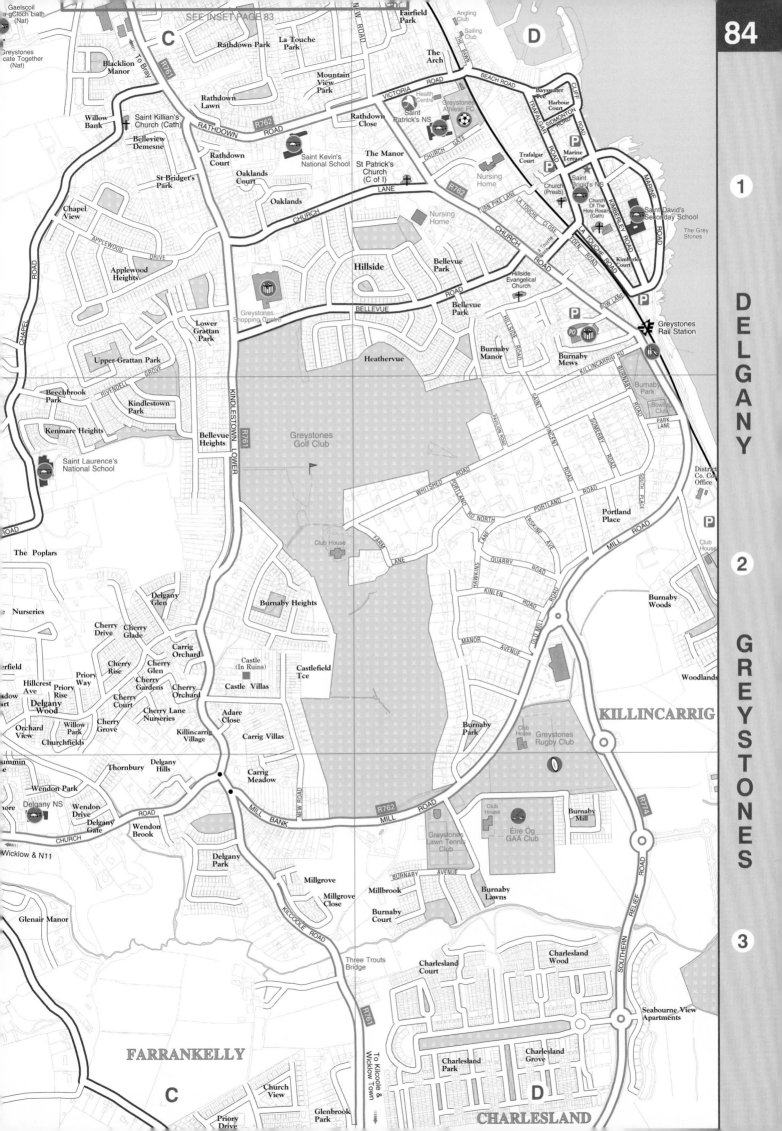

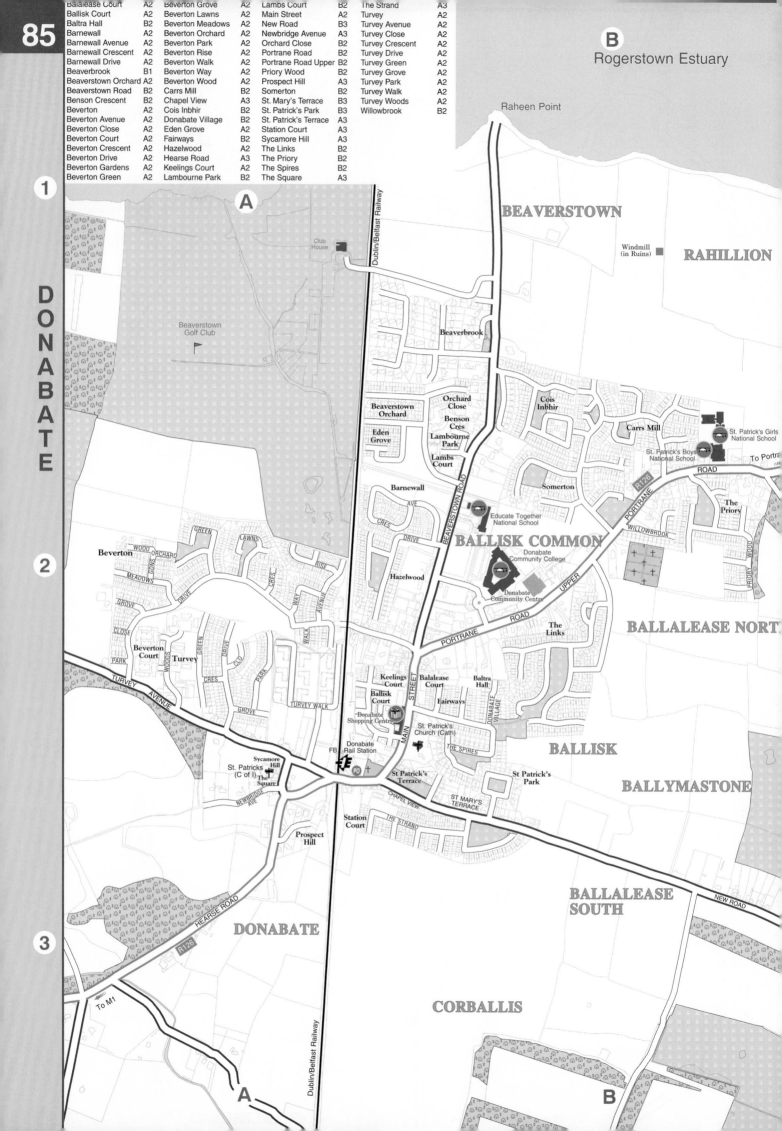

Balalease Court	A2	Beverton Grove	A2	Lambs Court	A2	The Strand	A3
Ballisk Court	A2	Beverton Lawns	A2	Main Street	B2	Turvey	A2
Baltra Hall	B2	Beverton Meadows	A2	New Road	B3	Turvey Avenue	A2
Barnewall	A2	Beverton Orchard	A2	Newbridge Avenue	A3	Turvey Close	A2
Barnewall Avenue	A2	Beverton Park	A2	Orchard Close	B2	Turvey Crescent	A2
Barnewall Crescent	A2	Beverton Rise	A2	Portrane Road	B2	Turvey Drive	A2
Barnewall Drive	A2	Beverton Walk	A2	Portrane Road Upper	B2	Turvey Green	A2
Beaverbrook	B1	Beverton Way	A2	Priory Wood	B2	Turvey Grove	A2
Beaverstown Orchard	A2	Beverton Wood	A2	Prospect Hill	A3	Turvey Park	A2
Beaverstown Road	B2	Carrs Mill	B2	Somerton	B2	Turvey Walk	A2
Benson Crescent	B2	Chapel View	A3	St. Mary's Terrace	A3	Turvey Woods	A2
Beverton	A2	Cois Inbhir	B2	St. Patrick's Park	B3	Willowbrook	B2
Beverton Avenue	A2	Donabate Village	B2	St. Patrick's Terrace	A3		
Beverton Close	A2	Eden Grove	A2	Station Court	A3		
Beverton Court	A2	Fairways	B2	Sycamore Hill	A3		
Beverton Crescent	A2	Hazelwood	A2	The Links	B2		
Beverton Drive	A2	Hearse Road	A3	The Priory	B2		
Beverton Gardens	A2	Keelings Court	A2	The Spires	B2		
Beverton Green	A2	Lambourne Park	B2	The Square	A3		

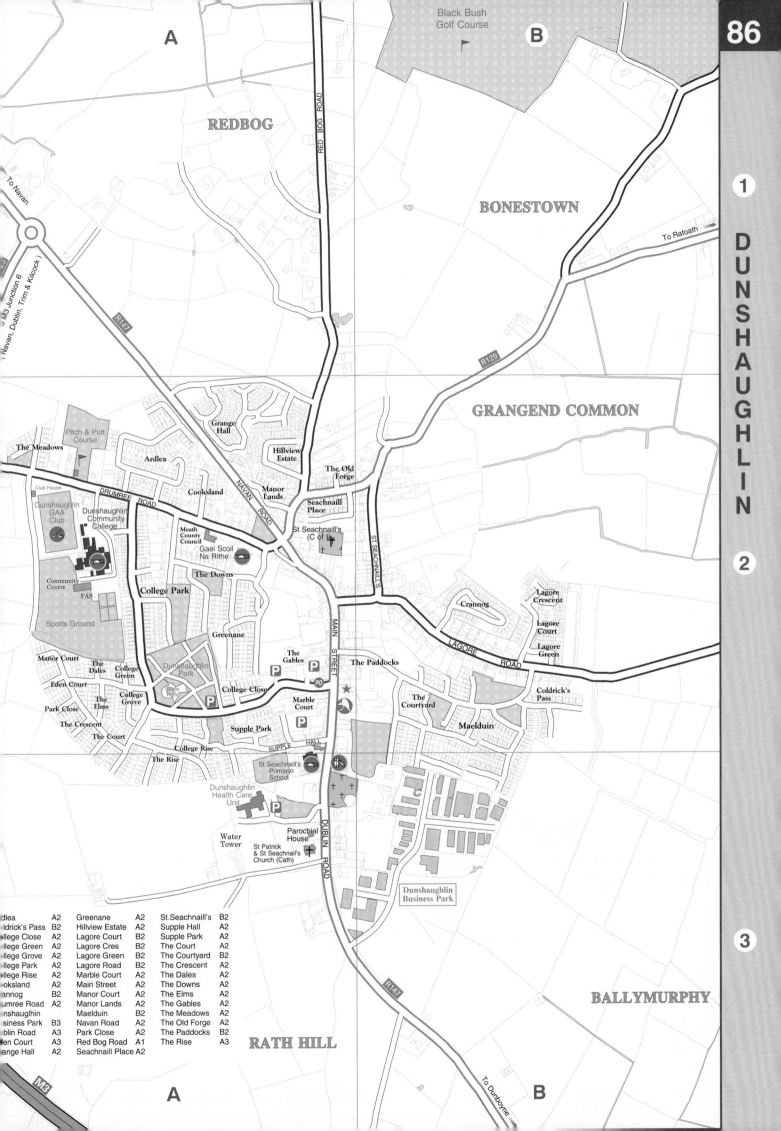

Black Bush
Golf Course

B

A

REDBOG

BONESTOWN

To Navan

To Ratoath

R147

To M3 Junction 6
(Navan, Dublin, Trim & Kilcock)

R125

GRANGEND COMMON

RED BOG ROAD

Grange
Hall

Pitch & Putt
Course

The Meadows

Ardlea

Hillview
Estate

Club House

Cooksland

Manor
Lands

The Old
Forge

Dunshaughlin
GAA Club

DRUMREE ROAD

Seachnaill
Place

ST SEACHNAILL'S

Dunshaughlin
Community College

Meath
County
Council

St Seachnaill's
(C of I)

Community
Centre

Gael Scoil
Na Rithe

Crannog

Lagore
Crescent

FÁS

The Downs

Lagore
Court

Sports Ground

College Park

Greenane

LAGORE ROAD

Lagore
Green

Manor Court

The
Dales

College
Green

Dunshaughlin
Park

Coldrick's
Pass

Eden Court

The Gables

P

P

The Paddocks

The
Courtyard

Park Close

The
Elms

College
Grove

P

PO

NAVAN ROAD

MAIN STREET

College Close

Marble
Court

Maelduin

The Crescent

P

The Court

Supple Park

College Rise

SUPPLE HALL

The Rise

St Seachnaill's
Primary School

Dunshaughlin
Health Care
Unit

P

Water
Tower

Parochial
House

St Patrick
& St Seachnaill's
Church (Cath)

Dunshaughlin
Business Park

DUBLIN ROAD

R147

BALLYMURPHY

RATH HILL

M3

A

B

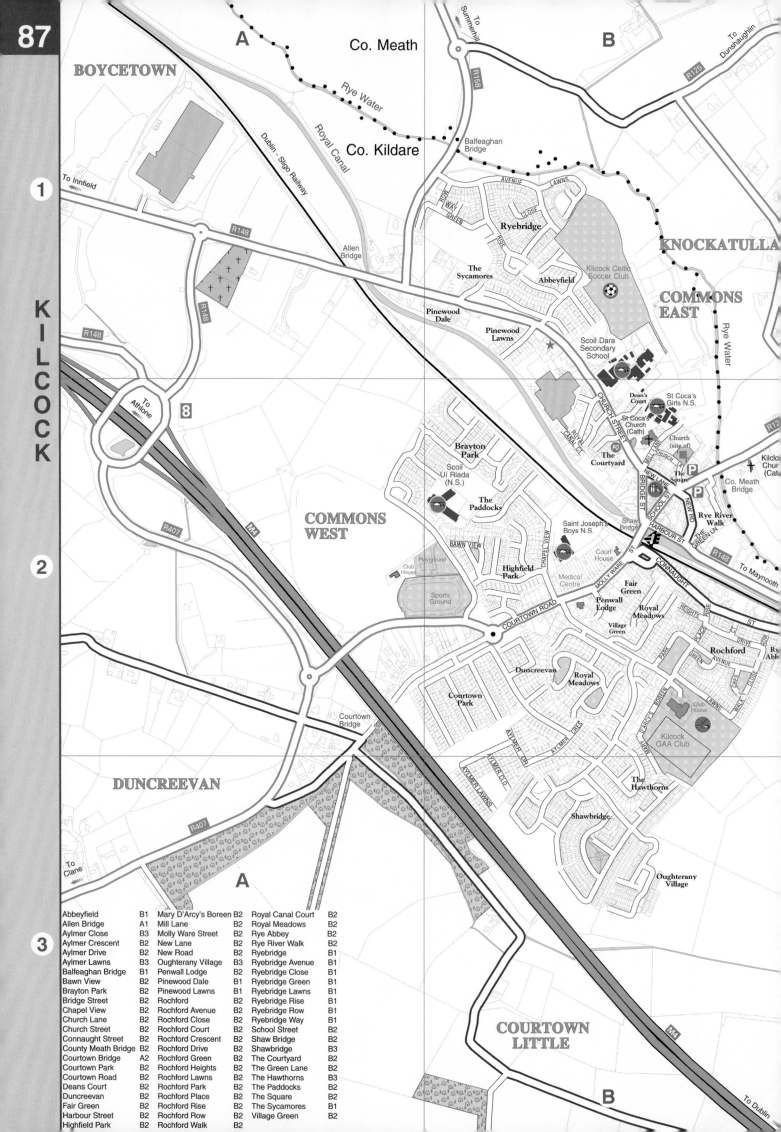

KILCOCK

BOYCETOWN

Co. Meath

Rye Water

Co. Kildare

To Innfield

KNOCKATULLA

Ryebridge

COMMONS EAST

Kilcock Celtic Soccer Club

The Sycamores

Abbeyfield

Pinewood Dale

Scoil Dara Secondary School

Pinewood Lawns

Allen Bridge

Dublin - Sligo Railway

Royal Canal

Balfeaghan Bridge

To Summerhill

To Dunshaughlin

Dean's Court

St Coca's Girls N.S.

St Coca's Church (Cath)

The Courtyard

Church (site of)

Kilclo Chur (Cath

Co. Meath Bridge

To Athlone

Brayton Park

Scoil Uí Riada (N.S.)

The Paddocks

COMMONS WEST

Saint Joseph's Boys N.S.

Shaw Bridge

Rye River Walk

Bawn View

Court House

Highfield Park

Medical Centre

Fair Green

Penwall Lodge

Royal Meadows

To Maynooth

Club House

Playground

Village Green

Rochford

Sports Ground

Courtown Road

Duncreevan

Royal Meadows

The Hawthorns

Courtown Park

Kilcock GAA Club

Courtown Bridge

DUNCREEVAN

Shawbridge

Oughterany Village

To Clane

COURTOWN LITTLE

To Dublin

bbeylands	B2	Dun Emer	A2	Perrin Way	B2
shgrove	A2	Dun Emer Avenue	A2	Post Office Road	A2
aker's Close	B2	Dun Emer Close	A2	Quickpennies Road	A1
alleally Lane	B3	Dun Emer Court	A2	Raheny Lane	B2
arrack Lane	B2	Dun Emer Crescent	A2	Rathmore Road	B3
elfry Place	B2	Dun Emer Dale	A2	Remount	B3
lackraven Court	B2	Dun Emer Drive	A2	Saddlers Place	B2
lacksmith's Road	B2	Dun Emer Gardens	A2	Scholar's Walk	B2
ramble Lane	B2	Dun Emer Glade	A2	Scribes Court	B2
hapel Farm	A2	Dun Emer Green	A2	Skerries Road	B1
hapel Farm Avenue	A2	Dun Emer Grove	A2	Station Road	B2
hapel Farm Close	A2	Dun Emer Lawn	A2	Stonemason's	B2
hapel Farm Copse	A2	Dun Emer Park	A2	Stonemason's Close	B2
hapel Farm Court	A3	Dun Emer Place	A2	Stonemason's Road	B2
hapel Farm Cresent	A2	Dun Emer Rise	A2	Sweetman Walk	B2
hapel Farm Drive	A3	Dun Emer Road	A2	Tanner's Way	B2
hapel Farm Green	A2	Dun Emer View	A2	Thatcher's Way	B2
hapel Farm Grove	A2	Dun Emer Walk	A2	The Green	A2
hapel Farm Lane	A2	Dun Emer Way	A2	The Square	B2
hapel Farm Lawn	A2	Forge Avenue	B3	T. Avenue Orlynn Park	B2
hapel Farm Mews	A2	Forge Lane	B2	The Close Orlynn Park	B2
hapel Farm Park	A2	Forge View	B3	The Drive Orlynn Park	B2
hapel Farm Place	A3	Gleann Ribh	B2	The Grove Orlynn Park	B2
hapel Farm Road	A2	Great Commons	B2	The Park Orlynn Park	B3
hapel Farm Row	A2	Hands Lane	A2	Thornigne-Foullard Ln.	A2
hapel Farm Square	A3	Hill Lane	B1	Tower View	A2
hapel Farm Terrace	A3	Huntsman's Road	B2	Treen Hill	A2
hapel Farm Walk	A2	Huntsman's Way	B2	Tyrell's Row	B2
hapel Farm Way	A2	Joyce Road	B2	Village Road	B2
hapel Farm Wood	A2	Kelly Park	A2	Weaver's Crescent	B2
hapel Green	A2	Kielys Lane	A3	Wendy Walsh Close	B2
hapel Lane	A2	Kilhedge Lane	A3	Whitethorn Walk	B2
hapel Road	A2	Little Commons	B2	Windward Way	B2
hurch Road	B2	Macullens Close	A2		
obbler's Walk	B2	Main Street	B2		
oleman	B2	Miller's Square	B2		
oleman Crescent	B2	Minister's Park	A2		
oleman Way	B2	Minister's Rise	A2		
ommon's Lane	B1	Minister's Road	A2		
oopers Walk	B2	Netterville Place	B2		
anes Court	B2	Norsemans Walk	B2		
ublin Road	B2	Orlynn Park	B2		

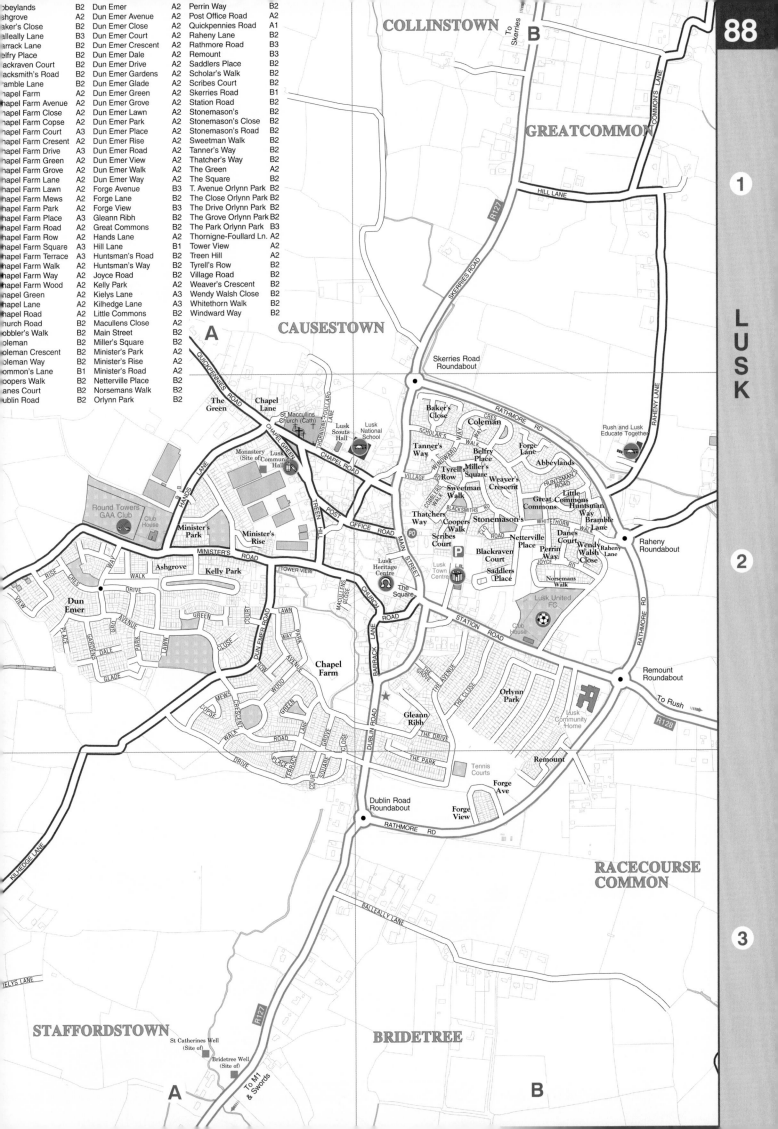

RUSH

An Tearmann	B3	Golden Ridge Close	C2	Mill Bank Court	B2	St Catherines Park	C1
Barrack Lane	C2	Golden Ridge Crescent	C2	Mill Bank Walk	B2	St Catherines View	C1
Bawn Road	C2	Golden Ridge Drive	C2	North Beach	C2	St Catherines Way	C1
Bayview Villas	C2	Golden Ridge Green	C2	Old Barrack Road	D3	St. Joseph's Road	C3
Bollum Lane	C2	Golden Ridge Lodge	C2	Old Haystown	B2	St. Maur's Park	C2
Brook Lane	B2	Golden Ridge Mews	C2	Old Road	B2	Sundrive Road	B3
Brookfield Park	C2	Golden Ridge Square	C2	Old Road Court	B2	Sunlock Court	C2
Brookford	B2	Golden Ridge View	C2	Old Road Grove	B2	Sunset Court	C2
Brookford Park	B2	Golden Ridge Walk	C2	Palmer Avenue	C1	Tayleurs Point	D3
Brookside Gardens	B2	Golden Ridge Way	C2	Palmer Court	C1	The Cairn	C1
Carthy's Lane	A3	Golf Road	B3	Palmer Road	C1	The Forge	D2
Carrig Leathan	C2	Hand Park	D2	Park Road	C2	The Mall	C2
Ceol na Mara	C2	Hands Lane	C3	Quay Road	D2	The Millbank	B2
Channel Road	A3	Harbour Road	D2	Ravenswell	D2	Thorn Chase	C1
Chapel Green	B2	Haystown	B2	Rogerstown Court	B3	Thornleigh	C2
Clann Beag	B3	Haystown Close	B2	Rogerstown Park	B3	Thornleigh Court	C2
Clifflands	C1	Haystown Road	B2	Sandy Lane	C3	Tower Street	D2
Clifflands Court	C1	Healy's Lane	B3	Sandy Road	C2	Upper Main Street	C2
Clifflands Rise	C1	Hoskyn Bank	C3	Sea Brook	B2	Whitestown Road	A3
Coast Guard Road	INSET	Kenure Crescent	C2	Seafield Court	D2	Woodbury	C2
Cois Tra	C2	Kenure Lawns	C1	Skerries Road	C1	Wooddale Road	C1
Congress Gardens	C3	Kenure Park	C2	Six Cross Lane	C1	Woodland Court	C2
Convent Lane	C3	Kilbush Lane	C2	South Shore Cove	B3	Woodland Park	C2
Cooper's Lane	C2	Kilbush View	C2	South Shore Road	C2		
Coopersfield	C2	Knockabawn	D2	South Strand	C3		
Crescent Road	B3	Lady Cove	C1	Spout Road	A3		
Daly's Lane	B3	Lambay View	C1	St Catherines Avenue	C1		
Doctor's Lane	B2	Linkside	INSET	St Catherines Close	C1		
Echlin Court	C2	Linn Ban	B2	St Catherines Court	C1		
Eden Terrace	C2	Linn Beag	B2	St Catherines Crescent	C1		
Farran's Lane	C2	Linn Cuin	B2	St Catherines Drive	C1		
Finistere	D2	Linn Dubh	B2	St Catherines Estate	C1		
Golden Ridge	C2	Lower Main Street	C2	St Catherines Green	C1		
Golden Ridge Avenue	C2	Melbourne Gardens	C3	St Catherines Grove	C1		
Golden Ridge Court	C2	Mill Bank	B2	St Catherines Lawn	C1		

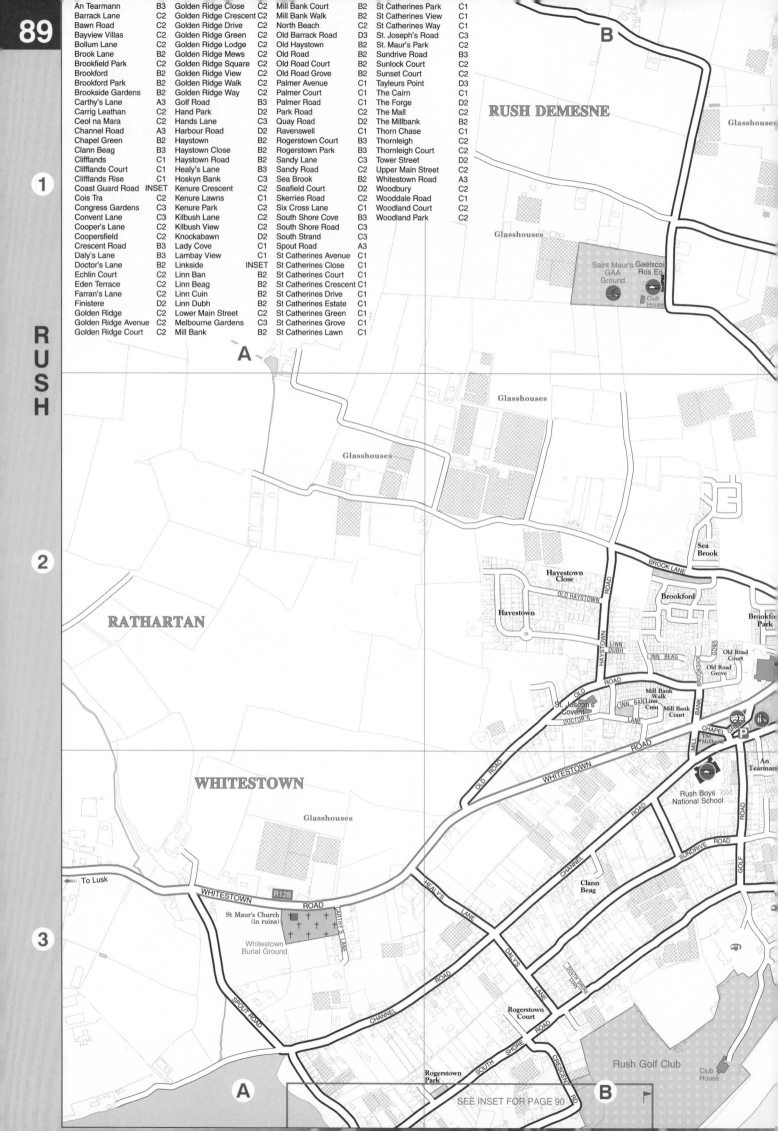

RUSH DEMESNE

Glasshouses

RATHARTAN

WHITESTOWN

To Lusk

WHITESTOWN ROAD R128

St Maur's Church (in ruins)

Whitestown Burial Ground

Saint Maur's GAA Ground

Gaelscoil Ros Eo

Club House

Hayestown Close

Hayestown

Brookford

Brookford Park

Sea Brook

St. Joseph's Convent

Rush Boys National School

An Tearmann

Clann Beag

Rogerstown Court

Rogerstown Park

Rush Golf Club

Club House

SEE INSET FOR PAGE 90

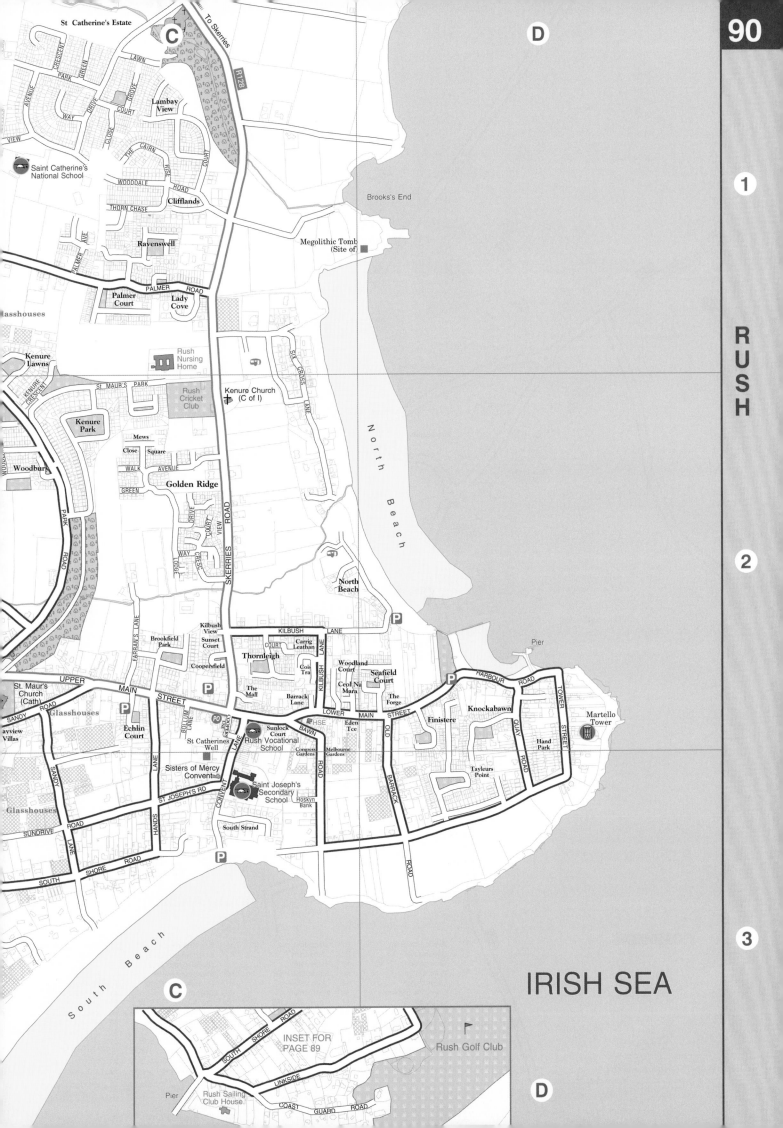

St Catherine's Estate

C

To Skerries

R128

CRESCENT
GREEN
PARK
LAWN

AVENUE
WAY
DRIVE
CLOSE
COURT
GROVE

Lambay View

VIEW

THE CAIRN
RISE
ROAD

Saint Catherine's
National School

WOODDALE

THORN CHASE

Clifflands

PALMER AVE

Ravenswell

D

Brooks's End

Megolithic Tomb
(Site of) ■

PALMER ROAD

Palmer Court

Lady Cove

Glasshouses

Kenure
Lawns

KENURE CRESCENT

ST MAUR'S PARK

Rush
Nursing
Home

Rush
Cricket
Club

Kenure Church
(C of I)

SIX CROSS LANE

Kenure Park

Mews

Close   Square

Woodbury

WALK   AVENUE

GREEN

Golden Ridge

SKERRIES ROAD

VIEW

DRIVE

WOOD

WAY

CRESC

COURT

PARK ROAD

North

Beach

North
Beach

P

KILBUSH LANE

**Kilbush
View**

**Brookfield
Park**

**Sunset
Court**

KILBUSH LANE

Thornleigh

COURT

**Carrig
Leathan**

Coopersfield

Cois
Tra

KILBUSH LANE

**Woodland
Court**

**Seafield
Court**

FARRAN'S LANE

**The
Mall**

**Barrack
Lane**

Ceol Na
Mara

**The
Forge**

Pier

HARBOUR ROAD

UPPER

St. Maur's
Church
(Cath)

MAIN

STREET

LOWER   MAIN   STREET

Finistere

Knockabawn

TOWER STREET

QUAY ROAD

Martello
Tower

SANDY

Glasshouses

BOLTON LANE

PO

CROMWELL

P

Echlin
Court

PQ

Sunlock
Court

HSE

St Catherines
Well

Rush Vocational
School

Eden
Tce

OLD

BARRACK ROAD

**Hand
Park**

ayview
Villas

Sisters of Mercy
Convent

CONVENT LANE

Congress
Gardens

Melbourne
Gardens

**Tayleurs
Point**

SANDY

LANE

ST JOSEPH'S RD

Saint Joseph's
Secondary
School

Hoskyn
Bank

Glasshouses

ROAD

HANDS

South Strand

SUNDRIVE

LANE

SHORE ROAD

P

SOUTH

*South
Beach*

IRISH SEA

C

INSET FOR
PAGE 89

SOUTH SHORE ROAD

Rush Golf Club

LINKSIDE

Pier

Rush Sailing
Club House

COAST GUARD ROAD

D

90

1

2

3

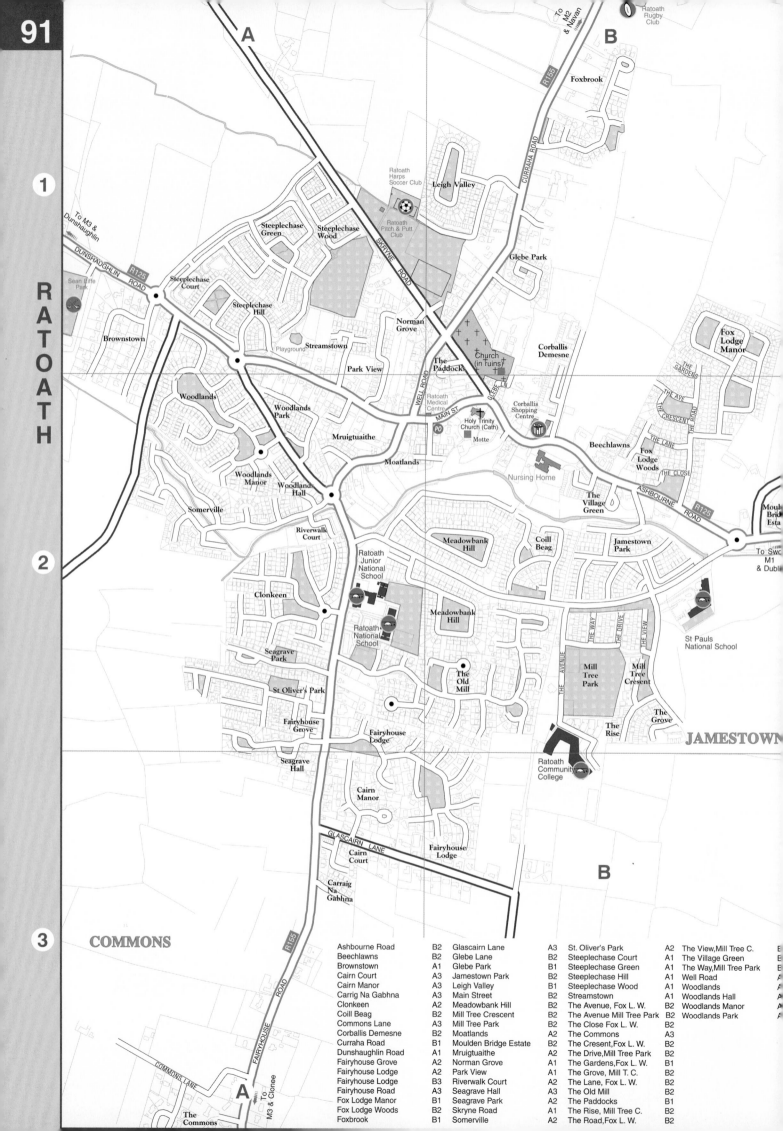

RATOATH

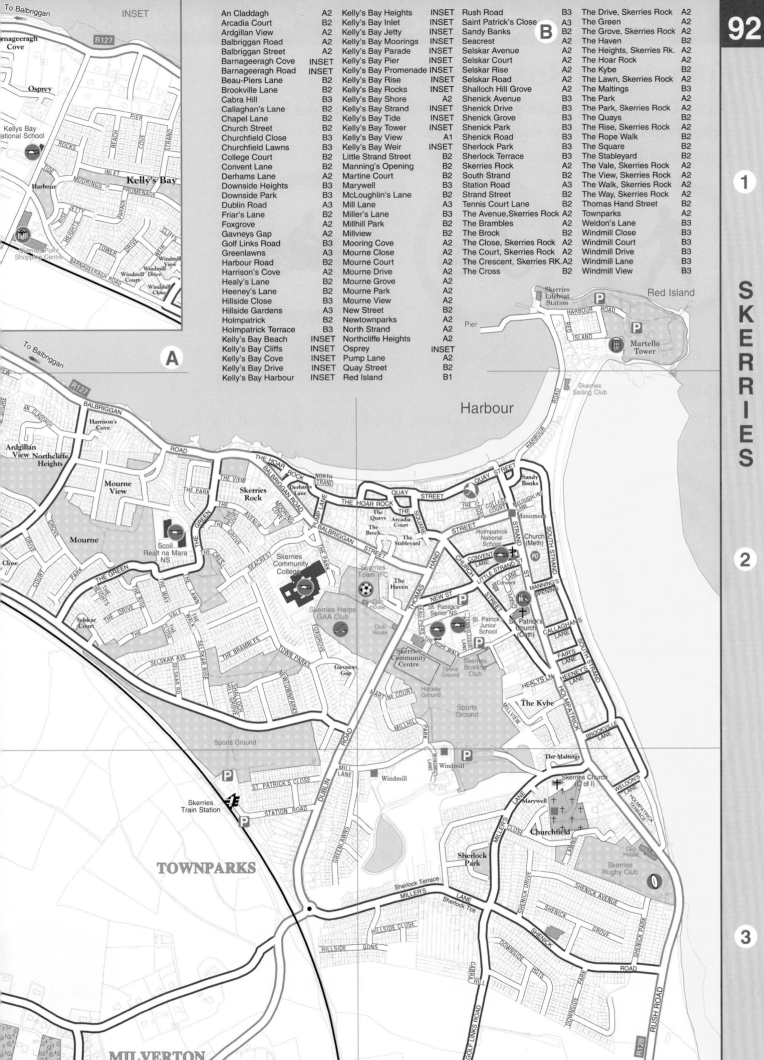

An Claddagh	A2	Kelly's Bay Heights	INSET	Rush Road	B3	The Drive, Skerries Rock	A2
Arcadia Court	B2	Kelly's Bay Inlet	INSET	Saint Patrick's Close	A3	The Green	A2
Ardgillan View	A2	Kelly's Bay Jetty	INSET	Sandy Banks	B2	The Grove, Skerries Rock	A2
Balbriggan Road	A2	Kelly's Bay Moorings	INSET	Seacrest	A2	The Haven	A2
Balbriggan Street	A2	Kelly's Bay Parade	INSET	Selskar Avenue	A2	The Heights, Skerries Rk.	A2
Barnageeragh Cove	INSET	Kelly's Bay Pier	INSET	Selskar Court	A2	The Hoar Rock	A2
Barnageeragh Road	INSET	Kelly's Bay Promenade	INSET	Selskar Rise	A2	The Kybe	B2
Beau-Piers Lane	B2	Kelly's Bay Rise	INSET	Selskar Road	A2	The Lawn, Skerries Rock	A2
Brookville Lane	B2	Kelly's Bay Rocks	INSET	Shalloch Hill Grove	A2	The Maltings	B3
Cabra Hill	B3	Kelly's Bay Shore	A2	Shenick Avenue	B3	The Park	A2
Callaghan's Lane	B2	Kelly's Bay Strand	INSET	Shenick Drive	B3	The Park, Skerries Rock	A2
Chapel Lane	B2	Kelly's Bay Tide	INSET	Shenick Grove	B3	The Quays	A2
Church Street	B2	Kelly's Bay Tower	INSET	Shenick Park	B3	The Rise, Skerries Rock	A2
Churchfield Close	B3	Kelly's Bay View	A1	Shenick Road	B3	The Rope Walk	A2
Churchfield Lawns	B3	Kelly's Bay Weir	INSET	Sherlock Park	B3	The Square	B2
College Court	B2	Little Strand Street	B2	Sherlock Terrace	B3	The Stableyard	B2
Convent Lane	B2	Manning's Opening	B2	Skerries Rock	A2	The Vale, Skerries Rock	A2
Derhams Lane	A2	Martine Court	B2	South Strand	B2	The View, Skerries Rock	A2
Downside Heights	B3	Marywell	B3	Station Road	A3	The Walk, Skerries Rock	A2
Downside Park	B3	McLoughlin's Lane	B2	Strand Street	B2	The Way, Skerries Rock	A2
Dublin Road	A3	Mill Lane	A3	Tennis Court Lane	B2	Thomas Hand Street	B2
Friar's Lane	B2	Miller's Lane	B3	The Avenue, Skerries Rock	A2	Townparks	A2
Foxgrove	A2	Millhill Park	B2	The Brambles	A2	Weldon's Lane	B3
Gavneys Gap	A2	Millview	B2	The Brock	B2	Windmill Close	B3
Golf Links Road	B3	Mooring Cove	A2	The Close, Skerries Rock	A2	Windmill Court	B3
Greenlawns	A3	Mourne Close	A2	The Court, Skerries Rock	A2	Windmill Drive	B3
Harbour Road	B2	Mourne Court	A2	The Crescent, Skerries RK.	A2	Windmill Lane	B3
Harrison's Cove	A2	Mourne Drive	A2	The Cross	B2	Windmill View	B3
Healy's Lane	B2	Mourne Grove	A2				
Heeney's Lane	B2	Mourne Park	A2				
Hillside Close	B3	Mourne View	A2				
Hillside Gardens	A3	New Street	B2				
Holmpatrick	B2	Newtownparks	A2				
Holmpatrick Terrace	B3	North Strand	A2				
Kelly's Bay Beach	INSET	Northcliffe Heights	A2				
Kelly's Bay Cliffs	INSET	Osprey	INSET				
Kelly's Bay Cove	INSET	Pump Lane	A2				
Kelly's Bay Drive	INSET	Quay Street	B2				
Kelly's Bay Harbour	INSET	Red Island	B1				

SKERRIES

Vulnerable Road Users

Since 2007, approximately 60% of Dublin's fatalities have been pedestrians, cyclists or motorcyclists.

Watch out for vulnerable road users

4 in 10 Fatalities

1 in 10 Fatalities

1 in 10 Fatalities

Speed Limits

To protect our Vulnerable Road Users, the following speed Limits apply within the Greater Dublin Area

High Concentration of Vulnerable Road Users

General built up areas

Primary approach roads to the city

Statistics show that:

◉ **85% of pedestrians would be killed if hit at 60kph**

◉ **45% of pedestrians would be killed if hit at 50kph**

◉ **5% of pedestrians would be killed if hit at 30kph**

Know your Speed Limits, know YOUR Speed!

Garda personnel conduct speed checks across the road network using handheld and in-car equipment as well as mobile safety camera vans. Safety camera vans are also operated by a service provider on behalf of An Garda Síochána in speed enforcement zones. These zones may be found at www.garda.ie

Take heed - do not speed!

Crime Prevention Advice

It pays to be careful. To reduce your chances of becoming a victim of crime, consider the following -

» Be aware of your surroundings

» Avoid travelling alone, where possible

» Avoid walking alone at night

» Keep cash on your person to the minimum required

» Keep wallets / purses out of sight

» Keep hand or shoulder bags close to the body and not dangling by the straps

» Where possible, take a mobile phone with you when out & about

» If travelling by public transport, sit as close as possible to the driver or exit

» If travelling by car, keep all doors locked

» Be alert when parking and getting out of your vehicle

» Be alert to pickpockets

» Ideally, do not leave property in cars or other vehicles

» Be especially careful with small electronic equipment e.g. Sat Navs, digital cameras, mobile phones, music players etc.

» Close all windows and lock all doors

» Do not leave property on view in your vehicle

» Do not leave cash, cheque books, credit/debit cards in your vehicle

» Do not leave personal/valuable documents in your vehicle e.g. utility bills, bank statements etc.

» Avoid parking in isolated places and, at night-time, park with care in a well-lit area

» Always secure bicycles to an immovable object

Apostolic Nunciature
183 Navan Road
Dublin 7
Tel: 838 0577
24 D4

Argentine Embassy
15 Ailesbury Drive
Dublin 4
Tel: 269 1546
48 D1

Australian Embassy
7th Floor,
Fitzwilton House
Wilton Terrace, Dublin 2
Tel: 664 5300
38 E4

Austrian Embassy
15 Ailesbury Court Apts.
93 Ailesbury Road
Dublin 4
Tel: 269 4577
48 D1

Belgian Embassy
1 Elgin Road
Dublin 4
Tel: 6315284
38 F4

Embassy of the Federative Republic of Brazil
Block 8 Sixth Floor
Harcourt Centre,
Charlotte Way.
Dublin 2.
Tel: 475 6000
38 D4

British Embassy
29 Merrion Road
Dublin 4
Tel: 205 3700
48 D1

Bulgarian Embassy
22 Burlington Road
Dublin 4
Tel: 660 3293
38 E4

Canadian Embassy
7/8 Wilton Terrace.
Dublin 2
Tel: 234 4000
38 E4

Chilean Embassy
44 Wellington Road
Ballsbridge
Dublin 4
Tel: 667 5094
38 F4

Embassy of the People's Republic of China
40 Ailesbury Road
Ballsbridge, Dublin 4
Tel: 269 1707
48 D1

Embassy of the Republic of Croatia
Adelaide Chambers
Peter Street
Dublin 8
Tel: 476 7181
38 D3

Embassy of the Republic of Cuba
32B Westland Square,
Pearse Street,
Dublin 2
Tel: 01 6718300
38 E2

Embassy of Republic of Cyprus
71 Lower Leeson Street
Dublin 2
Tel: 676 3060
38 E3

Embassy of The Czech Republic
57 Northumberland Road
Dublin 4
Tel: 668 1135
38 F4

Royal Danish Embassy
7th floor Block E
Iveagh Court
Harcourt Street
Dublin 2
Tel: 475 6404
38 D3

Embassy of the Arab Republic of Egypt
12 Clyde Road
Ballsbridge, Dublin 4
Tel: 660 6718
38 F4

Embassy of the Republic of Estonia
Block E, Iveagh Court,
Harcourt Road, Dublin 2.
Tel: 01 4788888
38 D4

Embassy of the Federal Democratic Republic of Ethiopia
26 Fitzwilliam Street Upper,
Dublin 2
Tel: 678 7062
38 E3

Finnish Embassy
Russell House
Stokes Place
St. Stephen's Green South
Dublin 2
Tel: 478 1344
38 D3

French Embassy
36 Ailesbury Road
Dublin 4
Tel: 277 5000
48 D1

Embassy of the Federal Republic of Germany
31 Trimleston Avenue
Booterstown, Co. Dublin
Tel: 269 3011
48 E2

Greek Embassy
1 Upper
Pembroke Street
Dublin 2
Tel: 676 7254
38 E3

Embassy of the Republic of Hungary
2 Fitzwilliam Place
Dublin 2
Tel: 661 2902
38 E4

Indian Embassy
6 Leeson Park
Dublin 6
Tel: 01 4970806
38 E4

Embassy of the Islamic Republic of Iran
72 Mount Merrion Avenue
Blackrock, Co. Dublin
Tel: 288 5881
48 F3

Israel Embassy
122 Pembroke Road
Dublin 4
2309400
38 F4

Embassy of Georgia
5 Marine Road,
Dun Laoghaire
Co Dublin.
Tel: 01 9059191
50 D4

Italian Embassy
63/65 Northumberland Road
Ballsbridge,
Dublin 4
Tel: 660 1744
38 F4

Japanese Embassy
Nutley Building
Merrion Centre
Nutley Lane, Dublin 4
Tel: 202 8300
48 E1

Embassy of the Republic of Kenya
11 Elgin Road
Ballsbridge, Dublin 4
Tel: 613 6380
38 F4

Embassy of the Republic of Korea
15 Clyde Road
Ballsbridge, Dublin 4
Tel: 660 8800
38 F4

Embassy of the Republic of Latvia
92 St Stephen's Green
Dublin 2
Tel: 478 0161
38 E4

Embassy of the Kingdom of Lesotho
52 Upper Mount Street,
Dublin 2.
Tel: 676 2233
38 E3

Embassy of the Republic of Lithuania
47Ailsbury Road,
Ballsbridge, Dublin 4.
Tel: 203 5737
48 D1

Embassy of Malaysia
Level 3A-5A
Shelbourne House
Shelbourne Road
Ballsbridge Dublin 4.
Tel: 667 7280
38 F3

Maltese Embassy
15 Leeson Street Lower
Dublin 2
Tel: 6762340
38 E4

Mexican Embassy
19 Raglan Road
Dublin 4
Tel: 667 3105
38 F4

Embassy of the Kingdom of Morocco
39 Raglan Road
Dublin 4
Tel: 660 9449
38 F4

Netherlands Embassy
160 Merrion Road
Dublin 4
Tel: 269 3444
48 D1

Embassy of the Federal Republic of Nigeria
56 Leeson Park
Dublin 6
Tel: 660 4366
38 E4

Royal Norwegian Embassy
34 Molesworth Street,
Dublin 2
Tel: 662 1800
38 E3

Embassy of the Islamic Republic of Pakistan
1B Ailesbury Road
Ballsbridge Dublin 4
Tel: 261 3032
48 D1

Embassy of the Republic of Poland
5 Ailesbury Road
Dublin 4
Tel: 283 0855
48 D1

Portuguese Embassy
15 Leeson Park
Dublin 6
Tel: 412 7040/5
38 E4

Embassy of Romania
26 Waterloo Road
Dublin 4
Tel: 668 1085
38 F4

Embassy of the Russian Federation
184/186 Orwell Road
Rathgar, Dublin 14
Tel: 492 2048
47 B3

Royal Embassy of Saudi Arabia
6/7 Fitzwilliam Square E
Dublin 2
Tel: 676 0704
76 D2

Embassy of the Slovak Republic
80 Merrion Square
Dublin 2
Tel: 01 6619594
38 E3

Embassy of the Republic of Slovenia
Morrison Chambers
2nd Floor,
32 Nassau Street Dublin 2
Tel: 670 5240
38 E3

Embassy of South Africa
Alexandra House,
Earlsfort Centre,
Earlsfort Terrace, Dublin 2
Tel: 661 5553
38 E3

Spanish Embassy
17A Merlyn Park
Dublin 4
Tel: 283 9900
48 E1

Swiss Embassy
6 Ailesbury Road
Ballsbridge
Dublin 4
Tel: 218 6382
48 D1

Embassy of the Republic of Turkey
8 Raglan Road
Ballsbridge, Dublin 4
Tel: 668 5240
38 F4

Embassy of Ukraine
16 Elgin Road,
Ballsbridge,
Dublin 4.
Tel: 668 8601
38 F4

Embassy of United Arab Emirates
45-47 Pembroke Road,
Dublin 4.
Tel: 01 6698588
38 F4

Embassy of the United States of America
42 Elgin Road
Ballsbridge, Dublin 4
Tel: 630 6200
38 F4

For further information contact:
Dept of Foreign Affairs,
80 St. Stephen's Green, Dublin 2.
Tel: 478 0822 / www.foreignaffairs.gov.

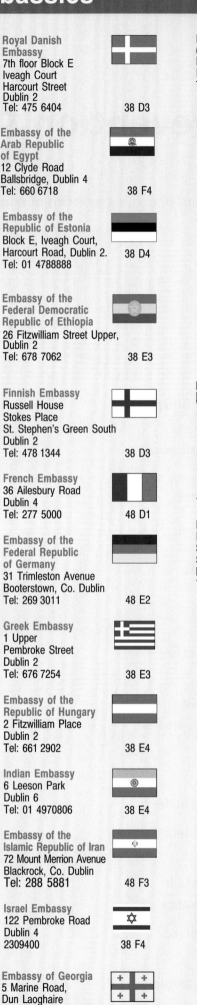

HOSPITAL		ADDRESS		TEL No.	GRID
Tallaght Hosp. Adelaide & Meath (A&E) Hosp. & The National Childrens Hosp.		Tallaght	Dublin 24	01 414 2000	**54F1**
Beaumont Hosp. (A&E)	Beaumont Road	Beaumont	Dublin 9	01 809 3000	**26D1**
Cherry Orchard Hosp.		Ballyfermot	Dublin 10	01 620 6000	**35C3**
Cheeverstown House	Kilvare	Templeogue	Dublin 6W	01 499 3700	**46D4**
City of Dublin Skin & Cancer Hosp.		Hume Street	Dublin 2	01 676 6935	**38E3**
Connolly Hosp. (A&E)		Blanchardstown	Dublin 15	01 646 5000	**22F2**
Dublin Dental School & Hosp.		Lincoln Place	Dublin 2	01 612 7200	**38E3**
Cappagh National Orthopaedic Hosp.	Cappagh	Finglas	Dublin 11	01 814 0400	**23C1**
National Rehabilitation Hosp.		Dun Laoghaire	Co. Dublin	01 235 5000	**59C2**
Incorporated Orthopaedic Hosp. of Ireland	Castle Ave	Clontarf	Dublin 3	01 833 2521	**26E4**
Peamount Hosp.		Newcastle	Co. Dublin	01 601 0300	**42E2**
Royal Hosp. Donnybrook	off Morehampton Road		Dublin 4	01 406 6600	**47B1**
Royal Victoria Eye & Ear Hosp.		Adelaide Road	Dublin 2	01 664 4600	**38E4**
St.Bricins Military Hosp.		Infirmary Road	Dublin 7	01 677 6112	**37B2**
St.Columcilles Hosp. (A&E)		Loughlinstown	Co. Dublin	01 282 5800	**64D2**
St.James's Hosp. (A&E)		James's Street	Dublin 8	01 410 3000	**37B3**
St.Joseph's Hosp.		Clonsilla	Dublin 15	01 821 7177	**21B2**
St.Joseph's Hosp.	Springdale Road	Raheny	Dublin 15	01 877 4900	**27A2**
St.Luke's Hosp	Highfield Road	Rathgar	Dublin 6	01 406 5000	**47A2**
St.Mary's Hosp.		Phoenix Park	Dublin 20	01 625 0300	**36E2**
St.Michaels Hosp. (A&E)	Lr. Georges Street	DunLaoghaire	Co. Dublin	01 280 6901	**50D4**
St.Vincent's		Elm Park	Dublin 4	01 221 4000	**48E1**
Stewart's Hosp.		Palmerston	Dublin 20	01 626 4444	**35C1**
The Mater Hosp. (A&E)		Eccles Street	Dublin 7	01 803 2000	**38D1**
MATERNITY HOSPITALS					
Coombe Women & Infants University Hospital		Cork Street	Dublin 8	01 408 5200	**37C4**
National Maternity Hosp.		Holles Street	Dublin 2	01 637 3100	**38E3**
Rotunda Hospital		Parnell Street	Dublin 1	01 817 1700	**38D1**
CHILDREN'S HOSPITALS					
University Hosp. (A&E)		Temple Street	Dublin 1	01 878 4200	**38D1**
National Childrens Hosp.		Tallaght	Dublin 24	01 414 2000	**54F1**
Our Lady's Hospital for Sick Children (A&E)		Crumlin	Dublin 12	01 409 6100	**46D1**
PSYCHIATRIC HOSPITALS					
Central Mental Hospital		Dundrum	Dublin 14	01 298 9266	**47C3**
Phoenix Care Centre		Nth Circular Rd	Dublin 7	01 827 6500	**37C1**
St.Edmundsbury Hospital	Old Lucan Road	Lucan	Co. Dublin	01 621 8200	**34E1**
St.John of God Hospital		Stillorgan	Co. Dublin	01 277 1400	**58F1**
St.Vincent's Hospital	Richmond Road	Fairview	Dublin 3	01 884 2400	**25B4**
St.Patrick's Hospital		James's Street	Dublin 8	01 249 3200	**37B3**
PRIVATE HOSPITALS					
Beacon Hospital	Bracken Road	Sandyford	Dublin 18	01 293 6600	**58D2**
Blackrock Clinic	Rock Road	Blackrock	Co. Dublin	01283 2222	**48F3**
Bon Secours Hospital Hospital		Glasnevin	Dublin 9	01 806 5300	**25A3**
Mater Private Hospital		Eccles Street	Dublin 7	01 885 8888	**38D1**
Hermitage Medical Clinic		Old Lucan Road	Dublin 20	01 645 9000	**35A1**
St Vincent's Private Hospital		Merrion Road	Dublin 4	01 263 8000	**48E2**
Sports Surgery Clinic		Santry Demesne	Dublin 9	01 526 2000	**12E4**

Name	Pg	Grid /Ref	No.
Abbey Business Park	14	F4	112
Advance Business Park	12	F3	179
Aerodrome Business Park	52	F1	60
Airport Business Park	13	A1	213
Airport Industrial Campus	12	E4	01
Airside Business Park	02	D3	266
Airside Retail Park	01	C3	295
Airton Business Park	45	A4	2
Airton Business Park	45	A4	3
Airton Business Park	45	A4	4
Airton Coporate Park	45	A4	38
Airways Ind Est	12	F4	5
Allied Ind Est	36	E4	6
Alltech Technology Park	06	E2	307
Ardee Court	67	B2	007
Ashgrove Ind Est	59	C1	008
Aughrim Lane Ind Est	37	C1	268
Avonbeg Enterprise Centre	55	A1	085
Avonbeg Ind Est	45	B1	277
Avondale	49	A4	167
Baldonnel Business Park	43	A4	241
Baldoyle Ind Est	27	C1	10
Balfe Road Ind Est	45	C1	196
Balheary Industrial Park	02	D1	11
Ballyboggan Ind Est	24	D3	12
Ballycoolin Business Park	10	D4	13
Ballymount Business Centre	45	B2	14
Ballymount Court Business Centre	45	B2	72
Ballymount Cross Ind Est	45	A2	15
Ballymount Ind Est	45	B2	16
Ballymount Road Ind Est	45	B2	17
Ballymount Trading Centre	45	B2	18
Ballymun Ind Est	12	D4	19
Barbeque Poultry Business Park	64	E3	300
Base Enterprise Centre	09	A4	301
Beech Hill Office Campus	47	C2	228
Beechlawn Ind Complex	45	B2	20
Beechwood Close Ind Est	67	C4	21
Belfield Office Park	47	C2	229
Belgard Ind Est	44	F4	22
Bellevue Industrial Park	24	E3	86
Benson Street Enterprise Centre	38	F2	24
Blackhorse Ind Est	37	B1	25
Blackrock Business Park	49	A3	169
Blanchardstown Corporate Park	09	C3	165
Blanchardstown Industrial Park	09	C4	26
Bluebell Ind Est	36	D4	28
Bluebell Business Centre	36	E4	273
Bluebell Business Park	36	E4	27
Bow Bridge Business Centre	37	B3	308
Bracetown Business Park	07	C1	29
Bray Ind Est	67	C4	30
Bray Businese Park	67	C4	255
Bridges Ind Est	45	A1	32
Bridgewater Business Centre	37	B2	31
Brookfield Enterprise Centre	54	D1	247
Broombridge Ind Est	24	E3	33
Broomfield Business Park	03	B4	271
Broomhill Business Park	45	A4	84
Broomhill Business Park Close	45	A4	35
Broomhill Business Park Drive	45	A4	36
Broomhill Business Park Road	45	A4	37
Burton Hall Campus	58	E2	39
Butterly Business Park	26	D2	66
Calmount Business Park	45	B2	197
Carrigalea Ind Est	45	B1	40
Cashel Business Centre	46	E2	293
Castleforbes Business Park	38	F2	41
Cedar Industrial Park, Bray	67	B4	258
Celbridge Industrial Est	31	C3	238
Central Park Business Park	58	E2	253
Century Business Park	11	B4	206
Chapelizod Ind Est	36	E2	90
Charlestown Centre	11	A4	160
Cherry Orchard Ind Est	35	C2	42
Cherrywood Business Park	64	D1	251
Churchtown Business Park	47	B4	225
Cian Park Ind Est	25	B4	43
City Junction Business Park	13	C4	212
City Link Business Park	36	E4	215
City West Business Campus	53	B1	44
Clondalkin Business Centre	35	B4	46
Clondalkin Commercial Park	35	B4	45
Clondalkin Enterprise Centre	35	A3	177
Clonshaugh Business & Technology Park	13	A4	311
Clonshaugh Ind Est	13	A4	47
Clonskeagh House Office Park	47	C2	226
Clonskeagh Square Office Park	47	C2	227
Cloverhill Ind Est	35	B4	48
College Business and Technology Park	09	C4	200
Collinstown Ind Est	12	F3	50
Collinstown Ind Est (Intel)	19	B3	92
Collinstown Cross Ind Est	12	F2	49
Concord Ind Est Naas Road	36	E4	272
Cookstown Ind Est	44	F4	52
Cookstown Ind Est The Extension	44	E4	243
Cookstown Business Centre	44	F4	245
Cookstown Enterprise Park	44	F4	51
Cookstown Square	44	F4	244
Coolmine Ind Est	22	D2	53
The Courtyard Business Park	43	B2	269
Crag Avenue Ind Centre	35	B4	219
Cranford Centre, Stillorgan	48	D2	274
Croke Park Ind Est	38	E1	55
Crosbie Business Centre	38	F1	262
Crossbeg Ind Est	45	A2	56
Crosslands Business Park	45	A2	297
Crosslands Industrial Park	45	A2	57
Cruiserath Business Park	09	C3	199
Crumlin Business Park	46	E1	292
Damastown Ind Est	08	F3	58
Damastown Industrial Park	08	F3	302
Damastown Technology Park	08	E3	166
Dartmouth House Ind Centre	36	E3	217
Deansgrange Business Park	59	B2	59
Docklands Innovation Park	39	A1	155
Donnelly Centre	37	C3	275
Dublin Ind Est Glasnevin/Broombridge	24	E3	61
Dun Laoghaire Ind Est	59	B2	63
Dunboyne Ind Est	07	B2	62
Dundrum Business Park	47	C3	231
Earlscourt Ind Est	47	B4	224
Earlsfort Centre	38	E3	276
East Point Business Park	39	A1	263
East Road Ind Est	38	F1	64
Elmfield Ind Est	44	E1	65
Fashion City	45	A3	69
Feltrim Industrial Park	02	E3	67
Finches Industrial Park	45	B1	68
Finglas Business Centre	11	B4	140
Finglas Business Park	24	E3	023
Fonthill Retail Park	35	A2	176
Frank Fahey Centre	45	B1	9
Furry Park Ind Est	12	E3	181
Gaywood Ind Est	09	B3	70
Glasnevin Business Centre	24	D3	220
Glasnevin Business Park	24	D3	221
Glen Ind Est	24	E3	73
Glen Abbey Complex	44	F4	71
Glenageary Office Park	60	D2	291
Glenview Ind Est	37	B4	74
Glenville Ind Est	48	E3	75
Goldenbridge Ind Est	36	F3	315
Grange Castle Business Park	34	D4	218
Grange Castle International Business Park	43	B1	239
Grattan Business Park	13	A4	210
Great Keppel Business Centre	15	A1	296
Green Isle Business Park	44	D3	242
Greenhills Ind Est	45	A4	77
Greenhills Business Centre	45	B4	193
Greenhills Business Park	45	B4	192
Greenhills Centre	45	B4	191
Greenmount Ind Est	37	C4	078
Greenogue Business Park	42	E4	235
Grove Ind Est, Dubber Cross	11	B3	079
Grove Ind Est, Finglas	24	E1	080
Harbour Ind Est	67	C1	081
The Harcourt Centre	38	D4	278
Hewlett Packard Ind Park	32	F2	234
Hibernian Ind Est	45	A4	82
Hillcrest Ind Est	45	B2	93
Hills Ind Est	34	D1	83
Hollywood Business Park	09	C3	303
Horizon Logistics	11	B2	204
Howth Junction Business Park	27	B1	270
The Hub Logistics Park	7	C1	313
I.D.A.Tallaght Business Park	54	F2	89
Industrial Yarns Complex	67	C1	91
International Financial Services Centre (IFSC)	38	E2	279
Irish Life Centre	38	E2	280
J.F.K. Ave	45	A1	96
J.F.K. Drive	45	B1	97
J.F.K. Park	36	D4	98
J.F.K. Road	36	D4	99
Jamestown Business Park	11	A4	208
Jamestown Ind Centre	36	F4	95
Jamestown Ind Est	36	E4	94
Jamestown Little Ind Est	11	A4	298
KCR Ind Est	46	E2	100
Kilbarrack Ind Est	27	B1	101
Kilcarbery Industrial Park	43	A1	283
Kileen Industrial Park	36	D4	216
Killarney Road Business Park	67	B3	257
Killinardin Enterprise Park	54	F2	246
Kingswood Business Park	43	B3	312
Kinsealy Business Park	14	D1	281
Knockmitten Business Park	44	F1	282
Kore Development Park	36	E4	314
Kylemore Ind Est	36	D4	102
Kylemore Park North	36	D3	103
Kylemore Park South	36	E4	104
Kylemore Park West	36	D4	105
Landys Ind Est	56	D1	106
Lansdown Valley	45	C1	107
Leopardstown Office Park	58	E2	261
Leopardstown Retail Park	58	E2	108
Liberties Craft & Small Industries Centre	37	C3	109
The Liffey Trust Enterprise Centre	38	F2	150
Lilmar Ind Est	12	F4	110
Loughlinstown Ind Est	64	D1	111
Maltings Business Park	37	C3	259
Manor Street Business Park	37	C1	309
Maynooth Business Campus	17	C4	211
Merrywell Business Park	45	A2	188
Merrywell Ind Est	45	A2	182
Mill Lane Business Park	33	B1	232
Millbank Business Park	34	D1	87
Millenium Business Park	10	E3	202
Monarch Ind Est	44	F4	114
Montone Business Park	44	F1	248
Mount Pleasant Ind Est	47	A1	284
Mulcahy Keane Estate	45	C2	115
Mygan Park Industrial Park	11	B4	207
Naas Road Business Park	36	F4	132
Naas Road Ind Est	36	E4	170
Nangor Road Business Centre	35	C4	174
Newcastle Business Centre	42	E1	088
Newcourt Business Park	11	A2	205
Newlands Business Centre	44	E2	116
Newtown Ind Est	13	C4	117
North Park Business & Office Park	11	A4	209
North Richmond Ind Est	38	E1	118
North Ring Business Park	12	F3	180
Northern Cross Business Park	11	A4	285
Northwest Business Park	10	D3	201
Nutgrove Enterprise Park	57	A1	252
Nutgrove Office Park	47	A4	223
Oak Road Business Park	44	F1	250
Oakfield Ind Est	44	E1	119
Old Court Ind Est	67	B4	120
Old Sawmills Ind Est	45	B2	121
Ossory Ind Est	38	F1	122
Palmgrove Ind Est	25	B2	265
Park West Business Park	35	C4	173
Park West Enterprise Centre	35	C4	172
Park West Industrial Park	36	D4	171
Parkmore Ind Est	45	B1	123
Parkway Business Centre	45	A2	183
Phoenix Ind Est	23	B3	124
Pineview Ind Est	55	C1	125
Pinewood Close Ind Est	67	C4	126
Plato Business Park	09	A3	198
Poppintree Ind Est	11	B4	127
Port Tunnel Business Park	13	A4	310
Portside Business Centre	38	F1	128
Red Cow Business Park	45	A1	184
The Red Cow Interchange Est	44	F2	233
Richmond Road Ind Est	25	B4	129
Richview Park	47	C2	230
Riversdale Ind Est	36	E4	130
Riverview Business Centre	35	C4	175
Robinhood Business Park	45	A1	294
Robinhood Ind Est	45	B1	131
Rock Enterprise Centre	43	B3	240
Rosemount Business Park	10	D4	133
Royal Liver Retail Park	36	E4	214
S.P.A.D.E. Unemployment Enterprise Centre	37	C2	287
Sandyford Business Centre	58	E2	137
Sandyford Ind Est	58	E2	135
Sandyford Office Park	58	E2	136
Sandyford Park	58	E2	163
Santry Avenue Ind Est	12	E4	138
Santry Hall Ind Est	25	B1	139
Shankhill Business Centre	64	E2	141
Shanowen Ind Est	25	B1	142
Sitecast Ind Est	45	B4	194
Solas Retail Park	67	C1	254
South City Business Park	54	F2	306
South City Executive Park	46	E1	288
South County Business Park	58	F2	143
Southern Cross Business Park	67	B4	256
The Square Ind Complex	54	F1	289
St Joans Ind Est	45	A2	134
St John's Court Office Park	25	B1	264
St Margaret's Business Park	11	A4	286
St. Anthony's Business Park	45	A2	54
Stadium Ind Est	10	E4	203
Stillorgan Industrial Park	58	D2	144
Sunbury Ind Est	45	B2	145
Sunshine Ind Est	37	A4	146
Swanward Business Centre	45	A2	185
Swiftbrook Ind Est	53	A2	147
Swords Business Campus	02	D1	267
Swords Business Park	02	E1	148
Tallaght Enterprise Centre	55	A1	149
Taurus Business Park	45	B4	195
Terenure Business Park	46	F2	290
Terenure Enterprise Centre	46	F2	304
Tolka Industrial Park	24	D3	34
Tolka Valley Business Park	24	D3	222
Turnpike Ind Est see Ballymount Cross	45	A2	151
Unidare/Jamestown Business Park	24	E1	152
Weatherwell Ind Est	35	A4	153
West Pier Business Campus	48	C4	168
Westend Retail Park	22	E2	237
Western Business Park	44	F1	249
Western Ind Est	45	A1	156
Western Office Park	22	E1	236
Western Parkway Business Centre	45	B2	157
Western Parkway Business Park	45	B2	190
Westgate Business Park	45	A3	186
Westland Square Business Park	38	E2	260
Westlink Ind Est	36	E3	154
Westpoint Buisness Park	08	F4	164
Westway Centre	45	B2	189
White Heather Ind Est	37	B4	158
White Swan Business Park	37	C4	159
Whitestown Ind Est	54	F1	305
Willow Business Park	45	A1	187
Woodford Business Park	12	F3	178
Woodlawn Ind Est	12	F3	162

No.	Name	Pg	Grid/Ref
1	Airport Industrial Campus	12	E4
2	Airton Business Park	45	A4
3	Airton Business Park	45	A4
4	Airton Business Park	45	A4
5	Airways Ind Est	12	F4
6	Allied Ind Est	36	E4
7	Ardee Court	67	B2
8	Ashgrove Ind Est	59	C1
9	Frank Fahey Centre	45	B1
10	Baldoyle Ind Est	27	C1
11	Balheary Industrial Park	02	D1
12	Ballyboggan Ind Est	24	D3
13	Ballycoolin Business Park	10	D4
14	Ballymount Business Centre	45	B2
15	Ballymount Cross Ind Est	45	A2
16	Ballymount Ind Est	45	B2
17	Ballymount Road Ind Est	45	B2
18	Ballymount Trading Centre	45	B2
19	Ballymun Ind Est	12	D4
20	Beechlawn Ind Complex	45	B2
21	Beechwood Close Ind Est	67	C4
22	Belgard Ind Est	44	F4
23	Finglas Business Park	24	E3
24	Benson Street Enterprise Centre	38	F2
25	Blackhorse Ind Est	37	B1
26	Blanchardstown Ind Park	09	C4
27	Bluebell Business Park	36	E4
28	Bluebell Ind Est	36	D4
29	Bracetown Business Park	07	C1
30	Bray Ind Est	67	C4
31	Bridgewater Business Centre	37	B2
32	Bridges Ind Est	45	A1
33	Broombridge Ind Est	24	E3
34	Tolka Industrial Park	24	D3
35	Broomhill Business Park Close	45	A4
36	Broomhill Business Park Drive	45	A4
37	Broomhill Business Park Road	45	A4
38	Airton Coporate Park	45	A4
39	Burton Hall Campus	58	E2
40	Carrigalea Ind Est	45	B1
41	Castleforbes Business Park	38	F2
42	Cherry Orchard Ind Est	35	C2
43	Cian Park Ind Est	25	B4
44	City West Business Campus	53	B1
45	Clondalkin Commercial Park	35	B4
46	Clondalkin Business Centre	35	B4
47	Clonshaugh Ind Est	13	A4
48	Cloverhill Ind Est	35	B4
49	Collinstown Cross Ind Est	12	F2
50	Collinstown Ind Est	12	F3
51	Cookstown Enterprise Park	44	F4
52	Cookstown Ind Est	44	F4
53	Coolmine Ind Est	22	D2
54	St. Anthony's Business Park	45	A2
55	Croke Park Ind Est	38	E1
56	Crossbeg Ind Est	45	A2
57	Crosslands Industrial Park	45	A2
58	Damastown Ind Est	08	F3
59	Deansgrange Business Park	59	B2
60	Aerodrome Business Park	52	F1
61	Dublin Ind Est / Glasnevin/Broombridge	24	E3
62	Dunboyne Ind Est	07	B2
63	Dun Laoghaire Ind Est	59	B2
64	East Road Ind Est	38	F1
65	Elmfield Ind Est	44	E1
66	Butterly Business Park	26	D2
67	Feltrim Industrial Park	02	E3
68	Finches Industrial Park	45	B1
69	Fashion City	45	A3
70	Gaywood Ind Est	09	B3
71	Glen Abbey Complex	44	F4
72	Ballymount Court Business Centre	45	B2
73	Glen Ind Est	24	E3
74	Glenview Ind Est	37	B4
75	Glenville Ind Est	48	E3
77	Greenhills Ind Est	45	A4
78	Greenmount Ind Est	37	C4
79	Grove Ind Est Dubber Cross	11	B3
80	Grove Ind Est	24	E1

No.	Name	Pg	Grid/Ref
81	Harbour Ind Est	67	C1
82	Hibernian Ind Est	45	A4
83	Hills Ind Est	34	D1
84	Broomhill Business Park	45	A4
85	Avonbeg Enterprise Centre	55	A1
86	Bellevue Industrial Park	24	E3
87	Millbank Business Park	34	D1
88	Newcastle Business Centre	42	E1
89	I.D.A.Tallaght Business Park	54	F2
90	Chapelizod Ind Est	36	E2
91	Industrial Yarns Complex	67	C1
92	Collinstown Ind Est (Intel)	19	B3
93	Hillcrest Ind Est	45	B2
94	Jamestown Ind Est	36	E4
95	Jamestown Ind Centre	36	F4
96	J.F.K. Ave	45	A1
97	J.F.K. Drive	45	B1
98	J.F.K. Park	36	D4
99	J.F.K. Road	36	D4
100	KCR Ind Est	46	E2
101	Kilbarrack Ind Est	27	B1
102	Kylemore Ind Est	36	D4
103	Kylemore Park North	36	D3
104	Kylemore Park South	36	E4
105	Kylemore Park West	36	D4
106	Landys Ind Est	56	D1
107	Lansdown Valley	45	C1
108	Leopardstown Retail Park	58	E2
109	Liberties Craft & Small Industries Centre	37	C3
110	Lilmar Ind Est	12	F4
111	Loughlinstown Ind Est	64	D1
112	Abbey Business Park	14	F4
114	Monarch Ind Est	44	F4
115	Mulcahy Keane Estate	45	C2
116	Newlands Business Centre	44	E2
117	Newtown Ind Est	13	C4
118	North Richmond Ind Est	38	E1
119	Oakfield Ind Est	44	E1
120	Old Court Ind Est	67	B4
121	Old Sawmills Ind Est	45	B2
122	Ossory Ind Est	38	F1
123	Parkmore Ind Est	45	B1
124	Phoenix Ind Est	23	B3
125	Pineview Ind Est	55	C1
126	Pinewood Close Ind Est	67	C4
127	Poppintree Ind Est	11	B4
128	Portside Business Centre	38	F1
129	Richmond Road Ind Est	25	B4
130	Riversdale Ind Est	36	E4
131	Robinhood Ind Est	45	B1
132	Naas Road Business Park	36	F4
133	Rosemount Business Park	10	D4
134	St Joans Ind Est	45	A2
135	Sandyford Ind Est	58	E2
136	Sandyford Office Park	58	E2
137	Sandyford Business Centre	58	E2
138	Santry Avenue Ind Est	12	E4
139	Santry Hall Ind Est	25	B1
140	Finglas Business Centre	11	B4
141	Shankhill Business Centre	64	E2
142	Shanowen Ind Est	25	B1
143	South County Business Park	58	F2
144	Stillorgan Industrial Park	58	D2
145	Sunbury Ind Est	45	B2
146	Sunshine Ind Est	37	A4
147	Swiftbrook Ind Est	53	A2
148	Swords Business Park	02	E1
149	Tallaght Enterprise Centre	55	A1
150	The Liffey Trust Enterprise Centre	38	F2
151	Turnpike Ind Est see Ballymount Cross	45	A2
152	Unidare/Jamestown Business Park	24	E1
153	Weatherwell Ind Est	35	A4
154	Westlink Ind Est	36	E3
155	Docklands Innovation Park	39	A1
156	Western Ind Est	45	A1
157	Western Parkway Business Centre	45	B2
158	White Heather Ind Est	37	B4
159	White Swan Business Park	37	C4
160	Charlestown Centre	11	A4
162	Woodlawn Ind Est	12	F3

No.	Name	Pg	Grid/Ref
163	Sandyford Park	58	E2
164	Westpoint Buisness Park	08	F4
165	Blanchardstown Corporate Park	09	C3
166	Damastown Technology Park	08	E3
167	Avondale	49	A4
168	West Pier Business Campus	48	C4
169	Blackrock Business Park	49	A3
170	Naas Road Ind Est	36	E4
171	Park West Industrial Park	36	D4
172	Park West Enterprise Centre	35	C4
173	Park West Business Park	35	C4
174	Nangor Road Business Centre	35	C4
175	Riverview Business Centre	35	C4
176	Fonthill Retail Park	35	A2
177	Clondalkin Enterprise Centre	35	A3
178	Woodford Business Park	12	F3
179	Advance Business Park	12	F3
180	North Ring Business Park	12	F3
181	Furry Park Ind Est	12	E3
182	Merrywell Ind Est	45	A2
183	Parkway Business Centre	45	A2
184	Red Cow Business Park	45	A1
185	Swanward Business Centre	45	A2
186	Westgate Business Park	45	A3
187	Willow Business Park	45	A1
188	Merrywell Business Park	45	A2
189	Westway Centre	45	B2
190	Western Parkway Business Park	45	B2
191	Greenhills Centre	45	B4
192	Greenhills Business Park	45	B4
193	Greenhills Business Centre	45	B4
194	Sitecast Ind Est	45	B4
195	Taurus Business Park	45	B4
196	Balfe Road Industrial Est	45	C1
197	Calmount Business Park	45	B2
198	Plato Business Park	09	A3
199	Cruiserath Business Park	09	C3
200	College Business and Technology Park	09	C4
201	Northwest Business Park	10	D3
202	Millenium Business Park	10	E3
203	Stadium Ind Est	10	E4
204	Horizon Logistics	11	B2
205	Newcourt Business Park	11	A2
206	Century Business Park	11	B4
207	Mygan Park Industrial Park	11	B4
208	Jamestown Business Park	11	A4
209	North Park Business & Office Park	11	A4
210	Finglas Business Park	09	C3
211	Maynooth Business Campus	17	C4
212	City Junction Business Park	13	C4
213	Airport Business Park	13	A1
214	Royal Liver Retail Park	36	E4
215	City Link Business Park	36	E4
216	Kileen Industrial Park	36	D4
217	Dartmouth House Ind Centre	36	E3
218	Grange Castle Business Park	34	D4
219	Crag Avenue Industrial Centre	35	B4
220	Glasnevin Business Centre	24	D3
221	Glasnevin Business Park	24	D3
222	Tolka Valley Business Park	24	D3
223	Nutgrove Office Park	47	A4
224	Earlscourt Ind Est	47	B4
225	Churchtown Business Park	47	B4
226	Clonskeagh House Office Park	47	C2
227	Clonskeagh Square Office Park	47	C2
228	Beech Hill Office Campus	47	C2
229	Belfield Office Park	47	C2
230	Richview Park	47	C2
231	Dundrum Business Park	47	C3
232	Mill Lane Business Park	33	B1
233	The Red Cow Interchange Est	44	F2
234	Hewlett Packard Ind Park	32	F2
235	Greenogue Business Park	42	E4
236	Western Office Park	22	E1
237	Westend Retail Park	22	E2
238	Celbridge Industrial Est	31	C3
239	Grange Castle International Business Park	43	B1
240	Rock Enterprise Centre	43	B3

No.	Name	Pg	Grid/Ref
241	Baldonnel Business Park	43	A4
242	Green Isle Business Park	44	D3
243	Cookstown Ind Est The Extension	44	E4
244	Cookstown Square	44	F4
245	Cookstown Business Centre	44	F4
246	Killinardin Enterprise Park	54	F2
247	Brookfield Enterprise Centre	54	D1
248	Montone Business Park	44	F1
249	Western Business Park	44	F1
250	Oak Road Business Park	44	F1
251	Cherrywood Business Park	64	D1
252	Nutgrove Enterprise Park	57	A1
253	Central Park Business Park	58	E2
254	Solas Retail Park	67	C1
255	Bray Business Park	67	C4
256	Southern Cross Business Park	67	B4
257	Killarney Road Business Park	67	B3
258	Cedar Industrial Park	67	B4
259	Maltings Business Park	37	C3
260	Westland Square Business Park	38	E2
261	Leopardstown Office Park	58	E2
262	Crosbie Business Centre	38	F1
263	East Point Business Park	39	A1
264	St John's Court Office Park	25	B1
265	Palmgrove Ind Est	25	B2
266	Airside Business Park	02	D3
267	Swords Business Campus	02	D1
268	Aughrim Lane Ind Est	37	C1
269	The Courtyard Business Park	43	B2
270	Howth Junction Business Park	27	B1
271	Broomfield Business Park	03	B4
272	Concord Ind Est Naas Road	36	E4
273	Bluebell Business Centre	36	E4
274	Cranford Centre	48	D2
275	The Donnelly Centre	37	C3
276	Earlsfort Centre	38	E3
277	Avonbeg Ind Est	45	B1
278	The Harcourt Centre	38	D4
279	International Financial Services Centre (IFSC)	38	E2
280	Irish Life Centre	38	E2
281	Kinsealy Business Park	14	D1
282	Knockmitten Business Park	44	F1
283	Kilcarberry Industrial Park	43	A1
284	Mount Pleasant Ind Est	47	A1
285	Northern Cross Business Park	11	A4
286	St Margaret's Business Park	11	A4
287	S.P.A.D.E. Unemployment Enterprise Centre	37	C2
288	South City Executive Park	46	E1
289	The Square Ind Complex	54	F1
290	Terenure Business Park	46	E1
291	Glenageary Office Park	60	D2
292	Crumlin Business Park	46	E1
293	Cashel Business Centre	46	E2
294	Robinhood Business Park	45	A1
295	Airside Retail Park	01	C3
296	Great Keppel Business Centre	15	A1
297	Crosslands Business Park	45	A2
298	Jamestown Little Ind Est	11	A4
300	Barbeque Poultry Business Park	64	E3
301	Base Enterprise Centre	09	A4
302	Damastown Industrial Park	08	F3
303	Hollywood Business Park	09	C3
304	Terenure Enterprise Centre	46	F2
305	Whitestown Ind Est	54	F1
306	South City Business Park	54	F2
307	Alltech Technology Park	06	E2
308	Bow Bridge Business Centre	37	B3
309	Manor Street Business Park	37	C1
310	Port Tunnel Business Park	13	A4
311	Clonshaugh Business & Technology Park	13	A4
312	Kingswood Business Park	43	B3
313	The Hub Logistics Park	7	C1
314	Kore Development Park	36	E4
315	Goldenbridge Ind Est	36	F3

Due to limitations imposed by scale it has not been possible to include all street names on the map pages. References in the index prefixed by * are not shown on the map but are given a grid square reference and a description referencing a feature shown on the map to give an approximate location.

ABBREVIATIONS USED IN THIS INDEX
Apartments .... Apts
Avenue .... Ave
Crescent .... Cres
Saint .... St.

A

STREET NAME	PAGE	GRID REF
1 Branch Road South	39	A2
2 Branch Road North	39	B2
2 Branch Road North Extension	39	B1
2 Branch Road South	39	A2
3 Branch Road South	39	A2
4 Branch Road South	39	B2
*A.W. Pugin House (off Stonepark Court)	46	F4
Abberley	64	E1
*Abberley Square Apts (off Belgard Road)	54	F1
Abbey Cottages	71	B4
Abbey Court (Killester)	26	E3
Abbey Court (Celbridge)	31	C4
*Abbey Court (off Abbey Road Monkstown)	59	B1
Abbey Drive	24	D4
Abbey Green	31	C4
Abbey House	8	D3
Abbey Lane	31	C4
Abbey Park (Killester)	26	E3
Abbey Park (Baldoyle)	27	C1
Abbey Park (Kill O'The Grange)	59	B1
Abbey Park (Celbridge)	31	C4
Abbey Road	59	B1
Abbey Street (Howth)	30	D1
Abbey Street Lower	71	C3
Abbey Street Middle	71	B4
Abbey Street Old	71	C3
Abbey Street Upper	71	B4
*Abbey Terrace (on Abbey Street)	30	D1
*Abbey Vale (Botanic Ave)	25	B4
Abbey View	59	B1
Abbeydale	34	F3
Abbeydale Close	34	F3
Abbeydale Cres	34	F3
Abbeydale Gardens	34	F3
Abbeydale Park	34	F3
Abbeydale Rise	34	F3
Abbeydale Walk	34	F3
Abbeyfarm	31	C4
Abbeyfield (Killester)	26	E3
Abbeyfield (Clonskeagh)	47	B2
Abbeyfield Lawns	26	E3
Abbeylea Ave	1	C1
Abbeylea Close	1	C1
Abbeylea Drive	1	C1
Abbeylea Green	1	C1
Abbeyvale Ave	1	B1
Abbeyvale Close	1	B1
Abbeyvale Court	1	B1
Abbeyvale Cres	1	B1
Abbeyvale Drive	1	B2
Abbeyvale Green	1	B2
Abbeyvale Grove	1	B1
Abbeyvale Lawn	1	B1
Abbeyvale Place	1	B1
Abbeyvale Rise	1	B1
Abbeyvale View	1	B2
Abbeyvale Way	1	B2
Abbeywood	34	F3
Abbeywood Ave	34	F3
Abbeywood Close	34	F3
Abbeywood Court	34	E3
Abbeywood Cres	34	F3
Abbeywood Park	34	F3
Abbeywood Way	34	F3
Abbots Hill	3	C3
Abbotstown Ave	23	C2
Abbotstown Drive	23	C1
Abbotstown Road	24	D2
Abby Well	14	D1
Abercorn Road	72	E3
*Abercorn Square (off Inchicore Terrace South)	36	F3
*Abercorn Terrace (off Inchicore Terrace South)	36	F3
Aberdeen Street	70	D3
Abington	2	F3
Accommodation Road	19	C4
Achill Road (Drumcondra)	25	B3
Achill Road (Loughlinstown)	64	E1
Acorn Drive	57	B1
Acorn Road	57	B1
Acres Road (Phoenix Park)	36	F2
*Adair (off Sandymount Ave)	39	A4
*Adair Lane (off Aston Place)	71	B4
*Adair Terrace (on Saint Joseph's Parade)	71	A1
Adam Court (off Grafton Street)	75	B1
Adams Town Court	34	D2
Adamstown Ave	33	C4
Adamstown Park	33	C3
Adamstown Road	34	D2
Adare Ave	26	E1
Adare Drive	26	E1
Adare Green	26	E1
Adare Park	26	E1
Adare Road	26	E1
Addison Ave	24	F3
Addison Drive	24	F3
*Addison Hall (off Addison Lane)	24	F3
*Addison Lane	24	F3
Addison Park	24	F3
*Addison Place (off Botanic Ave)	25	A3
Addison Road	25	C4
Adelaide Court	75	B3
Adelaide Mews	48	D1
Adelaide Road (Leeson Street)	75	B3
Adelaide Road (Dún Laoghaire)	60	E1
Adelaide Road (Bray)	67	C2
*Adelaide Square (Peter Street)	75	A1
Adelaide Street	50	D4
Adelaide Terrace (off Brookfield Road)	73	C2
*Adelaide Terrace (off Adelaide Road Dún Laoghaire)	60	E1
*Adelaide Villas (off Adelaide Road Dún Laoghaire)	60	E1
Adelaide Villas (Bray)	67	C2
Admiral Brown Walk	72	E4
Admiral Court (off Willie Nolan Road)	15	A4
Admiral Park	15	A4
Adrian Ave	46	F1
*Aengus Hall (off Belgard Square West)	54	F1
Affollus	5	C3
Aghards Road	31	C2
Aideen Ave	46	E2
Aideen Drive	46	E2
Aideen Place	46	E2
Aikenhead Terrace	39	A3
Aiken's Village	58	D3
*Ailesbury (off Shanowen Road)	25	B1
*Ailesbury Close (off Ailesbury Road)	48	D1
Ailesbury Drive	48	D1
Ailesbury Gardens	48	E1
Ailesbury Grove (Donnybrook)	48	D1
Ailesbury Grove (Dundrum)	57	B1
Ailesbury Lane (off Ailesbury Road)	48	D1
Ailesbury Lawn	57	B1
Ailesbury Mews	48	E1
Ailesbury Park	48	E1
Ailesbury Road	48	D1
Ailesbury Wood	48	D1
Airfield Court	48	D2
*Airfield Drive (off Churchtown Road)	47	B4
Airfield Park	48	D2
Airfield Road	46	F2
Airlie Heights	33	B2
Airpark Ave	56	E2
Airpark Close	56	E2
Airpark Court	56	E2
Airpark House	56	E2
Airpark Rise	56	E2
Airside	2	D3
Airton Close	45	A4
Airton Road	45	A4
*Airton Terrace (off Greenhills Road)	45	A4
Albany Ave	49	B4
Albany Court	64	E1
Albany Road	47	B1
Albert Ave	68	D2
Albert College Ave	25	A2
Albert College Court	25	A2
Albert College Cres	25	A2
Albert College Drive	25	A2
Albert College Grove	25	A2
Albert College Lawn	25	A2
Albert College Park	25	A2
Albert Court (Grand Canal Street Lower)	76	E1
Albert Court (Sandycove Road)	60	E1
*Albert Park (off Hudson Road)	60	E1
Albert Place East	76	E1
Albert Place West	75	B3
Albert Road Lower	60	E1
Albert Road Upper	60	E2
*Albert Terrace (Charlemont Street)	75	B3
*Albert Terrace (off Crofton Road)	50	D4
Albert Walk	67	C2
Aldborough House	72	D2
Aldborough Parade	72	D2
Aldborough Place	72	D2
Aldborough Square (off Aldborough Place)	72	D2
Aldemere	21	B2
Alden Drive	27	C1
Alden Park	27	C1
Alden Road	27	C1
Alder Court	4	D4
Alder Lodge	23	A4
Alderpark Court	54	F1
Alderwood Ave	54	E1
Alderwood Close	54	E1
Alderwood Court	54	E1
Alderwood Drive	54	F1
Alderwood Green	54	E1
Alderwood Grove	54	F1
Alderwood Lawn	54	E1
Alderwood Park	54	F1
Alderwood Rise	54	E1
Alderwood Way	54	F1
Aldrin Walk	26	E1
*Alen Hall (off Belgard Square West)	54	F1
Alensgrove	32	F2
Alexander Court Apts	76	D1
Alexander Terrace (North Wall)	72	F3
*Alexander Terrace (Novara Ave)	67	C2
Alexandra Court	47	C4
Alexandra Place	72	F2
Alexandra Quay (Alexandra Basin)	39	A2
*Alexandra Quay (off York Road, Ringsend)	39	A2
Alexandra Road	39	A2
Alexandra Road Extension	39	C2
*Alexandra Terrace (Portobello)	75	A3
Alexandra Terrace (Terenure)	46	F2
Alexandra Terrace (Dundrum)	47	C4
*Alexandra Villas (off Dundrum Road)	47	C4
*Alexandra Walk Apts (Wood Street)	75	A1
Alfie Byrne House	71	B2
Alfie Byrne Road	72	F1
All Hallows Green	25	B3
*All Hallows Lane (off All Hallows Square)	25	B3
All Hallows Square	25	B3
All Saint's Close	27	A3
All Saints Drive	27	A3
All Saints Park	27	A3
All Saints Road	26	F3
Allen Park Drive	58	E1
Allen Park Road	58	E1
Allen Terrace (off Avondale Ave)	70	F1
Allendale Close	21	B2
Allendale Copse	21	B1
Allendale Court	21	B1
Allendale Drive	21	B1
Allendale Elms	21	B1
Allendale Glen	21	B1
Allendale Green	21	B1
Allendale Grove	21	B1
Allendale Heath	21	B1
Allendale Lawn	21	B1
Allendale Place	21	B1
Allendale Rise	21	B1
Allendale Square	21	B2
Allendale Terrace	21	B1
Allendale View	21	B1
Allendale Walk	21	B1
Allenton Ave	55	A3
*Allenton Cres (off Allenton Road)	55	A2
Allenton Drive	55	A3
Allenton Gardens	55	A3
Allenton Green	55	A3
Allenton Lawns	55	A3
Allenton Park	55	A2
*Allenton Road (on Oldcourt Road)	55	B3
Allenton Way	55	A3
Allies River Road	67	A1
Allingham Street	74	E1
*Alma Court (off Alma Road)	49	B4
*Alma Park (off Carrickbrennan Road)	49	C4
*Alma Place (off Carrickbrennan Road)	49	C4
Alma Road	49	B4
*Alma Terrace (off Mountpleasant Ave Upper)	47	A1
Almeida Ave	73	C1
Almeida Terrace	73	C1
Alone Walk	26	E2
Alpine Heights	44	D1
Alpine Rise	44	E4
Altadore	60	D2
Altamont Hall	47	C4
Altham Court	73	A1
*Altham Court (Grattan Cres)	36	F3
*Alverno (off Castle Ave)	39	B1
Ambassador Court (off Herbert Road)	76	E3
Amber Vale	44	E4
Amberwood	9	A4
*Amiens Square Apts (Amiens Street)	72	D3
Amiens Street	72	D3
An Crannog	60	D3
Analands	64	D4
*Anastasia Lane (off Sorrento Road)	60	F2
Anglers Rest	47	C1
Anglesea Ave	49	A3
*Anglesea House (off Serpentine Ave)	39	A4
*Anglesea Lane (off Corrig Ave)	50	D4
Anglesea Park	60	E2
Anglesea Road	76	F4
Anglesea Row	71	A3
Anglesea Street	71	B4
Anley Court	34	E1
Ann Devlin Ave	46	E4
Ann Devlin Drive	46	E4
Ann Devlin Park	56	E1
Ann Devlin Road	46	E4
Anna Livia Apts	74	E1
Anna Villa	47	B1
*Annabeg (off Wyattville Road)	60	D4
Annacrivey	65	B3
*Annadale (off Churchtown Road Upper)	47	B4
*Annadale Ave (off Philipsburgh Ave)	25	C4
Annadale Cres	25	C3
Annadale Drive	25	C3
Annagh Court	22	F1
Annaghaskin	66	D1
Annaly Close	21	B1
Annaly Court	21	B1
Annaly Drive	21	B1
Annaly Grove	21	B1
Annaly Road	24	F4
Annaly Terrace	21	B1
Annamoe Drive	70	E1
Annamoe Parade	70	E1
Annamoe Park	70	E1
Annamoe Road	70	D1
Annamoe Terrace	70	E1
Annaville Ave	59	A1
Annaville Close	47	C4
*Annaville Grove (off Annaville Park)	47	C3
Annaville Lodge	47	C4
Annaville Park	47	C4
*Annaville Residence Apts (off Annaville Terrace)	47	C3
Annaville Terrace	47	C3
Anne Street North	71	A3
Anne Street South	75	B1

STREET NAME	PAGE	GRID REF
Anner Road	73	B2
Anne's Bridge	17	C1
Anne's Lane	75	B1
Annesley Ave	72	E1
Annesley Bridge (Tolka River)	72	E1
Annesley Bridge Road	72	E1
Annesley Close	72	E1
*Annesley Mews (off Annesley Park)	47	B1
Annesley Park	47	B1
Annesley Place	72	E1
Annfield	22	D3
Annfield Court	22	D3
Annfield Cres	22	D3
Annfield Drive	22	D3
Annfield Lawn	22	D4
Annsbrook	47	C2
Annville Drive	58	E1
Apollo Way	26	D1
*Appian Close (on Leeson Park)	76	D4
Apples Road	58	D2
Applewood Ave East	1	Inset
Applewood Ave West	1	Inset
Applewood Birch	1	Inset
Applewood Court	1	Inset
Applewood Cres	1	Inset
Applewood Drive (Swords)	1	Inset
Applewood Main Street	1	Inset
Applewood Mews	1	Inset
Applewood Place	1	Inset
Applewood Square	1	Inset
Aranleigh Court	56	F1
Aranleigh Dell	57	A1
Aranleigh Gardens	56	F1
Aranleigh Mount	56	F1
Aranleigh Park	57	A1
Aranleigh Vale	56	F1
Arás na Cluaine	35	B4
Aravon Court	68	D2
Arbour Court	70	D3
Arbour Hill	70	E3
Arbour Place	70	E3
Arbour Terrace	70	D3
Arbutus Ave	74	F4
*Arbutus Grove (off Beech Road)	67	B1
Arbutus Place	75	A3
Archers Wood	8	F4
*Archway Court (off Mountjoy Street)	71	A2
Ard Cluain	8	D3
Ard Lorcain	58	F1
*Ard Lorcain Villas (off Ard Lorcain Stillorgan)	58	F1
Ard Mhacha	54	F2
Ard Mhuire Park	60	E2
Ard Mor Ave	53	C1
Ard Mor Close	53	C1
Ard Mor Court	53	C1
Ard Mor Cres	53	C1
Ard Mor Dale	53	C1
Ard Mor Drive	53	C1
Ard Mor Green	53	C1
Ard Mor Lawn	53	C1
Ard Mor Park	53	C1
Ard Mor Walk	53	C1
Ard na Glaise	48	F4
*Ard Na Gréine (off Orwell Road Rathgar)	47	A3
Ard Na Gréine (Ballymorris)	67	B4
Ard na Mara	3	A3
Ard na Meala	12	D4
Ard Rí Place	70	E3
Ard Rí Road	70	E3
Ardagh Ave	59	A1
*Ardagh Close (off Ardagh Park Road)	59	A1
Ardagh Court	58	F1
Ardagh Cres	59	A1
Ardagh Drive	59	A1
Ardagh Grove	59	A1
Ardagh Park	59	A1
Ardagh Park Road	59	A1
Ardagh Road	73	C4
Ardara Ave	14	D4
Ardbeg Cres	26	E2
Ardbeg Drive	26	E2
Ardbeg Park	26	E2
Ardbeg Road	26	E2
*Ardbrugh Close (off Ardbrough Road)	60	F2
Ardbrugh Road	60	F2
*Ardbrugh Villas (off Ardbrough Road)	60	F2
Ardcian Park	1	C1
Ardcollum Ave	26	E2
*Ardee Court (Ardee Row)	74	F2
Ardee Grove	75	B4
Ardee Road	75	B4
Ardee Row	74	F2
Ardee Street (The Coombe)	74	F2
Ardee Street (Bray)	67	B2
Ardeen	33	C2
Ardeevin Ave	33	C2
Ardeevin Court	33	C2
Ardeevin Drive	33	C2
Ardeevin Road	60	F2
*Ardeevin Terrace (off Ardeevin Road)	60	F2
*Ardenza Park (off Seapoint Ave)	49	B3
*Ardenza Terrace (off Seapoint Ave)	49	B3
Ardglas Estate	57	C1
Ardilaun	14	F1
Ardilaun Road	72	D1
*Ardilaun Square (off Sackville Ave)	72	D1
Ardilea Downs	48	D4
Ardilea Wood	48	D4
Ardlea Road	26	E2
Ardlui Park	59	A1
Ardmeen Park	59	A1
Ardmore Ave	70	D1
Ardmore Close	26	D2
Ardmore Cres (Artane)	26	D2
Ardmore Cres (Bray)	67	B2
Ardmore Drive	26	D1
Ardmore Grove	26	D1
Ardmore Lawn	67	B3
Ardmore Park (Artane)	26	D2
Ardmore Park (Kill O'The Grange)	59	C1
Ardmore Park (Bray)	67	B2
Ardmore Wood	67	B3
Ardoyne Mews (off Claremont Road)	76	E4
Ardpatrick Road	24	D4
*Ardtona Ave (off Churchtown Road Lower)	47	B4
Arena Road	58	E2
Argus House	74	F4
*Argyle House Apts (off Claremont Road)	39	A4
Argyle Road	76	E4
*Argyle Square (off Marlborough Road)	47	C1
*Arkendale Court (off Arkendale Road)	60	E1
Arkendale Road	60	E1
*Arkendale Woods (off Arkendale Road)	60	E1
Arkle Road	58	E2
*Arkle Square (off Brewery Road)	58	F2
Arklow Street	70	D2
Armagh Road	46	D1
Armstrong Street (off Harold's Cross Road)	74	F4
Armstrong Walk	26	E1
Army Road	69	B3
Arnold Grove	60	D2
Arnold Park	60	D2
Arnott Street	75	A2
Arran Ave	64	E1
Arran Close	64	E1
Arran Court	22	F1
Arran Drive	64	E1
Arran Green	67	C2
Arran Quay	70	F4
Arran Quay Apts	70	F4
*Arran Quay Terrace (Arran Quay)	70	F4
Arran Road	25	B3
Arran Square Apts	70	F4
Arran Street East	71	A4
Arran Street West	70	F4
Arranmore Ave	71	A1
Arranmore Road	47	C1
Artane	26	E2
*Artane Cottages Lower (off Malahide Road)	26	E2
*Artane Cottages Upper (off Malahide Road)	26	E2
*Arthur Griffith Court (off Esker Road at Arthur Griffith Park)	34	D2
Arthur Griffith Park	34	D3
*Arundel (off Monkstown Valley)	49	B4
Asdill's Row (off Temple Bar)	71	B4
Asgard Apts	30	D1
Asgard Park	30	D2
Asgard Road (Grand Canal Dock)	72	E4
Asgard Road (Howth)	30	D2
Ash Grove (Meath Street)	74	F1
Ash Park Ave	34	E3
Ash Park Court	34	E3
Ash Park Grove	34	E2
Ash Park Heath	34	E2
Ash Street	74	F1
Ashberry	34	D3
Ashbrook (Ashtown)	23	C3
Ashbrook (Clontarf)	26	D4
Ashbrook (Bray)	67	C2
Ashbrook (Celbridge)	32	E3
*Ashbrook Terrace (Ranelagh)	47	B1
*Ashbrook Terrace (off Sallymount Ave)	47	B1
*Ashbrook Villas (Ranelagh)	47	B1
Ashbury Park	67	C2
Ashcroft	27	A2
*Ashcroft Court (adjacent Blakestown Drive)	22	D1
*Ashcroft Grove (adjacent Blakestown Drive)	22	D1
Ashdale Ave	46	F2
Ashdale Close	2	E3
Ashdale Gardens	46	F2
*Ashdale Park (off Ashdale Road)	46	F2
Ashdale Road (Swords)	2	E3
Ashdale Road (Terenure)	46	F2
Ashe Court	2	E2
Ashfield	46	D4
Ashfield Ave (Clondalkin)	44	F3
Ashfield Ave (Ranelagh)	47	B1
Ashfield Close (Clondalkin)	44	F3
Ashfield Court (Mulhuddart)	9	A4
Ashfield Court (Ballymorris)	67	B4
Ashfield Drive (Clondalkin)	44	F3
Ashfield Gardens	9	A4
Ashfield Green (Huntstown)	8	F4
Ashfield Grove	9	A4
Ashfield Lawn	8	F4
Ashfield Park (Huntstown)	9	A4
Ashfield Park (Clondalkin)	44	F3
Ashfield Park (Terenure)	46	F2
Ashfield Park (Booterstown)	48	E2
Ashfield Road (Ranelagh)	47	B1
Ashfield Way (Huntstown)	9	A4
Ashford Apts	24	F3
Ashford Cottages	70	D2
Ashford Place	70	D2
Ashford Street	70	D2
Ashgrove (Baskin Lane)	13	C1
Ashgrove (Celbridge)	31	C2
Ashgrove (Tallaght)	54	E1
Ashgrove (Kill O'The Grange)	59	C1
*Ashgrove Court (off Sandyford Road)	57	C1
*Ashgrove Terrace (off Sandyford Road)	57	C1
Ashington Ave	24	D3
Ashington Close	24	D3
Ashington Court	24	D3
Ashington Cres	23	C3
Ashington Dale	24	D3
Ashington Gardens	24	D3
Ashington Green	24	D3
Ashington Grove	24	D3
Ashington Heath	24	D3
Ashington Mews	24	D3
Ashington North	24	D3
Ashington Park	24	D3
Ashington Rise	23	C3
Ashlawn	57	C1
Ashlawn Court	67	B2
Ashlawn Park	60	D4
Ashleigh Court (Castleknock)	22	F3
Ashleigh Court (Celbridge)	32	D3
Ashleigh Green	22	F3
Ashleigh Grove (Maynooth)	17	B4
Ashleigh Grove (Blanchardstown)	22	F3
Ashleigh Lawn	3	B3
Ashley Ave	2	D2
Ashley Drive	2	D2
Ashley Grove	2	D2
*Ashley Heights (East of Dargle Heights)	67	B2
Ashley Rise	4	D4
Ashling Close	73	C4
Ashling Court	47	B1
Ashling Heights	22	E1
Ashmount	9	A4
Ashmount Court	73	B1
Ashton Ave (Swords)	1	Inset
Ashton Ave (Knocklyon)	56	D1
Ashton Close (Swords)	1	Inset
Ashton Close (Knocklyon)	56	D1
Ashton Court	1	Inset
Ashton Drive	1	Inset
Ashton Green	1	Inset
Ashton Grove (Swords)	1	Inset
Ashton Grove (Knocklyon)	56	D1
Ashton Lawn	56	D1
Ashton Lawns	1	Inset
Ashton Park	49	B4
Ashton Rise	1	Inset
Ashton Wood	67	A3
Ashtown	23	C3
Ashtown Court	23	C4
Ashtown Gate (Phoenix Park)	23	B4
Ashtown Gate Road (Phoenix Park)	23	B4
Ashtown Grove	23	C4
Ashtown Lodge	23	C4
Ashtown Road	23	B3
Ashtowngate	23	C3
*Ashurst (off Mount Merrion Ave)	48	E4
Ashurst (Ballybrack)	64	E1
Ashville Close	34	E1
Ashwood Ave	43	C1
Ashwood Close	43	C1
Ashwood Drive	44	D1
Ashwood Lawns	44	D1
Ashwood Park	44	D1
Ashwood Road	44	D1
Ashwood Way	44	D1
*Ashworth Place (off Mount Drummond Ave)	75	A4
Aspen Drive	2	E3
Aspen Park (Kinsealy Court)	2	E3
*Aspen Park (off Carriglea Ave)	59	C1
Aspen Road	2	E3
Aspen Wood	21	C2
Aspin Ave	21	C2
Aspin Lawns	22	D2
Assumpta Park	64	E3
Aston Place	71	B4
Aston Quay	71	B4
Astor Hall	71	C4
Athgoe	51	C1
*Athgoe Drive (off Beechfield Manor)	64	E2
Athgoe North	51	B1
Athgoe Road (Newcastle)	41	C4
Athgoe Road (Shankill)	64	E2
Athgoe South	51	B2
Atlumney Villas	75	B4
*Atmospheric Road (off Castlepark Road)	60	E1
Aubrey	64	E3
Aubrey Grove	64	E3
Aubrey Park	64	E3
Auburn	26	D4
Auburn Ave (Castleknock)	23	A3
Auburn Ave (Donnybrook)	47	C1
Auburn Ave (Cabinteely)	60	D3
Auburn Close (Castleknock)	23	A3
Auburn Close (Cabinteely)	60	D3
Auburn Drive (Castleknock)	23	A3
Auburn Drive (Cabinteely)	60	D3
Auburn Green	23	A3
Auburn Grove	3	A3
*Auburn House Apts (off Rathmines Road Upper)	47	A1
*Auburn Park Apts (off Navan Road / Auburn Ave)	23	A3
*Auburn Road (off Victoria Ave)	47	C1
*Auburn Road (off Churchview Road)	60	D3
Auburn Road (off Woodlands Road)	60	D3
Auburn Street	71	A2
Auburn Terrace (Old Kilmainham)	73	C1
Auburn Villas (Rathgar)	47	A2
Auburn Villas (Pearse Square, Bray)	67	B2
Auburn Walk	70	D2
Aughavannagh Road	74	E4
Aughrim Court	70	E3
Aughrim Lane	70	E2
Aughrim Place	70	D2
Aughrim Street	70	D2
Aughrim Villas	70	D2

STREET NAME	PAGE	GRID REF
Augustine Court (Saint Margaret'sTce)	74	F1
*Augustine Villas (near Meath Place)	67	C2
Aulden Grange	12	F4
Aungier Lane	75	B2
Aungier Place	75	B2
Aungier Street	75	B1
Austin's Cottages	72	E1
*Avalon (off Brighton Road Foxrock)	59	A3
Avalon Apts	29	B1
Ave Maria Road	74	D2
Ave Road	75	A3
*Avila Apts (off Carysfort Ave)	59	A1
Avila Park	23	C1
Avila Park Gardens	23	C1
Avoca Apts	32	D3
Avoca Ave (Stillorgan)	48	F4
Avoca Ave (Dún Laoghaire)	67	C3
Avoca Court	48	F4
*Avoca Hall (off Avoca Park)	49	A4
Avoca Park	48	F4
Avoca Place	49	A3
Avoca Road	48	F4
Avoca Terrace	48	F4
Avoca Wood	48	F4
*Avonbeg Court (off Avonbeg Drive)	55	A1
Avonbeg Drive	55	A1
Avonbeg Gardens	55	B1
Avonbeg Park	55	A1
Avonbeg Road	55	B1
Avondale	20	D4
*Avondale Apts (Lurgan Street)	71	A3
Avondale Ave	70	F1
Avondale Court (Blackrock)	49	A4
*Avondale Court (off Albert Road Lower)	60	E1
*Avondale Court Apts (Avondale Park)	09	A3
Avondale Cres	60	E2
Avondale House	71	C2
Avondale Lawn	49	A4
*Avondale Mews (off Kirkwood)	39	A4
Avondale Park (Raheny)	27	A2
*Avondale Park (off Carysfort Ave Blackrock)	49	A4
Avondale Park (Dalkey)	60	E2
Avondale Park (Dún Laoghaire)	67	B3
Avondale Park (Mulhuddart)	9	A3
Avondale Road (Phibsborough)	70	F1
Avondale Road (Dalkey)	60	D2
Avondale Square	7	B2
Avondale Terrace	45	C2
Avonmore	59	A2
*Avonmore Ave (off Avonmore Road)	55	B1
Avonmore Close	55	B1
Avonmore Drive	55	B1
*Avonmore Green (off Avonmore Close)	55	B1
Avonmore Grove	55	B1
Avonmore Park	55	B1
Avonmore Road	55	B1
Aylesbury	55	A2
Aylmer Ave	42	D4
Aylmer Heath	42	D4
Aylmer Road	42	D4
Ayrefield Ave	26	F1
Ayrefield Court	26	F1
Ayrefield Drive	26	F1
Ayrefield Grove	26	F1
*Ayrefield Park (off Ayrefield Road)	26	F1
Ayrefield Place	26	F1
Ayrefield Road	26	F1
Ayward Green	24	D2

B

STREET NAME	PAGE	GRID REF
Bachelor's Walk	71	B4
Bachelors Walk Apts	71	B4
Bachelors Way	71	B4
*Back Lane (off Sandwith Street Upper)	76	D1
Back Lane (High Street)	75	A1
*Back Lane		

STREET NAME	PAGE	GRID REF
(Between College Street and Main Street Baldoyle)	15	A4
Back Lane (Maynooth)	17	C3
Back Road	3	B4
Baggot Bridge Court	76	D2
Baggot Close	75	C2
Baggot Court	76	D2
Baggot Lane	76	E3
*Baggot Rath House (off Newbridge Ave)	39	A3
Baggot Road	23	C4
Baggot Street Lower	76	D2
Baggot Street Upper	76	E3
Baggot Terrace	23	C4
Baggotrath Place	76	D2
Bailey Green	30	E3
Bailey Green Road	30	E3
*Bailey View (off Harbour Road)	60	F1
Bailey's Row	72	D2
*Baker's Yard Apartment (Portland Street North)	71	C1
Balally Ave	58	D1
Balally Close	58	D1
Balally Drive	58	D1
Balally Grove	58	D2
Balally Hill	58	D2
Balally Park	58	D1
Balally Road	57	C1
*Balally Terrace (off Sandyford Road)	58	D2
Balbutcher Drive	11	C4
Balbutcher Lane	11	C4
Balbutcher Lane Lower	11	C4
Balbutcher Way	11	C4
Balcurris Close	12	D4
Balcurris Gardens	12	D4
Balcurris Park East	12	D4
Balcurris Park West	12	D4
Balcurris Road	12	D4
Baldoyle	15	A4
Baldoyle Road	28	D1
Balfe Ave	45	C1
Balfe Road	45	C1
Balfe Road East	46	D1
Balfe Street	75	B1
Balgaddy Road	34	F3
Balglass Road	30	D2
Balgriffin	14	D3
Balgriffin Cottages	14	D3
Balgriffin Park	14	D3
Balgriffin Road	14	D3
Balheary Road	2	D1
Balkill Grove	30	D2
Balkill Park	30	D2
Balkill Road	30	D2
Ballawley Court	57	C2
Ballentree	9	B2
Ballentree Ave	9	B2
Ballentree Close	9	B2
Ballentree Cres	9	B2
Ballentree Drive	9	B2
Ballentree Grove	9	B3
Ballentree Lodge Apts	9	B2
Ballentree Villa	9	B3
*Ballinakelly Edge (off Newcastle Boulevard)	42	D4
*Ballinakelly Mews (off Newcastle Boulevard)	42	D4
*Ballinakelly Rise (off Newcastle Boulevard)	42	D4
Ballinakelly Village	42	D4
Ballinclea Heights	60	E3
Ballinclea Road	60	D3
Ballinteer	57	B2
Ballinteer Ave	57	B2
Ballinteer Close	57	B2
*Ballinteer Court (off Ballinteer Ave)	57	B2
Ballinteer Cres	57	B2
Ballinteer Drive	57	B2
Ballinteer Gardens	57	C2
Ballinteer Grove	57	B2
Ballinteer Park	57	B2
Ballinteer Road (Dundrum)	57	C1
Ballinteer Road (Delbrook Park)	57	C2
Ballintrane Wood	1	C2
Ballintyre Demesne	57	B2
Ballintyre Downs	57	B2
*Ballintyre Grove (Ballintyre)	57	B2
Ballintyre Heath	57	B2
Ballintyre Meadows	57	B2
Ballintyre Square	57	B2
Ballintyre Walk	57	B2

STREET NAME	PAGE	GRID REF
Ballintyre Woods	57	B2
Ball's Lane	71	A3
Ballsbridge (River Dodder)	76	F4
*Ballsbridge Ave (off Merrion Road)	39	A4
*Ballsbridge Court	76	F3
Ballsbridge Gardens (off Merrion Road)	76	F3
*Ballsbridge Park (off Merrion Road)	39	A4
Ballsbridge Terrace (off Sandymount Ave)	76	F4
Ballsbridge Wood	76	F3
Ballybane	43	A1
Ballybetagh	62	F4
Ballybetagh Road	62	E4
Ballyboden	56	E1
Ballyboden Cres	56	E1
Ballyboden Road	56	E1
Ballyboden Way	56	E1
Ballyboggan Road	24	E3
Ballybough Ave	72	D1
Ballybough Court	72	D1
*Ballybough Lane (King's Ave)	72	D1
Ballybough Road	72	D1
Ballybrack (Village)	60	E4
Ballybrack (Two Rock Mountain)	61	B3
Ballybrew	65	C2
Ballybride	64	D3
Ballybride Road	64	D3
Ballycoolin Road	10	D4
Ballycorus	63	B3
Ballycorus Road	63	A2
Ballycullen Ave	55	B2
*Ballycullen Cottages (off Ballycullen Road)	55	C2
Ballycullen Drive	55	B2
Ballycullen Road	55	C1
Ballydowd Grove	34	E1
Ballydowd Manor	34	E2
Ballyedmonduff (Two Rock Mountain)	61	C2
Ballyedmonduff (Stepaside)	62	E1
Ballyedmonduff Road	62	D1
Ballyfermot	36	D3
Ballyfermot Ave	36	D3
Ballyfermot Cres	36	D3
Ballyfermot Drive	36	D3
Ballyfermot Parade	36	D3
Ballyfermot Road (Cherry Orchard)	35	C3
Ballyfermot Road (Ballyfermot)	36	E3
Ballygall Ave	24	E1
Ballygall Cres	24	E2
Ballygall Parade	24	E2
Ballygall Place	24	E2
Ballygall Road East	24	F2
Ballygall Road West	24	E1
Ballygihen Ave	60	E1
*Ballygihen Villas (off Sandycove Road)	60	E1
Ballygoran	18	E4
Ballygoran Court	31	C2
Ballygoran View	31	C2
Ballyhoy Ave	27	A3
Ballymacartle	13	C1
Ballymace Green	46	E4
Ballymacoll	6	D3
Ballymadrough Road	2	F1
Ballymakealy Grove	31	C4
Ballymakealy Lawns	31	C4
Ballyman	66	F1
Ballyman Lane (Carrickgollogan)	63	C4
Ballyman Lane (Ballyman)	66	F1
Ballyman Road	66	F2
Ballymana	54	E4
Ballymana Lane	54	E4
*Ballymanagin Lane (off Newlands Road)	35	A4
*Ballymorris (off Killarney Road)	67	B4
*Ballymoss Parade (off Brewery Road)	58	F2
Ballymoss Road	58	F2
Ballymount Ave	45	B2
*Ballymount Cottages (off Ballymount Road Lower)	45	B2
Ballymount Drive	45	B2
Ballymount Road	44	F3
Ballymount Road Lower	45	B2
Ballymount Road Upper	45	A2
Ballymount Square	45	B2

STREET NAME	PAGE	GRID REF
Ballymun	25	A1
Ballymun Road (M50 Junction 4)	12	D4
Ballymun Road (Ballymun)	25	A1
Ballymun Road (Glasnevin)	25	A3
Ballynakelly Cottages	42	D4
Ballynakelly Court	42	D4
Ballynakelly Edge	42	D4
Ballynakelly Green	42	D4
Ballynakelly Mews	42	D4
Ballynakelly Rise	42	D4
Ballynakelly View	42	D4
Ballynakelly Village	42	D4
Ballyneety Road	36	F3
*Ballynoe Court (South of Kilbride Lane)	67	B3
Ballyogan Ave	58	F4
Ballyogan Close	58	F4
Ballyogan Court	58	F4
Ballyogan Cres	58	F4
Ballyogan Drive	58	F4
Ballyogan Estate	58	F4
Ballyogan Green	58	F4
Ballyogan Lawn	58	F4
*Ballyogan Park (off Ballyogan Drive)	58	F4
Ballyogan Road	58	F4
Ballyogen Vale	59	A4
Ballyogen Wood	59	A4
*Ballyolaf Manor (off Parkvale)	57	C1
Ballyoulster Park	32	E3
Ballyowen Ave	34	F1
Ballyowen Court	34	F1
Ballyowen Cres	34	F1
Ballyowen Drive	34	F1
Ballyowen Green	34	F1
Ballyowen Grove	34	F1
Ballyowen Hall	34	F2
Ballyowen Lane	34	F2
Ballyowen Lawn	34	F1
Ballyowen Road	34	F1
Ballyowen Square	34	F2
Ballyowen View	34	F1
Ballyowen Way	34	F1
*Ballyroan Court (off Knocklyon Drive)	56	D1
Ballyroan Cres	56	E1
Ballyroan Heights	56	E1
Ballyroan Park	56	D1
Ballyroan Road	56	E1
Ballyshannon Ave	25	C1
Ballyshannon Road	26	D1
Ballystruan Lane	12	D3
Ballytore Road	46	F3
*Ballywaltrim Cottages (Ballywaltrim Road)	67	B4
Ballywaltrim Heights	67	B3
Ballywaltrim Lane	67	A4
Ballywaltrim Road	67	B4
Ballywilliam Close	67	B4
*Balnagowan (off Palmerston Park)	47	B2
*Balrothery Cottages (off Tallaght Road)	55	C1
Balrothery Estate	45	B4
Balscadden Road	30	E1
Balscott	41	C1
Bancroft Ave	55	A1
Bancroft Close	55	B1
*Bancroft Court (off Bancroft Grove)	55	B1
Bancroft Cres	45	B4
Bancroft Downs	45	A4
Bancroft Grove	55	B1
Bancroft Park	55	A1
Bancroft Road	55	B1
Bangor Circle	46	E1
Bangor Drive	73	C4
Bangor Road	46	E1
Bankside Cottages	47	B2
Bann Road	24	E3
Bannaville	75	B4
Bannow Road	24	E4
Banshee	51	A2
Bantry Road	25	A3
Bantry Square	22	F1
Banville Ave	36	D4
Barberstown Lane	1	A4
Barclay Court	49	A3
Bargy Road	72	F2
Barley Glen	54	F1
Barnacoille Park	60	F1
Barnamire	65	A4

STREET NAME	PAGE	GRID REF
Barnamore Cres	24	D3
Barnamore Grove	24	D3
Barnamore Park	24	D3
Barnaslingan Lane	63	A3
Barneville Green	35	C3
Barneville Walk	35	C4
Barnhall	32	F1
Barnhall Drive	32	F1
Barnhill Ave	60	E2
Barnhill Cross Road	34	D1
*Barnhill Grove (off Barnhill Road)	60	F2
*Barnhill Lawn (off Barnhill Road)	60	E2
*Barnhill Park (off Saval Park Gardens)	60	E2
Barnhill Road	60	E2
*Barnhill Villas (on Barnhill Road)	60	F2
Barnville Park	35	C4
Barnwell	21	A2
Barnwell Ave	21	A1
Barnwell Cres	21	A1
Barnwell Drive	24	F1
Barnwell Drive	21	A1
Barnwell Green	21	A1
Barnwell Lane	21	A1
Barnwell Lane	21	A1
Barnwell Road	21	A2
Barnwell Terrace	21	A1
Barnwell Way	21	A2
*Baroma (off Kimmage Road Lower)	46	E2
Barrack Bridge	3	A2
Barrack Court	52	F2
*Barrack Lane (off Irishtown Road)	39	A3
Barren Hill Cross Roads	29	C3
*Barrett Street (off York Road Dún Laoghaire)	49	C4
Barrogstown East	18	F4
Barrogstown West	18	E4
*Barron Place (off Walsh Road)	25	A3
Barrow Road	24	E3
Barrow Street	76	F1
Barry Ave	24	D1
Barry Close (off Barry Drive)	24	D1
Barry Drive	24	D1
Barry Green	24	D1
Barry Lane	21	A1
Barry Park	24	D1
Barry Road	24	D1
Barry's Park	2	D2
Barryscourt Road	26	E1
Barton Ave	56	F1
*Barton Court (off Barton Road East)	57	A1
Barton Drive	56	F1
Barton Road East	57	B1
Barton Road East Extension	57	A1
Barton Road Extension	57	A1
Barton Road West	56	F1
*Bartra Rock Apts (off Harbour Road)	60	F1
Basin Grove	74	D1
Basin Lane Flats	74	D1
Basin Street Lower	74	D1
Basin Street Upper	74	D1
Basin View (off Basin Street Upper)	74	D2
Baskin Cottages	13	C1
Baskin Lane	13	B1
Bass Place	76	D1
Bath Ave (Sandymount)	76	F2
Bath Ave (Malahide)	3	C2
Bath Ave Gardens	76	F2
Bath Ave Place	76	F2
Bath Lane	71	B2
*Bath Place (off Main Street Blackrock)	49	A3
Bath Street	39	A3
Bawnlea Ave	54	D2
Bawnlea Close	54	D2
Bawnlea Cres	54	D2
Bawnlea Drive	54	D2
Bawnlea Green	54	D2
*Bawnogue Cottages (off Cherrywood Villas)	43	C1
Bawnogue Road	43	C1
Bawnville Ave	55	A2
Bawnville Close	55	A2
Bawnville Drive	55	B2
Bawnville Park	55	B2
Bawnville Road	55	A2
Baymount Park	27	A4
Bayshore Lane	64	E1
Bayside Boulevard North	27	C1
Bayside Boulevard South	27	C1
*Bayside Cres (off Sarto Park)	27	C1
Bayside Park	27	C1
Bayside Square East	27	C1
Bayside Square North	27	C1
Bayside Square South	27	C1
Bayside Square West	27	C1
Bayside Walk	27	C1
*Bayswater Terrace (off Breffni Road)	60	F1
Baytownpark	6	E1
Bayview (Loughlinstown)	64	E1
*Bayview (near Bray Bridge)	67	C2
*Bayview (on Seapoint Road)	67	C2
Bayview Ave	72	D1
Bayview Close	64	E1
Bayview Court	64	E1
Bayview Cres	64	E1
Bayview Drive	64	E1
*Bayview Glade (Bayview)	64	E1
Bayview Glen	64	E1
Bayview Green	64	E1
Bayview Grove	64	E1
Bayview Lawn	64	E1
Bayview Rise	64	E1
Beach Ave	39	A3
Beach Drive	39	A3
Beach Park	15	A1
Beach Road	39	A3
Beach View	27	C2
Beacon Court	58	D2
*Beacon Hill (off Nerano Road)	60	F2
Beaconsfield Court	73	A1
Bealing	9	B2
Bealing Ave	9	B2
Bealing Close	9	B3
Bealing Cres	9	B2
Bealing Grove	9	B2
Bealing Mews	9	B2
Bealing View	9	B2
Bealing Walk	9	B2
Bealing Wood	9	B3
Bearna Park	58	D3
Beatty Grove	32	D2
Beatty Park	32	D3
Beatty's Ave (off Sandymount Ave)	76	F3
Beauchamp	64	E4
*Beaucourt (off Achill Road)	25	B3
Beaufield	17	C4
Beaufield Ave	17	C4
Beaufield Close	17	C4
Beaufield Cres	17	C4
Beaufield Drive	17	C4
Beaufield Gardens	17	C4
Beaufield Green	17	C4
Beaufield Grove	17	C4
Beaufield Lawn	17	C4
Beaufield Manor	48	E4
*Beaufield Mews (off Beaufield Manor)	48	E4
Beaufield Park	48	E4
*Beaufort (off Glasthule Road)	60	E1
*Beaufort Court (off Beaufort Downs)	46	F4
Beaufort Downs	46	F4
*Beaufort Villas (off Willbrook Road)	46	F4
Beaumont	26	D1
Beaumont Ave	47	B4
*Beaumont Close (off Beaumont Ave)	47	B4
Beaumont Cottages	34	D2
*Beaumont Court (off Ballyshannon Road)	25	C1
Beaumont Cres	26	D2
Beaumont Drive	47	B4
Beaumont Gardens	48	F4
Beaumont Grove	25	C2
*Beaumont Hall (off The Park)	25	C2
*Beaumont House (off Brighton Road)	46	F2
Beaumont Road	25	C2
*Beaumont Wood (off Ballyshannon Road)	25	C1
*Beaupark Downs (off Monkstown Valley)	49	B4
Beaupark Ave	14	E4
Beaupark Close	14	E4
Beaupark Cres	14	E4
Beaupark Mews	14	E4
Beaupark Place	14	E4
Beaupark Road	14	E4
Beaupark Row	14	E4
Beaupark Square	14	E4
Beaupark Street	14	E4
Beaupark Terrace	14	E4
Beauvale Park	26	D2
Beaver Close	72	D2
Beaver Row	47	C1
Beaver Street	72	D2
Beckett Hall	59	B4
Beckett Way	35	C4
Bective Square	70	F1
*Bedford Court (off Kimmage Road Lower)	46	E1
Bedford Lane (off Aston Quay)	71	B4
Bedford Row (off Aston Quay)	71	B4
Beech Drive	57	B1
Beech Grove (Lucan)	34	E2
Beech Grove (Blackrock)	48	F2
Beech Hill	47	C2
Beech Hill Ave	47	C2
Beech Hill Court	47	C1
*Beech Hill Cres (off Beech Hill Drive)	47	C2
Beech Hill Drive	47	C2
Beech Hill Road	47	C2
*Beech Hill Terrace (off Beech Hill Drive)	47	C2
*Beech Hill Villas (off Beech Hill Drive)	47	C2
Beech House (Sussex Road)	76	D3
Beech House (Swords)	1	Inset
Beech Lawn	57	B1
Beech Lodge	23	A4
Beech Park (Lucan)	34	E1
Beech Park (Cabinteely)	59	C4
Beech Park Ave (Deans Grange)	59	B2
Beech Park Drive	59	B2
Beech Park Grove	59	B2
Beech Park Road	59	B2
Beech Park Wood	32	E1
Beech Road (Fox and Geese)	45	A1
Beech Road (Shankill)	64	E3
Beech Road (Bray)	67	B1
Beech Row (Newlands Road)	35	A4
*Beech Row (off Nangor Road)	44	D1
*Beech Walk (off Brookwood)	56	E2
Beechbrook Grove	14	D4
Beechcourt	60	D3
Beechdale	7	B3
Beechdale Ave	55	B3
*Beechdale Close (off Beechdale Ave)	55	B3
Beechdale Court	55	B3
Beechdale Cres	55	B3
Beechdale Lawn	55	B3
*Beechdale Mews (off Palmerston Road)	47	B1
Beechdale Park	55	B3
Beechdale Place	55	C3
Beechdale Road	55	C3
Beechdale Way	55	B3
Beeches (opposite Knockmaroon Gate)	36	D1
Beeches Park	60	E1
Beeches Road	58	D1
Beechfield	8	D4
Beechfield Ave (Clonee)	8	D4
Beechfield Ave (Walkinstown)	45	C2
Beechfield Close (Clonee)	8	D4
Beechfield Close (Walkinstown)	46	D2
Beechfield Court	8	D4
Beechfield Drive	8	D4
Beechfield Green	8	D4
*Beechfield Haven (off Beechfield Manor)	64	E2
Beechfield Heights	8	D4
Beechfield Lawn	8	E4
Beechfield Manor	64	E2
Beechfield Meadows	8	E4
*Beechfield Mews (off Whitehall Road West)	46	D2
Beechfield Place	8	E4
Beechfield Rise	8	E4
Beechfield Road (Clonee)	8	D4
Beechfield Road (Walkinstown)	45	C2
Beechfield View	8	E4
Beechfield Way	8	E4
Beechlawn	48	F3
Beechlawn Ave (Coolock)	26	E1
Beechlawn Ave (Ballinteer)	57	B1
Beechlawn Close	26	E1
*Beechlawn Drive (Oscar Traynor Road)	26	E1
Beechlawn Green	26	E1
Beechlawn Grove	26	E1
*Beechlawn Manor (off Rathfarnham Road)	46	F2
*Beechlawn Mews (off Rathfarnham Road)	46	F2
Beechmount Drive (Windy Arbour)	47	C3
Beechpark	32	E1
Beechpark (Castleknock)	22	F3
Beechpark Ave	26	E1
Beechpark Ave (Castleknock)	23	A3
Beechpark Close	23	A3
Beechpark Court	26	E1
Beechpark Cres	23	A3
Beechpark Lawn	23	A3
Beechpark Orchard	23	A3
Beechurst	67	B2
*Beechview (off Edmondstown Road)	56	E2
Beechwood	14	F1
Beechwood Ave Lower	47	B1
Beechwood Ave Upper	47	B1
Beechwood Close (Hartstown)	21	C1
Beechwood Close (Boghall Road)	67	C4
Beechwood Court	58	F1
Beechwood Downs	21	C1
*Beechwood Grove (off Beechwood Park)	60	D1
*Beechwood House (at Eaton Wood Square)	64	E2
Beechwood Lawn	60	D2
Beechwood Lawns	52	F2
*Beechwood Park (off Dunville Ave Rathmines)	47	B1
Beechwood Park (Dún Laoghaire)	60	D1
Beechwood Road	47	B1
Beggar's Bush Buildings	76	F2
Beggars Bush Court	76	F2
Belarmine	58	D4
Belarmine Ave	58	D4
Belarmine Close	58	D4
Belarmine Court	58	D4
Belarmine Drive	58	D4
Belarmine Grange	58	D4
Belarmine Hall	58	D4
Belarmine Heath	58	D4
Belarmine Park	58	D4
Belarmine Place	58	D4
Belarmine Plaza	58	D4
Belarmine Square	58	D4
Belarmine Vale	58	D4
Belarmine Way	58	D4
Belcamp Ave	13	B4
Belcamp Cres	13	B4
Belcamp Gardens	13	B4
Belcamp Green	13	B4
Belcamp Grove	13	B4
Belcamp Lane	13	C4
Belcamp Park	13	A3
Belclare Ave	11	C4
Belclare Cres	11	C4
Belclare Drive	11	C4
Belclare Green	11	C4
Belclare Grove	11	C4
Belclare Lawns	11	C4
Belclare Park	11	C4
Belclare Terrace	11	C4
Belclare View	11	C4
Belclare Way	11	C4
*Belfield Close (off Roebuck Road)	47	C3
Belfield Court	48	D2
Belfield Downs	47	C4
Belfield Park Apts	48	E3
Belfry Ave	53	C2
Belfry Close	53	C2
Belfry Court	53	C2
Belfry Cres	53	C2
Belfry Dale	53	C2
Belfry Downs	53	C2
Belfry Drive	53	C2
Belfry Gardens	53	C2
Belfry Green	53	C2
Belfry Grove	53	C2
Belfry Hall	53	C2
Belfry Lawn	53	C2
Belfry Lodge	53	C2
Belfry Manor	53	C2
Belfry Meadows	53	C2
Belfry Park	53	C2
Belfry Place	53	C2
Belfry Rise	53	C2
Belfry Road	53	C2
Belfry Square	53	C2

STREET NAME	PAGE	GRID REF
Belfry Terrace	53	C2
Belfry Walk	53	C2
Belfry Way	53	C2
*Belgard Close (off Garrynisk Road)	44	F3
Belgard Green	44	E4
Belgard Heights	44	F4
Belgard Park	44	E4
Belgard Road	44	E3
Belgard Square	54	F1
Belgard Square East	54	F1
Belgard Square North	54	F1
Belgard Square South	54	F1
Belgard Square West	54	F1
Belgrave Ave	47	B1
*Belgrave Court (off Mountpleasant Ave Upper)	47	A1
*Belgrave Mews (off Castlewood Ave)	47	A1
*Belgrave Place (off Belgrave Square West)	47	A1
*Belgrave Place (off Seapoint Ave Monkstown)	49	B4
Belgrave Road (Rathmines)	47	A1
Belgrave Road (Monkstown)	49	B4
Belgrave Square (Rathmines)	47	A1
Belgrave Square (Monkstown)	49	B4
Belgrave Square East (Rathmines)	47	A1
Belgrave Square East (Monkstown)	49	B4
Belgrave Square North (Rathmines)	47	A1
Belgrave Square North (Monkstown)	49	B4
Belgrave Square South (Rathmines)	47	A1
Belgrave Square South (Monkstown)	49	B4
Belgrave Square West (Rathmines)	47	A1
Belgrave Square West (Monkstown)	49	B4
*Belgrave Terrace (off Eaton Place Monkstown)	49	B4
*Belgrave Terrace (east side of text Meath)	68	D2
*Belgrave View (off Belgrave Ave)	47	B1
*Belgrave Villas (off Belgrave Ave Rathmines)	47	B1
*Belgrave Villas (east side of text Meath)	68	D2
Belgree	9	B2
Belgree Ave	9	B2
Belgree Close	9	B2
Belgree Court	9	B2
Belgree Drive	9	B2
Belgree Green	9	B2
Belgree Grove	9	B2
Belgree Heights	9	B2
Belgree Lawns	9	B2
Belgree Rise	9	B2
Belgree Walk	9	B2
Belgree Woods	9	B2
Belgrove Lawn	36	D2
Belgrove Park (Vernon Ave)	26	F4
Belgrove Park (Chapelizod)	36	D2
Belgrove Road	26	F4
*Bella Ave (off Bella Street)	72	D2
Bella Place (off Bella Street)	72	D2
Bella Street	71	C2
*Bella Vista Lodge (opposite Owendore Ave)	46	F4
Belleview Maltings	69	B4
Belleville	23	C4
Belleville Ave	47	A2
Belleville Court	59	C3
Bellevue	74	E1
Bellevue Ave (Merrion)	48	E2
Bellevue Ave (Dalkey)	60	E2
Bellevue Copse	48	E2
Bellevue Cottages (off Finglas Road Old)	24	F3
*Bellevue Court (off Dornden Park)	48	E2
Bellevue Park	48	E2
Bellevue Park Ave	48	E2
Bellevue Road	60	D2
Bellman's Walk	72	E3
Bell's Lane (off Merrion Row)	75	C2
Bell's Lane (Swords)	1	C2
Belmayne Ave	14	D3
Belmayne Park North	14	D3
Belmayne Park South	14	D4
Belmont (Stillorgan)	59	A1
Belmont (Irishtown)	67	C4
Belmont Ave	47	C1
*Belmont Court (off Belmont Ave)	47	C1
Belmont Gardens	47	C1
Belmont Green	58	F1
Belmont Grove	58	F1
Belmont Lawn	58	F1
Belmont Park (Raheny)	27	A2
*Belmont Park (off Donnybrook Road)	47	C1
Belmont Place (off Gardiner Street Middle)	71	C2
Belmont Square	27	A2
*Belmont Terrace (off Stillorgan Road)	58	F1
Belmont Villas	47	C1
*Belmount Court (off Philipsburgh Ave)	25	C4
Belton Park Ave	26	D3
Belton Park Gardens	26	D3
Belton Park Road	26	D3
Belton Park Villas	26	D3
*Belton Terrace (off Castle Street)	67	C2
Belvedere Court	71	B2
Belvidere Ave	71	C1
Belvidere Court	71	B1
Belvidere Place	71	C1
Belvidere Road	71	B1
Belvidere Square	71	B1
*Belville Apts (off ailesbury Road)	48	D1
Belvue	54	E1
Ben Edar Road	70	D2
*Ben Inagh Park (off Rock Road)	49	A3
Ben Of Howth	30	D3
*Benamore Court (off Newtownpark Ave)	49	A4
Benbulbin Ave	73	B3
Benbulbin Road	73	B3
Benburb Street	70	E4
Beneavin Court	24	F2
Beneavin Drive	24	F2
Beneavin Park	24	F1
Beneavin Road	24	F2
Bengal Terrace	24	F4
Benildus Ave	58	D1
Benmadigan Road	73	A3
Benson Street	72	F4
*Bentley Ave (off Bentley Road)	67	C4
Bentley Park	67	C4
Bentley Road	67	C4
*Bentley Villas (off George's Place)	49	C4
Berach Lodge	27	C2
Berehaven Place	27	B2
Beresford	25	B3
Beresford Ave	25	B3
Beresford Green	25	B3
Beresford Lane	71	C3
Beresford Lawn	25	B3
Beresford Place	71	C3
Beresford Street	71	A3
Berkeley Ave	71	A1
Berkeley Place	71	A1
Berkeley Road	71	A1
Berkeley Street	71	A1
Berkeley Terrace	76	F1
Bernard Curtis Court	36	F4
*Bernard Curtis House (off Bluebell Ave)	36	F4
Berryfield	34	D3
Berryfield Cres	24	D2
Berryfield Drive	24	D2
Berryfield Lane	67	A3
Berryfield Road	24	D2
Berrys Court	73	A2
Bertram Court	74	E2
Bertram Court	74	F1
Berwick Ave	1	B2
Berwick Court	1	B1
Berwick Cres	1	B1
Berwick Drive	1	B1
Berwick Grove	1	B1
Berwick Hall	47	A4
Berwick Lawn	1	B1
Berwick Place	1	B1
Berwick Rise	1	B2
Berwick View	1	B1
Berwick Walk	1	B2
Berwick Way	1	B1
Berystede	76	D4
Bessborough Ave	72	E1
Bessborough Court (Rathmines)	75	B4
*Bessborough Court (The Laurels)	46	F2
Bessborough Parade	75	B4
Besser Drive	35	B4
*Bethany House (off Gilford Road)	39	B4
Bethesda Place	71	B2
Bettyglen	27	B2
*Bettysford (off Monastery Road)	44	E1
Bettystown Ave	26	F3
Beverly Ave	56	D1
Beverly Court	26	F4
Beverly Cres	55	C2
Beverly Downs	55	C2
Beverly Drive	56	D2
Beverly Green	55	C2
Beverly Grove	56	D1
Beverly Heights	56	D2
Beverly Lawns	56	D2
Beverly Park	55	C1
Beverly Rise	55	C2
Bewley	34	E2
Bewley Ave	34	E2
Bewley Drive	34	E2
Bewley Grove	34	E2
Bewley Lawn	34	E2
Bianconi Ave	53	B1
Big Lane	32	D3
Bigger Road	45	C2
Bill Shelly Park	23	C2
Binn Eadair	29	A1
Binn Eadair Court	29	A1
Binn Eadair Cres	29	A1
Binn Eadair View	29	A1
Binns Bridge (Royal Canal)	71	B1
Birch Ave	58	D2
*Birch Dale (off Pine Ave Foxrock)	59	A2
*Birch Dale (off Carriglea Ave)	59	C1
Birch Grove	59	C1
Birchdale Close	2	E3
Birchdale Drive	2	E3
Birchdale Park	2	F3
Birchdale Road	2	E3
Birches Road	58	D1
Birchfield Ave	47	C4
Birchfield Court	47	C4
Birchfield Heights	47	C4
Birchfield Lawn	47	C4
Birchfield Park	47	C4
Birch's Lane	47	C4
Birchview Ave	45	A4
Birchview Close	45	A4
Birchview Court	45	A4
Birchview Drive	45	A4
Birchview Heights	45	A4
Birchview Lawn	45	A4
Birchview Rise	45	A4
Birchwood Close	44	E4
Birchwood Drive	54	E1
Birchwood Heights	54	E1
Bird Ave	47	C3
Biscayne	3	C3
Bishop Street	75	A2
Bishops Lane	62	F2
Bishop's Orchard	9	B2
Bishop's Orchard Boulevard	9	B2
Bishop's Orchard House Apts	9	B2
Bishop's Square	75	A2
*Bishopsmede Apts (Clanbrassil Terrace)	75	A2
Bissett's Loft Apts	3	B2
Bissett's Strand	3	B2
Black Street	69	C3
Blackberry Lane (Rathmines)	75	B4
Blackberry Lane (Portmarnock)	15	A1
Blackberry Rise	15	A1
*Blackburn Square (off Main Street Rathfarnham)	46	F4
Blackcourt Road	22	E1
Blackditch Drive	35	C3
Blackditch Road (Cherry Orchard)	35	C3
Blackditch Road (Le Fanu Park)	36	D3
Blackglen Court	58	D3
Blackglen Road	57	C3
Blackhall Court	70	E3
Blackhall Green	70	E3
Blackhall Little	5	B1
Blackhall Parade (Blackhall Street)	70	F3
Blackhall Place	70	E4
Blackhall Place Apts	70	E3
*Blackhall Square Apts (Brunswick Street North)	70	F3
Blackhall Street	70	F4
Blackhall View	70	E3
Blackhall Walk	70	F4
Blackheath Ave	26	F4
Blackheath Court	26	F4
Blackheath Drive	26	E4
Blackheath Gardens	26	E4
Blackheath Grove	26	E4
Blackheath Park	26	E4
Blackhorse Ave (North Circular Road)	69	C2
Blackhorse Ave (Ashtown)	23	C4
Blackhorse Grove	70	D2
Blackpitts	74	F2
Blackrock	49	A3
Blackthorn Ave	58	E2
Blackthorn Close (Portmarnock)	4	D4
*Blackthorn Close (off Spruce Ave Sandyford)	58	D2
*Blackthorn Court (off Moreen Ave)	58	D2
Blackthorn Drive	58	D2
*Blackthorn Green (off Moreen Ave)	58	D2
*Blackthorn Grove (off Moreen Ave)	58	D2
Blackthorn Hall	57	C3
Blackthorn Hill Ave	52	E2
Blackthorn Hill Close	52	E2
Blackthorn Hill Cres	52	E2
Blackthorn Hill Drive	52	E2
Blackthorn Hill View	52	E2
Blackthorn Road	58	D2
Blackwater Road	24	E3
Blackwood Close	21	A1
Blackwood Cres	21	A1
Blackwood Drive	21	A1
Blackwood Lane	3	C4
Blackwood Lawn	21	A1
Blackwood Mews	21	A1
Blackwood Park	21	A1
Blackwood Place	21	A1
Blackwoods	3	B4
Blakeney House (Swords)	2	E2
Blakeney House Mews (Howth)	30	E3
Blake's Court	22	D1
*Blakes Villas (on Grangegorman Lower)	70	F2
Blakestown Cottages	22	D1
Blakestown Drive	22	D1
Blakestown Road (Mulhuddart)	9	A4
Blakestown Road (Hartstown)	22	D1
Blakestown Way	22	D1
Blanchardstown	22	F2
Blanchardstown ByPass	22	F2
Blanchardstown Interchange	23	A2
Blanchardstown Road North	9	B4
Blanchardstown Road South	22	D2
Blarney Park	46	E1
Blasket Square	22	F1
Blessington Court	71	A2
Blessington Lane	71	A2
Blessington Place (off Saint Joseph's Parade)	71	A2
Blessington Road	53	C2
Blessington Street	71	A2
*Blind Quay Apts (Exchange Street Lower)	71	A4
Blizzard Apts	2	F3
Blood Stoney Road	72	F4
Bloom Court	74	F3
Bloomfield Ave (Morehampton Road)	76	D4
Bloomfield Ave (Portobello)	75	A3
Bloomfield Cottages	75	A3
*Bloomfield Lane (on Georges Street Lower)	50	D4
Bloomfield Park (Morehampton Road)	76	E4
Bloomfield Park (Portobello)	75	A3
Bluebell	36	E4
Bluebell Ave	36	E4
Bluebell Road	36	E4
Blundelstown	42	E3
Blunden Drive	13	C4
Blythe Ave	72	E3
Boardman's Lane (off Cork Street)	74	D2
Boardwalk	71	B3
Boden Dale	56	F1

STREET NAME	PAGE	GRID REF
Boden Heath	56	E1
Boden Heath Apts	56	E1
Boden Mill	56	E2
Boden Park	56	E1
Boden Wood	46	F4
Boeing Road	12	F4
Boghall Road (Killarney Road)	67	B4
Boghall Road (off Vevay Road)	67	C4
Bohammer	13	C2
Boherboy	53	B2
Boherboy Road	53	B2
*Bohernabreena Cottages (off Bohernabreena Road)	55	A3
Bohernabreena Road	55	A3
*Bolbrook Ave (off Avonbeg Road)	55	B1
*Bolbrook Close (off Avonbeg Road)	55	B1
*Bolbrook Drive (off Avonbeg Road)	55	B1
Bolbrook Grove	55	B1
Bolbrook Park	55	B1
Bolbrook Villas	55	B1
Bolton Green	1	A2
*Bolton Square (Dominick Street Lower)	71	A3
Bolton Street	71	A3
Bond Drive	39	A1
Bond Road	39	A1
Bond Street	74	E1
Bonham Street	70	E4
Boolavogue Road	72	F2
Boot Road	44	D2
Booterstown	48	E2
Booterstown Ave	48	F3
*Booterstown Grove (off Booterstown Ave)	48	F2
*Booterstown Hall (Rock Road)	48	F2
Booterstown Park	48	F3
*Booterstown Woods (off South Hill Park)	48	E3
Boranaraltry	61	B4
Boranaraltry Bridge	61	B4
Boranaraltry Lane	61	C4
Boroimhe Alder	1	C3
Boroimhe Ash	1	C3
Boroimhe Aspen	1	C3
Boroimhe Beech	1	C3
Boroimhe Birches	1	C3
Boroimhe Blackthorn	1	C3
Boroimhe Cedars	1	C3
Boroimhe Cherry	1	C3
Boroimhe Elms	1	C3
Boroimhe Hawthorns	1	C3
Boroimhe Hazel	1	C3
Boroimhe Laurels	1	C3
Boroimhe Maples	1	C3
Boroimhe Oaks	1	C3
Boroimhe Pines	1	C3
Boroimhe Poplars	1	C3
Boroimhe Rowan	1	B3
Boroimhe Willows	1	C3
Borris Court (off High Street)	75	A1
Boru Court	1	C3
Botanic Ave	25	A4
*Botanic Court Apts (Prospect Way)	25	A4
Botanic Hall	24	F3
*Botanic Mews (off Prospect Ave)	25	A4
*Botanic Park (off Botanic Ave)	25	A4
Botanic Road	25	A4
*Botanic Square (off Botanic Ave)	25	A4
*Botanic Villas (off Botanic Ave)	25	A4
Bóthair Katherine Tynan	44	E4
Bottle Works	39	A3
Boulevard Mount Eustace	9	B2
Boundary Road	39	A1
Bow Bridge (Camac River)	74	D1
*Bow Bridge Court (Bow Bridge)	74	D1
*Bow Bridge Court (on Kilmainham Lane)	73	C1
*Bow Bridge House (Mount Brown)	74	D1
*Bow Bridge Place (Irwin Street)	74	D1
*Bow Bridge Place (off Military Road)	73	C1
Bow Lane East	75	B1
Bow Lane West	74	D1
Bow Street	70	F4
Boyd House	14	F4
Boyne Court	74	F4
Boyne Lane	76	D1
Boyne Road	24	E3
Boyne Street	76	D1
*Brabazon Buildings (Cork Street)	74	F2
*Brabazon Cottages (near Adelaide Villas)	67	C2
*Brabazon Court (off John Street South)	74	F2
Brabazon Hall	74	F2
Brabazon House	74	E2
Brabazon Place	74	F2
Brabazon Row	74	F2
Brabazon Square	74	F1
Brabazon Street	74	F2
Bracken Drive	4	D4
Bracken Hill	57	C3
Bracken Road	58	D2
Brackenbush Park	60	D4
Brackenbush Road	60	D4
Bracken's Lane	71	C4
Brackenstown Ave	1	C2
Brackenstown Road	1	C2
Bradogue Court	70	E1
Braeburn Terrace	1	Inset
Braemor Ave	47	A3
Braemor Drive	47	A3
Braemor Grove	47	A3
Braemor Park	47	A3
Braemor Road	47	A3
Braithwaite Street	74	E1
Bramblefield	8	F4
Bramblefield Court	8	F4
Bramblefield Cres	8	F4
Bramblefield Drive	8	F4
Bramblefield Park	8	F4
Bramblefield View	8	F4
Bramblefield Walk	8	F4
Bramley Ave	22	E3
Bramley Court	22	E3
Bramley Cres	22	E3
Bramley Garth	22	E3
Bramley Green	22	E3
Bramley Grove	22	E3
Bramley Heath	22	E3
Bramley Park	22	E3
Bramley Road	22	E3
Bramley View	22	E3
Bramley Walk	22	E3
Bramley Way	22	E3
Brandon Road	36	F4
Bray	68	D1
Bray Commons	67	B2
*Bray Head Terrace (Vevay Road, Putland Road)	67	C3
Bray Road (Cornelscourt)	59	B2
Bray Road (Shanganagh)	59	C4
Bray Southern Cross Road	67	B4
Breakwater Road North	39	B2
Breakwater Road South	39	B2
Breffini Terrace	60	E1
*Breffni Gardens (adjacent The Mall)	15	A4
Breffni Road	60	E1
Bregia Road	24	F4
Brehon Court	57	B3
Brehon Field Road	57	B2
Brehon's Chair	57	A3
Bremen Ave	39	A3
Bremen Grove	39	A3
Bremen Road	39	A3
Brendan Behan Court	71	C1
Brendan Road	47	C1
*Brennans Parade (between Sidmonton and Albert Ave)	68	D2
*Brennans Terrace (between Sidmonton and Albert Ave)	68	D2
Brennanstown Ave	59	C4
Brennanstown Court	59	C4
Brennanstown Road	59	B4
Brennanstown Square	59	C4
Brennanstown Vale	59	B4
Brewery Road	58	F2
Brian Ave	25	C4
Brian Boru Ave	39	C1
Brian Boru Street	39	C1
Brian Road	25	C4
Brian Terrace	25	C4
Briansboro Terrace	74	F3
Briar Walk	4	D4
Briar Wood	68	D3
Briarfield Grove	27	B1
Briarfield Road	27	B2
*Briarfield Villas (off Greendale Road)	27	B1
*Briarfield Villas (off Greendale Road)	27	B1
*Briarly Court (off Churchtown Road)	47	B4
*Briarsfield Walk (at Kilbarrack Station)	27	B1
Briarwood Ave	22	D1
Briarwood Close	9	A4
Briarwood Gardens	22	D1
Briarwood Green	22	D1
Briarwood Lawn	22	D1
Briarwood Park	22	D1
Briarwood Road	22	D1
Brickfield	67	B3
Brickfield Drive	73	C4
Brickfield Lane (The Coombe)	74	E2
*Brickfield Lane (near Brickfield)	67	B3
Bride Close	75	A1
Bride Road	75	A1
Bride Street	75	A1
Brides Glen	63	C2
Bride's Glen Ave	1	Inset
Brides Glen Park	1	C1
Bride's Glen Park	1	Inset
*Bridge Court	76	E2
*Bridge House Apts (off Lullymore Terrace)	74	E3
Bridge Street (Swords)	2	D2
Bridge Street (Ringsend)	39	A3
Bridge Street Lower	70	F4
Bridge Street Upper	74	F1
Bridgefoot Street	70	F4
Bridgeview	35	B3
*Bridgewater Hall (Clark's Bridge)	72	D1
Bridgewater Quay	69	B4
Bridon	62	F1
*Brighton Ave (off Charlemont Road Clontarf)	26	D4
Brighton Ave (Rathgar)	46	F2
Brighton Ave (Monkstown)	49	B4
Brighton Ave (Carrickmines)	59	A4
*Brighton Cottages (off Brighton Road Foxrock)	59	A3
Brighton Court	59	A4
Brighton Gardens	46	F2
*Brighton Green (off Brighton Square)	46	F2
Brighton Hall	59	A4
*Brighton Lane (off Monkstown Road)	49	B4
*Brighton Lodge (off Brighton Road Foxrock)	59	A3
Brighton Place	59	A4
Brighton Road (Terenure)	46	F2
Brighton Road (Foxrock)	59	A3
Brighton Square	46	F2
*Brighton Terrace (off Seapoint Ave Monkstown)	49	B4
*Brighton Terrace (off Glasthule Road)	60	E1
Brighton Vale	49	B3
Britain Place	71	B2
Britain Quay	72	F4
Broadfield Ave	52	E2
Broadfield Close	52	E2
Broadfield Court	52	E2
Broadfield Drive	52	E2
Broadfield Heath	52	E2
Broadfield Manor	52	E2
Broadfield Meadows	52	E2
Broadfield Park	52	E2
Broadfield View	52	E2
Broadford Ave	57	B2
Broadford Close	57	B2
Broadford Cres	57	B2
Broadford Drive	57	B2
Broadford Hill	57	B2
Broadford Lawn	57	B2
Broadford Park	57	B2
Broadford Rise	57	B2
Broadford Road	57	B2
Broadford Walk	57	B2
Broadmeadow	1	C1
*Broadmeadow Mews (adjacent to railway, Strand Street Malahide)	3	B2
Broadstone	70	F2
Broadstone Ave (off Royal Canal Bank)	71	A2
*Broadstone Hall Apts (near Whitaker Hall)	71	A2
*Broadstone Place (off Royal Canal Bank)	71	A2
Broadway Drive	22	E2
Broadway Grove	22	E2
Broadway Park	22	E2
Broadway Road	22	E2
*Broc Hall (off Beech Hill Ave)	47	C1
Brockey (Glencullen)	61	C4
Brockey (Glencullen Mountain)	65	A1
Brockey Lane	65	A1
Brodin Row	70	D3
*Bromley Court (off Francis Street)	74	F1
Brompton Court	22	E3
Brompton Green	22	E2
Brompton Grove	22	E3
Brompton Lawn	22	E2
Brook Court	49	B4
*Brook House (off Richmond Road)	25	B4
Brook Wood	67	B2
Brookdale	55	A2
Brookdale Ave	1	B3
Brookdale Close	1	B2
Brookdale Court	1	B3
Brookdale Drive	1	B2
Brookdale Green	1	B2
Brookdale Grove	1	B2
Brookdale Lawns	1	B2
Brookdale Park	1	B2
Brookdale Road	1	B2
Brookdale Walk	1	B2
Brookdale Way	1	B2
Brookdene	64	E2
Brookfield (Coolock)	26	F2
Brookfield (Lucan)	34	D3
Brookfield (Milltown)	47	B2
*Brookfield (off Anglesea Road Donnybrook)	47	C1
Brookfield (Blackrock)	48	F3
Brookfield Ave (Maynooth)	17	C2
Brookfield Ave (Blackrock)	49	A4
*Brookfield Ave (east side of Meath Road)	68	D3
*Brookfield Court (at Rialto Bridge)	73	C2
*Brookfield Court (off Ravensdale Park)	46	E2
*Brookfield Court (off Brookfield Place)	49	A4
*Brookfield Court (off Brookfield Road Tallaght)	54	D1
Brookfield Estate	46	E2
*Brookfield Green (off Ravensdale Park)	46	E2
*Brookfield Grove (off Brookfield Ave)	49	A4
Brookfield Park	17	C4
Brookfield Place	49	A4
Brookfield Road (Kilmainham)	73	C1
Brookfield Road (Tallaght)	54	D1
Brookfield Street	73	C2
Brookfield Terrace	49	A4
Brookfield View	54	D1
Brookhaven Drive	22	E1
Brookhaven Grove	22	E1
Brookhaven Lawn	22	E1
Brookhaven Park	22	E1
Brookhaven Rise	22	E1
Brooklands	48	E1
Brooklawn (Clontarf)	26	D4
Brooklawn (Lucan)	34	D3
Brooklawn (Blackrock)	48	F3
Brooklawn (Palmerston)	35	B1
*Brooklawn Ave (off Rockville Drive)	49	B4
*Brooklawn Wood (off Stradbrook Road)	49	B4
Brookmount Ave	55	C1
*Brookmount Court (off Butterfield Ave)	46	E4
*Brookmount Lawns (off Tallaght Road)	55	C1
Brookpark	34	D3
Brookstone Lane	15	A4
Brookstone Road	15	A4
Brookvale (off Lucan Road)	34	D1
Brookvale Downs	46	F3
Brookvale Road (Rathfarnham)	46	F3
*Brookvale Road (off Eglinton Road)	47	C1
Brookview Ave	54	D1
Brookview Close	54	D1
Brookview Court	54	D1

STREET NAME	PAGE	GRID REF
Brookview Cres	54	D1
Brookview Drive	54	D1
Brookview Gardens	54	D1
Brookview Green	54	D1
Brookview Grove	54	D1
Brookview Lawns	54	D1
Brookview Park	54	D1
Brookview Rise	54	D1
Brookview Terrace	54	D1
*Brookview Walk (Brookview Way)	53	C1
Brookview Way	54	D1
Brookville	24	D1
*Brookville Cres (off Brookville Park)	26	E1
Brookville Park (Coolock)	26	E1
Brookville Park (Artane)	26	E2
Brookville Park (Dean's Grange)	59	B1
Brookwood	56	E2
*Brookwood Abbey (off Gracefield Road)	26	E2
Brookwood Ave	26	E2
Brookwood Cres	26	F2
Brookwood Drive	26	E2
Brookwood Glen	26	F3
Brookwood Grove	26	E2
Brookwood Hall	26	E3
Brookwood Heights	26	F2
Brookwood Lawn	26	F2
Brookwood Meadow	26	E2
Brookwood Park	26	E3
Brookwood Rise	26	F3
Brookwood Road	26	E2
Broombridge Road	24	E4
Broomfield (Malahide)	3	B4
Broomfield (Lucan)	21	B4
Broomfield Court	64	E2
Broomfield Mews	3	B4
Broomhill Close	45	A4
Broomhill Drive	45	A4
Broomhill Road	45	A4
Broomhill Terrace (off Broomhill Road)	45	A4
Brown Street North	70	F3
Brown Street South	74	E2
Brownrath	5	B1
Brownsbarn	43	C4
Brownsbarn Court	43	C4
Brownsbarn Garden	43	C4
Brownsbarn Orchard	43	C4
Brownsbarn Wood	43	C4
Brownstown (Kilcloon)	5	A2
Brownstown (Peamount)	42	D1
*Bruce's Terrace (near Dargle Heights)	67	B2
*Brug Chroimlinn (off Saint Agnes RoadCrumlin)	46	D1
Brunswick Place	76	E1
Brunswick Street North	70	F3
Brunswick Villas (Pearse Street)	71	C4
*Brusna Cottages (off Main Street Blackrock)	49	A3
Buckingham Street Lower	72	D2
Buckingham Street Upper	72	D2
Buckingham Village	71	C2
*Buckley Hall (Buckingham Street Lower)	72	D2
Buckleys Lane	33	A1
Bulfin Court	73	A2
Bulfin Gardens	73	B1
*Bulfin House (off Bulfin Road)	73	B2
Bulfin Road	73	A2
Bull Alley Street	75	A1
*Bull Lane (Saint Kevin's Square)	67	C2
Bull Wall	40	D1
Bull Wall Cottages	40	D1
*Bullock Steps (off Harbour Road)	60	F1
Bunbury Gate Ave	1	Inset
Bunbury Gate Cres	1	Inset
Bunratty Ave	26	E1
Bunratty Drive	26	E1
Bunratty Road	26	E1
Bunting Road	45	C1
Burdett Ave	60	E1
Burg an Rí Glen	34	F3
Burg an Rí Terrace	34	F3
Burgage	13	C3
*Burgage Cres (Burgage Street)	42	D4
*Burgage Green (Burgage Street)	42	D4
*Burgage Green	56	E1
Burgage Street	42	D4
Burgess Lane	70	F4

STREET NAME	PAGE	GRID REF
Burgh Quay	71	C4
Burke Place (off Mount Brown)	74	D1
Burleigh Court	76	D3
Burleigh Mews	76	D3
Burlington Gardens	76	D3
Burlington Mews	76	D3
Burlington Road	76	D3
*Burmah Close (off Dalkey Ave)	60	F2
Burnell Park Ave	22	E4
Burnell Park Green	22	E4
Burnell Square	14	D4
Burnside	25	B1
Burren Court	11	C4
*Burris Court (off High Street)	75	A1
Burrow Court (Poppintree)	11	C4
Burrow Court (Portmarnock)	15	A1
Burrow Road (Sutton)	29	B1
Burrow Road (Stepaside)	58	D4
Burrowfield Road	28	D1
Burton Court	58	E2
Burton Hall Ave	58	E2
Burton Hall Road	58	E2
Burton Road	60	F2
*Bushfield Ave (off Marlborough Road)	47	B1
Bushfield Drive	44	D3
Bushfield Green	44	D2
Bushfield Grove	44	D3
Bushfield Lawns	44	D2
*Bushfield Place (off Bushfield Terrace)	47	B1
*Bushfield Square (off Philipsburgh Ave)	25	C4
Bushfield Terrace	47	B1
Bushy Park Gardens	46	E3
Bushy Park House	46	E3
Bushy Park Road	46	F3
Bustyhill	51	B3
*Butler's Place Apts (Benson Street)	72	F4
Butlerstown	5	C3
Butt Bridge (River Liffey)	71	C4
Buttercup Ave	13	C4
Buttercup Close	13	C4
Buttercup Drive	13	C4
Buttercup Green	13	C4
Buttercup Lawn	13	C4
Buttercup Mews	13	C4
Buttercup Park	13	C4
Buttercup Square	13	C4
Buttercup Terrace	13	C4
Butterfield Ave	46	E4
Butterfield Close	46	E4
Butterfield Court	46	F4
Butterfield Cres	46	F4
Butterfield Drive	46	F4
Butterfield Grove	46	E4
*Butterfield Meadow (off Butterfield Cres)	46	E4
Butterfield Orchard	46	E4
Butterfield Park	46	E4
*Byrne's Cottages (Francis Street)	74	E2
Byrnes Lane (Pearse Square West)	72	E4
Byrne's Lane (Jervis Street)	71	B4
*Byrne's Terrace (off Beech Hill Drive)	47	C2

C

STREET NAME	PAGE	GRID REF
Cabinteely	59	C4
Cabinteely Ave	59	C3
Cabinteely Bypass	59	C3
Cabinteely Close	59	C3
*Cabinteely Court (off Pottery Road)	59	C3
Cabinteely Cres	59	C3
Cabinteely Drive	59	C3
Cabinteely Green	59	C3
*Cabinteely Park (off Cabinteely Way)	59	C3
Cabinteely Way	59	C3
Cabra	69	C1
Cabra Drive	70	D1
Cabra Gate (Phoenix Park)	24	D4
Cabra Grove	70	D1
Cabra Park	70	F1
*Cabra Park Mews (Cabra Park)	24	F4
Cabra Road	70	D1

STREET NAME	PAGE	GRID REF
Caddell	14	F2
Cadogan Road	25	C4
Cairnbrook	63	A1
Cairnbrook Avenue	63	A1
Cairnbrook Hall	63	A1
Cairnbrook Manor	63	A1
Cairnbrook View	63	A1
Cairnbrook Way	63	A1
Cairn Court	12	D4
Cairn Hill	59	B2
Cairnfort	62	E1
Cairnwood Ave	44	E4
Cairnwood Court	44	E4
Cairnwood Green	44	E4
Caldbeck Way	44	E2
Calderwood Ave	25	C3
*Calderwood Grove (off Calderwood Road)	25	C3
Calderwood Road	25	C3
Caledon Court	72	F2
Caledon Road	72	F2
Callaghan Bridge	21	C2
Callary Road	48	D3
Callender's Mill	32	D4
Calmount Ave	45	B2
Calmount Park	45	B2
Calmount Road	45	B2
Camac Close	73	A1
Camac Court	73	A1
*Camac Cres Apts (off Turvey Ave)	73	A1
*Camac House (on Bow Bridge)	73	C1
Camac Park	36	E4
*Camac View Apts (on Kilmainham Lane)	73	C1
*Camac Way Apts (on Rowserstown Lane)	73	C1
Camaderry Road	68	D3
*Camberley Elms (off Churchtown Road Upper)	47	B4
*Camberley Oaks (off Churchtown Road Upper)	47	B4
*Cambridge Ave (off Pigeon House Road)	39	A3
*Cambridge Court (off Cambridge Park)	39	A3
Cambridge Park	39	A3
Cambridge Road (Ringsend)	39	A3
Cambridge Road (Rathmines)	47	A1
*Cambridge Square (off Thorncastle Street)	39	A3
*Cambridge Street (off Cambridge Park)	39	A3
Cambridge Terrace (Ranelagh)	75	C4
*Cambridge Terrace (off York Road Dún Laoghaire)	49	C4
*Cambridge Villas (off Castlewood Park)	47	A1
Camden Ave	23	C3
Camden Buildings	75	B2
Camden Court	75	B3
Camden Lock	76	F1
Camden Market	75	B3
Camden Place	75	B2
Camden Row	75	A2
Camden Street Lower	75	B2
Camden Street Upper	75	B3
Camden Villas	75	B2
Cameron Square	73	C1
Cameron Street	74	E2
Cammock Apts	73	C1
Camogie Road (Phoenix Park)	69	B3
*Campbell Court (streets between Tuckett's Lane and Main Street)	30	D2
Campbell's Court	71	A3
Campbell's Lane (off Belvidere Ave)	71	C1
Campbell's Row (off Portland Street North)	71	C1
Campfield Terrace	57	C1
Campshire Hall	72	D4
Campshire Mews	72	D4
Canal Road	75	B4
Canal Terrace	36	E4
Canal Turn	35	B4
*Canal View (off Lullymore Terrace)	74	E3
Canal Walk	36	D4
*Cannon Mews (off Herbert Road)	39	A4
Cannon Mews East	76	F2
Cannon Mews West	76	F2

STREET NAME	PAGE	GRID REF
*Cannon Place (off Herbert Road)	39	A4
Cannon Rock Estate	30	E2
Cannon Rock View	30	E2
Cannonbrook	34	D2
Cannonbrook Ave	34	D2
Cannonbrook Court	34	D2
Cannonbrook Lawn	34	D2
Cannonbrook Park	34	D2
*Canon Court (Bride Street)	75	A1
Canon Lillis Ave	72	E2
*Canon Mooney Gardens (off Cambridge Road)	39	A3
Canon Troy Court	36	D2
Capel Street	71	A3
Cappagh Ave	24	D1
Cappagh Drive	24	D1
Cappagh Green	24	D1
Cappagh Road (Cappoge)	10	E4
Cappagh Road (Finglas)	24	D1
Cappaghmore Estate	35	A4
Cappoge	10	F4
Cappoge Cottages	10	E4
Captain's Ave	46	D1
Captain's Drive	46	D2
Captain's Hill	20	D4
Captain's Road	46	D2
Cara Park	13	B3
*Caragh Court (off Philipsburgh Ave)	25	C4
Caragh Road	69	C1
Carberry Road	25	C3
*Carbury Place (off Newtown Ave Blackrock)	49	A3
Carbury Terrace	72	F3
Cardiff Castle Road	24	D2
Cardiff Lane	72	E4
Cardiffs Bridge	24	D3
Cardiffsbridge Ave	24	D2
Cardiffsbridge Grove (off Cappagh Road)	24	D1
Cardiffsbridge Road	24	D2
Card's Lane (Pearse Street)	71	C4
Carleton Road	25	C4
Carlingford Court	76	E1
Carlingford Parade	76	E1
Carlingford Road	25	A4
Carlisle Ave	47	B1
*Carlisle Court (off Terenure Road North)	46	F2
Carlisle Street	75	A3
*Carlisle Terrace (off North Circular Road)	70	F1
Carlisle Terrace (Malahide)	3	B3
*Carlisle Terrace (off Corrig Road)	60	D1
*Carlisle Terrace (on Seymour Road)	67	C2
Carlton Court (Swords)	02	D1
Carlton Court (Clontarf)	26	D4
*Carlton Terrace (Novara Ave)	67	C2
Carlton Villas (off Sandymount Ave)	76	F3
*Carlton Villas (Novara Ave)	67	C2
Carmanhall Court	58	E2
Carmanhall Road	58	E2
*Carman's Court (off Carman's Hall)	74	F1
Carman's Hall	74	F1
Carna Road	35	C3
Carndonagh Drive	27	B1
Carndonagh Lawn	27	B1
Carndonagh Park	27	B1
Carndonagh Road	27	B1
Carne Court	8	F4
Carnegie Court	2	D1
Carnew Street	70	D2
Carnlough Road	70	D1
Carnlough Road	24	E4
Caroline Court (off Sandymount Road)	76	E3
*Caroline Row (off Irishtown Road)	39	A3
Carpenterstown	22	D3
Carpenterstown Ave	22	E3
Carpenterstown Manor	22	E3
Carpenterstown Park East	22	E3
Carpenterstown Road	22	E4
Carraig Close	11	C4
Carraig Glen	59	C4
Carraig Grennane	60	E4
Carraroe Ave	27	A1
Carrick Court	14	F1
*Carrick Lawn (off Kilmacud Road Upper)	58	D1

STREET NAME	PAGE	GRID REF
Carrick Terrace	74	D2
Carrickaspinkeen	65	A3
Carrickbrack Heath	29	B2
Carrickbrack Hill	29	B2
Carrickbrack Lawn	29	B2
Carrickbrack Park	29	B2
Carrickbrack Road (Sutton)	29	B2
Carrickbrack Road (The Summit Howth)	30	D4
Carrickbrennan Lawn	49	C4
Carrickbrennan Road	49	C4
Carrickfoyle Terrace	73	B1
Carrickhill Close	4	D4
Carrickhill Drive	15	A1
Carrickhill Heights	15	A1
Carrickhill Rise	4	D4
Carrickhill Road	15	A1
Carrickhill Road Middle	15	A1
Carrickhill Road Upper	3	C4
Carrickhill Walk	4	D4
Carrickmines	59	B4
Carrickmines Ave	59	B4
Carrickmines Chase	59	B4
Carrickmines Dale	59	B4
Carrickmines Garth	59	B4
Carrickmines Green	63	A1
Carrickmines Little	59	A4
Carrickmines Manor	63	A1
Carrickmines Oaks	59	B4
Carrickmount Ave	57	A1
Carrickmount Drive	57	A1
Carrig Court	53	B1
Carrig Road	11	C4
Carrigallen Drive	24	E3
Carrigallen Park	24	E3
Carrigallen Road	24	E3
Carrigeen	52	D3
Carriglea	55	B2
Carriglea Ave (Tallaght)	55	B2
Carriglea Ave (Kill O'The Grange)	59	C2
Carriglea Court (Tallaght)	55	B2
*Carriglea Court (off Carriglea Gardens)	59	C1
Carriglea Downs (Tallaght)	55	B2
Carriglea Downs (Kill O'The Grange)	59	C2
Carriglea Drive	55	B2
Carriglea Gardens	59	C1
Carriglea Grove	55	B2
Carriglea Rise	55	B2
Carriglea View	55	B2
Carriglea Walk	55	B2
Carrigmore Ave	53	B2
Carrigmore Close (Saggart)	53	B2
Carrigmore Close (Oldbawn)	54	F3
Carrigmore Court	53	C2
Carrigmore Cres	53	C1
Carrigmore Dale	53	B2
Carrigmore Downs	53	B1
Carrigmore Drive	54	F2
Carrigmore Elms	53	B2
Carrigmore Gardens	53	B1
Carrigmore Glen	53	B1
Carrigmore Green	53	B3
Carrigmore Grove (Saggart)	53	B2
Carrigmore Grove (Oldbawn)	54	F3
Carrigmore Lawns	53	B1
Carrigmore Manor	53	B2
Carrigmore Meadows	53	B2
Carrigmore Oak	53	B2
Carrigmore Park	54	F3
Carrigmore Place	53	B2
Carrigmore Road	54	F2
Carrigmore Terrace	53	B2
Carrigmore View	54	F3
Carrigmore Way	53	C2
Carrigwood	55	C2
Carrington	12	E4
Carrow Road	73	A3
Carton Ave	18	D2
Carton Bridge	18	E2
Carton Court	17	C4
Carton Demesne	18	F2
Carton Square	17	C2
Carwell Court	2	E2
Carysfort Ave	49	A4
Carysfort Downs	59	A1
*Carysfort Drive (off Carysfort Road)	60	F1
Carysfort Grove	59	A1
Carysfort Hall	49	A4
Carysfort Park	49	A4
Carysfort Road	60	F1
Carysfort Woods	59	A1

STREET NAME	PAGE	GRID REF
Casana View	30	E2
*Casement Close (beside school on Barry Road)	24	D1
Casement Drive	24	D1
Casement Green	24	D1
Casement Grove	24	D1
Casement Park	24	D1
Casement Road (Mellows Park)	24	D1
Casement Road (Finglas South)	24	D2
Casement Villas	59	B1
Cashel Ave	46	E2
Cashel Road	46	D1
Casimir Ave	46	F1
*Casimir Court (off Casimir Ave)	46	F1
Casimir Road	46	F1
Casino Drive	3	B2
Casino Park	26	D3
Casino Road	25	C4
*Cassian Court (at Lockkeeper's Walk)	24	D3
Castaheany	8	E4
Castilla Park	26	F4
Castle Ave (Swords)	2	D2
Castle Ave (Clontarf)	26	E4
Castle Ave (Clondalkin)	44	E1
Castle Ave (Churchtown)	47	A4
Castle Close (Clondalkin)	44	E1
Castle Close (Dalkey)	60	F1
Castle Court (Clontarf)	26	D4
*Castle Court (off Cypress Lawn)	46	D4
*Castle Court (off Main Street Rathfarnham)	46	F4
*Castle Court (off Whitehall Road Rathfarnham)	47	A4
Castle Court (Booterstown)	48	F2
*Castle Court (off Dundrum Castle)	57	C1
Castle Court (Stepaside)	58	E4
Castle Court (Loughlinstown)	64	E1
Castle Court Apts (Dublin Castle)	75	A1
*Castle Court Apts (off Saint Margarets Ave Malahide)	3	B3
Castle Cove (Malahide)	3	A2
*Castle Cove (off Castle Street Dalkey)	60	F2
*Castle Cres (off Monastery Road)	44	E1
Castle Dawson	17	B3
Castle Down Croft	2	F2
Castle Down Grove	2	F2
Castle Down Road	2	F2
Castle Drive (Swords)	2	D2
Castle Drive (Clondalkin)	44	E1
Castle Drive (Ballyogan Road)	58	E4
Castle Elms	26	E1
Castle Farm	64	E3
Castle Farm Wood	64	E3
Castle Gate Apts	75	A1
Castle Grove (Swords)	2	D2
Castle Grove (Clontarf)	26	E4
Castle Grove (Clondalkin)	44	E1
Castle Heath	3	A3
Castle Lawn	58	E4
Castle Lawns (Malahide)	2	F2
Castle Lawns (Tallaght)	45	B4
Castle Market (off Drury Street)	75	B1
*Castle Mews Apts (Castle Street Dalkey)	60	F2
*Castle Oaks (adjacent to Lawson Spinney)	3	A3
Castle Park (Swords)	2	D2
Castle Park (Leixlip)	33	A1
Castle Park (Clondalkin)	44	E1
Castle Park (Tallaght)	45	B4
Castle Park (Monkstown)	49	C4
Castle Park Estate (Tallaght)	55	B1
*Castle Place (on Breffni Road)	60	F1
Castle Riada Ave	34	E2
Castle Riada Cres	34	E2
Castle Riada Drive	34	E3
Castle Riada Grove	34	E2
Castle Road (Clontarf)	26	E4
Castle Road (Lucan)	34	E2
Castle Road (Saggart)	53	A2
Castle Rosse	14	F4
*Castle Side (off Castlefield Ave)	55	C1
Castle Steps (off Castle Street)	75	A1
Castle Street (Cork Hill)	75	A1
Castle Street (Dalkey)	60	F2
Castle Street (Bray)	67	C2
Castle Terrace (Phibsborough Ave)	70	F1

STREET NAME	PAGE	GRID REF
Castle Terrace (Malahide)	3	B2
*Castle Terrace (off Ulverton Road)	60	F1
Castle View (Clondalkin)	44	E1
*Castle View (off Dundrum Castle)	57	C1
Castle View (Carrickmines)	59	A4
*Castle View (off Oldcourt Road)	55	B3
*Castle View Apts (opposite Fade Street)	75	B1
Castle View Road	44	E1
Castle Village	31	C2
Castle Village Ave	31	C2
Castle Village Close	31	C2
Castle Village Court	31	C2
Castle Village Cres	31	C2
Castle Village Drive	31	C2
Castle Village Green	31	C2
Castle Village Grove	31	C2
Castle Village Lawns	31	C2
Castle Village Park	31	C2
Castle Village Place	31	C2
Castle Village Rise	31	C2
Castle Village Walk	31	C2
Castle Village Way	31	C2
Castle Village Woods	31	C2
Castle Villas (Dalkey)	60	F2
*Castle Way Apts (Golden Lane)	75	A1
Castlebridge	18	D3
Castlebrook	57	C1
Castlebyrne Park	49	A4
Castlecurragh Heath	9	A4
Castlecurragh Park	9	B4
Castlecurragh Vale	9	B4
Castledawson Ave	48	F3
Castlefarm	1	C1
Castlefield Ave	55	C1
Castlefield Court (Clonsilla)	21	C2
Castlefield Court (Firhouse)	55	C1
Castlefield Drive	55	C2
Castlefield Green	55	C2
Castlefield Grove	55	C2
Castlefield Lawn	55	C1
Castlefield Manor (Malahide)	3	B3
Castlefield Manor (Firhouse)	55	C1
Castlefield Orchard	55	C1
Castlefield Park (Clonsilla)	21	C2
Castlefield Park (Firhouse)	55	C2
Castlefield Way	55	C2
Castlefield Woods	21	C2
Castleforbes Road	72	F3
Castleforbes Square	72	F3
Castlegate (Monkstown)	59	C1
Castlegate (Shankill)	64	D3
Castlegate Chase	33	C3
Castlegate Close	33	C3
Castlegate Copse	33	C4
Castlegate Court	33	C4
Castlegate Cres	33	C3
Castlegate Dene	33	C3
Castlegate Downs	33	C4
Castlegate Drive	33	C3
Castlegate Elms	33	C3
Castlegate Grange	33	C4
Castlegate Green	33	C3
Castlegate Grove	33	C3
Castlegate Heath	33	C4
Castlegate Lawn	33	C4
Castlegate Mews	33	C4
Castlegate Park	33	C3
Castlegate Place	33	C3
Castlegate Row	33	C4
Castlegate Square	34	D3
Castlegate Terrace	33	C4
Castlegate Walk	33	C3
Castlegate Way	33	C3
Castlegrange	21	B1
Castlegrange Ave (Swords)	2	D1
Castlegrange Ave (Clonsilla)	21	B1
Castlegrange Close (Swords)	2	D1
Castlegrange Close (Clondalkin)	43	B1
Castlegrange Court (Clondalkin)	43	C1
Castlegrange Drive (Clonsilla)	21	B1
Castlegrange Drive (Clondalkin)	43	B1
Castlegrange Gardens	21	B1
Castlegrange Green (Swords)	2	D1
Castlegrange Green (Clonsilla)	21	B1
Castlegrange Green (Clondalkin)	43	B1
Castlegrange Heights	2	D1
Castlegrange Hill	2	D1
Castlegrange Lawn (Clonsilla)	21	B1
Castlegrange Lawn (Clondalkin)	43	C1
Castlegrange Park	21	B1
Castlegrange Road (Swords)	2	D1

STREET NAME	PAGE	GRID REF
Castlegrange Road (Clondalkin)	43	C1
Castlegrange Row	21	B1
Castlegrange Square (Clondalkin)	43	C1
Castlegrange Terrace	21	B1
Castlegrange Way	2	D1
Castlekevin Road	26	D1
Castleknock	22	F3
Castleknock Ave	22	F3
Castleknock Brook	22	F3
Castleknock Close	22	E3
Castleknock Court	22	F3
Castleknock Cres	22	F3
Castleknock Dale	22	F3
Castleknock Downs	22	E3
Castleknock Drive	22	E3
Castleknock Elms	22	F3
Castleknock Gate (Phoenix Park)	23	B4
Castleknock Glade	22	F3
Castleknock Grange	22	F3
Castleknock Green	23	A3
Castleknock Grove	22	F3
Castleknock Laurels	22	F3
Castleknock Lodge	23	A4
Castleknock Manor	23	A3
Castleknock Meadows	22	F3
Castleknock Oaks	22	F3
Castleknock Park	23	A3
Castleknock Rise	22	E3
Castleknock Road (Blanchardstown)	22	F3
Castleknock Road (Phoenix Park)	23	A4
Castleknock Vale	22	F3
Castleknock View	22	F3
Castleknock Walk	22	E3
Castleknock Way	22	F3
Castleknock Wood	22	F3
*Castlelands (off Hyde Road)	60	F1
*Castlelands Grove (off Hyde Road)	60	F1
Castlelyons	42	D4
Castlemoyne	14	D3
*Castlepark Court (off Castlepark Road)	60	E2
Castlepark Road	60	E1
Castlerosse Cres	14	F4
Castlerosse Drive	14	F4
Castlerosse View	14	F4
Castleside Drive	46	F3
Castletimon Ave	25	C1
Castletimon Drive	25	C1
Castletimon Gardens	25	C1
Castletimon Green	25	C1
Castletimon Park	25	C1
Castletimon Road	25	C1
Castletown	32	F1
Castletown Court	32	D3
Castletown Drive	32	D3
Castletown Grove	32	D3
Castletown Lawn	32	D3
Castletymon Court	45	B4
Castletymon Gardens	45	B4
Castletymon Green	45	B4
Castleview (Artane)	26	E2
Castleview (Clontarf)	26	E4
Castleview Court	1	Inset
Castleview Ave	1	Inset
Castleview Close	1	Inset
Castleview Cres	1	Inset
Castleview Drive	1	Inset
Castleview Estate	7	B3
Castleview Green	1	Inset
Castleview Grove	1	Inset
Castleview Heights	1	Inset
Castleview Lawns	1	Inset
Castleview Meadows	1	Inset
Castleview Park (Swords)	1	Inset
Castleview Park (Malahide)	3	A3
Castleview Place	1	Inset
Castleview Rise	1	Inset
Castleview Row	1	Inset
Castleview Walk	1	Inset
Castleview Way	1	Inset
Castlewarden	51	A3
Castlewarden North	51	A3
Castlewood	21	C1
Castlewood Ave	47	A1
*Castlewood Close (off Castlewood Ave)	47	A1
*Castlewood Court (off Oakley Road)	47	B1
Castlewood Park	47	A1

STREET NAME	PAGE	GRID REF
*Castlewood Place (off Church Gardens)	47	A1
*Castlewood Terrace (off Castlewood Ave)	47	A1
Cathal Brugha Street	71	B3
*Cathedral Court (New Street South)	75	A2
Cathedral Lane	75	A2
Cathedral Street	71	B3
Cathedral View Court	75	A2
Cathedral View Walk	75	A2
Catherine Court (off William Street North)	72	D1
Catherine Lane	70	F3
Catherine Street (Swift's Alley)	74	F1
Catherines Close	74	F1
Catherine's Well	22	F2
*Cats Ladder (off Torca Road)	60	F2
Causeway Road	27	B3
Cavalry Row	70	D3
Cavendish Row	71	B2
Caves Strand	3	A2
Ceanchor Road	30	D4
Ceannt Fort (off Mount Brown)	74	D1
Cecil Ave	26	D4
Cecilia Street (off Temple Bar)	71	B4
Cedar Ave	45	A3
Cedar Ave	1	B3
Cedar Brook	35	C4
Cedar Brook Ave	35	B3
Cedar Brook Place	35	B3
Cedar Brook Walk	35	B3
Cedar Close	1	B3
Cedar Court (Terenure)	46	F2
Cedar Court (Loughlinstown)	64	D1
Cedar Drive (Dunboyne)	7	B2
Cedar Drive (Palmerstown)	35	B2
*Cedar Grove (off Shelerin Road adjacent Lohonda Cres)	21	C2
Cedar Grove	1	B3
*Cedar Grove Apts (off Knocklyon Ave)	55	C1
*Cedar Hall (off Milltown Road)	47	C1
Cedar House	76	D3
Cedar House	1	Inset
Cedar Lawn	1	B3
Cedar Lodge	23	A4
Cedar Lodge Apts	56	E2
Cedar Park (Leixlip)	19	C4
Cedar Park (Donaghmede)	27	A1
Cedar Place	1	B3
Cedar Square (Swords)	1	B3
*Cedar Square (off Linden Grove)	48	F4
Cedar Walk	27	B2
Cedarhurst Green	23	B3
Cedarhurst Road	23	B3
Cedarmount Road	48	E4
Cedars (opposite Knockmaroon Gate)	36	D1
Cedarwood	32	D3
Cedarwood Ave	24	F1
Cedarwood Close	24	F1
Cedarwood Green	24	F1
Cedarwood Grove	24	F1
Cedarwood Park	24	F1
Cedarwood Rise	24	F1
Cedarwood Road	24	F1
Ceder Park	1	B3
Ceder View	1	B3
Celbridge	32	D3
Celbridge Abbey	31	C4
Celbridge Road (Maynooth)	18	D4
Celbridge Road (Leixlip)	32	F2
Celbridge Road (Lucan)	33	B2
*Celestine Ave (off Dermot O'Hurley Ave)	39	A3
Celtic Park Ave	25	C2
Celtic Park Road	25	C2
Cenecle Grove	64	E1
Chalet Gardens	34	E1
Chalfont Ave	3	B2
Chalfont Park	3	B2
Chalfont Place	3	B2
Chalfont Road	3	A2
*Chamber Court (off Chamber Street)	74	F2
Chamber Street	74	F2
*Chamberlain Court (off Richmond Ave)	25	C4
*Chamberlain Court (Richmond Ave)	25	B4
Chamley Gardens	2	F3
Chamley Park	2	F3

STREET NAME	PAGE	GRID REF
Champions Ave	71	C3
Chancel Mews	24	D4
*Chancery Court (Chancery Lane)	75	A1
*Chancery Hall (John Street North)	70	E4
*Chancery Hall Apts (Ellis Quay / John Street North)	70	F4
Chancery Lane	75	A1
Chancery Place	71	A4
Chancery Street	71	A4
Chandlers Guild Apts	74	D1
Chandlers Mill	32	D4
Chanel Ave	26	E2
Chanel Grove	26	E1
Chanel Road	26	E2
*Chapel Ave (off Bath Street)	39	A3
*Chapel Cres	24	D3
Chapel Hill	34	D1
Chapel Lane (Parnell Street)	71	B3
Chapel Lane (Swords)	2	D2
Chapel Lane (Bray)	67	B1
*Chapel Manor (Knockmaroon Hill)	36	D1
Chapel Road (Kinsaley)	14	D1
Chapel View Apts	34	D1
Chapelizod	36	E2
Chapelizod Bypass	36	E2
Chapelizod Court	36	E2
Chapelizod Hill Road	36	E2
Chapelizod Road	69	A4
Chapelizod Gate (Phoenix Park)	36	E2
Chapelton	9	B1
*Chaplains Place (near Community Centre)	35	A3
*Chaplains Terrace (near Harelawn Green)	35	A3
Chaplegate	25	A4
Chaplewood Ave	9	C1
Chaplewood Cres	9	C1
Chaplewood View	9	C1
Charlemont	25	C3
*Charlemont Ave (off George's Place Dún Laoghaire)	50	D4
Charlemont Bridge (Grand Canal)	75	B3
Charlemont Court	75	B3
Charlemont Gardens	75	B3
Charlemont Mall	75	B4
Charlemont Parade	72	D1
Charlemont Place	75	C3
Charlemont Road	26	D4
Charlemont Street	75	B3
*Charlemont Terrace (off George's Place Dún Laoghaire)	50	D4
Charles Lane	71	C1
*Charles Sheils Houses	58	F2
Charles Street Great	71	C2
Charles Street West (off Ormond Quay Upper)	71	A4
Charleston Ave	47	B1
*Charleston Court Flats (off Charleston Road)	47	B1
Charleston Road	47	B1
Charlestown Ave	11	B4
Charlestown Court	11	B4
Charlestown Drive	11	B4
Charlestown Green	11	B4
Charlestown Mews	11	B4
Charlestown Park	11	B4
Charlestown Place	11	A4
Charlestown Way	11	B4
Charleville	47	B4
Charleville Ave	72	D1
Charleville Close	47	A1
Charleville Mall	72	D1
Charleville Road (Phibsborough)	70	E1
Charleville Road (Rathmines)	47	A1
Charleville Square	46	E4
*Charleville Terrace (on Charleville Road)	70	E1
Charlotte Quay	76	F1
*Charlotte Quay Apts	76	E1
*Charlotte Terrace (off Victoria Road Dalkey)	60	F2
Charlotte Way	75	B3
Charlton Lawn	48	D4
Charnwood (Clonsilla)	21	C2
Charnwood (Bray)	67	C3
Charnwood Ave	21	C2
Charnwood Court	21	C2
Charnwood Dale	21	C2
Charnwood Gardens	21	C2
Charnwood Green	21	C2

STREET NAME	PAGE	GRID REF
Charnwood Grove	21	C2
Charnwood Heath	21	C2
Charnwood Meadows	21	C2
Charnwood Park	21	C2
*Charter House (on Convent Lane)	17	C3
Chatham Court (on Chatham Street)	75	B1
Chatham Lane (off Chatham Street)	75	B1
Chatham Row	75	B1
Chatham Street	75	B1
*Chaworth Terrace (Hanbury Lane)	74	F1
Cheeverstown Road	54	D1
Chelmsford Ave	75	C4
*Chelmsford Lane (off Chelmsford Road)	47	B1
Chelmsford Road	47	B1
Chelsea Gardens	26	F4
Cheltenham Place	75	B4
Cherbury Court	48	F3
Cherbury Gardens	48	F3
*Cherbury Mews (off Cherbury Court)	48	F3
Cherbury Park Ave	34	D2
Cherbury Park Road	34	D2
Cherries Road	58	D2
Cherrington Close	64	E3
Cherrington Drive	64	E3
Cherrington Road	64	E3
Cherry Ave (Swords)	1	C3
Cherry Ave (Carpenterstown)	22	E3
Cherry Court (Terenure)	46	F2
*Cherry Court (off Loughlinstown Drive)	64	D1
Cherry Drive (Coolmine)	22	E3
Cherry Garth (Swords)	1	C2
Cherry Garth (Stillorgan)	48	E4
Cherry Grove (Swords)	1	B3
Cherry Grove (Crumlin)	45	C2
Cherry House	76	D3
Cherry Lawn	22	E3
Cherry Lawns	33	C2
Cherry Lodge	23	A4
Cherry Orchard Ave	35	C3
Cherry Orchard Ave	36	D4
Cherry Orchard Court	35	C4
Cherry Orchard Cres	35	C4
Cherry Orchard Drive	35	C4
Cherry Orchard Green	35	C4
Cherry Orchard Grove	35	C4
Cherry Orchard Parade	35	C4
*Cherry Orchard Way (off Cherry Orchard Drive)	35	C4
Cherry Park (Swords)	1	B3
Cherry Park (Carpenterstown)	22	E3
*Cherry Tree Drive (off Boghall Road)	67	C3
Cherry Wood	64	D1
Cherryfield Ave	45	C2
Cherryfield Ave Lower	47	B1
Cherryfield Ave Upper	47	B1
Cherryfield Close	21	C1
Cherryfield Court	21	B1
Cherryfield Drive	45	C2
Cherryfield Lawn	21	C1
Cherryfield Park	21	C1
Cherryfield Road	45	C2
Cherryfield View	21	B1
Cherryfield Walk	21	C1
Cherryfield Way	46	D4
*Cherrymount Cres (off Casino Park)	26	D3
*Cherrymount Grove (off Casino Park)	26	D3
Cherrymount Park	70	F1
Cherrywood	32	D3
Cherrywood Ave	44	D1
Cherrywood Cres	43	C1
Cherrywood Drive	43	C1
Cherrywood Grove	44	D1
Cherrywood Lawn	43	C2
Cherrywood Park (Clondalkin)	43	C2
Cherrywood Park (Loughlinstown)	64	D1
Cherrywood Road	64	D2
Cherrywood Villas (Cherrywood)	43	C1
*Cherrywood Villas (off Tower Road)	44	D1
Chester Downs	60	D1
Chester Road	47	B1
*Chester Square (off Albert Road Lower)	60	E1
Chesterfield Ave (Phoenix Park)	69	B3

STREET NAME	PAGE	GRID REF
Chesterfield Ave (Phoenix Park)	23	B4
Chesterfield Ave (Castleknock)	23	B4
Chesterfield Close	23	B4
Chesterfield Copse	23	B4
Chesterfield Grove	23	B4
Chesterfield Park	23	B4
Chesterfield View	23	B3
*Chestnut Court (off Collinswood)	25	C2
Chestnut Grove (Dunboyne)	7	B3
Chestnut Grove (Celbridge)	32	D3
Chestnut Grove (Clondalkin)	44	F3
Chestnut Grove (Ballinteer)	57	B2
Chestnut House (Swords)	1	Inse
*Chestnut Park (off Pine Ave Foxrock)	59	A2
Chestnut Road (Clondalkin)	45	A1
Chestnut Road (Mount Merrion)	48	E3
Chipping Row	21	A1
Chipping Terrace	21	A1
Christchurch Hall	74	F1
Christchurch Place	75	A1
Christchurch Square	75	A1
Church Ave (Portmarnock)	14	F2
Church Ave (Blanchardstown)	22	F2
*Church Ave (off Ballymun Road)	25	A3
Church Ave (Drumcondra)	25	B3
Church Ave (Irishtown)	39	A3
Church Ave (Rathmines)	47	A1
Church Ave (Killiney)	60	E4
Church Ave South (Dolphin's Barn)	74	D2
Church Ave West (Church Street)	70	F4
Church Court (East Wall)	72	F2
Church Court (Castleknock)	22	F3
Church Gardens	47	A1
Church Green	46	F1
Church Grove	55	A2
Church Lands	67	C3
Church Lane (College Green)	71	B4
Church Lane (Rathfarnham)	46	F2
*Church Lane (off Church Ave)	47	A1
Church Lane South	75	A2
Church Park	46	F1
Church Park Ave	46	F1
Church Park Court	46	F1
Church Park Drive	46	F1
Church Park Lawn	46	F1
Church Park Way	46	F1
Church Place (off Irvine Terrace)	72	F3
Church Road (East Wall)	72	F2
Church Road (Swords)	2	D2
Church Road (Malahide)	3	B3
Church Road (Mulhuddart)	9	A4
Church Road (Finglas)	24	D2
Church Road (Sutton)	29	B1
Church Road (Celbridge)	32	D4
Church Road (Rathcoole)	52	F2
Church Road (Killiney)	60	D3
Church Road (Ballybrack)	60	E4
Church Road (Dalkey)	60	F1
Church Road (Bray)	67	C3
Church Road (Saggart)	53	A2
*Church Row (off Irvine Terrace)	72	F3
Church Square	72	F2
Church Street (Four Courts)	70	F4
Church Street (Finglas)	24	E2
Church Street (Howth)	30	D1
Church Street East	72	F3
Church Street New	70	F4
Church Street Upper	70	F3
*Church Terrace (off Church Street)	70	F3
Church Terrace (Finglas)	24	E2
*Church Terrace (Main Street, Herbert Road)	67	C2
*Church View (adjacent Church Road)	24	D2
Church View (Drumcondra)	25	B3
Church View (Hollystown)	9	B1
*Church View (off Oak Way Clondalkin)	44	D2
*Church Villas (off Brennanstown Road)	59	C4
Church Walk	24	D4
Churchfields (Clonskeagh)	47	C2
*Churchgate Ave (off Vernon Ave)	39	C1
*Churchill Mews (off Church Road)	60	F1
*Churchill Terrace (off Sandymount Ave)	39	A4

STREET NAME	PAGE	GRID REF
*Churchlands (off Sandyford Road)	58	D3
Churchtown	47	B4
Churchtown Ave	47	B3
Churchtown Close	47	B3
Churchtown Drive	47	B3
Churchtown Road	47	B4
Churchtown Road Lower	47	B3
Churchtown Road Upper	47	A4
Churchview Ave	60	D3
Churchview Drive	60	D3
Churchview Park	60	D3
Churchview Road	60	D3
Churchwell Ave	14	D3
Churchwell Close	14	D3
Churchwell Court	14	D3
Churchwell Drive	14	D3
Churchwell Mews	14	D3
Churchwell Place	14	D4
Churchwell Road	14	D4
Churchwell Square	14	D3
Cian Park	25	B4
Cianlea	1	B1
Cill Cais	54	F2
Cill Eanna	26	F2
*Cill Manntan Park (near Market House)	67	C2
Cill Sarain	67	B3
*City Gate Apts (near Brazen Head)	70	F4
City Quay	72	D4
Citywest Ave	53	C1
Citywest Interchange (Junction 3)	43	B4
Citywest Road	53	C1
*Claddagh Court	35	C3
Claddagh Green	35	C3
Claddagh Road	35	C3
*Claddagh Terrace (at Esplanade)	68	C2
Clanawley Road	26	E3
Clanboy Road	26	E3
Clanbrassil Close	74	F4
Clanbrassil Street Lower	74	F3
Clanbrassil Street Upper	74	F3
Clanbrassil Terrace	74	F2
Clancarthy Road	26	D3
Clancy Ave	24	E1
Clancy Quay	69	B4
Clancy Road	24	E1
Clandonagh Road	26	D3
Clane Road	31	B4
Clanfadda Wood	48	F3
Clanhugh Road	26	E3
Clanmahon Road	26	E3
Clanmaurice Road	26	D3
Clanmawr	64	E2
Clanmoyle Road	26	D3
Clanranald Road	26	D3
Clanree Road	26	D3
Clanwilliam Court	76	E2
Clanwilliam Place	76	E2
Clanwilliam Square	76	E1
Clanwilliam Terrace	76	E1
Clare Hall	14	D4
Clare Lane	75	C1
*Clare Park Villas (off Achill Road)	25	B3
Clare Road	25	B3
Clare Street	75	C1
*Claremont Ave (off Ballymun Road)	25	A3
Claremont Close	24	F4
Claremont Court (Finglas)	24	F4
*Claremont Court (off Shelbourne Road)	39	A4
*Claremont Court (off Claremont Road)	39	A4
Claremont Cres	24	F4
Claremont Drive	24	F2
Claremont Grove	60	E3
Claremont Lawn	24	F4
Claremont Mews	29	C1
Claremont Park	39	A4
Claremont Road (Sutton)	29	B1
Claremont Road (Sandymount)	39	A4
Claremont Road (Carrickmines)	59	B4
Claremont Road (Killiney)	60	E3
*Claremont Terrace (off Main Street Dundrum)	47	C4
*Claremont Villas (off Adelaide Road)	60	E1
Claremont Villas (Glenageary)	60	E1
Claremount (Shankill)	64	E3
Claremount (Cornelscourt)	59	B3

STREET NAME	PAGE	GRID REF
Claremount Pines	59	B4
*Claremount Terrace (west side of text Meath)	68	D2
Clarence Mangan Road	74	F2
Clarence Mangan Square (off John Dillon Street)	75	A1
Clarence Place Great	76	E1
Clarence Street	49	C4
Clarence Street Great North	72	D2
Clarendon Market (off William Street South)	75	B1
Clarendon Row (off King Street South)	75	B1
Clarendon Street	75	B1
*Clareville Court (off Claremont Lawn)	24	F4
Clareville Grove	24	F4
Clareville Road	46	F1
Clarinda Manor	60	D1
Clarinda Park East (Dún Laoghaire)	50	D4
Clarinda Park North	50	D4
Clarinda Park West	50	D4
Clarion Quay	72	D3
Clarke Terrace	74	D2
*Clarke's Bridge (Royal Canal)	72	D1
*Clarkeville Terrace (off Lucan Road Palmerston)	35	C1
Classon's Bridge	47	B3
Claude Road	25	A4
*Clayton Terrace (off Saint Laurence Road)	36	E2
Clearstream Court	24	E1
*Clearwater Apts (off Bath Ave Malahide)	3	C2
*Clearwater Court (at Lockkeeper's Walk)	24	D3
*Clearwater Cove (off Dunleary Road)	49	C4
Cleggan Ave	35	C3
Cleggan Park	35	C3
Cleggan Road	35	C3
Clifden Drive	35	C3
Clifden Road	36	D3
*Cliff Terrace (off Breffni Road)	60	E1
Clifford's Lane	2	E2
*Clifton Ave (off Monkstown Cres)	49	C4
Clifton Court Apts	70	E4
*Clifton Lane (off Monkstown Road)	49	C4
Clifton Mews	75	B4
Clifton Park	64	E2
*Clifton Terrace (off Seapoint Ave)	49	C4
Cliftonville Road	25	A4
Clinch's Court	72	D1
*Clipper Court (Liffey Street West)	70	E4
*Clipper Court Apts (off Liffey Street West)	70	E4
*Clipper View (Liffey Street West)	70	E4
*Clipper View Apts (off Liffey Street West)	70	E4
Clogher Green	74	F4
Clogher Road	74	D4
Cloghran	1	C4
Cloghran Roundabout	1	C4
Cloister Ave	49	A4
Cloister Close	48	F4
Cloister Court	24	D3
Cloister Gate	49	A4
Cloister Green	49	A4
Cloister Grove	49	A4
Cloister Park	49	A4
Cloister Square	49	A4
Cloister Way	49	A4
Clon Burgh	58	D3
*Clonallen (off Kimmage Road Lower)	46	E2
Clonard Ave	57	C2
Clonard Close	57	C2
*Clonard Court (off Poddle Close)	46	E2
Clonard Drive	57	C2
Clonard Grove	57	C2
Clonard Lawn	57	C2
Clonard Park	57	C2
Clonard Road (Crumlin)	73	B4
Clonard Road (Sandyford)	57	C2
*Clonasleigh (off Beechfield Manor)	64	E2
Cloncourt Apts	8	D3
Clondalkin	44	D1

STREET NAME	PAGE	GRID REF
Clonee	8	D3
Clonee Bridge	8	D3
Clonee Bypass	8	D3
Cloneen	5	A2
Clonfert Road	46	E1
Clongriffin	14	E4
*Clonkeen Court	59	B3
Clonkeen Cres	59	B2
Clonkeen Drive	59	B2
Clonkeen Grove	59	B2
*Clonkeen Lawn (off Clonkeen Road)	59	B3
Clonkeen Road	59	B2
Clonlara Ave	43	A4
*Clonlara Road (off Pine Road)	39	A3
Clonlara Road (Naas Road)	43	A4
Clonlea	57	C2
*Clonlea Wood (off Ballinteer Road)	57	C2
Clonliffe Ave	72	D1
Clonliffe Gardens	25	B4
Clonliffe Road	25	B4
*Clonliffe Square (off Distillery Road)	25	B4
*Clonmacnoise Grove (off Clonmacnoise Road)	46	E1
Clonmacnoise Road	46	E1
Clonmel Road	25	A2
Clonmel Street	75	B2
Clonmellon Grove	14	D4
*Clonmore Court (off Ballymun Road)	25	A3
Clonmore Road (Ballybough)	72	D1
Clonmore Road (Goatstown)	48	E4
Clonmore Terrace	72	D1
*Clonmore Villas (Clonmore Road)	72	D1
Clonrosse Court	26	F1
Clonrosse Drive	26	F1
Clonrosse Park	26	F1
Clonshaugh	13	B3
Clonshaugh Ave	13	A4
Clonshaugh Close	13	B4
*Clonshaugh Court (off Clonshaugh Cres)	13	B4
Clonshaugh Cres	13	A4
Clonshaugh Drive	13	B4
Clonshaugh Glen	13	B4
Clonshaugh Green	13	B4
Clonshaugh Grove	13	B4
Clonshaugh Heights	13	A4
Clonshaugh Lawns	13	B4
Clonshaugh Meadow	13	A4
Clonshaugh Park	13	B4
Clonshaugh Rise (off Clonshaugh Ave)	13	B4
Clonshaugh Road (Belcamp)	13	A3
Clonshaugh Road (Kilmore)	13	A4
Clonshaugh Walk	13	B4
Clonsilla	21	C2
Clonsilla Close	22	E2
Clonsilla Link Road	21	C2
Clonsilla Park	22	E2
Clonsilla Road	22	E2
Clonskeagh	47	C2
*Clonskeagh Drive (off Clonskeagh Road)	47	C2
Clonskeagh Road	47	C2
*Clonskeagh Square (off Clonskeagh Road)	47	C2
Clontarf	39	C1
Clontarf Park	39	C1
Clontarf Road (Fairview)	26	D4
Clontarf Road (Clontarf)	39	C1
*Clonturk Ave (off Drumcondra Road Upper)	25	B3
*Clonturk Court (off Church Ave)	25	B3
*Clonturk Gardens (off Clonturk Park)	25	B4
Clonturk Park	25	B4
Cloonlara Cres	24	E3
Cloonlara Drive	24	E3
Cloonlara Road	24	E3
Cloonlara Square	23	B3
Cloonmore Ave	54	E2
Cloonmore Close	54	E2
Cloonmore Cres	54	D2
Cloonmore Drive	54	D2
Cloonmore Gardens	54	D2
Cloonmore Green	54	D2
Cloonmore Grove	54	D2
Cloonmore Lawn	54	D2
Cloonmore Park	54	D2
Cloonmore Road	54	D2

STREET NAME	PAGE	GRID REF
*Cloragh Mills (South of Springvale)	56	E2
*Cloragh Mills Apts (Edmonstown Park)	56	E2
Cloragh Road	56	E4
*Clounties Court (adjacent Chamley Park)	2	F3
Clover Hill	67	A3
Clover Hill Drive	36	D3
Clover Hill Road	36	D4
Cloverhill Road (Clondalkin)	35	A4
Cloverhill Road (Cherry Orchard)	35	B3
*Cloyne Road (off Blarney Park)	46	E1
Cluain Aoibhinn	17	C4
Cluain Mhuire (Glenageary)	60	D1
Cluain Mhuire (Shankill)	64	D3
*Cluain na Greine Court (at The Bridge)	64	E3
Cluain Rí	34	F2
Cluain Shee	58	D3
Club Road	45	A1
Clune Road	24	E1
Cluny Grove	60	D3
Cluny Park	60	E2
Clutterland	42	F1
Clyde Court (off Seafort Ave)	76	E4
*Clyde House (off Serpentine Ave)	39	A4
Clyde Lane	76	F4
Clyde Road	76	E4
Cnoc Aoibhean	33	B2
Coast Road (Malahide)	3	C2
Coast Road (Baldoyle)	15	A4
*Coates Lane (off main street and Pound Lane)	17	C3
Coburg	67	B2
Coburg Place	72	D2
*Coghill's Court (off Dame Street)	71	B4
Cois Cairn	67	B1
*Cois Coillte (off Loughlinstown Drive)	64	D1
Cois Eala	75	A4
Cois Na hAbhann	54	F2
Cois Sleibhe	67	B4
Coke Lane	70	F4
Coke Ovens Cottages	24	F4
Colbert's Fort (off Saint James Walk)	74	D2
Colbert's Fort (Tallaght)	44	F4
*Coldbeck Way (off Fonthill Road South)	46	E2
*Coldcut Cres (Coldcut Road)	35	B2
Coldcut Cres	35	B2
Coldcut Park	35	B2
Coldcut Road	35	B2
Coldwell Street	60	D1
Colepark Ave	36	D3
Colepark Drive	36	D3
Colepark Green	36	D3
Colepark Road	36	D3
Coleraine Street	71	A3
Colganstown	41	B2
Coliemore Apts.	60	G2
Coliemore Road	60	G2
*Coliemore Villas (off Coliemore Road)	60	F2
College Cres	46	D3
College Drive	46	E3
College Fort	22	F4
College Gate	22	F3
*College Gate Apts (Tara Street)	71	C1
College Green (Trinity College)	71	B4
College Green (Maynooth)	17	C4
College Grove (Castleknock)	22	F4
College Lane (Trinity College)	76	D1
College Lane (Rathcoole)	52	F1
*College Manor (off Millmount Ave)	25	B4
*College Mews (off Clonliffe Road)	25	B4
College Park (Castleknock)	23	A4
College Park (Kimmage)	46	E3
College Park Ave	57	C2
College Park Close	57	C2
*College Park Court (off College Park Ave)	57	C2
*College Park Drive (off College Park Ave)	57	C2
College Park Grove	57	C2
College Park House	75	C1
College Park Way	57	C2
College Road (Castleknock)	22	F4

STREET NAME	PAGE	GRID REF
College Road (Greenogue Industrial Estate)	42	E4
College Road (Whitechurch Road)	57	A3
College Square	46	D3
College Street (Trinity College)	71	C4
College Street (Baldoyle)	15	A4
College View (Drumcondra)	25	B3
*College View (off Main Street Tallaght)	55	A1
College Wood	22	F4
Collegeland	42	F4
*Collier's Ave (off Anna Villa)	47	B1
Colliersland	6	F2
*Collindale (off Beaumont Road)	25	C2
Collins Ave	25	C2
Collins Ave East	26	D3
Collins Ave Extension	25	A2
Collins Ave West	25	B2
Collins Bridge	20	F4
*Collins Close (off Collins Ave)	25	C3
*Collins Court (off Collins Ave)	25	C3
*Collins Court (off Temple Road)	49	A3
Collins Drive	24	E1
Collins Green	24	E1
Collins Park	26	D3
Collins Place	24	E1
*Collins Row (Glasaree Road)	24	E2
*Collinstown Cres (off Collinstown Road)	35	A3
Collinstown Cross	12	F3
Collinstown Grove	35	B3
Collinstown Road	35	A3
Collinswood	25	C2
Colmanstown	51	C2
Colmanstown Lane	51	C2
Colmcille Court	2	D2
Colthurst Close	34	F2
Colthurst Cres	34	F2
Colthurst Gardens	34	F2
Colthurst Green	34	F2
Colthurst Mews	34	F2
Colthurst Park	34	F2
Colthurst Rise	34	F2
Colthurst Road	34	F2
Colthurst Way	34	F2
Comeragh Road	36	F4
Comeran Court	74	E2
Commons (Hazelhatch)	41	C2
Commons (Rathcoole)	52	E1
Commons East	2	D3
Commons Little	42	D4
Commons Lower	41	A1
Commons Road (Saint John's Gate)	44	D2
Commons Road (Loughlinstown)	64	E2
Commons Street	72	D3
Compass Court	23	C3
*Compass Court Apts (at Lockkeeper's Walk)	24	D3
*Comyn Place (off Walsh Road)	25	A3
Con Colbert Road (Kilmainham)	73	A1
Con Colbert Road (Inchicore)	36	F3
Confey	20	D4
*Congress Gardens (off Hudson Road)	60	E1
Congress Hall	7	B3
Congress Park	7	B3
Connaught Parade (off Connaught Street)	24	F4
*Connaught Place (off Crofton Road)	50	D4
Connaught Street	24	F4
Connawood	67	B1
Connawood Copse	67	B1
Connawood Cres	67	B1
Connawood Drive	67	B1
Connawood Green	67	B1
Connawood Grove	67	B1
Connawood Lawn	67	B1
Connawood Walk	67	B1
Connawood Way	67	B1
Connolly Ave (Kilmainham)	73	A2
Connolly Ave (Malahide)	3	A4
Connolly Gardens	73	A2
Connolly's Folly	18	E4
Conor Clune Road	23	C4
Conquer Hill Ave	39	C1
Conquer Hill Road	39	C1
Constellation Road	12	F4
Constitution Hill	71	A3
Convent Ave (Marino)	25	B4
Convent Ave (Bray)	68	D2
Convent Close	76	D2
*Convent Court (off Coolnevaun Kilmacud)	58	E1
*Convent Hall Apts (off Milltown Ave)	47	B2
Convent Lane (Portmarnock)	4	D4
Convent Lane (Maynooth)	17	C3
Convent Lane (Willbrook)	46	F4
*Convent Lawns (off Kylemore Road)	36	E3
Convent Lodge	26	F2
Convent Place	75	C3
Convent Road (Clondalkin)	44	E2
Convent Road (Blackrock)	49	A4
Convent Road (Dún Laoghaire)	50	D4
Convent Road (Dalkey)	60	F4
Convent View (Oldcourt)	67	C3
*Convent View (Sidmonton Road Bray)	68	D2
Convent View Cottages (off Ratoath Road Cabra)	24	D4
Convent View Cottages (Saint John's Gate)	44	D2
*Convent View Cres (adjacent Convent View Cottages)	24	D4
Convent Way	24	D4
Conway Court	76	E1
Conyngham Road	69	C4
Cook Street	71	A4
Cooks Road	1	A4
Cookstown	66	E3
Cookstown Court	44	F4
Cookstown Road	44	E4
Cookstown Way	44	E4
*Coolamber Court (off Knocklyon Road)	56	D1
Coolamber Drive	52	F2
Coolamber Park	56	D1
Coolamber Road	52	F2
Coolatree Close	25	C2
Coolatree Park	25	C2
Coolatree Road	25	C2
Cooldrinagh Lane	33	B1
Cooldrinagh Terrace	33	B1
Cooldríona Court	2	D2
Cooleen Ave	25	C1
Coolevin (Ballybrack)	60	D4
Coolevin Road	75	A2
Cooley Close	36	F4
Cooley Road	73	A4
Coolgariff Road	25	C1
*Coolgraney (off Nutgrove Park)	47	C2
*Coolgraney Court (off Nutgrove Park)	47	C2
Coolgreena Close	25	C2
Coolgreena Road	25	C1
Coolkill	58	D3
Coolmine	52	F3
Coolmine Boulevard	22	E2
Coolmine Close	22	D2
Coolmine Cottages	9	A4
Coolmine Court	22	E2
Coolmine Green	22	D3
Coolmine Lawn	22	D2
Coolmine Mews	22	E2
Coolmine Park	22	E2
Coolmine Road (Carpenterstown)	22	E3
Coolmine Road (Saggart)	52	F3
Coolmine Woods	22	E2
Coolnevaun	58	E1
Coolock	26	E1
Coolock Drive	26	E1
Coolock Lane (Santry)	12	F4
Coolock Village	26	E1
*Coolock Village Close (off Coolock Village)	26	E1
Coolrua Drive	25	C1
Coolwater Lakes	53	B2
Coombe Court	74	F1
Coopers Way	70	F3
*Coopers Yard (Smithfield)	70	F3
Coopers Yard Apts	70	F3
Cope Bridge	20	D3
Cope Street	71	B4
Copeland Ave	26	D4
Copeland Grove	26	D4
Copper Alley (Eustace Street)	71	A4
*Copper Beech Grove (East of Hazelwood)	67	B2
Coppinger	49	A4
Coppinger Close	48	F4
Coppinger Glade	48	F4
Coppinger Row	75	B1
Coppinger Walk	49	A4
Coppinger Wood	48	F4
Corbally	53	C3
Corbally Ave	53	C2
Corbally Close	53	C2
Corbally Downs	53	C2
Corbally Drive	53	C2
Corbally Glade	53	C2
Corbally Green	53	C2
Corbally Heath	53	C2
Corbally Lawn	53	C2
Corbally Park	53	C2
Corbally Rise	53	C2
Corbally Square	53	C2
Corbally Vale	53	C2
Corbally Way	53	C2
Corbawn Ave	64	E2
Corbawn Close	64	F2
Corbawn Court	64	F2
Corbawn Dale	64	F2
Corbawn Drive	64	F2
*Corbawn Glade (near Corbawn Wood)	64	E2
Corbawn Grove	64	F2
Corbawn Lane	64	E2
Corbawn Lawn	64	E3
Corbawn Wood	64	E2
Corduff	22	F1
Corduff Ave	22	F1
Corduff Close	22	F1
Corduff Cottages	22	E1
Corduff Cres	22	F1
Corduff Gardens	22	F1
Corduff Green	22	F1
Corduff Grove	9	B4
Corduff Park	9	B4
Corduff Place	22	F1
Corduff Way	22	F1
Cork Hill (off Dame Street)	71	A4
Cork Street	74	E2
Corkagh View	44	D2
Corke Abbey	67	C1
Corke Abbey Ave	67	B1
Cormac Terrace	46	F2
Corn Exchange Apts	71	C4
Corn Exchange Place	71	C4
*Corn Mill (off Distillery Road)	25	B4
*Corn Mill (Blank Tony)	25	B4
*Corn Mill Apts. (Distillery Road)	25	B4
Cornelscourt	59	B3
Cornelscourt Hill Road	59	B3
Cornelstown	6	D2
Cornerpark	42	D3
Cornmarket	74	F1
Corporation Street 71 C3	71	C3
Corr Castle	29	B1
Corr Castle Apts	29	B1
Corrbridge Terrace	29	B1
Corrib Road	46	E2
Corrig Ave	50	D4
Corrig Close	45	B3
*Corrig Court (off Corrig Road)	58	E2
Corrig Hall	57	C3
Corrig Park	50	D4
Corrig Road (Stillorgan)	58	E2
Corrig Road (Dún Laoghaire)	60	D1
Corrig Road (Dalkey)	60	F1
Corrybeg	46	D4
*Cosy Lodge (off William's Park)	47	A1
Coulson Ave	46	F2
Coultry Ave	25	B1
Coultry Close	25	A1
Coultry Court	12	D4
Coultry Cres	12	D4
Coultry Drive	12	D4
Coultry Gardens	12	D4
Coultry Green	12	D4
Coultry Grove	12	E4
Coultry Lawn	12	E4
Coultry Park	12	E4
Coultry Road	12	D4
Coultry Terrace	12	D4
Coultry Way	25	B1
Coundon Court	60	E4
Countess Markievicz House	72	D4
Countybrook Lawns	66	E2
*Court House Square (off Doctors Lane)	17	C3
Courthill	7	B2
Courthill Drive	7	B2
*Courthouse Square Apts (off Main Street Tallaght)	55	A1
Courtlands	59	C3
*Courtney House	76	D4
Courtney Place	72	E1
Court View	23	C3
Cow Parlour	74	E2
Cowbooter Lane	30	E2
Cowper Downs	47	A1
Cowper Drive	47	B2
Cowper Gardens	47	B2
*Cowper Mews (off Cowper Road)	47	A2
Cowper Road	47	B2
Cowper Street	70	D2
Cowper Village	47	A2
Cows Lane	71	A4
Crag Ave	35	B4
Crag Cres	35	B4
Crag Terrace	35	B4
Craigford Ave	26	E3
Craigford Drive	26	E3
Craigie Court	24	E2
*Craiglands (off Ardeevin Road)	60	F2
*Craigmore Gardens (off Temple Road)	49	A3
Crampton Ave (off Park Lane)	76	F3
Crampton Court (off Dame Street)	71	B4
Crampton Quay	71	B4
Crane Lane (off Dame Street)	71	A4
Crane Street	74	E1
*Crane Yard Apts (Crane Lane)	71	A4
Cranfield Place	39	A3
*Cranford Court (off Terenure Road West Kimmage)	46	E2
Cranford Court (Stillorgan Road)	48	D2
Cranmer Lane	76	E2
*Cranmer Place	76	E2
*Crannagh (off Milltown Road)	47	C2
*Crannagh Castle (off Crannagh Road)	46	F3
*Crannagh Court (off Crannagh Road)	46	F3
Crannagh Grove	47	A3
Crannagh Hall	47	A3
Crannagh Park	46	F3
Crannagh Road	46	F3
*Crannagh Way (off Crannagh Road)	47	A3
Crannogue Close	11	C4
Crannogue Road	11	C4
Crawford Ave	25	A4
*Crawford Terrace (off Kings Ave)	72	D1
Creighton Street	72	D4
Cremona Road	36	E3
Cremore Ave	24	F3
Cremore Cres	24	F3
Cremore Drive	24	F3
*Cremore Heights	24	F2
Cremore Lawn	24	F3
Cremore Park	25	A3
Cremore Road	24	F3
Cremore Villas (off Cremore Cres)	24	F3
Cremorne (Terenure Road East)	46	F2
Cremorne (Knocklyon)	56	D1
Cres Gardens	72	E1
*Cres House (off Marino Cres)	26	D4
Cres Place	26	D4
Cres Villas	25	A4
Crestfield Ave	25	B2
Crestfield Close	25	B2
Crestfield Drive	25	B2
Crestfield Park	25	B2
Crestfield Road	25	B2
Creston	11	B3
Crewhill	17	B1
Crinan Strand	72	D3
Crinken Glen	64	E3
Crinken Lane	64	D4
Crinstown	17	A4
Croaghpatrick Road	24	D4
Crockshane	52	E3
Crodaun Court	31	C2
Crodaun Forest Park	32	D2
Crofton Ave	50	D4
*Crofton Mansions (off Crofton Road)	50	D4
Crofton Road	50	D4
*Crofton Terrace (off Crofton Road)	50	D4
Croftwood Cres	35	C3
Croftwood Drive	35	C3
Croftwood Gardens	35	C3

STREET NAME	PAGE	GRID REF
Croftwood Green	36	D3
Croftwood Grove	35	C3
Croftwood Park	36	D3
Croke Villas	72	D1
Cromcastle Ave	26	D1
*Cromcastle Close (off Cromcastle Green)	26	D1
*Cromcastle Court (off Kilmore Road)	26	D1
Cromcastle Drive	26	D1
Cromcastle Green	26	D1
Cromcastle Park	26	D1
Cromcastle Road	26	D1
Cromlech Close	62	F2
Cromlech Court	11	C4
Cromlech Fields	64	E1
Cromwellsfort Road	45	C2
Crooksling	53	B4
Crosbie House	75	C4
*Crosbie's Yard Apts (near Ossory Industrial Estate)	72	E2
Crosforge	53	A2
Cross Ave (Booterstown)	48	F3
Cross Ave (Dún Laoghaire)	50	D4
*Cross Guns Quay Apts (Prospect Road)	25	A4
Cross Lane	17	C3
Crosstrees Court	30	D2
Crosthwaite Park East	60	D1
Crosthwaite Park South	60	D1
Crosthwaite Park West	60	D1
*Crosthwaite Terrace (off Clarinda Park West)	50	D4
Crostick Alley (off Meath Street)	74	F1
Crotty Ave	45	C1
Crow Street (off Dame Street)	71	B4
Crown Alley (off Temple Bar)	71	B4
Croydon Gardens	25	C4
Croydon Green	25	C4
Croydon Park Ave	25	C4
*Croydon Terrace (off Griffith Ave)	25	C3
Cruagh Ave	62	E1
Cruagh Close	62	E1
Cruagh Court	62	E1
Cruagh Green	62	E1
Cruagh Lane	56	E4
Cruagh Rise	62	E1
Cruagh Road	56	E4
Cruagh Wood	62	E1
Cruise Park	9	A2
Cruise Park Ave	9	A2
Cruise Park Close	9	A2
Cruise Park Court	9	A2
Cruise Park Cres	9	A2
Cruise Park Drive	9	A2
Cruise Park Hall	9	A2
Cruise Park Rise	9	A2
Cruise Park Square	9	A2
Cruise Park Walk	9	A2
Cruiserath Road	9	C3
Crumlin	73	A4
*Crumlin Park (off Crumlin Road)	46	D1
Crumlin Road	73	C4
Cuala Grove	68	D3
Cuala Road (Cabra)	24	F4
Cuala Road (Bray)	68	D3
*Cuan na Mara (off Harbour Road, close to Post Office)	30	D1
Cuckoo Lane	71	A3
Cuffe Lane	75	B2
Cuffe Street	75	B2
Cuilenn Park	24	F1
Cul na Greine	54	F2
*Cullen's Cottages (off Annaville Ave)	49	A4
Cullen's Wood House	75	C4
*Cullenswood Court (off Cullenswood Park)	47	B1
Cullenswood Gardens	47	B1
Cullenswood Park	47	B1
*Cullenswood Road (off Charleston Road)	47	B1
*Culmore Park (off Culmore Road)	35	C2
Culmore Road	35	C2
*Cumberland Place North (on North Circular Road)	70	F1
Cumberland Road	76	D3
Cumberland Street	49	C4
Cumberland Street North	71	C2
Cumberland Street South	76	D1
Cunningham Drive	60	F2

STREET NAME	PAGE	GRID REF
Cunningham Park	59	B3
Cunningham Road	60	F2
Curlew Road	73	A4
*Curracloe Drive (off Kilfenora Drive)	27	A1
Curragh Hall	9	B3
Curragh Hall Ave	9	B3
Curragh Hall Close	9	B3
Curragh Hall Court	9	B3
Curragh Hall Cres	9	B3
Curragh Hall Drive	9	B3
Curragh Hall Gate	9	B3
Curragh Hall Green	9	B3
Curragh Hall Grove	9	B3
Curragh Hall House	9	B3
Curragh Hall Lane	9	B3
Curragh Hall Lodge	9	B3
Curragh Hall Road	9	B3
Curragh Hall View	9	B3
Curragh Hall Way	9	B3
Curragh Hall Wood	9	B3
Curtlestown	65	B4
Curved Street	71	B4
Curzon Street	75	A3
Cushinstown	6	F1
Cushlawn Ave	54	F2
Cushlawn Close	54	F3
Cushlawn Dale	54	F3
Cushlawn Drive	54	F2
Cushlawn Grove	54	F2
Cushlawn Park	54	F2
Cushlawn Walk	54	F3
Cushlawn Way	54	F3
Custom Hall	71	C3
Custom House Harbour	72	D3
Custom House Quay	71	C3
Custom House Square	72	E3
Cymric Road	39	A3
*Cypress Ave (off Brookwood)	56	E2
Cypress Court	64	E1
Cypress Drive	46	D3
Cypress Garth	46	D4
Cypress Grove North	46	D3
Cypress Grove Road	46	D3
Cypress Grove South	46	D4
Cypress House	28	D1
Cypress Lawn	46	D4
Cypress Park	46	D4
Cypress Road	48	E3
Cypress Springs	20	D4

D

STREET NAME	PAGE	GRID REF
*Daisy Market (off Arran Street)	71	A4
Dakota Ave	12	F4
Dakota Court	25	A4
Dal Riada	3	C4
Dalcassian Downs	24	F4
*Dale Close (off Dale Drive)	58	E1
Dale Drive	58	E1
Dale Road	58	E1
Dale View	60	E4
*Dale View Park (off Madden's Lane)	60	E4
Dalepark Road	55	A2
Daletree Ave	55	B2
Daletree Close	55	C3
Daletree Court	55	C3
Daletree Cres	55	C2
Daletree Drive	55	C2
Daletree Park	55	C3
Daletree Place	55	C3
Daletree Road	55	C3
Daletree Terrace	55	C3
Daletree View	55	B3
Daleview Road	1	C1
Dalkey	60	F1
Dalkey Ave	60	F2
*Dalkey Court (off Barnhill Road)	60	F2
*Dalkey Grove (off Dalkey Park)	60	F2
Dalkey Park	60	E2
Dalkey Rock	60	F2
Dalriada Avanue	55	C3
Dalriada Close	55	C3
Dalriada Court	55	C3
*Dalriada Square (Dalriada Estate)	55	C3
Dalton Mews	3	B3
Dalymount	70	F1

STREET NAME	PAGE	GRID REF
Damastown Ave	8	F3
Damastown Close	8	F3
Damastown Court	9	A3
Damastown Drive	8	E3
Damastown Green	8	F3
Damastown Road	8	F3
Damastown Walk	8	E3
Damastown Way	9	A3
Dame Court	75	B1
Dame Lane	71	B4
Dame Street	71	B4
Damer Court	71	A2
Damer House	2	E2
Dane Close	11	C4
Dane Road	11	C4
Danes Court (Dollymount)	27	A4
Danesfort	39	B1
Daneswell Road	25	A4
Dangan	41	A2
Dangan Ave	46	D2
Dangan Drive	46	D2
Dangan Park	46	D2
Daniel Street	75	A3
Danieli Drive	26	E2
Danieli Road	26	E2
Dara Court	32	D3
Dara Cres	32	D3
*Dargan Court (between Sidmonton and Albert Ave)	68	D2
*Dargan Street (near Ardee Street)	67	B2
Dargle Bridge	67	A3
*Dargle Court (East of Dargle Heights)	67	B2
*Dargle Cres (East of Hazelwood)	67	B2
Dargle Drive	57	A1
Dargle Heights	67	B2
Dargle Lodge	56	D1
Dargle Road (Drumcondra)	25	A4
Dargle Road (Dean's Grange)	59	A1
*Dargle Terrace (on Lower Dargle Road)	67	B2
Dargle Valley	57	A1
Dargle View	57	A1
Dargle Wood	56	D1
*Darley Cottages (off Vevay Road)	67	C2
Darley Court	70	D3
Darley Street	74	F4
Darley's Terrace	74	E2
Darling Estate	23	C4
Darndale	13	C4
Dartmouth Lane	75	C4
Dartmouth Place	75	C4
Dartmouth Road	75	C4
Dartmouth Square	75	C3
Dartmouth Square East	75	C3
Dartmouth Square North	75	C3
Dartmouth Square South	75	C4
Dartmouth Square West	75	C4
Dartmouth Terrace	75	C4
*Dartmouth Walk (Grand Parade)	75	C3
*Dartry Cottages (off Dartry Road)	47	B3
Dartry Park	47	B2
Dartry Road	47	A2
David Park	25	A4
David Road	25	A4
*Davis Court (Thomas Davis Street West)	36	F3
*Davis Court Apts (off Thomas Davis Street West)	36	F3
Davis Place (off Thomas Davis Street South)	74	F1
Davitt House	73	A3
Davitt Park	60	D4
Davitt Road (Inchicore)	73	B2
Davitt Road (Bray)	67	C2
Davitt Terrace	73	A3
*Dawson Court (off Stephen Street Lower)	75	B1
Dawson Court (Mount Merrion Ave)	48	F3
Dawson Lane	75	C1
Dawson Street	75	C1
*De Bret House (off Stonepark Court)	46	F4
De Burgh Road	70	D4
*De Courcy Square (off Prospect Ave)	25	A4
De Selby	54	D2
De Selby Close	54	D2

STREET NAME	PAGE	GRID REF
De Selby Court	54	D2
De Selby Cres	54	D2
De Selby Downs	54	D2
De Selby Drive	54	D2
De Selby Green	54	D2
De Selby Lane	54	D2
De Selby Lawns	54	D2
De Selby Park	53	C2
De Selby Rise	54	D2
De Selby Road	54	D2
De Velara Place	71	B1
*De Vesci Court (off Sloperton)	49	C4
*De Vesci Court (off Sloperton)	49	C4
*De Vesci House (on Old Dunleary Road)	49	C4
De Vesci Terrace	49	C4
Dean Court	75	A1
*Dean Court (off Back Lane)	75	A1
Dean Street	75	A2
Dean Swift Green	25	A2
Dean Swift Road	25	A2
Dean Swift Square	74	F1
*Deans Court (off Kill Lane)	59	B1
Deans Grange	59	B2
Dean's Grange Road	59	B1
Deansrath Ave	34	F4
Deansrath Cres	43	C1
Deansrath Green	43	C1
Deansrath Grove	34	F4
Deansrath Lawn	34	F4
Deansrath Park	43	C1
Deansrath Road	43	C1
Deanstown Ave	24	D2
Deanstown Drive	24	D2
Deanstown Green	24	D2
Deanstown Park	24	D2
Deanstown Road	24	D2
Decies Road	36	E3
Deepdales	67	B4
Deerhaven	8	F4
Deerhaven Ave	8	F4
Deerhaven Close	8	F4
Deerhaven Cres	8	F4
Deerhaven Green	8	F4
Deerhaven Park	8	F4
Deerhaven View	8	F4
Deerhaven Walk	8	F4
Deerpark	67	B4
*Deerpark Apts (Killarney Street)	72	D2
Deerpark Ave (Castleknock)	23	A4
Deerpark Ave (Kiltipper)	54	F3
Deerpark Close (Castleknock)	23	A3
Deerpark Close (Kiltipper)	54	F3
Deerpark Downs	54	F3
Deerpark Drive (Castleknock)	23	A3
Deerpark Drive (Kiltipper)	54	F3
Deerpark Green	54	F3
*Deerpark House (off Thomas Davis Street West)	36	F3
Deerpark Lawn	23	B3
Deerpark Lodge	54	F3
Deerpark Place	54	F3
Deerpark Rise	54	F3
Deerpark Road (Castleknock Road)	23	A3
Deerpark Road (Mount Merrion)	48	D4
Deerpark Road (Kiltipper)	54	F3
Deerpark Square	54	F3
Deerpark Terrace	54	F3
*Deerpark View (off Deerpark Way)	54	F3
*Deerpark View (Deerpark Way)	54	F3
Deerpark Walk (Kiltipper)	54	F3
Deerpark Way	54	F3
Deey Bridge	19	A4
Del Val Ave	27	C2
Del Val Court	27	C2
Delaford Ave	55	C1
Delaford Drive	55	C1
Delaford Grove	55	C1
Delaford Lawn	55	C1
Delaford Park	55	C1
Delbrook Manor	57	C2
Delbrook Park	57	C2
Delhurst Ave	21	B1
Delhurst Close	21	B1
Delhurst Mews	21	B1
Delhurst Terrace	21	B1
Delville Road	25	A2
*Delvin Road (off Fassaugh Road)	24	F4
*Delvin Terrace (near Maunsell Place)	71	A2
Delwood Close	22	E3

STREET NAME	PAGE	GRID REF
Delwood Drive	22	E3
Delwood Grove	22	E3
Delwood Lawn	22	E3
Delwood Park	22	E3
Delwood Road	22	E3
Delwood Walk	22	E3
Demesne	26	E3
Denewood Castleknock	23	A3
Denmark Street Great	71	B2
Denville Court	60	D4
Denzille Lane	76	D1
*Derby Square		
(off Werburgh Street)	75	A1
Dermot O'Hurley Ave	39	A3
Derravaragh Road	46	E2
Derry Drive	46	D1
Derry Park	46	D1
Derry Road	46	D1
Derrynane Court	71	B1
Derrynane Gardens	39	A3
Derrynane Parade	71	B1
Derrynane Square	71	B1
*Desmond Ave (off Cross Ave)	50	D4
*Desmond Cottages		
(off Ardbrough Road)	60	F2
Desmond Street	75	A3
Devenish Road	46	E1
Deverell Place	71	C3
*Devery's Lane		
(off Phibsborough Road)	25	A4
*Devitt Villas		
(off Eden Road Lower)	60	E1
Devlin's Place	76	D1
*Devon Close (off Kill Lane)	59	B1
Devoy Road	73	B2
Dewberry Park	4	D4
Dexter Terrace	75	C4
*Diamond Terrace		
(north of River Lane)	67	B2
Diamond Valley Apts	67	B2
*Digges Lane		
(Longford Street Little)	75	B1
Digges Street Upper	75	B2
*Dillon Place South		
(off John Dillon Street)	75	A1
Dillon's Row	17	C2
Dingle Glen	63	A2
Dingle Road	24	E4
*Dispensary Lane		
(off Main Street Lucan)	34	D1
Dispensary Lane (Willbrook)	46	F4
*Distillery House Apts		
(off Martin's Row Chapelizod)	36	E2
Distillery Lane	20	D4
*Distillery Loft Apts		
(off Richmond Road)	25	B4
Distillery Road	25	B4
Diswellstown Cottages	22	E4
Diswellstown Road	22	D3
Dixon Lane	63	A2
*Dixon Villas		
(off Adelaide Road)	60	E1
Doctor's Lane (Maynooth)	17	C3
Dodder Ave	55	B2
*Dodder Bank		
(off Dundrum Road)	47	B2
Dodder Court	55	B2
*Dodder Court		
(on Dundrum Road)	47	C3
Dodder Cres	55	B2
Dodder Dale	46	F4
Dodder Green	55	B2
Dodder Lawn	55	B2
*Dodder Park Drive		
(off Dodder Road Lower		
Rathfarnham)	46	F3
Dodder Park Grove	46	F3
Dodder Park Road	46	F3
Dodder Road Lower	47	A3
*Dodder Terrace		
(off Irishtown Road)	39	A3
*Dodder Vale		
(off Orwell Gardens)	47	A3
Dodder View Cottages		
(off Herbert Road)	76	F3
Dodder View Road	46	E4
Dodsboro Cottages	33	B2
Dodsboro Road	33	C2
D'Olier Street	71	C4
Dollymount	27	A4
Dollymount Ave	27	A4
Dollymount Grove	26	F4
Dollymount Park	27	A4
Dollymount Rise	27	A4
Dolly's Grove	5	C2

STREET NAME	PAGE	GRID REF
Dolmen Court	12	D4
Dolphin Ave	74	E3
Dolphin Court	73	C3
Dolphin House	74	D3
*Dolphin Market		
(off Dolphin's Barn Street)	74	D3
Dolphin Park	74	D3
Dolphin Road	73	C3
Dolphin's Barn	74	D3
Dolphins Barn Bridge		
(Grand Canal)	74	D3
Dolphin's Barn Street	74	D3
*Dominick Court		
(off Dominick Street Upper)	71	A2
Dominick Lane	71	A3
Dominick Place	71	B3
Dominick Street	50	D4
*Dominick Street Court		
(Dominick Street Upper)	71	A2
Dominick Street Lower	71	A3
Dominick Street Upper	71	A2
*Domville Court		
(near Santry Villas)	12	E4
Domville Drive	46	D4
Domville Green	46	D4
*Domville Grove		
(opposite Cenacle Grove)	64	E1
Domville Road	46	D4
Donaghmede	14	F4
Donaghmede Ave	27	B1
Donaghmede Drive	27	B1
Donaghmede Park	27	B1
Donaghmede Road	27	B1
Donaghmore	18	F3
Donard Road	36	F4
Donnelan Ave		
(Saint Johns Terrace)	73	C1
Donnybrook	47	C1
*Donnybrook Castle		
(off Stillorgan Road)	47	C1
*Donnybrook Close		
(off Stillorgan Road)	48	D2
Donnybrook Court	47	C2
*Donnybrook Green		
(off Greenfield Park U.C.D.)	48	D2
Donnybrook Manor	47	C1
Donnybrook Mews	47	C1
Donnybrook Road	47	C1
Donnycarney	26	D3
Donnycarney Road	26	D3
Donomore Ave	54	E2
Donomore Cres	54	E2
Donomore Green	54	E2
Donomore Park	54	E2
Donore Ave	74	E2
Donore Road	74	E2
Donore Terrace	74	E2
Donovan Lane	74	F3
Doon Ave	70	D1
Doon Court	11	C4
Doonamana Road	60	D3
Doonanore Park	60	D3
Doonsalla Drive	60	D3
Doonsalla Park	60	D3
Doreen House Apts		
(off Nephin Road)	24	D4
Doris Street	76	F1
Dornden Park	48	E2
Dorney Court	64	E3
Dorset Lane	71	B1
Dorset Place	71	B1
Dorset Square	71	B1
Dorset Street Lower	71	B1
Dorset Street Upper	71	A2
Double Lane	17	C3
Dowland Road	46	D1
Dowling's Court	72	D4
Downpatrick Road (Crumlin)	73	C4
Downpatrick Road	46	E1
Dowth Ave	24	F4
Doyles Lane (off Clontarf Road)	27	A4
*Drapier Green		
(off Drapier Road)	24	F2
Drapier Road	24	F2
*Drayton Close		
(off Monkstown Road)	49	B4
Drimnagh	73	A3
Drimnagh Road	45	C1
Drinagh Park	58	F4
Drinaghmore	58	F4
Drinaghmore Ave	58	F4
Drinaghmore Close	58	F4
Drinaghmore Court	58	F4
Droim Na Coile Drive	34	F2
Droim na Coille Ave	34	F2

STREET NAME	PAGE	GRID REF
Droim na Coille Court	34	F2
Droim na Coille Place	34	F2
Droim na Coille Place	34	F2
Dromard Road	36	F4
*Dromard Terrace		
(off Seafort Ave)	39	A4
Dromartin Castle	47	C4
Dromawling Road	25	C2
Drombawn Ave	25	C2
Dromcarra Ave	54	E2
Dromcarra Drive	54	E2
Dromcarra Green	54	D2
Dromcarra Grove	54	E2
Dromeen Ave	25	C2
Dromheath Ave	9	B4
Dromheath Drive	9	B4
Dromheath Gardens	9	B4
Dromheath Grove	9	B4
Dromheath Park	9	B4
Dromlee Cres	25	C2
*Dromnanane Park		
(off Dromawling Road)	25	C2
*Dromnanane Road		
(off Dromawling Road)	25	C2
Dromore Road	73	A4
Druid Court	11	C4
Druid Valley	64	E1
Drumahill	58	D1
Drumalee Ave	70	D2
Drumalee Court	70	D2
Drumalee Drive	70	D2
Drumalee Grove	70	D2
Drumalee Park	70	D2
Drumalee Road	70	D2
Drumcairn Ave	54	E1
Drumcairn Drive	54	D1
Drumcairn Gardens	54	D1
Drumcairn Green	54	E1
Drumcairn Parade	54	E1
Drumcairn Park	54	E1
Drumcliffe Drive	24	E4
Drumcliffe Road	24	E4
Drumcondra	25	A4
Drumcondra Park	71	C1
Drumcondra Road Lower	25	B4
Drumcondra Road Upper	25	B3
Drumderg Court	25	C2
Drumfinn Ave	35	C2
Drumfinn Park	36	D3
Drumfinn Road	36	D2
Drumkeen Manor	60	D3
Drummartin Close	48	D4
*Drummartin Cres		
(off Drummartin Park)	58	D1
Drummartin Link Road	58	D1
Drummartin Park	58	D1
Drummartin Road	48	D4
Drummartin Terrace	48	D4
Drummond Place		
(off Mount Drummond Ave)	75	A4
Drumnigh	14	E3
Drumnigh Road	14	E3
Drumnigh Wood	14	E2
*Drury Hall Apts		
(Stephen Street Lower)	75	B1
Drury Street	75	B1
Drynam Ave	2	E3
Drynam Close	2	E3
Drynam Copse	2	E3
Drynam Court	2	D2
Drynam Cres	2	E3
Drynam Drive	2	E3
Drynam Glen	2	E3
Drynam Green	2	E3
Drynam Grove	2	E3
Drynam Hall	2	E3
Drynam Mews	2	E3
Drynam Place	2	E4
Drynam Rise	2	E4
Drynam Road	2	D2
Drynam Square	2	E3
Drynam View	2	E3
Drynam Walk	2	E3
Drynam Way	2	E3
Drysdale Close	55	A2
Dualla Court	48	E4
Dubber Cross	11	B3
Dublin Airport	12	E1
Dublin Road (Swords)	1	C3
Dublin Road (Malahide)	3	A3
Dublin Road (Dunboyne)	7	C2
Dublin Road (Maynooth)	18	D3
Dublin Road (Donaghmore)	18	F3
Dublin Road (Kilbarrack)	27	C2
Dublin Road (Sutton)	29	A1

STREET NAME	PAGE	GRID REF
Dublin Road (Celbridge)	32	D3
Dublin Road (Shankill)	64	E3
Dublin Road (Bray)	67	B1
Dublin Street (Baldoyle)	15	A4
Duck Lane (Smithfield)	70	F3
Dufferin Ave	74	F3
Duke Lane Lower	75	C1
Duke Lane Upper	75	B1
Duke Row	72	D2
Duke Street	75	B1
Dun Aengus	54	F2
Dun an Oir	54	F2
Dun Emer Drive	57	C1
Dun Emer Park	57	C1
Dun Emer Road	57	C1
Dun Gaoithe	58	E3
Dun Laoghaire	50	D4
Dunard Ave	69	B1
Dunard Court	69	C1
Dunard Drive	69	C1
Dunard Park	69	C1
Dunard Road	69	C1
Dunard Walk	69	C1
Dunawley Ave	44	D1
Dunawley Drive	44	D1
Dunawley Grove	44	D1
Dunawley Way	44	D1
Dunbavin Bridge	51	A4
*Dunbo Hill (at Saint		
Laurence Road, Police Station)	30	D1
*Dunbo Terrace (at Saint		
Laurence Road, Police Station)	30	D1
Dunboy	59	A4
Dunboyne	7	C3
Dunboyne Bridge	7	C3
Dunboyne Road	18	D2
Dunbro Lane	11	C1
*Dunbur Terrace		
(near Duncairn Ave)	67	C2
Duncairn Ave	67	C2
Duncairn Terrace	67	C2
Duncarraig	29	B2
Dundaniel Road	26	D1
Dundela Ave	60	E1
Dundela Cres	60	E1
*Dundela Haven		
(off Dundela Park)	60	E1
Dundela Park	60	E1
Dundrum	57	C1
Dundrum By Pass	57	C1
*Dundrum Gate Apts		
(off Ballinteer Road)	57	C1
Dundrum Road	47	C3
Dundrum Wood	57	B1
Dunedin Court	59	C1
*Dunedin Drive		
(off Saint Patrick's Cres)	59	C1
Dunedin Park	59	C1
Dunedin Terrace	59	C1
*Dungar Terrace		
(off Northumberland Ave		
Dún Laoghaire)	50	D4
Dungriffan Road	30	D2
*Dungriffan Villas		
(off Dungriffan Road)	30	D2
Dunleary Hill	49	C4
Dunleary Road	49	C4
Dunluce Road	26	E3
Dunmanus Court	24	E4
Dunmanus Road	24	E4
Dunmore Grove	44	F3
Dunmore Lawn	44	F3
Dunmore Park	44	F2
Dunne Street	72	D2
Dunree Park	26	F1
Dunsandle Court	23	A3
Dunsandle Grove	23	A3
Dunseverick Road	26	E3
Dunsinea Lane	23	B3
Dunsink Ave	24	D2
Dunsink Drive	24	D2
Dunsink Gardens	24	D2
Dunsink Green	24	D2
Dunsink Lane	23	A2
Dunsink Park	24	D2
Dunsink Road	24	D2
Dunsoghly	23	C1
Dunsoghly Ave	23	C1
Dunsoghly Close	23	C1
Dunsoghly Court	23	C1
Dunsoghly Drive	23	C1
Dunsoghly Green	23	C1
Dunsoghly Grove	23	C1
Dunsoghly Park	23	C1

STREET NAME	PAGE	GRID REF
*Dunstaffnage Hall Apts (off Church Road)	58	F1
Dunville Ave	47	B1
*Dunville Close (off Annesley Park)	47	B1
*Dunville Court (off Moyne Road)	47	B1
*Durham Place (off Corrig Road)	60	D1
Durham Road	39	B4
Durrow Road	46	E1
Dursey Row	22	F1
Dwyer Park	67	C1

E

STREET NAME	PAGE	GRID REF
*Eagle Hill (off George's Ave)	49	A3
*Eagle Hill Ave (off Terenure Road North)	46	F2
Eagle Park	26	D1
*Eagle Terrace (off Sandyford Road)	57	C1
*Eagle Terrace (Dalkey)	60	F2
Eagle Valley	66	E4
Eagle's Nest	68	D3
*Eaglewood Apts (off Rochestown Ave)	59	C2
*Eaglewood House (off Rochestown Ave)	59	C2
*Eaglewood Mews (off Rochestown Ave)	59	C2
Earl Place	71	B3
Earl Street North	71	B3
Earl Street South	74	F1
Earls Court (Dolphins Barn)	74	D3
Earls Court (Cabra)	69	C1
*Earls Court (off Terenure Road East)	46	F2
Earlscroft	67	C4
*Earlsfield Court (off Francis Street)	74	F1
Earlsfort	34	F3
Earlsfort Ave	34	F3
Earlsfort Close	34	F3
*Earlsfort Court (Earlsfort Terrace)	75	C3
Earlsfort Court	34	F2
Earlsfort Drive	34	F3
Earlsfort Gardens	34	F2
Earlsfort Green	34	F3
Earlsfort Grove	34	F3
Earlsfort Lane	34	F3
Earlsfort Lawn	34	F2
Earlsfort Meadows	34	F2
Earlsfort Park	34	F2
Earlsfort Rise	34	F3
Earlsfort Road	34	F2
Earlsfort Terrace	75	C3
Earlsfort Vale	34	F3
Earlsfort View	34	F3
Earlsfort Way	34	F3
Earman's Wood	14	E2
East Pier (Howth)	30	D1
East Pier (Dún Laoghaire)	50	E3
East Road	72	F3
East Wall	72	F1
East Wall Road (Fairview)	72	F1
East Wall Road (Alexandra Basin)	39	A2
*Eastmore (Bushy Park Road)	46	F3
Eastmoreland Court	76	E3
Eastmoreland Lane	76	E3
Eastmoreland Place	76	E3
Easton	32	E1
*Easton Drive (Easton)	32	E1
*Easton Green (Easton)	32	E1
Easton House	19	B4
*Easton Mews (Easton)	32	E1
Easton Park	19	C4
Easton Road	19	B4
*Easton Row (Easton)	32	E1
Eastwood	23	C2
Eaton Brae (Orwell Road)	47	A3
Eaton Brae (Shankill)	64	E2
Eaton Close	52	F2
*Eaton Court (off Terenure Road North)	46	F2
*Eaton Court (Newcourt Ave)	68	D3
Eaton Green	52	F2
*Eaton Hall (off Terenure Road North)	46	F2
*Eaton House (beside Eaton Terrace)	52	F2
Eaton Place	49	B4
Eaton Road	46	F2
Eaton Square (Terenure)	46	F2
Eaton Square (Monkstown)	49	B4
Eaton Terrace	52	F2
Eaton Way	52	F2
Eaton Wood Ave	64	E3
Eaton Wood Court	64	E3
Eaton Wood Green	64	E3
Eaton Wood Grove	64	E3
Eaton Wood Square	64	E2
Ebenezer Terrace	74	E2
Eblana Ave	50	D4
Eblana Villas (Lower Grand Canal Street)	76	E1
Eblana Villas (off Arbour Hill)	70	E3
Eccles Court	71	B1
Eccles Place	71	B1
Eccles Street	71	A1
Echlin Street	74	E1
Eden Ave	57	A1
Eden Court	57	A1
Eden Cres	57	A1
Eden Grove	57	A1
Eden Park	60	D1
Eden Park Ave	58	D1
Eden Park Drive	48	D4
Eden Park Road	58	D1
Eden Quay	71	C4
Eden Road Lower	60	D1
Eden Road Upper	60	D1
Eden Terrace (Botanic Ave)	25	A4
Eden Terrace (Dún Laoghaire)	60	D1
*Eden Villas (off Coldwell Street)	60	D1
*Edenbrook Court (off Ballyboden Road)	56	F1
Edenbrook Drive	46	E4
Edenbrook Park	46	E4
Edenmore	26	D1
Edenmore Ave	26	F1
Edenmore Cres	27	A2
Edenmore Drive	26	F2
Edenmore Gardens	26	F2
Edenmore Green	26	F2
Edenmore Grove	26	F2
Edenmore Park	26	F2
Edenvale	57	A2
Edenvale Road	47	B1
*Edenwood (off Eden Park Drive Goatstown)	48	D4
*Edgewood (off Richmond Road)	25	B4
Edgewood Lawns	22	E1
Edmondsbury Court (off Esker Lane)	34	E1
Edmondstown	56	E3
Edmondstown Green	56	E2
Edmondstown Road	56	E3
Edward Lane	76	D4
Edward Place	76	D4
Edward Road	68	D3
Edward Square	76	D4
*Edward Terrace (off Nerano Road)	60	F2
Edwards Court	56	E2
*Edwin Court (off Albert Road Upper)	60	E2
Effra Road	47	A1
*Eglington Park (off Tivoli Road Dun Laoghaire)	49	C4
*Eglinton Road (off Quinnsborough Road)	67	C2
Eglinton Court	47	C1
Eglinton Park (Donnybrook)	47	C1
Eglinton Road	47	C1
*Eglinton Square (off Eglinton Road)	47	C1
*Eglinton Terrace (Royal Canal Bank)	71	A2
Eglinton Terrace (Donnybrook)	47	C1
Eglinton Terrace (Dundrum)	47	C4
*Eglinton Wood (off Eglinton Road)	47	C1
Eklad Close	13	C4
Eklad Park	13	C4
*El Greco Apts (off Serpentine Ave)	39	A4
*Elbin House (off Serpentine Ave)	39	A4
Elder Park	54	E3
Elderberry	34	D3
Elderwood Road	35	B2
*Elford Terrace (off Donore Ave)	74	E2
Elgin Heights	67	A4
Elgin Road	76	E3
Elgin Wood	67	B4
*Elizabeth O'Farrell Park (Lombard Street East)	72	D4
Elizabeth Street	25	B4
Elkwood	56	E1
*Ellen Hall (off Emmet Road)	73	A2
Ellenfield Road	25	C2
Ellensborough	54	F3
Ellensborough Close	54	F3
Ellensborough Copse	54	F3
Ellensborough Court	54	F3
Ellensborough Cres	54	F3
Ellensborough Dale	54	F3
Ellensborough Downs	54	F3
Ellensborough Drive	54	F3
Ellensborough Grange	54	F3
Ellensborough Green	54	F3
Ellensborough Grove	54	F3
Ellensborough Lane	54	F3
Ellensborough Lawn	54	F3
Ellensborough Lodge	54	F3
Ellensborough Meadows	54	F3
Ellensborough Park	54	F3
Ellensborough Rise	54	F3
Ellensborough View	54	F3
Ellensborough Walk	54	F3
Ellensborough Way	54	F3
Ellerslie	64	D3
*Ellesmere (off Brewery Road)	58	F2
Ellesmere Ave	70	D1
Ellis Court	70	E4
Ellis Quay	70	E4
Ellis House Apts	70	E4
Ellis Street	70	E4
Elm Close	34	E3
Elm Court (Lucan)	34	E3
Elm Court (Jobstown)	54	D2
Elm Dene	34	E3
Elm Drive (Lucan)	34	E3
Elm Drive (Jobstown)	54	D2
Elm Green	34	E3
Elm Grove (Lucan)	34	E3
Elm Grove	49	A4
Elm Grove (Jobstown)	54	D2
Elm House	76	D3
*Elm House Apts (off Elm Drive)	54	D2
Elm Mount Ave	25	C2
Elm Mount Close	26	D2
Elm Mount Court	26	D2
Elm Mount Cres	26	D2
Elm Mount Drive	26	D2
Elm Mount Grove	26	D2
Elm Mount Heights	26	D2
Elm Mount Lawn	26	D2
Elm Mount Park	26	D2
Elm Mount Rise	26	D2
Elm Mount Road	26	D2
Elm Mount View	26	D2
Elm Park (Celbridge)	32	D3
Elm Park (Nutley Lane)	48	D1
Elm Park Terrace	46	F2
Elm Road (Donnycarney)	26	D3
Elm Road (Fox and Geese)	45	A1
Elm Road (Newtown)	11	A2
Elm Vale	34	E3
Elm Way (Lucan)	34	E3
*Elm Way (off Grange Wood)	57	A2
Elm Wood	34	E3
Elmbrook	34	E2
Elmbrook Cres	34	E2
Elmbrook Lawn	34	E2
Elmbrook Walk	34	E2
Elmcastle Close	45	A3
Elmcastle Court	45	A3
Elmcastle Drive	45	A3
Elmcastle Green	45	A3
Elmcastle Park	45	A3
Elmcastle Walk	45	A3
Elmdale Cres	35	C3
Elmdale Drive	35	C3
Elmdale Park	35	C3
*Elmfield (adjacent Kilgobbin Wood)	58	E4
Elmfield Ave	14	D4
Elmfield Close	14	D4
Elmfield Court (Clarehall)	14	D4
Elmfield Court (Clondalkin)	44	E1
Elmfield Cres	14	E4
Elmfield Drive	14	E4
Elmfield Green	14	D4
Elmfield Grove	14	D4
Elmfield Lawn	14	E4
Elmfield Park	14	E4
Elmfield Rise	14	D4
Elmfield Vale	14	D4
Elmfield Walk	14	D4
Elmfield Way	14	D4
Elmgrove	60	D4
*Elmgrove Terrace (near Duncairn Ave)	67	C2
Elmpark Apts	48	E2
Elmpark Ave	47	B1
Elmpark Green	48	E2
Elms	48	F3
Elms (opposite Knockmaroon Gate)	36	D1
Elmwood Ave Lower	47	B1
Elmwood Ave Upper	47	B1
Elmwood	21	B1
*Elmwood Court (On Elmwood Road)	1	C1
Elmwood Drive	1	C1
Elmwood Park	1	C1
Elmwood Road	1	C1
Elner Court	4	D4
*Elton Court (off Philipsburgh Ave)	25	C4
*Elton Court (off Clonrosse Drive)	26	F1
Elton Court (Leixlip)	32	F1
Elton Court (Dalkey)	60	E1
Elton Drive (Dunboyne)	7	B2
Elton Drive (Coolock)	27	A1
Elton Grove (Dunboyne)	7	B3
Elton Park (Coolock)	27	A1
Elton Park (Dalkey)	60	E1
*Elton Walk (off Clonrosse Drive)	27	A1
*Elvenden House (off Cameron Street)	74	E2
Ely Close	55	B3
*Ely Cres (off Allenton Road)	55	B3
Ely Drive	55	B3
*Ely Green (off ElyClose)	55	B3
Ely Green	55	B3
Ely Grove	55	B3
Ely Place	75	C2
Ely Place Upper	75	C2
Ely View	55	B3
Embassy Lawn	47	C2
Emerald Cottages	76	F2
Emerald Place	72	D3
Emerald Square	74	D2
Emerald Street	72	E3
Emerald Terrace	74	E2
*Emily Lawless Court (off Bayside Square South)	27	C1
Emmet Court	73	A2
Emmet Cres	73	A2
*Emmet Manor (Emmet Cres)	36	F3
Emmet Place	70	F4
Emmet Road	73	A1
Emmet Square	48	F3
Emmet Street (Harold's Cross)	74	F4
Emmet Street (North Circular Road)	71	C1
*Emmet Street (off Parnell Street Sallynoggin)	60	D1
*Emmett Buildings (Watling Street)	70	E4
Emor Street	75	A3
Emorville Ave	75	A3
Empress Place	72	D2
Enaville Ave (off Annesley Place)	72	E1
Enaville Road	72	E1
Engine Alley (off Meath Street)	74	F1
*Engleberg Court (opposite Glandore Park)	59	C1
English Row	32	D4
Ennafort Ave	26	F3
Ennafort Court	26	F3
Ennafort Drive	26	F3
Ennafort Grove	26	F3
Ennafort Park	26	F3
Ennafort Road	26	F3
Ennel Ave	26	F2
*Ennel Court (beside Inagh Court)	64	E1
Ennel Drive	26	F2
Ennel Park	26	F2

STREET NAME	PAGE	GRID REF
*Ennis Grove (off Londonbridge Road)	39	A3
Enniskerry	66	D3
Enniskerry Bridge	66	E3
Enniskerry Demense	66	E4
*Enniskerry Road (off Phibsborough Road)	25	A4
Enniskerry Road (Sandyford)	58	D4
Erne Place (Lansdowne Park)	76	E1
Erne Place Little	76	D1
Erne Place Lower	72	D4
Erne Street Lower	72	D4
Erne Street Upper	76	D1
Erne Terrace Front	76	D1
Erne Terrace Rere	76	D1
Errigal Gardens	73	A4
Errigal Road	36	F4
Erris Road	24	E4
Erris Square	22	F1
Esker Drive	34	D2
Esker Glebe	34	D2
Esker Lane	34	E2
Esker Lawns	34	D1
Esker Lodge	34	E2
Esker Lodge Ave	34	E2
Esker Lodge Close	34	E2
Esker Lodge View	34	E2
Esker Manor	34	E2
Esker Meadow	34	E2
Esker Meadow Close	34	E2
Esker Meadow Court	34	E2
Esker Meadow Green	34	E2
Esker Meadow Grove	34	E2
Esker Meadow Lawn	34	E2
Esker Meadow Rise	34	E2
Esker Meadow View	34	E2
Esker Park	34	E2
Esker Pines	34	E1
Esker Road	34	D2
Esker South	34	D3
*Esker Villas (off Summerville Park)	47	A1
Esker Woods	34	E2
Esker Woods Close	34	E2
Esker Woods Court	34	E2
Esker Woods Drive	34	E2
Esker Woods Grove	34	E2
Esker Woods Rise	34	E2
Esker Woods View	34	E2
Esker Woods Walk	34	E2
Esmond Ave	25	C4
*Esmonde Terrace (Upper Dargle Road)	67	B2
*Esplanade Terrace (Strand Road, Convent Ave)	68	D2
*Esposito Road (off John Mc Cormack Ave)	45	C1
Essex Gate (off Essex Quay)	71	A4
Essex Quay	71	A4
Essex Street East	71	A4
Essex Street West (off Fishamble Street)	71	A4
Estate Ave	48	E1
Estate Cottages (Northumberland Road)	76	E2
Estate Cottages (Ballsbridge)	76	F3
Estuary Court	2	D1
Estuary Road	2	F2
Estuary Roundabout (Swords)	2	D1
Estuary Row	3	B2
Estuary Walk	2	F2
Eugene Street	74	E2
Eustace Bridge (Grand Canal)	75	C3
Eustace Street	71	B4
Everton Apts	56	E1
Everton Ave	70	D2
Evora Cres (end of Grace O' Malley Road)	30	D1
Evora Park	30	D1
Evora Terrace (at Saint Laurence Road, Police Station)	30	D1
Ewington Lane	74	D1
Exchange Court	71	C4
Exchange Street Lower (off Wood Quay)	71	A4
Exchange Street Upper (off Lord Edward Street)	71	A4
Exchequer Street	75	B1
Excise Walk	72	E3
Eyre Court	2	E2
*Faber Grove (off Rory O'Connor Park)	59	B1
Fade Street	75	B1
*Fagan's Lane (off main street and Pound Lane)	17	C3

F

STREET NAME	PAGE	GRID REF
*Fair Haven (on Strand Street Malahide)	3	B2
Fairacre	2	F3
Fairbrook Lawn	46	F4
Fairfield Ave	72	E2
*Fairfield Court (off Newbridge Ave)	39	A3
*Fairfield House (off Harrison Row)	46	F2
Fairfield Park	47	A2
Fairfield Road	25	A4
Fairgreen	53	A2
*Fairgreen Court (near Adelaide Villas)	67	C2
*Fairgreen Road (near Maitland Street)	67	B2
*Fairgreen Terrace (near Adelaide Villas)	67	C2
Fairlawn Park	24	E2
Fairlawn Road	24	E2
*Fairlawns (off Saval Park Road)	60	E2
*Fairview Ave (off Irishtown Road)	39	A3
Fairview Ave Lower	25	C4
Fairview Ave Upper	25	C4
Fairview Close	25	C4
*Fairview Court (off Fairview Ave Lower)	25	C4
*Fairview Green (off Fairview Ave Upper)	25	C4
Fairview Lawn	64	D1
*Fairview Passage (off Fairview Strand)	25	C4
Fairview Strand	25	C4
*Fairview Terrace (off Fairview Ave Lower)	25	C4
Fairways	46	E4
Fairway's Ave	24	F2
Fairway's Green	24	F2
*Fairways Grove	24	E2
Fairway's Park	24	F2
Fairy Castle	61	B2
Fairy Grove	12	E3
Fairyhill (Stillorgan)	59	A1
Fairyhill (Oldcourt)	67	B3
Faith Ave	72	E1
Falcarragh Road	25	B2
*Falcons View Apts (adjacent Blanchardstown Town Centre)	22	E1
Falls Road	64	D2
Farmhill Drive	47	C4
Farmhill Park	47	C4
Farmhill Road	47	C4
Farmleigh	23	A4
Farmleigh Ave (Castleknock)	23	A4
Farmleigh Ave (Stillorgan)	58	F1
Farmleigh Close (Castleknock)	23	A4
Farmleigh Close (Stillorgan)	58	F1
Farmleigh Court	23	A4
Farmleigh Park (Castleknock)	23	A4
Farmleigh Park (Stillorgan)	58	F1
Farmleigh View	23	A4
Farmleigh Woods	23	A4
Farney Park	39	A4
Farnham Cres	24	E2
Farnham Drive	24	E2
Farrenboley Cottages	47	B3
Farrenboley Park	47	B3
Fassaroe	66	F3
Fassaroe	67	A2
Fassaroe Ave	67	A3
Fassaroe Glen	67	A2
Fassaroe Lane	67	A3
*Father Bidone Court (off Father Mary's Ave West)	36	F3
*Father Colohan Terrace (near Market House)	67	C2
*Father Didone Court (off Saint Mary's Ave West)	36	F3
*Father Kit Court (off Saint Agnes Road Crumlin)	46	D1
Father Lemass Court	36	D3
Father Mathew Square	70	F3
Father Matthew Bridge (River Liffey)	70	F4
Father Scully House	71	C2
Fatima Terrace	67	C2

STREET NAME	PAGE	GRID REF
*Faughart Road (off Kells Road)	46	E1
Faulkner's Terrace	73	C1
Faussagh Ave	24	E4
Faussagh Road	24	F4
Fawn Lodge	23	A4
Feltrim	3	A4
Feltrim Hall	2	D3
Feltrim Road	2	F4
Fenian Street	76	D1
Fergus Road	46	F2
Ferguson Road	25	A3
*Fernbrook (north of Connawood)	67	B1
Ferncarrig Ave	58	D3
Ferncarrig Court	58	D3
Ferncarrig Rise	58	D3
Ferncourt Ave	55	B3
Ferncourt Close	55	B3
*Ferncourt Cres (off Ferncourt Ave)	55	B3
*Ferncourt Drive (off Ferncourt Drive)	55	B3
Ferncourt Green	55	B3
Ferncourt Park	55	B3
Ferncourt View	55	B3
Ferndale (Tallaght)	55	A2
Ferndale	8	F4
Ferndale Ave	24	F2
Ferndale Glen	64	D3
Ferndale Hill	64	D4
Ferndale Road (Glasnevin)	24	F2
Ferndale Road (Shankill)	64	D3
Ferndale Road (Bray)	67	A1
Fernhill Ave	45	C3
Fernhill Park	45	C3
Fernhill Road	45	C2
Fernleigh	22	D3
Fernleigh Close	22	D3
Fernleigh Court	22	D3
Fernleigh Cres	22	D3
Fernleigh Dale	22	D3
Fernleigh Dene	22	D4
Fernleigh Drive	22	D3
Fernleigh Grange	22	D4
Fernleigh Green	22	D3
Fernleigh Grove	22	D4
Fernleigh Heath	22	D4
Fernleigh Lawn	22	D3
Fernleigh Park	22	D3
Fernleigh Place	22	D3
Fernleigh Vale	22	D3
Fernleigh View	22	D4
Fernleigh Way	22	D4
Fernley Court	75	A2
Ferns Road	46	E1
Fernvale Drive	46	D1
Fernwood Ave	54	E1
Fernwood Close	54	E1
Fernwood Court	54	E1
Fernwood Lawn	54	E1
Fernwood Park	54	E1
Fernwood Way	54	E1
Ferrard Road	46	F2
Ferrycarrig Ave	13	B4
Ferrycarrig Drive	13	B4
Ferrycarrig Green	13	B4
Ferrycarrig Park	13	B4
Ferrycarrig Road	13	B4
Ferryman's Crossing	72	E3
*Fertullagh Road (off Leix Road)	24	F4
Fettercairn	44	E4
Fettercairn Cres	54	D1
Fettercairn Road	44	E4
*Fey Yerra (off Leopardstown Road)	58	F2
Fforster	34	E2
Fforster Close	34	E2
Fforster Court	34	E2
Fforster Cres	34	E2
Fforster Lawn	34	E2
Fforster Park	34	E2
Fforster Walk	34	E2
Fforster Way	34	E2
*Field Ave (off Balfe Road)	45	C1
*Field's Terrace (off Charleston Road)	47	B1
*Fieldview Cottages (off Annaville Ave)	49	A4
Fiery Lane	62	D4
*Findlater Building Apts (off Harbour Road, opposite west pier)	30	D1
Findlater Place	71	B3
Findlater Street (North Circular Road)	70	D3

STREET NAME	PAGE	GRID REF
*Findlater Street (off Eden Terrace Dún Laoghaire)	60	E1
Fingal Place	70	E2
Fingal Street	74	E2
Finglas	24	E1
Finglas East	24	E1
Finglas Park	24	E1
Finglas Place	24	E2
Finglas Road	24	E2
Finglas Road Old	24	F3
Finglas South	24	D2
*Finglas Square (off Owenstown Park Fosters Ave)	48	D3
Finglas West	24	D1
Finglaswood Road	24	D1
Finn Street	70	D3
Finneber Fort	24	E2
Finneber Fort Square	24	E2
Finnscourt	34	D3
Finnsgreen	34	D3
Finnsgrove	34	D3
Finnslawn	34	D3
Finnspark	34	D3
Finnstown Cloisters	34	D3
Finnstown Fairways	34	D3
Finnstown Hall	34	D3
Finnsvale	34	D3
Finnsview	34	D3
Finnswalk	34	D3
Finnswood	34	D3
Finsbury Green	47	B4
Finsbury House (off Herbert Road)	76	F3
Finsbury Park	47	B4
*Firgrove (off Military Road Ballybrack)	60	E4
Firhouse	55	C1
Firhouse Road	55	B2
Firhouse Road West	55	A2
First Ave (Seville Place)	72	E3
First Ave (Sarsfield Road)	36	F3
First Ave (Belgard Heights)	44	F4
Fishamble Street	71	A4
*Fisherman's Green (off Gasyard Lane Malahide)	3	B2
*Fishermans Wharf (off York Road)	39	A2
*Fitzgerald Park (off Mounttown Road Lower)	59	C1
Fitzgerald Street	75	A4
Fitzgibbon Lane	71	C1
Fitzgibbon Street	71	C1
Fitzmaurice Road (Glasnevin)	24	F2
Fitzmaurice Road (Rathcoole)	52	F2
*Fitzpatrick's Cottages (off Harold's Cross Road)	46	F1
Fitzroy Ave	25	B4
Fitzwilliam Court (Leeson Park)	76	D4
Fitzwilliam Court (Fitzwilliam Square)	75	C2
Fitzwilliam Court (Stillorgan Road)	48	E3
Fitzwilliam Lane	76	D2
Fitzwilliam Place	75	C3
Fitzwilliam Place North (Grangegorman)	70	F3
*Fitzwilliam Point (off Fitzwilliam Quay)	39	A3
*Fitzwilliam Quay (off Fitzwilliam Quay)	39	A3
Fitzwilliam Square	75	C2
Fitzwilliam Square East	76	D2
Fitzwilliam Square North	76	D2
Fitzwilliam Square South	75	C2
Fitzwilliam Square West	75	C2
*Fitzwilliam Street (off Cambridge Park)	39	A3
Fitzwilliam Street Lower	76	D2
Fitzwilliam Street Upper	76	D2
*Fitzwilliam Terrace (at Esplanade)	68	D2
Fleet Street	71	B4
Fleming Road	25	A3
Fleming's Hall Apts	76	D3
Fleming's Place	76	D3
Flemingstown Park	47	B4
Flemming House	76	D3
Fleurville	49	A4
Fleurville & Benamore Road	49	A4
Fleurville Road	49	A4
Floraville Ave	44	E1
Floraville Drive	44	E2
Floraville Estate	44	E1
Floraville Lawn	44	E1
Florence Road	67	C2

STREET NAME	PAGE	GRID REF
Florence Street	75	A3
*Florence Terrace (Leeson Park Ave)	76	D4
*Florence Terrace (Florence Road)	67	C2
*Florence Villas (Sandymount)	39	A4
*Florence Villas (Florence Road)	67	C2
Flower Grove	60	D2
Foley Street	71	C3
Fontenoy Street	71	A2
Fontenoy Terrace	68	D3
*Fonthill Abbey (off Fonthill Park)	56	F1
Fonthill Abbey	56	F1
Fonthill Park	56	F1
Fonthill Road (Clondalkin)	35	A2
Fonthill Road (Rathfarnham)	56	F1
Fonthill Road North	35	A3
Fonthill Road South	44	D2
Forbes Lane	74	E2
*Forbes Quay Apts (Forbes Street)	72	E4
Forbes Street	72	E4
Forest Ave (Swords)	1	B3
Forest Ave (Kilnamanagh)	45	A3
Forest Boulevard	1	B3
Forest Close	45	A3
Forest Court	1	B2
Forest Cres	1	B3
Forest Dale	1	B2
Forest Drive (Swords)	1	B3
Forest Drive (Kilnamanagh)	45	A3
Forest Green (Swords)	1	B3
Forest Green (Kilnamanagh)	45	A3
Forest Grove	1	B3
Forest Hills (Swords)	1	C3
Forest Hills (Rathcoole)	52	E2
Forest Lawn	45	A3
Forest Park (Swords)	1	B2
Forest Park (Leixlip)	32	F1
Forest Park (Kilnamanagh)	45	A3
Forest Road	1	B4
Forest View	1	B3
Forest Walk	1	C3
Forest Way	1	C3
Forester Drive	34	F2
Forestfields Road	1	C3
Forestwood Ave	12	D4
Forestwood Close	12	E4
*Forge Court (south of Church on Main Street Howth)	30	D2
Forster Way	2	D2
Fort Ostman	73	C4
*Fort Ostman Wood (off Old County Road)	73	C4
Fortescue Lane	75	B4
Fortfield Ave	46	E3
*Fortfield Court (off Fortfield Road)	46	E3
Fortfield Cres	46	E3
Fortfield Drive	46	E3
Fortfield Gardens	47	A2
Fortfield Grove	46	E3
Fortfield Park	46	E3
Fortfield Road (Kimmage)	46	E2
Fortfield Road (Bushy Park)	46	E3
Fortfield Square	46	E3
Fortfield Terrace	47	A2
Forth Road	72	F2
*Forthill Court (off Fonthill Road)	56	F1
Fortlawn Ave	22	D1
Fortlawn Cres	22	D1
Fortlawn Drive	22	D1
Fortlawn Park	22	D1
Fortlawns	60	E2
Fortrose Park	46	E4
Fortunestown	53	C1
Fortunestown Close	53	C1
Fortunestown Cres	53	C1
Fortunestown Lane	53	B1
Fortunestown Road	54	D2
Fortunestown Way	54	D2
Fortview Ave	39	C1
Fortwilliam	48	E4
Foster Place North	72	D1
Foster Place South (College Green)	71	B4
Foster Terrace	72	D1
Fosterbrook	48	E2
Fosters Ave	48	D3
Fountain Place	70	F3
Fountain Road (Phoenix Park)	69	C3
*Fountain View Apts (James's Street)	74	D1
Fourth Ave (Seville Place)	72	E3
Fourth Ave (Tallaght)	44	F4
Fownes Street Lower (off Temple Bar)	71	B4
Fownes Street Upper	71	B4
Fox and Geese	45	A1
Fox Hill	55	A4
Foxborough Ave	34	E3
Foxborough Close	34	F3
Foxborough Court	34	F3
Foxborough Cres (off Foxborough Road)	34	F3
Foxborough Downes	34	E3
Foxborough Drive	34	E3
Foxborough Gardens	34	F3
Foxborough Glade	34	F3
Foxborough Glen	34	F3
Foxborough Green	34	F3
Foxborough Grove	34	F3
Foxborough Hall (off Newlands Road)	34	F3
Foxborough Heights	34	F3
Foxborough Hill	34	E3
Foxborough Lane	34	F3
Foxborough Lawn	34	F3
Foxborough Manor	34	F3
Foxborough Meadows	34	E3
Foxborough Park	34	E3
Foxborough Place	34	E3
Foxborough Rise	34	E3
Foxborough Road	34	E3
Foxborough Row	34	F3
Foxborough Walk	34	F3
Foxborough Way	34	E3
Foxdene Ave	34	F3
Foxdene Drive	34	F3
Foxdene Gardens	34	F3
Foxdene Green	34	F3
Foxdene Grove	34	F3
Foxdene Park	34	F3
Foxes Grove	64	E3
Foxe's Lane	27	B2
Foxfield	34	D3
Foxfield Ave	27	B2
Foxfield Cres	27	B2
Foxfield Drive	27	B2
Foxfield Green	27	B2
Foxfield Grove	27	B2
Foxfield Heights	27	B2
Foxfield Lawn	27	B2
Foxfield Park	27	B2
Foxfield Road	27	B2
Foxfield Saint John	27	B2
Foxford	34	F2
Foxford Court (off Ballyowen Lane)	34	F2
Foxhill Ave	27	A1
Foxhill Close	27	A1
Foxhill Court	27	A1
Foxhill Cres	27	A1
Foxhill Drive	27	A1
Foxhill Green	14	D4
Foxhill Grove	27	A1
Foxhill Lawn	27	A1
Foxhill Park	27	A1
Foxhill Way	27	A1
Foxpark	34	D3
Foxrock	59	A3
Foxrock Ave	59	A2
Foxrock Close	59	B2
Foxrock Court	59	A2
Foxrock Cres	59	B2
Foxrock Green	59	A2
Foxrock Grove	59	B2
Foxrock Manor	58	F2
*Foxrock Mount (off Foxrock Park)	59	A2
Foxrock Park	59	A2
Foxrock Wood	59	B2
Foxwood (Swords)	2	D2
Foxwood (Lucan)	34	D3
Foyle Road	25	C4
*Frances Ball House (off Stonepark Court)	46	F4
*Francis Court (off Mark's Alley west)	74	F1
Francis Street	74	F1
Frank Sherwin Bridge (River Liffey)	70	D4
*Frankfort (off Dundrum Road)	47	B4
Frankfort Ave	47	A2
Frankfort Cottages	72	D2
*Frankfort Court (off Rathgar Ave)	46	F2
*Frankfort Flats (off Rathgar Ave)	46	F2
Frankfort Mews	47	B4
Frankfort Park	47	B4
*Frascati Court (off George's Ave)	49	A3
*Frascati Hall (off Frascati Road Blackrock)	49	A3
Frascati Park	49	A3
Frascati Road	49	A3
Frederick Court	71	B2
*Frederick House (Fredrick Street South)	75	C1
Frederick Lane North	71	B2
Frederick Street North	71	B2
Frederick Street South	75	C1
*French Mullen Flats (Charlemont Street)	75	B3
French Park	9	B2
Frenchman's Lane	71	C3
*Friar's Walk (off Monastery Park)	44	E1
*Friarsland Ave (off Larchfield Road)	47	C3
Friarsland Cres	47	C3
Friarsland Road	47	C3
Friary Ave	70	F3
*Friary Close (near Cook Street)	71	A4
Friary Court	70	F3
Friary Grove	70	F3
Friel Ave	36	D4
Fumbally Court	75	A2
Fumbally Lane	75	A2
*Fumbally Square (Fumbally Lane)	75	A2
Furry Glen	36	D1
*Furry Hill (off Sandyford Road)	58	D2
Furry Park Court	26	E3
Furry Park Road	26	E3
Furze Road (Phoenix Park)	36	E1
Furze Road (Sandyford)	58	E2

G

Gables	27	A1
Gaelic Street	72	E2
Gainsborough	2	F3
Gainsborough Ave	2	F3
Gainsborough Close	2	F3
Gainsborough Court	2	F3
Gainsborough Cres	2	F3
Gainsborough Downs	2	F3
Gainsborough Green	2	F3
Gainsborough Lawn	2	F3
Gainsborough Park	2	F3
Gallaun Road	11	C4
Gallery Quay Apts	76	E1
Galloping Green (Stillorgan)	58	F1
*Galloping Green (off Belmont)	59	A1
Gallows Hill	1	C2
Galmoy Road	24	F4
Galtrim Park	67	C2
Galtrim Road	67	C2
Galtymore Close	36	F4
Galtymore Drive	73	B3
Galtymore Park	36	F4
Galtymore Road	73	B3
*Gandon Close (off Harold's Cross Road)	46	F1
*Gandon Court (off Main Street Lucan)	34	D1
Gandon Hall	71	C3
*Gandon Mews (off Main Street Lucan)	34	D1
Garda Terrace (Phoenix Park)	69	C3
Garden Lane	74	F1
Garden Terrace (off Clanbrassil Street Upper)	74	F3
Garden View	75	B4
Garden View Court	74	F1
Gardiner Lane	71	C2
Gardiner Place	71	B2
Gardiner Row	71	B2
Gardiner Street Lower	71	C2
Gardiner Street Middle	71	C2
Gardiner Street Upper	71	B1
Garnett Hall	7	A2
Garnett Vale	7	A2
Garnish Square	22	F1
Garrison Mews	64	D1
Garrynisk Close	44	F3
Garrynisk Road	44	F3
Garrynure	47	B2
Garryowen Road	36	E3
Gartan Ave	25	A4
Gartan Court	2	E1
Gartan Drive	2	E1
Garter Ave	53	C1
Garter Lane	53	B1
Garthy Wood Apts	56	D1
Garville Ave Upper	46	F2
*Garville Court (off Garville Road)	47	A2
*Garville Drive (off Garville Ave)	47	A2
Garville Lane	47	A2
*Garville Place (off Garville Ave)	47	A2
Garville Road	47	A2
Gas Yard Lane	3	B2
*Gascoigne Court (Camden Row)	75	A2
*Gateway Apts (Gateway)	25	A1
Gateway Ave	25	A1
Gateway Court	25	A1
Gateway Cres	25	A1
Gateway Gardens	25	A1
Gateway Mews	25	A1
Gateway Place	25	A1
Gateway View	25	A1
Gaybrook Lawns	3	A3
Gazelle Ave	9	B2
Gazelle Lane	9	B2
Gazelle Mews	9	B2
Gazelle Terrace	9	B2
Gazelle Walk	9	B2
Geoffrey Keating Road	74	F2
*George Reynolds Flats (off Oliver Plunkett Ave)	39	A3
George's Ave (Blackrock)	49	A3
Georges Court	72	D4
George's Dock	72	D3
George's Hill	71	A3
George's Lane	70	F3
George's Place (Temple Street)	71	B1
*George's Place (off George's Ave)	49	A3
George's Place (Dún Laoghaire)	50	D4
George's Quay	71	C4
*Georges Quay House (Georges Quay)	71	C4
George's Street Lower	50	D4
George's Street Upper	50	D4
George's Wharf	71	A1
Georgian Hamlet	15	A4
Georgian Village	23	A4
Gerald Street	76	F1
*Geraldine Court (off Doctors Lane)	17	C3
Geraldine Street	71	A1
Geraldstown Woods	12	D4
*Gertrude Terrace (near Ardee Street)	67	B2
*Gibbon's Cottages (beside De Selby Road)	54	D2
Gilbert Road	74	F2
Gilford Ave	39	B4
*Gilford Court (off Gilford Road)	39	A4
Gilford Drive	39	A4
Gilford Park	39	A4
*Gilford Pines (off Gilford Road)	39	A4
Gilford Place	72	D2
Gilford Road	39	A4
*Gilford Terrace (off Gilford Road)	39	B4
Giltspur Heights	67	B4
Giltspur Lane	67	B4
Giltspur Wood	67	B3
Glandore Park	59	C1
Glandore Road	25	C3
Glasanaon Court	24	E2
Glasanaon Park	24	E2
Glasanaon Road	24	E2
Glasaree Court	24	E2
Glasaree Road	24	E2
Glasilawn Ave	24	F2
Glasilawn Road	24	F2
Glaslyn	26	D4
Glasmeen Road	24	F2
Glasmore Park	1	C1
*Glasnamana Place (off Glasnamana Road)	24	F2
Glasnamana Road	24	F2
Glasnevin	24	F3
Glasnevin Ave	24	F1

STREET NAME	PAGE	GRID REF
Glasnevin Court	24	E3
Glasnevin Downs	24	F3
Glasnevin Drive	25	A1
Glasnevin Hill	25	A3
Glasnevin North	24	F1
Glasnevin Oaks (off Finglas Road Old)	24	F3
Glasnevin Park	24	F1
Glasnevin Woods	24	E3
Glasson Court	47	B3
*Glasthule Buildings (off Glasthule Road)	60	E1
Glasthule Road	60	E1
*Glaunsharoon (off Eglinton Road)	47	C1
Gleann na Rí	63	C1
Gleann na Smol (Monkstown)	49	B4
Gleann na Smól (Tallaght)	54	F2
Glebe (Airport)	13	B1
Glebe (Newcastle)	41	C3
Glebe (Rathcoole)	52	D3
Glebe Close	41	C3
Glebe Green	41	C3
Glebe Hall	59	C1
Glebe Heights	41	C4
Glebe Square	41	C4
*Glebe View (Church Street Finglas)	24	E2
Glebe Way	41	C4
Gledswood Ave	47	C3
Gledswood Close	47	C3
*Gledswood Drive (off Bird Ave)	47	C3
Gledswood Park	47	C3
Glen Ave	59	B3
Glen Close	59	B3
Glen Dale	59	B3
Glen Drive	59	B3
Glen Druid	64	E1
Glen Ellan Ave	1	C1
Glen Ellan Close	1	C1
Glen Ellan Court	1	C1
Glen Ellan Cres	1	C1
Glen Ellan Drive	1	C1
Glen Ellan Gardens	1	C1
Glen Ellan Green	1	C1
Glen Ellan Grove	1	C1
Glen Ellan Park	1	C1
Glen Ellan Pines	1	C1
Glen Ellan Walk	1	C1
Glen Garth	59	B3
Glen Grove	59	B3
Glen Lawn Drive	59	B3
Glen na Smol	67	C4
*Glen Terrace (off Link Road)	60	E1
Glen Walk	59	B3
Glenaan Road	25	B2
Glenabbey Road	48	E4
Glenacre	62	E4
Glenageary Ave	60	D2
Glenageary Court	60	D2
Glenageary Hall	60	E2
Glenageary Lodge	60	D2
Glenageary Park	60	D2
Glenageary Road Lower (Sallynoggin)	60	D1
Glenageary Road Lower (Dun Laoghaire)	50	D4
Glenageary Road Upper	60	D1
Glenageary Woods	60	D1
Glenalbyn Road	58	F1
Glenalua Heights	60	E3
Glenalua Road	60	E3
Glenalua Terrace	60	E3
Glenamuck Cottages	63	A2
Glenamuck North	62	F1
Glenamuck Road (Golden Ball)	62	F2
Glenamuck Road (Carrickmines)	63	A1
Glenamuck Road North (Brighton Road)	59	B4
Glenamuck Road South (Carrickmines)	63	A1
Glenamuck Road South (Kilternan)	62	F2
*Glenann (off Willbrook Road)	46	F4
Glenanne	46	F2
Glenard Ave (Cabra)	70	D1
Glenard Ave (Bray)	67	C2
*Glenard Hall (off Roebuck Downs)	47	C3
Glenarm Ave	25	B4
*Glenarm Square Apts (Dargle Road)	25	A4
Glenarriff Road	23	C3
Glenart Ave	48	F4

STREET NAME	PAGE	GRID REF
Glenaulin	36	D2
Glenaulin Drive	36	D2
*Glenaulin Green (off Oakcourt Ave)	35	C2
Glenaulin Park	36	D2
Glenaulin Road	35	C2
*Glenavon Court (off Griffith Ave)	25	A3
Glenavon Park	64	D1
Glenavy Park	46	E2
Glenayle Road	26	F1
Glenayr Road	46	F2
Glenbeigh Park	69	C1
Glenbeigh Road	70	D2
Glenbourne Ave	58	F4
Glenbourne Close	58	F4
Glenbourne Cres	58	F4
Glenbourne Drive	58	F4
Glenbourne Green	58	F4
Glenbourne Grove	58	F4
Glenbourne Park	58	F4
Glenbourne Road	58	F4
Glenbourne View	58	F4
Glenbourne Walk	58	F4
Glenbourne Way	58	F4
*Glenbower Park (off Churchtown Road)	47	B4
Glenbrae	64	E2
*Glenbrian Hall (off Howth Road)	26	D4
Glenbrook (Enniskerry)	66	E3
*Glenbrook (South of Glenlucan)	67	B3
Glenbrook Park	46	F4
Glenbrook Road	23	C3
*Glenburgh Terrace (on River Lane)	67	B2
Glencairn	58	E3
Glencairn Ave	58	E3
Glencairn Chase	58	E3
Glencairn Close	58	E3
Glencairn Copse	58	E4
Glencairn Court	58	E4
Glencairn Cres	58	E4
Glencairn Dale	58	E3
Glencairn Drive	58	E3
*Glencairn Garth (off Glencairn Road)	58	E3
Glencairn Glade	58	E4
Glencairn Glen	58	F4
Glencairn Green	58	E3
Glencairn Grove	58	F4
Glencairn Heath	58	E3
Glencairn Heights	58	E3
Glencairn Lawn	58	E3
Glencairn Oaks	58	E4
Glencairn Park	58	E3
Glencairn Place	58	E4
Glencairn Rise	58	E3
Glencairn Road	58	E3
Glencairn Thicket	58	F3
Glencairn View	58	E3
Glencairn View	58	E3
Glencairn Walk	58	E3
Glencairn Way	58	E3
Glencar Road	69	C2
*Glencarr Court (beside Glencarr Lawn)	64	E1
Glencarr Lawn	64	E1
Glencarraig	29	B1
Glencarrig Court	55	B2
*Glencarrig Court (Near Grace Park Ave)	25	B4
Glencarrig Drive	55	B2
Glencarrig Green	55	B2
Glencarthy Court Apts	26	D3
Glencloy Road	25	B2
Glencorp Road	25	C2
Glencourt Estate	67	C3
Glencullen	62	E4
Glencullen Bridge	65	B1
Glendale	20	D4
Glendale Drive	67	C3
Glendale Meadows	20	E4
Glendale Park	46	D3
*Glendalough Road (off Hollybank Road)	25	A4
Glendhu Park	23	C3
Glendhu Road	23	C3
Glendinning Lane (off Wicklow Street)	75	B1
Glendoher Ave	56	F1
Glendoher Close	56	E1
Glendoher Drive	56	F1
Glendoher Park	56	E1

STREET NAME	PAGE	GRID REF
Glendoher Road	56	E1
Glendoo Close	45	B3
Glendown Ave	46	D3
Glendown Close	46	D3
Glendown Court	46	D3
Glendown Cres	46	D3
Glendown Drive	46	D3
Glendown Green	46	D3
Glendown Grove	46	D3
Glendown Lawn	46	D3
Glendown Park	46	D3
Glendown Road	46	D3
Glendun Road	25	B2
Glenealy Downs	8	F4
Glenealy Road	74	D4
Gleneaston	19	B4
Gleneaston Ave	19	B4
Gleneaston Close	19	B4
Gleneaston Court	19	B4
Gleneaston Cres	19	B4
Gleneaston Drive	19	B4
Gleneaston Gardens	19	B4
Gleneaston Green	19	B4
Gleneaston Grove	19	B4
Gleneaston Lawns	19	B4
Gleneaston Manor	19	B4
Gleneaston Park	19	B4
Gleneaston Rise	19	B4
Gleneaston Square	19	B4
Gleneaston View	19	B4
Gleneaston Way	19	B4
Gleneaston Woods	19	B4
*Glenesk Court (off Claremont Road)	39	A4
Glenfarne Road	26	F1
Glenfield Ave	35	A2
Glenfield Close	35	A2
Glenfield Drive	35	A2
Glenfield Grove	35	A2
Glenfield Park	35	A2
*Glengara Close (off Glenageary Road Lower)	60	D1
Glengara Park	60	D1
Glengariff Parade	71	A1
Glengarriff Cres	71	B1
Glengarriff Parade	71	B1
Glenhill Ave	24	E2
Glenhill Court	24	E2
Glenhill Drive	24	E2
Glenhill Grove	24	E2
Glenhill Road	24	E2
Glenhill Villas	24	E2
Glenlucan	67	B2
Glenlyon Cres	55	C2
Glenlyon Grove	55	C2
Glenlyon Park	55	C2
*Glenmalure Court (off James's Walk)	73	C2
Glenmalure Park	73	C2
Glenmalure Square	47	B2
*Glenmalure Villas (off Saint Jame's Walk)	74	D2
Glenmaroon Park	35	C2
Glenmaroon Road	35	C2
Glenmore Court	56	F2
Glenmore Green	56	F2
Glenmore Park	56	F2
Glenmore Road	69	C1
Glenmurry Park	45	C3
Glenomena Grove	48	E2
Glenomena Park	48	E2
Glenpark Close	35	B1
Glenpark Drive	35	B1
Glenpark Road	35	B1
Glenshane Close	54	D1
Glenshane Cres	54	D1
*Glenshane Dale (off Glenshane Lawns)	54	D1
Glenshane Drive	54	D1
Glenshane Gardens	54	D1
Glenshane Green	54	D1
Glenshane Grove	54	D1
Glenshane Lawns	54	D1
Glenshane Park	54	D1
*Glenshane Place (off Glenshane Lawns)	54	D1
Glenshesk Road	25	C2
*Glenside Villas (off Lucan Road Palmerston)	35	C1
Glenthorn	67	B4
Glenties Drive	24	D2
Glenties Park	24	D2
Glentow Road	25	B2
*Glentworth Park (off Slademore Ave)	27	A1

STREET NAME	PAGE	GRID REF
Glenvale	34	E3
Glenvar Park	48	F3
Glenvara Park	55	C2
Glenview (Rochestown Ave)	60	D3
Glenview (Enniskerry)	66	D3
Glenview Drive	55	B1
*Glenview House Apts (opposite Brookmount Ave)	55	C1
Glenview Lawns	55	B1
Glenview Park	55	B1
Glenville Ave	22	E2
Glenville Court	22	E3
Glenville Drive	22	E3
Glenville Garth	22	E3
Glenville Green	22	E2
Glenville Grove	22	E2
Glenville Lawn	22	E2
Glenville Road	22	E3
*Glenville Terrace (off Main Street Dundrum)	47	C4
Glenville Way	22	E2
Glenwood (Bray)	67	B2
Glenwood (Laragcon Lucan)	33	C1
*Glenwood (off Landscape Road)	47	A3
Glenwood Road	26	F1
Glin Ave	13	B4
Glin Close	13	B4
Glin Court	13	B4
Glin Cres	13	B4
Glin Drive	13	B4
Glin Grove	13	B4
Glin Park	13	B4
Glin Road	13	B4
Glitspur Brook	67	C3
Gloucester Diamond	71	C2
Gloucester Lane (off Sean McDermott Street Lower)	71	C2
Gloucester Place North	71	C2
Gloucester Place Lower	71	C2
Gloucester Place Upper	71	C2
*Gloucester Square Apts (Gloucester Place Lower)	71	C2
Gloucester Street South	72	D4
Glovers Alley	75	B1
Glovers Court (off York Street)	75	B1
Goatstown	48	D4
Goatstown Ave	47	C4
Goatstown Close	48	D4
Goatstown Road	47	C4
Gobán Saor	58	E4
Godfrey Place (off Oxmanstown Road)	70	D2
Gofton Hall (off Mckee Ave)	24	E1
Golden Ball	62	F2
Golden Lane	75	A1
Goldenbridge Ave	73	B2
Goldenbridge Gardens	73	A2
Goldenbridge Terrace	73	A2
Goldenbridge Walk (Goldenbridge)	73	A2
Goldenbridge Walk (Tyrconnell Road)	36	F4
Goldsmith Hall Apts	72	D4
Goldsmith Street	71	A1
*Goldsmith Terrace (off Quinnsborough Road)	67	C2
Goldstone Court Apts	74	D4
Golf Links Road (Portmarnock)	15	A2
Gordon Ave	59	A3
Gordon Place	75	B1
Gordon Street	76	F1
*Gorsefield Court (off McAuley Road)	26	F2
Gort na Mona Drive	59	B3
Gortbeg Ave	24	E3
Gortbeg Drive	24	E3
Gortbeg Park	24	E3
Gortbeg Road	24	E3
Gortmore Ave	24	E2
Gortmore Drive	24	E2
Gortmore Park	24	E3
Gortmore Road	24	E3
Gosworth Park	60	E1
*Goulding Mews (Cadogan Road)	25	C4
Gowrie Park	60	D1
Grace O'Malley Drive	30	D2
Grace O'Malley Road	30	D2
Grace Park Ave	25	B4
Grace Park Court	25	B4
Grace Park Gardens	25	B4
Grace Park Heights	25	C3
*Grace Park Lawns (off Grace Park Heights)	25	C2

STREET NAME	PAGE	GRID REF
Grace Park Manor	25	B3
Grace Park Meadows	25	C3
Grace Park Road	25	C3
Grace Park Terrace	25	C3
Gracefield Ave	26	F2
Gracefield Road	26	E2
Grafton Street	75	B1
Graham Court	71	B2
Graham's Row	71	A2
Graigue Court	11	C4
Granby Lane	71	A2
Granby Place	71	B3
Granby Row	71	A2
Grand Canal Bank	74	D2
*Grand Canal Court		
(off Herberton Road)	73	C3
Grand Canal Docks	76	F1
Grand Canal Place	74	E1
Grand Canal Plaza	76	E1
Grand Canal Quay	76	E1
Grand Canal Square 72 E4	72	E4
Grand Canal Street Lower	76	E1
Grand Canal Street Upper	76	E2
Grand Canal View	73	B2
Grand Central Apts	58	E2
Grand Parade	75	C3
Grange (Meath)	6	E4
Grange (Malahide)	14	E1
Grange	43	A1
Grange Abbey Cres	14	E4
Grange Abbey Drive	14	E4
Grange Abbey Grove	14	E4
Grange Abbey Road	14	E4
Grange Ave	14	F4
Grange Brook	56	F2
Grange Close (Kilbarrack)	27	C1
Grange Close (Pottery Road)	59	C3
*Grange Cottages		
(off Brewery Road)	58	F1
Grange Court	57	A1
*Grange Court Apts		
(Stanhope Street)	70	F3
Grange Cres	59	B2
Grange Downs	57	A1
Grange Drive	27	C1
*Grange Grove		
(off Dean's Grange Road)	59	B1
Grange Hall	57	B3
Grange Hall Apts	27	A2
Grange Lodge Ave	14	E4
Grange Lodge Court	14	E4
Grange Manor	34	D3
Grange Manor Ave	57	A1
Grange Manor Close	57	A1
Grange Manor Drive	57	A1
Grange Manor Grove	57	A1
Grange Manor Road	57	A1
Grange Parade	27	C1
Grange Park (Baldoyle)	14	F4
Grange Park (Willbrook)	56	F1
Grange Park (Cornelscourt)	59	B2
Grange Park Ave	27	A2
Grange Park Close	27	B2
Grange Park Cres	27	B2
Grange Park Drive	27	A2
Grange Park Green	27	B2
Grange Park Grove	27	A2
Grange Park Rise	27	B1
Grange Park Road	27	A2
Grange Park View	27	B1
Grange Park Walk	27	A2
Grange Rise	14	F4
Grange Road (Baldoyle)	14	F4
Grange Road (Rathfarnham)	46	F4
Grange Road (The Priory)	56	F1
Grange Road (Marley Park)	57	A2
*Grange Terrace		
(off Dean's Grange Road)	59	B1
Grange View Close	43	B1
Grange View Court	43	B1
Grange View Green	43	B1
Grange View Grove	43	B1
Grange View Lawn	43	B1
Grange View Park	43	B1
Grange View Place	34	E4
Grange View Road	43	B1
Grange View Walk	43	B1
Grange View Way	43	B1
Grange View Wood	43	B1
Grange Way	27	C1
Grange Wood (Ballinteer)	57	A2
Grangebrook Ave	56	F2
Grangebrook Close	56	F2
Grangebrook Park	56	F2
Grangebrook Vale	56	F2

STREET NAME	PAGE	GRID REF
Grangefield	57	B3
Grangegorman Lower	70	F3
Grangegorman Upper	70	F2
Grangegorman Villas	70	F3
Grangemore	14	E4
Grangemore Ave	14	E4
Grangemore Court	14	D4
Grangemore Cres	14	D4
Grangemore Drive	14	E4
Grangemore Grove	14	E4
Grangemore Lawn	14	E4
Grangemore Park	14	E4
Grangemore Rise	14	D4
Grangemore Road	14	D4
Grangewood	59	C1
*Granite Hall		
(off Rosmeen Gardens)	60	D1
Granite Place (off Gilford Road)	76	F4
*Granite Terrace		
(off Inchicore Terrace South)	36	F3
Granitefield	59	C3
Granitefield Manor	59	C3
Granitefield Mews	59	C3
Grantham Place	75	B3
Grantham Street	75	A3
Grants Ave		
(Greenogue Industrial Estate)	42	E4
Grants Court		
(Greenogue Industrial Estate)	42	E4
Grants Cress		
(Greenogue Industrial Estate)	42	E4
Grants Drive		
(Greenogue Industrial Estate)	42	E4
Grants Hill		
(Greenogue Industrial Estate)	42	E4
Grants Lane		
(Greenogue Industrial Estate)	42	E4
Grants Park		
(Greenogue Industrial Estate)	42	E4
Grants Place		
(Greenogue Industrial Estate)	42	E4
Grants Rise		
(Greenogue Industrial Estate)	42	E4
Grants Road		
(Greenogue Industrial Estate)	42	E4
Grants Row		
(Greenogue Industrial Estate)	42	E4
Grant's Row	76	D1
Grants View		
(Greenogue Industrial Estate)	42	E4
Grants Way		
(Greenogue Industrial Estate)	42	E4
Granville Close	60	D3
*Granville Cres		
(off WoodleyRoad)	60	D3
Granville Park	59	A1
Granville Road (Deans Grange)	59	A2
Granville Road (Cabinteely)	59	C3
Grattan Ave	25	A4
Grattan Bridge (River Liffey)	71	A4
Grattan Court (off Mount Street)	76	E1
Grattan Court (Celbridge)	31	C4
Grattan Court East	76	E1
Grattan Cres	36	F3
Grattan Hall	14	E4
Grattan Lodge	14	E4
Grattan Parade	25	A4
Grattan Place	76	E1
Grattan Street	76	E1
*Gravel Walk Apts		
(Hendrick Street)	70	E4
*Gravel Walk Church Apts		
(Hendrick Street)	70	E4
Gray Square	74	F1
Gray Street (off Meath Street)	74	F1
Great Western Ave	70	F1
Great Western Square	70	F1
Great Western Villas	70	F1
Greeg Court	71	B3
Greek Street	71	A4
Green Acre Court	56	D1
Green Court View Apts	71	A3
*Green Isle Court		
(off Bushfield Lawns)	44	D2
Green Lane (Leixlip)	19	C4
Green Lane (Rathcoole)	52	E2
Green Park (Rathgar)	47	B3
Green Park Road	67	B2
Green Road (Blackrock)	48	F3
Green Street	71	A3
Green Street East	72	F4
Green Street Little	71	A3
Greencastle Ave	26	E1
Greencastle Cres	26	E1
Greencastle Drive	13	B4

STREET NAME	PAGE	GRID REF
Greencastle Parade	26	F1
Greencastle Park	13	B4
Greencastle Road	13	B4
Greendale Ave	27	C2
*Greendale Court		
(off Thornville Drive)	27	B2
Greendale Road	27	B2
Greenfield Close	17	C4
Greenfield Cres	48	D2
Greenfield Drive	18	D4
*Greenfield Manor		
(off Greenfield Park U.C.D.)	48	D2
Greenfield Park		
(Stillorgan Road)	48	D2
Greenfield Park		
(Ballycullen Road)	55	C2
Greenfield Place		
(off Mount Drummond Ave)	75	A4
Greenfield Road (Sutton)	29	B1
Greenfield Road		
(Mount Merrion)	48	E4
Greenfort Ave	35	A2
Greenfort Close	35	A2
Greenfort Cres	35	A2
Greenfort Drive	35	A2
Greenfort Gardens	35	A2
Greenfort Lawns	35	A2
Greenfort Park	35	A2
Greenfort Walk	35	A2
Greenhills	45	B3
Greenhills Court	55	A1
Greenhills Road	45	A4
Greenisle Road	43	C3
Greenlands	58	D2
*Greenlawns (off Macroom Ave)	13	B4
Greenlea Ave	46	E2
Greenlea Drive	46	E2
Greenlea Grove	46	E2
Greenlea Park	46	E3
*Greenlea Place		
(off The Laurels)	46	F2
Greenlea Road	46	E3
Greenmount Ave	74	F4
Greenmount Court	74	F4
Greenmount Lane	74	F4
Greenmount Lawns	46	F2
Greenmount Lodge	62	F2
Greenmount Road	46	F2
Greenmount Square	74	F4
Greenoge	42	F4
Greenogue Drive	52	F2
Greenore Court	76	E1
Greenore Terrace	76	E1
Greenpark Road	33	C2
Greenridge Court	22	E1
Greentrees Drive	45	C2
Greentrees Park	45	C2
Greentrees Road	45	C2
Greenview	14	E2
Greenville Ave	74	F3
Greenville Parade (Blackpitts)	74	F3
Greenville Place	74	F3
Greenville Road	49	B4
Greenville Terrace	74	F3
Greenwood	13	C1
Greenwood Ave	14	D4
Greenwood Close	14	D4
Greenwood Court	14	D4
Greenwood Drive	14	D4
*Greenwood Heights Apts		
(near The Orchard)	14	D4
*Greenwood Lawn		
(on Greenwood Drive)	14	D4
Greenwood Lawn	14	D4
Greenwood Park	14	D4
Greenwood Walk	14	D4
Greenwood Way	14	D4
Grenville Lane	71	B2
Grenville Street	71	B2
*Greygates (off Sycamore Cres)	48	E4
Grey's Lane	30	D2
Greythorn Park	60	D1
Griannan Fidh	58	D3
Griffeen	34	E3
Griffeen Ave	34	D3
Griffeen Glen Ave	34	E3
Griffeen Glen Boulevard	34	E3
Griffeen Glen Chase	34	E3
Griffeen Glen Close	34	E3
Griffeen Glen Court	34	E3
Griffeen Glen Court Yard	34	E3
Griffeen Glen Cres	34	E3
Griffeen Glen Dale	34	E3
Griffeen Glen Dene	34	E3
Griffeen Glen Drive	34	E3

STREET NAME	PAGE	GRID REF
Griffeen Glen Green	34	E3
Griffeen Glen Grove	34	E3
Griffeen Glen Lawn	34	E3
Griffeen Glen Park	34	E3
Griffeen Glen Road	34	E3
Griffeen Glen Vale	34	E3
Griffeen Glen View	34	E3
Griffeen Glen Way	34	E3
Griffeen Glen Wood	34	D3
Griffeen Road	34	E3
Griffeen Way	34	E2
Griffin Rath Hall	18	D4
Griffin Rath Manor	18	D4
Griffin Rath Road	18	D4
Griffith Ave	25	B3
Griffith Bridge (Grand Canal)	73	B2
Griffith Close	24	F2
Griffith Court	25	C4
Griffith Cres	24	F2
Griffith Downs	25	B3
Griffith Drive	24	F2
Griffith Hall	25	C3
Griffith Heights	24	F2
Griffith Lawns	25	A3
Griffith Parade	24	F2
Griffith Road	24	F2
Griffith Square	74	F3
Griffith Terrace	74	F1
*Grosvenor Ave		
(on Newcourt Road)	68	D3
Grosvenor Court (Clontarf)	26	E4
Grosvenor Court		
(Templeville Road)	46	D3
*Grosvenor House Apts		
(off Pakenham Road)	49	C4
Grosvenor Lane	47	A1
Grosvenor Lodge	47	A1
*Grosvenor Park		
(off Leinster Road)	47	A1
Grosvenor Place	47	A1
Grosvenor Road	47	A1
Grosvenor Square	47	A1
*Grosvenor Terrace		
(off The Hill Dún Laoghaire)	49	C4
*Grosvenor Terrace		
(off Sorrento Road)	60	F2
Grosvenor Villas (Rathmines)	47	A1
*Grosvenor Villas		
(off Sorrento Road)	60	F2
Grotto Ave	48	F2
Grotto Place	48	F2
Grove Ave (Harold's Cross)	75	A4
Grove Ave (Malahide)	3	C3
Grove Ave (Finglas)	24	E1
Grove Ave (Mount Merrion)	48	F4
Grove Court (Blanchardstown)	22	D1
*Grove Court		
(off Naas Road Bluebell)	36	F4
*Grove Hall (Linden Court)	48	F4
*Grove House (Grove Ave)	75	A4
*Grove House Apts		
(off Grove Wood)	59	A3
*Grove House Gardens		
(off Stillorgan Grove)	48	F4
Grove Lane	13	C4
Grove Lawn (Malahide)	3	C3
Grove Lawn (Stillorgan)	48	F4
Grove Mews	70	F1
Grove Paddock	48	F4
Grove Park (Rathmines)	75	B4
Grove Park (Coolock)	13	C4
Grove Park Ave	24	F1
Grove Park Cres	24	F1
Grove Park Drive	24	F1
Grove Park Road	24	F1
Grove Road (Rathmines)	75	A4
Grove Road (Malahide)	3	C3
Grove Road (Blanchardstown)	22	D2
Grove Road (Finglas)	24	E1
Grove Wood (Finglas)	24	E1
Grove Wood (Foxrock)	59	A3
Grovedale	63	B2
Guild Street	72	E3
*Guilford Terrace		
(off Lower Road)	64	E3
Gulistan Cottages	47	A1
Gulistan Place	47	A1
Gulistan Terrace	47	A1
Gunny Hill	55	D3
Gurteen Ave	36	D3
Gurteen Park	36	D3
Gurteen Road	36	D2

H

STREET NAME	PAGE	GRID REF
Hacketsland	64	E1
Haddington Lawns	60	E2
Haddington Park	60	E2
Haddington Place	76	E2
Haddington Road	76	E2
Haddington Square	76	F2
*Haddington Terrace (off Adelaide Street)	50	D4
*Haddington Way East (Canon Mews East)	76	F2
*Haddington Way West (Canon Mews West)	76	F2
*Haddon Court (off Haddon Road)	39	B1
*Haddon Park (Seaview Ave North)	26	D4
Haddon Road	26	E4
Hadleigh Court	23	A3
*Hadleigh Green (near The Pines)	23	A3
*Hadleigh Park	23	A3
Hagan's Court	76	D2
Haigh Terrace	50	D4
Hainault Drive	59	B3
Hainault Grove	59	B3
Hainault Lawn	59	B3
Hainault Park	59	A3
Hainault Road	59	A3
Halliday Road	70	E3
Halliday Square	70	D3
Hallscourt	67	C2
Halston Street	71	A3
Hamilton Court (off Strand Street Little)	71	A4
*Hamilton Court (at Hamilton Hall Dunboyne)	7	B3
*Hamilton Court (Seaview Terrace)	48	D1
Hamilton Hall	7	B3
*Hamilton House (Wellington Lane)	76	E4
Hamilton Street	74	E3
Hammond Lane	70	F4
Hammond Street	74	F2
Hampstead Ave	25	A2
Hampstead Court	25	A2
Hampstead Park	25	A3
Hampton Court	76	E4
Hampton Court (Clontarf)	26	F4
*Hampton Court (off Tyrconnell Road)	36	F3
Hampton Cres	48	E3
Hampton Green (Cabra)	69	B1
*Hampton Lodge Apts (off Grace Park Road)	25	B3
Hampton Park	48	E3
Hampton Square	69	C1
Hampton Wood	11	C4
Hampton Wood Ave	11	B4
*Hampton Wood Court	11	C4
Hampton Wood Cres	11	B4
Hampton Wood Drive	11	C4
Hampton Wood Green	11	B4
Hampton Wood Lawn	11	C4
Hampton Wood Park	11	B4
Hampton Wood Road	11	B4
*Hampton Wood Square	11	C4
Hampton Wood Way	11	C4
Hamwood	6	F3
Hanbury Court	74	F1
*Hanbury Hall (off Hanbury Lane)	74	F1
Hanbury Lane (The Coombe)	74	F1
*Hanbury Lane (off Main Street Lucan)	34	D1
*Hanbury Mews (Hanbury Lane)	74	F1
Hanlon's Lane	61	B1
Hanna Square	35	A1
Hannaville Park	46	F2
*Hanover Dock Apts (Forbes Street)	72	E4
Hanover Lane	75	A1
Hanover Quay	72	F4
*Hanover Reach Apts (Forbes Street)	72	E4
Hanover Square	75	A1
Hanover Street East	72	D4

STREET NAME	PAGE	GRID REF
Hanover Street West	74	F1
*Hanover Waterfront Apts (Hanover Quay)	72	F4
*Hanover Wharf Apts (Asgard Road)	72	E4
Hansfield	8	E4
Hansted Close	34	D4
Hansted Cres	34	D4
Hansted Dale	34	D4
Hansted Drive	34	D4
Hansted Park	34	D4
Hansted Place	34	D4
Hansted Road	34	D4
Hansted Way	34	D4
Ha'penny or Liffey Bridge (River Liffey)	71	B4
Harbour Court	71	C4
Harbour Cres	60	F1
*Harbour House Apts (off Bond Street)	74	E1
Harbour Master Place	72	D3
Harbour Road (Howth)	30	D1
Harbour Road (Dún Laoghaire)	50	D4
Harbour Road (Dalkey)	60	F1
Harbour Square	50	D4
*Harbour Terrace (off Harbour Road)	49	C4
Harbour View	30	D1
Harbour View (Dún Laoghaire)	50	D4
Harcourt Green	75	B3
Harcourt Hall	75	B3
Harcourt Lane	75	B3
Harcourt Lodge	73	B3
Harcourt Place	75	B3
Harcourt Road	75	B3
Harcourt Square	75	B3
Harcourt Street	75	B2
Harcourt Terrace	75	C3
Harcourt Terrace Lane (Charlemont Place)	75	C3
*Harcourt Villas (off Dundrum Rosd / Mulvey Park)	47	C3
*Harcourt Villas (on Dundrum Road)	47	C3
Hardebeck Ave	45	C1
Hardiman Road	25	A3
Hardwicke Arch (off Hardwicke Street)	71	B2
Hardwicke Lane	71	B2
Hardwicke Place	71	B2
Hardwicke Street	71	B2
*Hardwicke Street Flats (Hardwicke Street)	71	B2
Harelawn Ave	35	A3
Harelawn Cres	35	A3
Harelawn Drive	35	A2
Harelawn Green	35	A3
Harelawn Grove	35	A2
Harelawn Park	35	A2
Harlech Cres	48	D3
Harlech Downs	47	C3
Harlech Grove	48	D3
*Harlech Villas (off Harlech Downs)	47	C3
Harmac Court	46	F2
Harman Street	74	E2
Harmoney Court	76	E1
Harmonstown Road	26	F2
*Harmony Ave (off Eglinton Road)	47	C1
*Harmony Court (off Eglinton Road)	47	C1
Harmony Row	76	D1
Harold Bridge Court	74	F4
*Harold Cres (off Eden Road Lower)	60	E1
Harold Road	70	E3
Harold's Cross	74	F4
Harold's Cross Cottages	74	F4
Harold's Cross Road	74	F4
Harold's Grange Road	57	B3
Haroldville Ave	74	D2
Harrington Court	75	B3
Harrington Street	75	A3
Harrison Row	46	F2
Harristown	5	A2
Harry Street	75	B1
Hartstown Road	21	C1
Harty Ave	45	C1
Harty Court (off Daniel Street)	75	A2
*Harty Court (off Harty Ave)	45	C1
Harty Place	75	A2
Harvard	48	D3
Hastings Street	76	F1

STREET NAME	PAGE	GRID REF
*Hastings Terrace (off Glasthule Road)	60	E1
Hatch Lane	75	C3
Hatch Place	75	C3
Hatch Street Lower	75	C3
Hatch Street Upper	75	B3
Hatter's Lane	74	F4
Havelock Place	76	F2
Havelock Square	76	F2
*Havelock Terrace (off O'Connell Gardens)	39	A3
*Haven View (adjacent The Haven Malahide)	3	B2
Haverty Road	25	C4
Hawkins Street	71	C4
Hawkridge	33	B2
Hawthorn Ave	72	E2
*Hawthorn Drive (off Acorn Road)	57	B1
Hawthorn Lawn	22	F3
Hawthorn Lodge (Castleknock Road)	22	F3
Hawthorn Lodge (Farmleigh)	23	A4
*Hawthorn Manor (off Newtown Park)	59	A1
Hawthorn Park	1	C2
Hawthorn Road (Clondalkin)	44	F1
Hawthorn Road (Bray)	67	B1
Hawthorn Terrace	72	E2
Hawthorn View	32	D2
Hawthorns Road	58	D2
*Hayden Square (off Owenstown Park Fosters Ave)	48	D3
Haydens Lane	34	D4
Hayden's Lane	34	D3
Haydens Lane Place	34	D4
Haydens Park	34	D3
Haydens Park Ave	34	D3
Haydens Park Close	34	D3
Haydens Park Dale	34	D3
Haydens Park Drive	34	D3
Haydens Park Glade	34	D3
Haydens Park Green	34	D3
Haydens Park Grove	34	D3
Haydens Park Lawn	34	D3
Haydens Park View	34	D3
Haydens Park Walk	34	D3
Haydens Park Way	34	D3
Haymarket	70	F4
Haymarket House	70	F4
*Hayworth Close (off Hayworth Drive)	21	B1
Hayworth Court	21	B1
Hayworth Drive	21	B1
Hayworth Mews	21	A1
Hayworth Place	21	A1
Hayworth Rise	21	A1
Hayworth Terrace	21	A1
Hazel Ave	58	D1
Hazel Court	14	F2
Hazel Grove	14	F2
Hazel Lane	26	F4
Hazel Lawn (Blanchardstown)	22	E2
*Hazel Lawn (off Carriglea Ave Kill O'The Grange)	59	C2
*Hazel Park (off Kimmage Road Lower)	46	E2
Hazel Road	26	D3
Hazel Villas	58	D1
Hazelbrook (Malahide)	14	E1
Hazelbrook (Tymon North)	45	B4
Hazelbrook (Kilmacud)	58	D1
*Hazelbrook Apts (off Hazelbrook Court)	46	E2
Hazelbrook Court	46	E2
Hazelbrook Drive	46	E2
Hazelbrook Road	46	E2
Hazelbrook Square	47	A4
Hazelbury Green	8	E4
Hazelbury Park	8	E4
Hazelcroft Gardens	24	E2
Hazelcroft Green	24	E2
Hazelcroft Park	24	E2
Hazelcroft Road	24	E2
Hazeldene	47	C1
Hazeldine Apts	67	C4
Hazelgrove	54	D2
Hazelgrove Court	54	E2
Hazelhatch	41	B1
Hazelhatch Park	32	F2
Hazelhatch Road	41	C3
Hazelwood (Santry Ave)	12	D4
Hazelwood (Shankill)	64	E2
Hazelwood (Bray)	67	B2
Hazelwood Ave	21	C1

STREET NAME	PAGE	GRID REF
Hazelwood Bank	44	D2
Hazelwood Close	44	D2
Hazelwood Court (Hartstown)	21	C1
Hazelwood Court (Beaumont)	26	D1
Hazelwood Cres (Hartstown)	21	C1
Hazelwood Cres (Clondalkin)	44	D2
Hazelwood Cres (Bray)	67	B4
Hazelwood Drive	26	D2
Hazelwood Green	21	C1
Hazelwood Grove	26	D1
Hazelwood House	75	B4
Hazelwood Lane	44	D2
Hazelwood Park	26	D1
Hazelwood View	44	D2
Hazlebury Park	8	E4
Headford Grove	47	B4
Headfort Court (Hill Street)	71	C2
Healthfield Road	46	F2
Healy Street (off Rutland Place North)	71	C2
Heaney Ave	35	C4
*Heany Ave (off Coliemore Road)	60	F2
Heath Square (off Mckee Ave)	24	E1
Heather Close	57	A2
Heather Court	58	E2
Heather Drive	57	A2
Heather Gardens	4	D4
Heather Grove (Palmerston)	35	B2
Heather Grove (Ballinteer)	57	B2
Heather Lawn	57	A2
Heather Park	57	B2
Heather Road (Ballinteer)	57	A2
Heather Road (Burton Hall)	58	E2
Heather View Ave	54	F2
Heather View Close	54	F2
Heather View Drive	54	F2
Heather View Lawn	54	F2
Heather View Park	54	F2
Heather View Road	54	F2
Heather Walk	4	D4
Heatherwood	67	B4
*Heathfield (off Monkstown Road)	49	B4
Heathfield	23	C1
Heathfield Ave	23	C1
Heathfield Cres	23	C1
Heathfield Green	23	C1
Heathfield Park	23	C1
Heathfield Terrace	23	C1
Heathfield View	23	C1
Heathfield Way	23	C1
*Heatley Villas (on Pearse Road)	59	C2
Heidelberg	48	D3
*Hempenstal Terrace (off Durham Road)	39	B4
Hendrick Lane	70	E4
Hendrick Place	70	E4
Hendrick Street	70	F4
*Henley Court (off Henley Villas)	47	B4
Henley Park	47	B4
Henley Villas	47	B4
Henrietta Lane	71	A2
Henrietta Place	71	A3
Henrietta Street	71	A3
Henry Place	71	B3
Henry Road	36	D4
Henry Street	71	B3
Herbert Ave	48	E1
Herbert Cottages (off Merrion Road)	76	F3
*Herbert Court (off Hollyrood Park)	39	A4
Herbert Cres	22	F2
Herbert House	76	E1
Herbert Lane	76	D2
Herbert Park (Ballsbridge)	76	F4
Herbert Park (Oldcourt)	67	B3
Herbert Park Lane	76	F4
Herbert Park Mews	47	C1
Herbert Place (Baggot Street Lower)	76	D2
*Herbert Place (off Bath Street)	39	A3
Herbert Road (Blanchardstown)	22	F2
Herbert Road (Sandymount)	39	A4
Herbert Road (Oldcourt)	67	B3
Herbert Street	76	D2
*Herbert View (Pearse Square, Bray)	67	B2
Herberton Apts	74	D2
Herberton Bridge (Grand Canal)	73	C3
Herberton Drive	74	D3
Herberton Park	73	C2
Herberton Road	73	C2

STREET NAME	PAGE	GRID REF
Herberton Street	74	D2
Herberton Walk	74	D2
Hermitage Ave	56	F1
Hermitage Close	56	F1
Hermitage Court	57	A1
Hermitage Cres	34	F1
Hermitage Downs	57	A1
Hermitage Drive	56	F1
Hermitage Garden	34	F1
Hermitage Green	34	F1
Hermitage Grove	56	F1
Hermitage Lawn	56	F1
Hermitage Manor	34	F1
Hermitage Park (Lucan)	34	F1
Hermitage Park (Grange Road)	56	F1
Hermitage Place	34	F1
Hermitage Road	34	F1
Hermitage Road	34	F1
Hermitage Valley	34	F1
Hermitage View	56	F1
Hermitage Way	34	F1
Heronford Lane	63	C2
Heskin Court	48	E2
Heuston Square	73	A1
*Heuston Square South (Military Road)	69	C4
Hewardine Terrace (off Killarney Street)	72	D2
Heymarket Way	70	F4
Heytesbury Court (off Merrion Road)	76	E3
Heytesbury Lane	76	E4
Heytesbury Street	75	A3
Hibernian Ave	72	E2
Hibernian Road	72	E4
*Hibernian Terrace (off Chapelizod Road)	36	E2
High Park	25	C2
High Street (Christ Church)	75	A1
*High Street (off Old Blessington Road)	55	A1
Highdownhill	51	C1
Highfield Ave (Dundrum)	57	A2
Highfield Close	1	C2
*Highfield Court (off Highfield Road)	47	A2
Highfield Cres	1	C2
Highfield Downs	1	C2
Highfield Drive	57	A2
Highfield Green	1	C2
Highfield Grove	47	A2
Highfield Lawn	1	C2
Highfield Manor	47	A2
*Highfield Mews (off Rathmines Road Upper)	47	A2
Highfield Park (Celbridge Road)	33	A1
Highfield Park (Churchtown)	47	B3
Highfield Road	47	A2
Highland Ave	59	B3
Highland Grove	59	B3
Highland Lawn	59	B3
Highland View	59	B3
Highridge Green	58	E1
Highthorn Park	59	C1
*Highthorn Woods (off Highthorn Park)	59	C1
*Hill Cottages (off Killiney Hill Road)	60	E3
Hill Court	14	F1
Hill Crest	3	C4
Hill Drive	3	B3
Hill Street	71	B2
Hillbrook Woods	22	D1
Hillcourt	47	A2
Hillcourt Park	60	D2
Hillcourt Road	60	D2
Hillcrest (Malahide)	3	A2
Hillcrest (Lucan)	34	D2
*Hillcrest (off Templeogue Road)	46	D4
Hillcrest (Rathgar)	47	A2
Hillcrest Ave	33	C2
Hillcrest Close	33	C2
*Hillcrest Court (off Griffith Ave)	25	A3
Hillcrest Court	34	D2
Hillcrest Downs	58	D3
Hillcrest Drive	33	C2
Hillcrest Green	33	C2
Hillcrest Grove	34	D2
Hillcrest Heights	33	C2
Hillcrest Lawns	33	C2
*Hillcrest Manor (off Templeogue Road)	46	D4
Hillcrest Park (Glasnevin)	24	F2
Hillcrest Park (Lucan)	33	C2
Hillcrest Road (Lucan)	34	D2
Hillcrest Road (Sandyford)	58	D3
Hillcrest View	33	C2
Hillcrest Walk	33	C2
Hillcrest Way	33	C2
Hillsbrook Ave	46	D2
Hillsbrook Cres	46	D2
Hillsbrook Drive	46	D2
Hillsbrook Grove	46	D2
Hillside	60	E2
Hillside Drive	47	A3
Hillside Park	56	E1
*Hillside Terrace (south of Church on Main Street Howth)	30	D2
Hilltop Lawn	64	D3
Hilltown	1	B3
Hilltown Close	1	C2
Hilltown Court	1	C2
Hilltown Cres	1	A2
Hilltown Green	1	C2
Hilltown Grove	1	C2
Hilltown Lawn	1	C2
Hilltown Park	1	C2
Hilltown Road	1	C2
Hilltown Way	1	C2
Hillview	52	E2
*Hillview Cottages (off Hillview Drive)	59	C2
*Hillview Court (off Beech Lawn Ave)	57	B1
Hillview Drive	59	C2
Hillview Estate	57	B1
*Hillview Glade (off Beech Lawn Ave)	57	B1
Hillview Grove	57	B1
Hillview Lawns	59	C2
Hilton Gardens	57	C2
Hilton Mews (Harcourt Terrace)	75	C3
Hoey Close	14	E4
Hoey Court	14	E4
Hoey Place	14	E4
*Hoeys Court (off Werburgh Street)	75	A1
Hogan Ave	76	E1
*Hogan House (off Stonepark Court)	46	F4
Hogan Place	76	D1
Hogan Square	76	E1
*Hogan View Apts (Convent Ave)	25	B4
Holles Place	76	D1
Holles Row	76	D1
Holles Street	76	D1
Holly Ave	58	D1
Holly Court	64	D1
Holly Park	64	E2
Holly Park Ave	59	A1
Holly Road (Donnycarney)	26	D3
Holly Road (Fox and Geese)	44	F1
Holly Tree Square	11	C4
Holly Tree Terrace	11	C4
Hollybank Ave Lower	47	B1
Hollybank Ave Upper	47	B1
Hollybank Road	25	A4
Hollybrook	59	A3
*Hollybrook Court (off Hollybrook Road)	26	D4
*Hollybrook Court Drive (off Hollybrook Road)	26	D4
Hollybrook Grove	26	D4
Hollybrook Manor	26	D4
*Hollybrook Mews (off Hollybrook Park)	26	D4
*Hollybrook Mews (Copeland Grove)	26	D4
Hollybrook Park (Clontarf)	26	D4
Hollybrook Park (Irishtown)	67	C4
Hollybrook Road (off Hollybrook Park)	26	D4
*Hollybrook Wood (off Hollybrook Park)	26	D4
*Hollybrook Wood (Hollybrook Grove)	26	D4
*Hollybrooke (off Bluebell Ave)	36	E4
*Hollyrood Apts (off Hollyrood Park)	39	A4
Hollystown	9	B1
Hollystown Demesne	9	B1
Hollystown Park	9	B1
Hollyville Lawn	35	C1
Hollywell	11	C4
Hollywood Drive	48	D4
Hollywood Park	48	D4
*Holme's Cottages (on Church Ave Rathmines)	47	A1
Holmston Ave	60	D1
Holmwood	59	B4
*Holycross Ave (off Clonliffe Road)	25	B4
*Holycross Cottages (off Holycross Ave)	25	B4
Holyrood Park	39	A4
Holywell	58	D1
Holywell Ave (in Holywell Estate)	2	E3
Holywell Ave (Kilbarrack)	27	B1
Holywell Close	2	E3
Holywell Court	2	D3
Holywell Cres (Kilbarrack)	27	B1
Holywell Cres North	2	D3
Holywell Cres South	2	D3
Holywell Dale	2	D3
Holywell Dene	2	D3
Holywell Drive	2	D3
Holywell Gardens	2	D3
Holywell Green	2	E3
Holywell Grove	2	E3
Holywell Heath	2	D3
Holywell Heights	2	D3
Holywell Lawn	2	E4
Holywell Manor	2	D3
Holywell Meadow	2	E4
*Holywell Mews (in Holywell Estate)	2	D3
Holywell Park	2	D3
Holywell Place	2	D3
Holywell Rise	2	D3
Holywell Road (in Holywell Estate)	2	D3
Holywell Road (Kilbarrack)	27	B1
*Holywell Row (in Holywell Estate)	2	D3
Holywell Square	2	E3
Holywell View	2	E3
Holywell Villas	2	D3
Holywell Walk	2	D3
Holywell Way	2	E3
Holywell Wood	2	D3
Home Farm Park	25	B3
Home Farm Road	25	A3
Home Villas	47	C1
Homelawn Ave	55	B1
Homelawn Drive	55	B1
Homelawn Gardens	55	B1
Homelawn Road	55	A1
Homelawn Villas	55	A1
*Homelee (off Serpentine Park)	39	A4
Homeleigh	22	D4
Homestead Court	24	E4
*Homeville (off Ballycullen Road)	55	C1
*Homeville Court (off Ballycullen Road)	55	C1
*Honey Park (off Sallynoggin Road)	60	D2
Hope Ave	72	E1
Hope Street (off Gordon Street)	76	F1
*Hopkins Square (off Owenstown Park Fosters Ave)	48	D3
*Horan Hall (off Belgard Square West)	54	F1
Horan's Lane	54	E3
Horse Fair	72	E4
Horton Court	46	F2
Hotel Yard	71	B3
Houghton Terrace	70	E3
Howard Street (off Gordon Street)	76	F1
Howth	30	D2
Howth Harbour	30	D1
*Howth House Apts (off Harbour Road, close to Post Office)	30	D1
Howth Junction Cottages (off Kilbarrack Road)	27	B1
Howth Lodge Apts	29	C1
*Howth Peninsula Apts (off Harbour Road, opposite west pier)	30	D1
Howth Road (Marino)	26	D4
Howth Road (Killester)	26	E3
Howth Road (Saint Anns Park)	26	F3
Howth Road (Raheny)	27	B2
Howth Road (Sutton)	29	B1
Howth Road (Howth)	29	C1
Howth Road Apts	26	E3
*Howth Terrace (at Saint Laurence Road, Police Station)	30	D1
Howth View Park	27	B1
Huband Bridge (Grand Canal)	76	E2
Huband Road	36	F4
Hudson Road	60	E1
Hughes Road East	45	C1
Hughes Road North	45	C1
Hughes Road South	45	C1
Hume Ave	35	C4
Hume Ave	36	D4
Hume Street	75	C2
Hunters Ave	55	C3
Hunters Court	55	C3
Hunters Cres	55	C3
Hunters Green	55	C3
Hunters Grove	55	C3
*Hunters Hall (off Hunters Place)	55	C3
Hunters Hill	55	C3
Hunters Lane	55	C3
Hunters Meadow	55	C3
Hunters Parade	55	C3
Hunters Place	55	C3
*Hunter's Row (off Seapark Road)	26	F4
Hunters Run	8	E4
Hunters Run The Close	8	E4
Hunters Run The Drive	8	E4
Hunters Run The Glade	8	E4
Hunters Run The Grove	8	E4
Hunters Run The Park	8	E4
Hunters Run The Rise	8	E4
Hunters Run The View	8	E4
Hunters Run The Way	8	E4
Hunters Walk	55	C3
Hunters Way	55	C3
Huntstown Ave	21	C1
Huntstown Close	8	F4
Huntstown Court	8	F4
Huntstown Drive	8	F4
Huntstown Glen	8	F4
Huntstown Green	8	F4
Huntstown Grove	8	F4
Huntstown Lawn	22	D1
Huntstown Park	8	F4
Huntstown Rise	9	A4
Huntstown Road	21	C1
Huntstown Way	9	A4
Huntstown Wood	8	F4
Hutchinson's Strand	2	E1
Huttonread	51	C4
Huxley Court	74	E2
Huxley Cres	74	E2
Hyacinth Street	72	E2
Hybla Court	23	C4
Hybreasal	73	B2
Hybreasal Apts	73	B2
Hyde Park (Templeogue)	46	E3
Hyde Park (Dalkey)	60	E1
Hyde Park Ave	48	F3
Hyde Park Gardens	48	F3
Hyde Road	60	F1
*Hyde Square (Kilmainham)	73	B2
*Hyde Square (off Owenstown Park Fosters Ave)	48	D3
*Hyde Square Apts (off South Circular Road)	73	B2
Hynestown	42	D2

I

STREET NAME	PAGE	GRID REF
Idrone Ave	56	D1
Idrone Close	56	D1
Idrone Drive	56	D1
*Idrone Mews (off Idrone Terrace)	49	A3
Idrone Park	56	D1
Idrone Terrace	49	A3
Imaal Road	70	E1
Inagh Court	64	E1
Inagh Road	36	D3
Inbhir Ide	3	A2
Inbhir Ide Close	3	A2
Inbhir Ide Drive	3	A2
Inchicore	73	A1
Inchicore Road	73	A1
*Inchicore Square (off Inchicore Terrace South)	36	F3
*Inchicore Terrace North (off Inchicore Terrace South)	36	F3
Inchicore Terrace South	36	F3

STREET NAME	PAGE	GRID REF
Infirmary Road	69	C3
Inglewood Close	21	C2
Inglewood Cres	21	C2
Inglewood Drive	21	C2
Inglewood Road	21	C2
Ingram Road	74	F3
Inis Fáil	54	F2
Inis Thiar	54	F2
Inishowen	12	F3
*Inkerman Cottages (off Amiens Street)	72	D2
Innisfallen Parade	71	B1
Innishmaan Road	25	B2
Innishmore Terrace (Saint Mary's Road)	46	D1
Innismore	46	D1
*Inns Court (on Winetavern Street)	75	A1
Inns Quay	70	F4
Inver Road	24	E4
*Invermore Grove (off Carraroe Ave)	27	A1
Inverness Road	25	C4
Iona Ave	25	A4
Iona Cres	25	A4
Iona Drive	25	A4
Iona Park	25	A4
Iona Road	25	A4
Iona Villas	25	A4
Iris Grove	48	E3
Irishtown (Ringsend)	39	A3
Irishtown (Bray)	67	C4
Irishtown Road	39	A3
Irvine Cottages	72	F3
Irvine Terrace	72	F3
Irwin Court	73	C1
Irwin Street	73	C1
Island Key	72	F2
Island Street	70	E4
Island View (Malahide)	3	C3
Island View (Kilbarrack)	27	C2
*Island View Apts (off Harbour Road, close to Post Office)	30	D1
Island View Court Apts	27	C2
Island Villa	76	E1
Islandbridge	69	B4
Islandbridge Court	69	B4
Islandbridge Gate (Phoenix Park)	69	A4
Islington Ave	50	E4
Isolda Road	39	A3
*Isolde Gardens (off Martin's Row Chapelizod)	36	E2
*Isolde House Apts (off Martin's Row Chapelizod)	36	E2
Ivar Street	70	E3
Iveagh Buildings	75	A2
Iveagh Court	75	B3
*Iveagh Exchange Apts (Granby Place)	71	B3
Iveagh Gardens	73	B4
*Iveagh Trust (Bride Road)	75	A1
Iveleary Road	25	B2
Iveragh Court (off Seafort Ave)	76	F3
Iveragh Road	25	B2
Ivy Cottages	75	C4
*Ivy Court (off Ballyshannon Road)	25	C1
Ivy Terrace	74	E2

J

Jackson's Bridge	17	A3
James Connolly Park	35	A4
*James Connolly Square (Saint Kevin's Square)	67	C2
James Everett Park	67	B2
James Joyce Bridge (River Liffey)	70	E4
*James Joyce Court (off Ferguson Road)	25	A3
James Joyce Court (off Sutton Downs)	27	C1
James Joyce Street	71	C3
James Larkin Road	27	B2
*James McCormack Gardens (off Burrowfield Road)	29	A1
James Plunkett House	36	F3
James's Place East	76	D2

STREET NAME	PAGE	GRID REF
James's Street	74	D1
James's Street East	76	D2
James's Street North	72	E1
James's Terrace	3	B2
*James's Terrace Upper (off James Terrace)	3	B2
Jamestown	62	F1
Jamestown Ave	36	F4
Jamestown Cottages	62	F1
Jamestown Court	36	F4
Jamestown Road (Poppintree)	11	B4
Jamestown Road (Finglas)	24	F1
Jamestown Road (Inchicore)	36	F4
Jamestown Road (Grand Canal)	36	E4
*Jamestown Square (Jamestown Road)	36	F4
*Jane-Ville (off Tivoli Road)	50	D4
Jerome Connor Place	69	C3
Jervis Lane Lower	71	A4
Jervis Lane Upper	71	A3
Jervis Street	71	A3
Jobstown	54	D2
Jobstown Road	54	D2
*Jobstown Village Square (off Jobstown Road)	54	D1
*Joe Sartini Court (near Temple Buildings)	71	A2
John Dillon Street	75	A1
John F Kennedy Ave	45	A1
John F Kennedy Drive	45	A1
John F Kennedy Park	36	D4
John F Kennedy Road	36	D4
John Field Road	75	A1
John MacCormack Ave	45	C1
John McCormack Bridge (Tolka River)	72	F1
John Street North (off Ellis Quay)	70	E4
John Street South	74	F2
John Street West	74	F1
Johns Court (Christchurch)	74	F1
*John's Court (Dolphins Barn Street)	74	E2
John's Lane East	75	A1
John's Lane West	74	F1
Johnsbridge	34	D3
Johnsbridge Ave	34	D3
Johnsbridge Close	34	D3
Johnsbridge Green	34	D3
Johnsbridge Grove	34	D3
Johnsbridge Meadows	34	D3
Johnsbridge Park	34	D3
Johnsbridge Walk	34	D3
Johnson Place	75	B1
Johnson's Court	75	B1
Johnstown	51	C4
Johnstown Ave	59	C3
Johnstown Court	59	C2
Johnstown Gardens	24	E2
Johnstown Grove	59	C3
*Johnstown House (off Johnstown Park)	24	F2
Johnstown Lane	59	C3
Johnstown Park (Glasnevin)	24	F2
Johnstown Park (Cornelscourt)	59	C3
Johnstown Road (Rathcoole)	52	E2
Johnstown Road (Cornelscourt)	59	C3
*Jones Terrace (Sidmonton Ave)	68	D2
Jones's Road	71	C1
Jordanstown	42	F4
Jordanstown Ave (Greenogue Industrial Estate)	42	F4
Jordanstown Drive (Greenogue Industrial Estate)	42	F4
Jordanstown Road (Greenogue Industrial Estate)	42	F4
Josephine Ave	71	B1
Joy Street (off Gordon Street)	76	F1
Joyce Ave	59	A3
Joyce Hall	59	B4
Joyce Road (Drumcondra)	25	A3
Joyce Way	35	C4
Jugback Close	1	C1
Jugback Court	1	C1
Jugback Cres	1	C1
Jugback Green	1	Inset
Jugback Lane	1	C1
Juliet Square	35	B1

K

STREET NAME	PAGE	GRID REF
Kavanagh Ave	36	D4
Keadeen Ave	45	B2
Kearneystown Lower	41	A3
Kearn's Place	73	B1
Keatingspark	52	D2
*Keegan's Cottages (off Merrion Road)	48	E1
Keeloges	42	D3
Keeper Road	73	C3
Kells Road	46	E1
Kelly's Ave	50	D4
Kelly's Lane (Phibsborough)	71	A1
*Kelly's Lane (off main street and Pound Lane)	17	C3
Kelly's Row	71	B1
Kelly's Square	71	B1
Kellystown Lane	19	A3
Kellystown Road	57	B4
Kelston Ave	59	A2
Kelston Drive	59	A2
*Kelston Hall (off Kelston Drive)	59	A2
Kelston Park	59	A2
Kelston View	59	A2
Kelvin Close	4	D4
Kempton	23	C3
Kempton Ave	23	C3
Kempton Court	23	C3
Kempton Green	23	C3
Kempton Grove	23	C3
Kempton Heath	23	C3
Kempton Lawn	23	C3
Kempton Park	23	C3
Kempton Rise	23	C3
Kempton View	23	C3
Kempton Way	23	C3
Kenah Court	60	E3
*Kengar Mews (off Rathgar Ave)	46	F1
Kenilworth Lane	46	F1
*Kenilworth Manor (off Harold's Cross Road)	46	F1
Kenilworth Park	46	F1
Kenilworth Road	47	A1
Kenilworth Square	46	F1
Kenilworth Square East	47	A1
Kenilworth Square North	46	F1
Kenilworth Square South	46	F1
Kenilworth Square West	46	F1
Kenmare Parade	71	B1
*Kennedy Court (off Pembroke Street)	39	A3
*Kennedy Park (off Boghall Road)	67	C3
Kennelsfort Green	35	B2
Kennelsfort Road Lower	35	C1
Kennelsfort Road Upper	35	C2
*Kennilworth Lodge (off Harold's Cross Road)	46	F1
Kennington Close	45	C4
Kennington Cres	45	C4
Kennington Lawn	45	C4
Kennington Road	45	C3
*Kensington Lodge (off Rochestown Ave)	59	C2
*Kent Terrace (on Barnhill Road)	60	F2
Kentfield	64	E2
Kerlogue Road	39	A3
*Kerrygold House (off Harold's Cross Road)	46	F1
Kerrymount Ave	59	A4
*Kerrymount Close (off Kerrymount Rise)	59	B3
Kerrymount Green	59	B3
Kerrymount Mall	59	B3
Kerrymount Rise	59	B3
Kettles Drive	2	E4
Kettles Lane	2	E4
Kettles Place	2	E4
Kevin Barry Flats (off Church Street Upper)	70	F3
*Kevin Street Cross (on New Bride Street)	75	A2
Kevin Street Lower	75	A2
Kevin Street Upper	75	A2
Kew Park	33	C1
Kew Park Ave	33	B2

STREET NAME	PAGE	GRID REF
Kew Park Cres	33	B1
Kickham Road	73	B2
Kilakee Close	45	B3
Kilakee Drive	45	B3
Kilbarrack	27	C1
Kilbarrack Ave	27	C2
Kilbarrack Gardens	27	C2
Kilbarrack Grove	27	C2
Kilbarrack Parade	27	B1
Kilbarrack Road	27	B1
Kilbarrack Way	27	B1
Kilbarron Ave	26	D1
*Kilbarron Court (off Kilbarron Park)	26	D1
Kilbarron Drive	26	D1
Kilbarron Park	26	D1
Kilbarron Road	26	D1
*Kilbegnet Close (off Castle Street Dalkey)	60	F2
Kilbogget Grove	59	C4
*Kilbogget Villas (off Bray Road)	59	C4
Kilbride	43	A3
Kilbride Grove	67	B3
Kilbride Lane	67	B3
Kilbride Road (Killester)	26	E3
Kilbrina	7	B2
Kilcarberry Ave	43	C2
Kilcarberry Close	43	C2
Kilcarberry Court	43	C2
Kilcarberry Lawn	43	C2
Kilcarbery	43	B2
Kilcarrig Ave	44	E4
Kilcarrig Close	54	E1
Kilcarrig Cres	44	E4
Kilcarrig Green	44	E4
Kilclare Ave	54	E2
Kilclare Cres	54	E2
Kilclare Drive	54	E2
Kilclare Gardens	54	E2
Kilcloon	5	A2
Kilcloon Lawns	5	A2
Kilcock Maynooth Leixlip ByPass	32	E1
Kilcock Road	17	C3
Kilcock-Maynooth-Leixlip Bypass	33	A1
*Kilcolman Court (off Glenageary Road Upper)	60	E2
Kilcronan Ave	34	E4
Kilcronan Close	34	E4
Kilcronan Court	34	E4
Kilcronan Cres	34	E4
Kilcronan Grove	34	E4
Kilcronan Lawns	34	E4
Kilcronan View	34	E4
Kilcroney Lane	67	A4
Kilcross Ave	58	D3
Kilcross Close	58	D3
Kilcross Court	57	C3
Kilcross Cres	57	C3
Kilcross Drive	57	C3
Kilcross Grove	57	C3
Kilcross Lawn	58	D3
Kilcross Park	57	C3
Kilcross Road	58	D3
Kilcross Square	57	C3
Kilcross Way	57	C3
Kildare Bridge	18	D2
Kildare Park	46	D1
Kildare Place	75	C1
Kildare Road	46	D1
Kildare Street	75	C1
Kildonan Ave	24	D1
Kildonan Court	24	D1
Kildonan Drive	24	D1
Kildonan Road	24	D1
Kildress House	76	D2
Kilfenora Drive	27	A1
Kilfenora Road	46	E1
Kilgarran	66	D3
Kilgarron Park	66	D3
Kilgobbin Grove	58	E4
*Kilgobbin Heights	58	E4
Kilgobbin Lane	58	D4
*Kilgobbin Lawn (off Kilgobbin Grove)	58	E4
Kilgobbin Road	58	E3
Kilgobbin Wood	58	E4
Kilgraigue	5	B3
*Kilgrastor Court (Oldcourt Park)	67	B3
Kilkieran Court	24	E4
Kilkieran Road	24	E4
Kill Abbey	59	B1
Kill Ave	59	B1

STREET NAME	PAGE	GRID REF
Kill Lane	59	B2
Kill O' the Grange	59	C1
Killadoon Park	31	C4
Killakee Ave	55	B2
Killakee Close	45	B3
Killakee Court	55	B2
Killakee Drive	45	B2
Killakee Gardens	55	B2
Killakee Green	55	B2
Killakee Grove	55	B2
Killakee Lawns	55	B2
Killakee Park	55	B2
Killakee Rise	55	B2
Killakee Road	56	D4
Killakee View	55	B2
Killakee Walk	55	B2
Killakee Way	55	B2
Killala Road	24	E4
Killan Court	72	F3
Killan Road	72	F3
Killarney Ave	72	D2
Killarney Court (on Killarney Ave)	72	D2
*Killarney Court (Oldcourt Park)	67	B3
Killarney Glen	67	B2
Killarney Heights	67	B3
Killarney Lane	67	B3
Killarney Parade	71	B1
Killarney Park	67	B3
Killarney Road	67	B3
Killarney Street	72	D2
*Killarney Villas (near Market House)	67	C2
Killary Grove	27	B1
Killeany	5	A4
Killeck	1	A2
Killeck Lane	1	A3
Killeen	2	F3
Killeen Ave	2	F3
Killeen Court	2	F3
Killeen Cres	2	F3
Killeen Mews	3	B3
Killeen Park	2	F3
Killeen Road (Bluebell)	36	D4
Killeen Road (Fox and Geese)	45	A1
Killeen Road (Rathmines)	47	B1
Killeen Terrace	3	B3
Killegar	65	C1
*Killery Terrace (on Upper Dargle Road)	67	B2
Killester	26	E3
Killester Ave	26	E3
*Killester Court (off Killester Park)	26	E3
*Killester Park (off Killester Park)	26	E3
Killester Park	26	E3
Killinarden	54	E3
Killinarden Estate	54	E2
Killinarden Heights	54	E2
Killinarden Road	54	E3
Killiney	60	E3
Killiney Ave	60	E4
*Killiney Court (Seafield Road near Seafield Court)	64	E1
Killiney Gate	60	E4
Killiney Grove	60	E4
Killiney Heath	60	E4
Killiney Hill Road	60	E3
Killiney Hill Road	64	E1
*Killiney Oaks (Seafield Road near Seafield Court)	64	E1
Killiney Road	60	E2
*Killiney Terrace (off Breffni Road)	60	E1
*Killiney Towers (off Killiney Road)	60	E2
Killiney View	60	E1
Killininny Cottages	55	B2
*Killininny Court Apts (off Kilakee Grove)	55	B2
Killininny Road	55	B2
*Killshannig (on Crinken Lane)	64	D4
Kilmactalway	42	F3
Kilmacud	58	E1
Kilmacud Ave	58	E1
Kilmacud Park	58	E1
Kilmacud Road Upper	58	E1
Kilmahuddrick Ave	43	B1
Kilmahuddrick Close	43	B1
Kilmahuddrick Court	43	B1
Kilmahuddrick Cres	43	B1
Kilmahuddrick Drive	43	B1
Kilmahuddrick Green	43	B1
Kilmahuddrick Grove	43	B1
Kilmahuddrick Lawn	43	B1
Kilmahuddrick Place	43	B1
Kilmahuddrick Road	43	B1
Kilmahuddrick Walk	43	B1
Kilmahuddrick Way	43	B1
Kilmainham	73	B1
Kilmainham Bank	73	A1
Kilmainham Lane	73	C1
Kilmainham Orchard	73	B1
Kilmainham Square (South Circular/Inchicore Road)	73	B1
Kilmalin	65	C3
*Kilmantain Place (near Market House)	67	C2
Kilmartin Ave	54	D1
Kilmartin Cres	44	D4
Kilmartin Drive	54	D1
Kilmartin Gardens	54	D1
Kilmartin Green	54	D1
Kilmartin Park	54	D1
Kilmashogue Bridge	56	F3
Kilmashogue Close	45	B3
Kilmashogue Drive	45	B3
Kilmashogue Grove	45	B3
Kilmashogue Lane	56	F3
Kilmore	26	D1
Kilmore Ave (Coolock)	26	E1
Kilmore Ave (Killiney)	60	E4
Kilmore Close	26	E1
*Kilmore Court (off Kilmore Road)	26	D1
Kilmore Cres	26	E1
Kilmore Drive	26	E1
Kilmore Place Apts	26	D1
Kilmore Road	26	D1
Kilmorony Close	27	A1
Kilnamanagh	45	A3
Kilnamanagh Court	45	C1
Kilnamanagh Estate	45	A3
Kilnamanagh Road	45	C1
Kilrock Road	30	E2
*Kilronan Court (off Howth Road)	26	D4
Kilshane	10	E2
Kilshane Ave	10	D2
*Kilshane Court (Ratoath Ave)	23	C2
Kilshane Cross	10	F2
Kilshane Drive	10	E3
Kilshane Drive	23	C2
Kilshane Park	10	D2
Kilshane Road (North Road)	10	E3
Kilshane Road (Rathoath Road)	23	C2
Kilshane View	10	D2
Kilshane Way	10	D3
Kiltalown	54	D3
Kiltalown Ave	54	D2
Kiltalown Close	54	D2
Kiltalown Cottages	54	D2
Kiltalown Court	54	D2
Kiltalown Cres	54	D2
Kiltalown Drive	54	D2
Kiltalown Green	54	D2
Kiltalown Grove	54	D2
Kiltalown Heights	54	D2
Kiltalown Hill	54	D2
Kiltalown Park	54	D2
Kiltalown Path	54	D2
Kiltalown Road	54	D2
Kiltalown View	54	D2
Kiltalown Walk	54	D2
Kiltalown Way	54	D2
Kilteel Road	52	E2
Kilteragh Drive	59	A3
*Kilteragh Pines (off Westminister Road)	59	A3
Kilteragh Road	59	A3
Kilternan	62	F2
Kilternan Bridge	62	F3
Kiltipper	54	E2
Kiltipper Ave	55	A2
Kiltipper Close	55	A2
Kiltipper Drive	55	A2
Kiltipper Gate	54	F3
Kiltipper Rise	54	F3
Kiltipper Road	55	A3
Kiltipper View	54	F3
Kiltipper Way	54	F3
*Kiltuck Park (beside Medical Centre)	64	E4
Kilvere	46	E4
Kilvere Park	46	D4
Kilwogan Manor	31	C2
Kilworth Road	36	F4
Kimmage	46	D2
*Kimmage Court (off Kimmage Road Lower)	46	E2
Kimmage Grove	46	E2
Kimmage Manor Way	46	D2
Kimmage Road Lower	46	F1
Kimmage Road West	46	D2
Kinahan Street	70	D3
Kincora Ave	26	E4
Kincora Court	39	C1
Kincora Drive	26	E4
Kincora Grove	26	E4
Kincora Park	26	E4
Kincora Road	26	E4
*Kincora Walk (on Hazel Lane)	26	F4
*King Edward Court (King Edward Lane)	67	C2
King Edward Lawn	67	C2
King Edward Park	67	B2
King Edward Road	67	B2
King Street North	70	F3
King Street South	75	B1
King William's Rampart	24	D2
Kingram Place	75	C3
King's Ave	72	D1
King's Court	70	E2
*Kings Court Apts (Beside Chapel Lane)	71	B3
*Kings Court Apts (Brunswick Street North)	70	F3
King's Hall	36	E2
*Kings House Apts (off Bow Bridge)	74	D1
Kings Inns	71	A3
King's Inns Court	71	A2
King's Inns Street	71	A3
Kingsbry	17	C4
Kingsland Parade	75	A3
Kingsland Park Ave	75	A3
*Kingsmill Court (near Yarnhall Street)	71	A3
*Kingsmill Court Apts (Yarnhall Street)	71	A3
Kingsmill Road	67	C2
Kingston	57	B3
Kingston Ave	57	B3
Kingston Close	57	B3
Kingston Court	56	F2
Kingston Cres	57	B3
Kingston Drive	57	C3
Kingston Green	57	B3
Kingston Grove	57	B3
Kingston Hall	57	B3
Kingston Heights	57	C3
Kingston Lawn	57	B3
*Kingston Lodge (off Clonliffe Road)	25	B4
Kingston Park	57	B3
Kingston Rise	57	B3
Kingston View	57	B3
Kingston Walk	57	B3
Kingswood	43	C3
Kingswood Ave (Citywest)	43	C4
Kingswood Ave (Kilnamanagh)	44	F3
Kingswood Castle	45	A2
Kingswood Drive (Citywest)	43	C4
Kingswood Drive (Kilnamanagh)	44	F3
Kingswood Heights	44	F3
Kingswood Interchange (Junction 2)	43	C3
Kingswood Manor	44	F3
Kingswood Manor Apts	44	F3
Kingswood Road	43	C4
Kingswood View	44	F3
Kinsaley	14	D1
Kinsaley Bridge	14	D1
Kinsaley Lane	3	A4
Kinsealy Court	2	E3
Kinsealy Downs	2	E3
Kinsealy Lane	14	D1
Kinvara Ave	24	D4
Kinvara Drive	23	C4
Kinvara Grove	23	C4
Kinvara Park	24	D4
Kinvara Road	23	C4
Kippure Ave	45	B3
Kippure Park	24	D3
Kirbrensis Manor	21	A1
Kirkfield	22	D2
Kirkpatrick Ave	22	D3
Kirkpatrick Drive	22	D3
Kirkwood	39	A4
Kirwan Street	70	E3
Kirwan Street Cottages	70	E2
Kitestown Road	30	E3
*Knapton Court (off York Road Dún Laoghaire)	49	C4
*Knapton Lawn (off Knapton Road)	49	C4
Knapton Road	49	C4
*Knapton Terrace (off Knapton Road)	49	C4
*Knapton Villas (on Knapton Road)	49	C4
*Knights Bridge (off Castle Ave Clontarf)	26	E4
Knights Wood	12	E4
Knock Riada	36	D2
Knockaire	56	D1
Knockandinny	52	E4
Knockaulin	20	D4
Knockcullen	56	D1
Knockcullen Drive	56	D1
Knockcullen Lawn	56	D1
Knockcullen Park	56	D1
Knockcullen Rise	56	D1
Knockdara	3	C3
Knockfield Manor	55	C1
Knocklyon	56	D1
Knocklyon Ave	55	C1
Knocklyon Close	56	D1
Knocklyon Court	56	D1
Knocklyon Drive	56	D1
*Knocklyon Gate Apts (off Knocklyon Hill)	55	C2
Knocklyon Green	56	D1
Knocklyon Grove	56	D1
Knocklyon Heights	55	C1
*Knocklyon Mews (off Knocklyon Ave)	55	C1
Knocklyon Park	55	C1
Knocklyon Road	55	C1
Knockmaree Apts	36	E2
Knockmaroon Gate (Phoenix Park)	36	D1
Knockmaroon Hill	36	D1
Knockmaroon Road (Phoenix Park)	36	D1
Knockmeenagh Lane	44	E2
Knockmeenagh Road	44	E2
*Knockmitten Close (off Knockmitten Lane)	44	F1
Knockmitten Lane	45	A1
*Knockmitten Lane North (off Knockmitten Lane)	44	F1
Knockmore Ave	54	E2
Knockmore Cres	54	E2
Knockmore Drive	54	E2
Knockmore Gardens	54	E2
Knockmore Green	54	E2
Knockmore Grove	54	E2
Knockmore Park	54	E2
Knock-na-Cree Grove	60	F2
Knock-na-Cree Park	60	F2
Knock-na-Cree Road	60	F2
*Knocknagow (off Stradbrook Road)	49	B4
Knocknarea Ave	73	B4
Knocknarea Road	73	A4
*Knocknarrow Terrace (Kilmainham Lane)	73	C1
Knocknashee	48	D4
Knocksedan Bridge	1	A2
Knocksedan Drive	1	A2
Knocksedan Wood	1	A2
Knocksink Bridge	66	E3
Knocksinna	59	A2
*Knocksinna Court (off Granville Road)	59	A2
Knocksinna Cres	59	A2
*Knocksinna Grove (off Knocksinna Park)	59	A2
Knocksinna Park	59	A2
Knowth Court	11	C4
Kyber Road (Phoenix Park)	36	F2
*Kyle-Clare Road (off Pine Road)	39	A3
Kylemore Ave	36	D3
Kylemore Drive	36	D3
Kylemore Park North	36	D4
Kylemore Park South	36	D4
Kylemore Park West	36	D4
Kylemore Road (Ballyfermot)	36	D2
Kylemore Road (Grand Canal)	36	E4
Kylemore Way	36	E4

STREET NAME	PAGE	GRID REF

L

STREET NAME	PAGE	GRID REF
La Rochelle Apts	74	F1
*La Touche Court (off Bluebell Ave)	36	F4
La Touche Court (Ballinteer)	57	A2
La Touche Drive	36	E4
La Touche Road	36	F4
La Vallee	67	A3
La Vista Ave	29	B2
Labre Park	36	E4
Laburnum Road	47	C2
Laburnum Walk	35	B2
Lad Lane	76	D2
Lad Lane Apts	76	D3
Lad Lane Upper	76	D3
Lady's Lane	73	B1
Lady's Well Road	9	A4
Lagan Road	24	E3
Lake Drive	53	C1
Lakelands Ave	58	D1
Lakelands Close	58	D1
Lakelands Cres	58	E1
Lakelands Drive	58	E1
Lakelands Grove	58	D1
Lakelands Lawn	58	D1
Lakelands Park	46	E3
*Lakelands Place	58	D1
Lakelands Road	58	E1
Lakeshore Drive	2	D3
Lakeview Drive	2	D3
Lally Road	36	E3
Lamb Alley	74	F1
Lambay Close	64	E1
Lambay Court	3	C3
Lambay Drive	64	E1
Lambay Road	25	A3
*Lambda Apts (on Monkstown Farm)	59	C1
Lambourne Park (Clonsilla)	21	C2
Lambourne Ave	21	C2
Lambourne Court	21	C2
Lambourne Drive	21	C2
Lambourne Road	21	C2
*Lambourne Village (off Kincora Grove)	26	E4
Lambourne Wood	59	C4
Lamb's Brook	58	D3
Lamb's Court (off James Street)	74	D1
Landen Road	36	E3
*Landore (off Orwell Road Rathgar)	47	A3
Landscape Ave	47	A3
*Landscape Court (off Landscape Road)	47	A3
Landscape Cres	47	A4
Landscape Gardens	47	B4
Landscape Park	47	A4
Landscape Road	47	A3
Landsdown Valley Place	45	C1
*Landsdowne Gate (Blank Tony)	45	C1
*Landsdowne Valley (off Slieve Bloom Park)	45	C1
*Landsdowne Valley Apts (Landsdowne Valley)	45	C1
*Landsdowne Valley Cres (off Kilworth Road)	36	F4
*Landsdowne Valley Park (off Davitt Road)	36	F4
Lanesborough Ave	11	B4
Lanesborough Castle	11	B4
Lanesborough Court	11	B4
Lanesborough Drive	11	B4
Lanesborough Gardens	11	B4
Lanesborough Grove	11	B4
Lanesborough Mews	11	B4
Lanesborough Park	11	B4
Lanesborough Road	11	B4
Lanesborough Square	11	B4
Lanesborough Terrace	11	B4
Lanesborough View	11	B4
Lanesville	59	B1
*Lanesville Mews (off Lanesville)	59	C1
Lanesville Terrace	59	B1
Lanewood Mews (off Wellington Road)	76	E3
Langrishe Place	71	C2
Lanndale Lawns	54	E1

STREET NAME	PAGE	GRID REF
*Lansdowne Court (Lansdowne Park)	76	F3
Lansdowne Cres	76	F2
Lansdowne Gardens (off Sandymount Ave)	76	F3
*Lansdowne Hall (off Sandymount Road)	39	A3
Lansdowne Lane	76	F2
Lansdowne Park (Ballsbridge)	76	F2
Lansdowne Park (Templeogue)	56	D1
Lansdowne Road	76	F3
*Lansdowne Square (off Herbert Road)	39	A4
Lansdowne Terrace	76	F2
Lansdowne Village	39	A3
Lansdowne Villas	76	F2
Lansdowne Woods (off Merrion Road)	76	F3
Lapwing Apts	48	E3
*Laracor Gardens (off Ardara Ave adjacent Kilmorony Close)	27	A1
Laragh	60	E4
Laragh Close	27	A1
*Laragh Flats (off Grace Park Court)	25	C2
Laragh Grove	27	A1
Laraghbryan East	17	B2
Laraghbryan West	17	A2
Laraghcon	34	D1
*Larch Drive (off Brookwood)	56	E2
Larch Grove	21	C2
Larch Grove	47	B1
Larch Hill	12	F4
Larch House (Swords)	1	Inset
Larchfield	7	C3
Larchfield	47	C4
Larchfield Park	47	C4
Larchfield Road	47	C4
Larchford Place	21	B1
Larkfield	34	D1
Larkfield Ave (Liffey Valley)	34	F2
Larkfield Ave (Harold's Cross)	46	F1
Larkfield Close	34	F2
Larkfield Court	34	F2
Larkfield Gardens	46	F1
Larkfield Green	34	F2
Larkfield Grove (Liffey Valley)	34	F2
Larkfield Grove (Harold's Cross)	46	F1
Larkfield Mews	32	D3
Larkfield Park	46	F1
Larkfield Place	34	F2
Larkfield Rise	34	F2
Larkfield Square	34	F2
Larkfield View	34	F2
Larkfield Way	34	F2
Larkhill Road	25	B2
*Larkspur Hall (at Levmoss Estate)	58	F3
*Larrisa Court (off Kimmage Road Lower)	46	E1
Latchford	21	B1
Latchford Close	21	B1
Latchford Court	21	B1
Latchford Green	21	B1
Latchford Park	21	B1
Latchford Row	21	B1
Latchford Square	21	B1
Latchford Terrace	21	B1
Latouche Bridge (Grand Canal)	75	B4
Latouka Apts (off Ballyowen Lane)	34	F1
Lauderdale Estate	67	C3
Lauderdale Terrace (New Row South)	75	A2
*Lauderdale Terrace (Lauderdale Estate)	67	C3
Lauder's Lane	29	A1
Laundry Lane	46	F1
Laurel Ave (Dundrum)	57	B1
Laurel Ave (Ballybrack)	64	E1
Laurel Bank	59	C1
Laurel Court	22	E3
Laurel Drive	57	B1
*Laurel Hill (off Glenageary Road Upper)	60	D1
Laurel Lodge Road	22	F3
Laurel Park	44	E1
Laurel Place	46	F2
Laurel Road	57	B1
Laurelton (Rathbeale Road)	1	C1
Laurelton (Terenure)	46	F3
Laurence Brook	36	E2
Laurence Court	46	F1
Laurleen	58	F1
Lavarna Grove	46	E2

STREET NAME	PAGE	GRID REF
Lavarna Road	46	E2
Laverna Ave	22	E3
Laverna Dale	22	E3
Laverna Grove	22	E3
Laverna Way	22	E3
Laverty Court	75	C2
Lavery Ave	35	C4
Lavista Ave	26	E3
Lawnswood Park	58	F1
Lawrence Grove	26	D4
*Lawrence Walk (Saint James)	26	D4
Lawrence's Ave	18	D4
Lawson Spinney	3	A3
*Lawson Terrace (off Sandycove Road)	60	E1
Lazer Lane	72	E4
*Le Bas Terrace (off Leinster Road West)	46	F1
*Le Brett Terrace (off Main Street Rathfarnham)	46	F3
Le Brocquy Ave	36	D4
*Le Fanu Drive (off Clover Hill Road)	36	D3
Le Fanu Road	36	D3
Le Vere Terrace	74	F4
Lea Cres	39	B4
Lea Road	39	B4
Leahy's Terrace	39	A3
Lealand Ave	43	C1
Lealand Close	43	C1
Lealand Cres	43	C1
Lealand Drive	43	C1
Lealand Gardens	43	C1
Lealand Grove	43	C1
Lealand Road	43	C1
Lealand Walk	43	C1
Leda Mews (off Waterloo Road)	76	E3
Ledwidge Cres	67	B1
Lee Road	24	E3
Leeson Close	75	C3
Leeson Court	76	D4
Leeson Lane	75	C2
Leeson Mews	75	C4
Leeson Park	75	C4
Leeson Park Ave	76	D4
Leeson Place	75	C3
Leeson Street Lower	75	C2
Leeson Street Upper	76	D4
Leeson Village	76	D4
Leeson Walk	75	C4
Lehaunstown Road	63	C1
Leicester Ave	47	A1
*Leicester Court (off Leicester Ave)	47	A1
Leighlin Road	46	E1
Lein Gardens	26	F2
Lein Park	26	F2
Lein Road	26	F2
Leinster Ave	72	E1
*Leinster Cottages (on Convent Lane)	17	C3
*Leinster Court (adjacent O'Neill's Park)	18	D3
Leinster Lane	75	C1
Leinster Lawn	47	C3
*Leinster Lodge Apts (adjacent O'Neill's Park)	18	D3
Leinster Market	71	C4
Leinster Park (Maynooth)	18	D3
Leinster Park (Harold's Cross)	46	F1
Leinster Place	46	F1
Leinster Road	47	A1
Leinster Road West	46	F1
*Leinster Square (Leinster Road)	47	A1
Leinster Street	17	C3
Leinster Street East	72	E1
Leinster Street North	24	F4
Leinster Street South	75	C1
*Leinster Terrace (off Nangor Road)	44	D1
Leinster Wood (in Carton Demesne)	18	F1
Leitrim Place	76	E2
Leix Road	70	D1
Leixlip	33	B1
Leixlip Bridge	33	A1
Leixlip Gate	32	E1
Leixlip Park	32	F1
Leixlip Road	33	B1
Lemon Street	75	B1
Lennox Place	75	A3
Lennox Street	75	B3
Lennox Terrace	75	B3
Lentisk Lawn	27	A1

STREET NAME	PAGE	GRID REF
Leo Ave	71	B1
Leo Street	71	B1
Leonard's Court	74	F3
Leopardstown	58	F3
Leopardstown Abbey	58	F4
Leopardstown Ave	58	F2
*Leopardstown Court (off Brewery Road)	58	F2
Leopardstown Drive	58	F2
Leopardstown Gardens	58	F2
Leopardstown Grove	58	F2
Leopardstown Heights	58	E3
*Leopardstown Lawn (off Leopardstown Drive)	58	F2
Leopardstown Oaks	58	F2
Leopardstown Park	58	F2
Leopardstown Rise	58	E3
Leopardstown Road (Leopardstown)	58	D3
Leopardstown Road (Stillorgan Road)	58	F2
Leopardstown Valley	58	F4
*Les Buissonets Apts (off Sweetman's Ave)	49	A3
Leslie Ave	60	F1
Leslie's Buildings	70	F1
*Leukos Road (off Pine Road)	39	A3
Levmoss Estate	58	F3
*Levmoss Hall (at Levmoss Estate)	58	F3
*Liberty Court (Clanbrassil Terrace)	74	F2
*Liberty Court (Corporation Street)	71	C3
*Liberty Court Apts (Clanbrassil Terrace)	75	A2
*Liberty Court Apts (on Clanbrassil Street Lower)	74	F2
Liberty House	71	C2
Liberty Lane	75	B2
Liberty Lane	74	F1
Liberty Square	74	F1
Library Road (Dún Laoghaire)	50	D2
Library Road (Shankill)	64	E2
Library Square	52	F2
Library View Villas	71	A1
Liffey Ave	34	F2
Liffey Close	34	F2
Liffey Court	34	F2
Liffey Cres	34	F2
Liffey Dale	34	F2
Liffey Downs	34	F2
Liffey Drive	34	F2
Liffey Gardens	34	F2
Liffey Glen	34	F2
Liffey Green	34	F2
Liffey Grove	34	F2
Liffey Hall (off Liffey Cres)	34	F2
Liffey Junction	24	E4
Liffey Lawn	34	F2
Liffey Park	34	F2
Liffey Place	34	F2
Liffey Rise	34	F2
Liffey Road	34	F2
Liffey Row	34	F2
Liffey Street Lower	71	B4
Liffey Street South	36	F3
Liffey Street Upper	71	B3
Liffey Street West	70	E4
*Liffey Terrace (off Saint Laurence Road)	36	E2
Liffey Terrace	34	F2
Liffey Vale	34	F2
Liffey Valley Park	34	F2
Liffey View	34	F2
*Liffey View Apts (off Main Street Leixlip)	33	A1
Liffey Villas	34	F2
Liffey Walk	34	F2
Liffey Way	34	F2
Liffey Wood	34	F2
Lighthouse Apts	72	F1
Lilys Way	21	A1
Lime Street	72	E4
Limekilin Court	45	B3
Limekiln Ave	45	B3
Limekiln Close	45	C3
Limekiln Drive	45	C3
Limekiln Green	45	B3
Limekiln Grove	45	C3
Limekiln Lane (Harold's Cross)	74	F4
Limekiln Lane (Kimmage)	45	C2
Limekiln Park	45	C3
Limekiln Road	45	C3
Limelawn Court	22	D2

STREET NAME	PAGE	GRID REF
Limelawn Glade	22	D2
Limelawn Green	22	D2
Limelawn Hill	22	D2
Limelawn Park	22	D2
Limelawn Rise	22	D2
Limelawn Wood	22	D2
Limes Road	58	D2
Limetree Ave	4	D4
Limewood Ave	26	F1
Limewood Park	26	F1
Limewood Road	27	A1
Lincoln Hall (Swords)	1	Inset
Lincoln House	70	F4
Lincoln Lane	70	F4
Lincoln Place	76	D1
Linden Court	48	F4
Linden Grove	48	F4
Linden Lea Park	58	F1
Linden Square	48	F4
*Lindenvale (off Proby Square)	49	A4
Lindisfarne Ave	43	C1
Lindisfarne Drive	43	C1
Lindisfarne Green	43	C1
Lindisfarne Grove	43	C1
Lindisfarne Lawns	43	C1
Lindisfarne Park	34	F4
Lindisfarne Vale	43	C1
Lindisfarne Walk	43	C1
*Lindsay Grove (off Prospect Road)	25	A4
Lindsay Road	25	A4
Linenhall Parade	71	A3
Linenhall Street (off King Street North)	71	A3
Linenhall Terrace	71	A3
Link Road (off Monkstown Cres)	49	C4
Link Road (Glasthule)	60	E1
*Linnbhlá (adjacent Santry Cross Junction)	12	D4
Linnetfields	21	A1
Linnetfields Ave	8	E4
Linnetfields Close	8	E4
Linnetfields Court	21	A1
Linnetfields Drive	8	E4
Linnetfields Park	21	A1
Linnetfields Rise	8	E4
Linnetfields Square	8	E4
Linnetfields View	8	D4
Linnetfields Walk	21	A1
Lios na Sídhe	54	F2
Lioscian	1	B1
*Lisalea (off Frascati Park Blackrock)	49	A3
*Lisburn Court (King Street North)	71	A3
Lisburn Street	71	A3
Liscannor Road	24	E4
*Liscanor (off Harbour Road)	60	F1
Liscarne Court	35	A3
*Liscarne Dale (off Collinstown Road)	35	A3
Liscarne Dale	35	A3
Liscarne Gardens	35	A3
Lisin Glen Apts	24	F3
Lisle Road	46	D1
*Lismeen Grove (off Beechpark Ave)	26	E1
Lismore	18	E4
Lismore Road	46	D1
Lissadel Ave	73	B4
Lissadel Court	73	A4
Lissadel Cres	2	F2
Lissadel Drive	73	A4
Lissadel Green	73	A3
Lissadel Grove	2	F2
Lissadel Park	2	F2
Lissadel Road	73	A4
Lissadel Wood	2	F2
Lissane Apts	22	E1
Lissen Hall	2	E1
Lissen Hall Drive	2	E1
Lissenfield	75	B4
Lissenhall Ave	2	D1
Lissenhall Bridge	2	E1
Lissenhall Court	2	D1
Lissenhall Drive	2	D1
Lissenhall Park	2	D1
Little Britain Street	71	A3
Little Fitzwilliam Place	76	D2
*Little Meadow (off Pottery Road)	59	C3
*Little Orchard (off Pottery Road)	59	C3
Littlepace	8	E4
Littlepace Close	8	E4
Littlepace Court	8	E4
Littlepace Cres	8	E4
Littlepace Drive	8	E4
Littlepace Gallops	8	E4
Littlepace Meadow	8	E4
Littlepace Park	8	E4
Littlepace Road	8	E4
Littlepace View	8	E4
Littlepace Walk	8	E4
Littlepace Way	8	E4
Littlepace Woods	8	E4
Littlewood	58	D4
Litton Lane	71	B4
Llewellyn Close	57	A1
Llewellyn Court	57	A1
Llewellyn Grove	57	A1
Llewellyn Lawn	57	A1
Llewellyn Park	57	A1
Llewellyn Way	57	A1
Llex House	76	D3
Lock Road	34	D3
Lockkeeper's Walk	24	D3
*Loftus Hall (off Belgard Square West)	54	F1
Loftus Lane	71	A3
*Loftus Square (off Main Street Rathfarnham)	46	F4
Lohunda Close	22	D2
Lohunda Court	22	D2
Lohunda Cres	21	C2
Lohunda Dale	22	D2
Lohunda Downs	22	D2
Lohunda Drive	22	D2
Lohunda Green	22	D2
Lohunda Grove	22	D2
Lohunda Park	21	C2
Lohunda Park View	22	D2
Lohunda Road	22	D2
Lombard Court (Clanbrassil Street)	74	F3
Lombard Court (Lombard Street East)	72	D4
Lombard Street East	72	D4
Lombard Street West	75	A3
Lomond Ave	25	C4
*Londonbridge Drive (off Londonbridge Road)	39	A3
Londonbridge Road	39	A3
Long Lane (New Bride Street)	75	A2
*Long Lane (off Mountjoy Street)	71	A2
Long Lane Close (off Long Lane)	75	A2
Long Meadow Apts	69	C4
Long Mile Road	45	B1
*Longboat Quay North Apts (Asgard Road)	72	E4
*Longboat Quay South Apts (Asgard Road)	72	E4
Longdale Terrace	25	A1
Longdale Way	25	A1
Longford Lane	75	B1
Longford Place	49	C4
Longford Street Great	75	A1
Longford Street Little	75	B1
Longford Terrace	49	C4
Longlands	2	D2
Longmeadow	59	C3
Longmeadow Grove	59	C3
Long's Place	74	E1
Longwood Ave	75	A3
Longwood Park	46	F4
*Looceville Court (off Saint Agnes Road Crumlin)	46	D1
Lorcan Ave	25	C1
Lorcan Cres	25	C1
Lorcan Drive	25	B1
Lorcan Green	25	C1
Lorcan Grove	25	C1
*Lorcan O'Toole Court (off Lorcan O'Toole Park)	46	D2
Lorcan O'Toole Park	46	D2
Lorcan Park	25	C1
Lorcan Road	25	B1
Lorcan Villas	25	C1
Lord Edward Street	75	A1
Lordello	64	D3
Lordello Road	64	D3
Lords Walk (Phoenix Park)	69	B2
Loreto Abbey	47	A4
Loreto Ave (Nutgrove Ave)	47	A4
Loreto Ave (Dalkey)	60	F1
Loreto Court	47	A4
Loreto Cres	47	A4
Loreto Grange	67	C3
Loreto Park	47	A4
Loreto Road	74	E2
Loreto Row	47	A4
Loreto Terrace	46	F4
*Loretto Ave (Sidmonton Road)	67	C2
*Loretto Terrace (Sidmonton Road)	67	C2
*Loretto Villas (Sidmonton Road)	67	C2
Lorne Terrace (off Almeida Ave)	73	C2
*Losset Hall (off Belgard Square West)	54	F1
Lough Conn Ave	36	D2
Lough Conn Drive	36	D2
Lough Conn Road	36	D2
Lough Conn Terrace	36	D2
Lough Derg Road	27	A2
Lough na Mona	19	C4
Loughlinstown	64	D1
Loughlinstown Drive	64	D1
Loughlinstown Park	64	D1
Loughlinstown Wood	64	D1
*Loughmorne House (off Terenure Road West)	46	F2
Loughoreen Hills	30	D3
Loughsallagh Bridge	7	C3
Loughtown Lower	41	C1
Loughtown Upper	42	D1
*Louis Lane (off Leinster Road)	47	A1
Louisa Bridge	19	C4
Louisa Manor	19	C4
Louisa Vally	19	C4
Lourdes Road	71	C2
Lourdes Road	74	D2
Louvain	48	D3
Louvain Glade	48	D3
Love Lane	76	E2
Love Lane East	76	E2
Lower Dargle Road	67	B2
Lower Glen Road (Phoenix Park)	36	D1
Lower Kilmacud Road (Goatstown)	48	D4
Lower Kilmacud Road (Stillorgan)	58	D1
Lower Lucan Road (Strawberry Beds)	21	C4
Lower Lucan Road (Lucan)	34	D1
Lower Road (Strawberry Beds)	35	B1
Lower Road (Shankill)	64	E3
Loyola	67	A3
Luby Road	73	A2
Lucan	34	D2
Lucan Bridge	34	D1
Lucan Bypass	34	D2
Lucan Heights	34	E1
Lucan Newlands Road (Esker)	34	D2
Lucan Newlands Road (Ronanstown)	35	A4
Lucan Road (Ballydowd)	34	E1
Lucan Road (Palmerstown)	35	C1
Lucan Road (Lucan)	34	D1
Lucan Road (near Qaurryvale)	35	A1
Lucan Road (Chapelizod)	36	D2
Lucan-Newlands Road	34	F3
Lucky Lane	70	D2
Ludford Drive	57	B1
Ludford Park	57	B1
Ludford Road	57	B2
Lugg	52	F4
Lugmore	54	D3
Lugmore Lane	53	C3
Lugnaquilla Ave	45	B3
Luke Street	71	C4
Lullymore Terrace	74	E3
Lurgan Street	71	A3
Lutterell Hall	7	B2
Luttrell Park	22	D3
Luttrell Park Close	22	D3
Luttrell Park Court	22	D3
Luttrell Park Cres	22	E3
Luttrell Park Drive	22	E3
Luttrell Park Green	22	E3
Luttrell Park Grove	22	D3
*Luttrell Park Heath (adjacent Oldfarm off Carpenterstown Road)	22	E3
Luttrell Park Lawn	22	D3
Luttrell Park View	22	D3
Luttrellstown Ave	22	E4
Luttrellstown Chase	22	D4
Luttrellstown Close	22	E4
Luttrellstown Court	22	D4
Luttrellstown Dale	22	D4
Luttrellstown Drive	22	D4
Luttrellstown Glade	22	D4
Luttrellstown Green	22	D4
Luttrellstown Grove	22	D4
Luttrellstown Heath	22	D4
Luttrellstown Heights	22	D4
Luttrellstown Lawn	22	D4
Luttrellstown Oaks	22	D4
Luttrellstown Park	22	D4
Luttrellstown Place	22	D4
Luttrellstown Rise	22	D3
Luttrellstown Road (Castleknock)	22	D4
Luttrellstown Road (Clonsilla)	21	C3
Luttrellstown Thicket	22	D4
Luttrellstown View	22	E4
Luttrellstown Walk	22	D4
Luttrellstown Way	22	D4
Luttrellstown Wood	22	E4
Lymewood Mews	12	E4
Lynchs Lane	34	E4
*Lynch's Lane (off Ballyfermot Road)	36	E3
Lynch's Place	71	A1
Lyndon Gate (off Blackhorse Ave)	24	D4
*Lynton Court (off Sandymount Ave)	39	A4
Lynwood	57	C1
Lyons	41	A4
Lyons Ave	42	D4
*Lyons Ave North (off Newcastle Boulevard)	42	D4
*Lyons Ave South (off Newcastle Boulevard)	42	D4
Lyons Lane	42	D4
Lyons Road	41	B4
Lyons Street (off Newcastle Boulevard)	42	D4
*Lyre House (off Thomas Davis Street West)	36	F3
Lyreen Court	17	C3
Lyreen Park	18	D2

M

STREET NAME	PAGE	GRID REF
M1 Junction 1 (M50/M1)	13	A3
M1 Junction 2 (Dublin Airport)	13	A1
M1 Junction 3 (Swords)	2	E3
M4 Junction 5 (Leixlip)	33	B1
M4 Junction 6 (Celbridge)	32	D1
M4 Junction 7 (Maynooth)	17	C4
M50 Junction 1 (Dublin Port)	39	A1
M50 Junction 10 (Ballymount)	45	A3
M50 Junction 11 (N81 Tallagh)	45	C4
M50 Junction 12 (Firhouse)	55	C2
M50 Junction 13 (Dundrum)	57	C3
M50 Junction 14 (N31 Dun Laoghaire)	58	E3
M50 Junction 15 (Carrickmines)	59	A4
M50 Junction 16 (Cherrywood)	63	C2
M50 Junction 17 (M50/M11)	64	D3
M50 Junction 2 (Santry)	13	A1
M50 Junction 3 (M1/M50)	12	F3
M50 Junction 4 (Ballymun)	12	D3
M50 Junction 5 (N2/M50 Finglas)	11	A4
M50 Junction 6 (N3/M50 Blanchardstown)	22	F2
M50 Junction 7 (N4/M50)	35	B1
M50 Junction 9 (N7/M50 Red Cow)	44	F1
Ma Tuire Apts	48	D4
Mabbot House	71	C3
Mabbot Lane	71	C3
Mabel Street	25	B4
Mac Mahon Bridge (Grand Canal)	76	E1
Mac Ullaim	53	C1
*Mac Ulliam Ave (Mac Ulliam)	53	C1
*Mac Ulliam Close (Mac Ulliam)	53	C1
*Mac Ulliam Court (Mac Ulliam)	53	C1
*Mac Ulliam Cres (Mac Ulliam)	53	C1
*Mac Ulliam Dale (Mac Ulliam)	53	C1
*Mac Ulliam Drive (Mac Ulliam)	53	C1
*Mac Ulliam Gardens (Mac Ulliam)	53	C1
*Mac Ulliam Green (Mac Ulliam)	53	C1
*Mac Ulliam Lane (Mac Ulliam)	53	C1
*Mac Ulliam Lawns (Mac Ulliam)	53	C1
*Mac Ulliam Mews (Mac Ulliam)	53	C1

STREET NAME	PAGE	GRID REF
*Mac Ulliam Parade (Mac Ulliam)	53	C1
*Mac Ulliam Road (Mac Ulliam)	53	C1
*Mac Ulliam Walk (Mac Ulliam)	53	C1
*Mac Ulliam Way (Mac Ulliam)	53	C1
*Macken House (near The Point)	72	F3
Macken Street	76	E1
Macken Villa	76	E1
Mackies Place	75	C2
Mackintosh Park	59	C2
Macroom Ave	13	B4
Macroom Road	13	B4
Madden Road	74	F2
*Madden's Court (off Thomas Street)	74	E2
Madden's Lane	60	E4
*Madison Court Apts	76	E1
Madison Road	73	C2
*Magdalen Terrace (off Oliver Plunkett Ave)	39	A3
Magennis Place	72	D4
Magennis Square	72	D4
Magenta Cres	25	B1
Magenta Hall	25	B1
*Magenta Place (off Eden Road Upper)	60	D1
Magna Ave	53	C2
Magna Drive	53	C2
*Maher's Terrace (on Main Street Dundrum)	47	C4
*Maidens Row (off Martin's Row Chapelizod)	36	E2
Main Road (Tallaght)	55	A1
Main Street (Clongriffin)	14	E4
Main Street (Swords)	2	D2
Main Street (Malahide)	3	B2
Main Street (Dunboyne)	7	B2
Main Street (Ballymun)	12	D4
Main Street (Baldoyle)	15	A4
Main Street (Maynooth)	17	C3
Main Street (Blanchardstown)	22	E2
Main Street (Finglas)	24	E2
Main Street (Raheny)	27	A2
Main Street (Howth)	30	D2
Main Street (Celbridge)	32	D3
Main Street (Leixlip)	33	A1
Main Street (Lucan)	34	D1
Main Street (Newcastle)	42	D4
Main Street (Clondalkin)	44	E1
Main Street (Rathfarnham)	46	F4
Main Street (Dundrum)	47	C4
Main Street (Blackrock)	49	A3
Main Street (Rathcoole)	52	F2
Main Street (Tallaght)	55	A1
Main Street (Bray)	67	C2
Main Street (Saggart)	53	A2
Main Street (Ongar)	21	A1
Main Street (Chapelizod)	36	E2
Maitland Street	67	B2
Malachi Place	72	E2
Malachi Road	70	E3
Malahide	3	B2
Malahide Demesne	3	A3
Malahide Road (Darndale)	13	C4
Malahide Road (Swords)	2	E4
Malahide Road (Balgriffin)	14	D3
Malahide Road (Marino)	26	D4
Malahide Road (Artane)	26	E2
Malahide Road (Coolock)	26	F1
Malahide Roundabout (Swords)	2	D2
Malin House	22	F1
Mallin Ave	74	D2
Malone Gardens	76	F2
Malpas Court	75	A2
Malpas Place (off Malpas Street)	75	A2
Malpas Street (off New Street)	75	A2
Malpas Terrace	75	A2
Mandalay	20	D4
Mander's Terrace	75	C4
Mangerton Road	36	F4
Mannix Road	25	A4
Manor Ave	46	E3
Manor Close	57	A2
Manor Court	17	C3
Manor Cres	21	B1
Manor Drive	14	D4
Manor Green	57	A2
Manor Grove	46	D2
*Manor Hall (Adjacent Cromwells Quarter)	73	C1
*Manor Hall Apts (Mount Brown)	74	D1
Manor Heath	57	A1
Manor House View	27	A3

STREET NAME	PAGE	GRID REF
Manor Mews (off Norseman Place)	70	E3
Manor Park (Palmerston)	35	C2
Manor Park (Ballinteer)	57	A2
Manor Place (Stoneybatter)	70	E3
Manor Place (Clonsilla)	21	A1
Manor Rise	57	A2
Manor Road	35	C2
Manor Square	21	A1
Manor Street	70	E3
*Manor Villas (off Mount Argus Grove)	46	F1
Manorfields	21	B1
Mantua Park	2	D1
Maolbuille Road	25	A2
Mapas Ave	60	E2
Mapas Road	60	E2
Mapel House	1	Inset
Maple Ave (Carpenterstown)	22	E3
Maple Ave (off Blackthorn Drive)	58	D2
Maple Close	22	E3
Maple Drive (Dunboyne)	7	B2
Maple Drive (Carpenterstown)	22	E3
*Maple Drive (off The Cloisters)	46	F2
Maple Glen	22	E3
Maple Green	22	E3
Maple Grove (Carpenterstown)	22	E3
Maple Grove (Rathcoole)	52	F2
Maple Grove (Bray)	67	B2
Maple House	76	D3
Maple Lawn	22	E3
Maple Lodge	23	A4
Maple Manor	59	C3
Maple Road	47	C2
Maples (opposite Knockmaroon Gate)	36	D1
Maples Road	58	D2
Maplewood Ave	54	E1
Maplewood Close	54	E1
Maplewood Court	54	E1
Maplewood Drive	54	E1
Maplewood Green	54	E1
Maplewood Lawn	54	E1
Maplewood Park	54	E1
Maplewood Road	54	E1
Maplewood Way	54	E1
Maquay Bridge (Grand Canal)	76	E2
Maretimo Gardens East	49	A3
*Maretimo Gardens West (off Newtown Ave Blackrock)	49	A3
*Maretimo Place (off Newtown Ave Blackrock)	49	A3
*Maretimo Road (off Newtown Ave Blackrock)	49	A3
*Maretimo Terrace (off Newtown Ave Blackrock)	49	A3
*Maretimo Villas (off Temple Road)	49	A3
Marewood Cres	24	F1
Marewood Drive	11	C4
Marewood Grove	24	F1
Margaret Place	76	F2
Marguerite Road	25	A4
Marian Court	14	F4
Marian Cres	46	E4
Marian Drive	46	E4
Marian Grove	46	E4
Marian Park (Baldoyle)	27	C1
Marian Park (Templeogue)	46	E4
Marian Park (Blackrock)	59	A1
Marian Road	46	E4
Marianella	47	A2
Mariavilla	17	C2
*Marie Villas (Sidmonton Road)	67	C2
Marigold Ave	13	C4
Marigold Court	13	C4
Marigold Cres	13	C4
Marigold Grove	13	C4
Marigold Park	13	C4
Marigold Road	13	C4
*Marina House Apts (off Clarence Street Dún Laoghaire)	49	C4
Marina Village	3	B2
Marine Ave	60	E1
*Marine Court (off Crofton Road)	50	D4
Marine Court (Dalkey)	60	E1
Marine Cove (off Baldoyle Road)	28	D1
Marine Drive	39	A4
Marine Parade	60	E1
Marine Road	50	D4
*Marine Terrace (off Park Road Dún Laoghaire)	50	D4
*Marine Terrace (at Esplanade)	68	D2

STREET NAME	PAGE	GRID REF
Marine View	48	F3
*Marine Villas (off Harbour Road, opposite Howth Station)	30	D1
Mariners Court (off Kilbarrack Road)	27	C2
Mariners Cove	30	E2
Mariner's Port	72	E3
Marino	25	C4
Marino Ave	26	D4
Marino Ave East	60	E4
Marino Ave West	60	E4
*Marino Court (off Fairview Ave Lower)	25	C4
Marino Cres	25	C4
Marino Green	25	C4
*Marino Mart (off Haverty Road)	25	C4
Marino Park	25	C4
Marino Park Ave	25	C4
*Marino Villa (off Casino Park)	26	D3
Marion Villas	74	E2
Mark Street	72	D4
Market House	67	C2
Market Square (Smithfield)	70	F3
*Market Square (near Market House)	67	C2
Market Square Apts	71	A3
Market Street South	74	E1
Mark's Alley West	74	E1
Mark's Lane	72	D4
Marlay View	57	B2
Marlborough Court (Marlborough Street)	71	C3
Marlborough Court (Blackhorse Ave)	70	D2
*Marlborough Court (off Sharavogue)	60	E2
*Marlborough Lane (off Marlborough Road)	47	B1
Marlborough Mews	70	D2
*Marlborough Park (off Adelaide Road)	60	D1
Marlborough Place	71	C3
Marlborough Road (North Circular Road)	70	D2
Marlborough Road (Donnybrook)	47	B1
Marlborough Road (Glenageary)	60	E1
Marlborough Street	71	C3
*Marlborough Terrace (at Esplanade)	68	D2
Marley	3	C3
Marley Ave	57	A1
Marley Close	57	A1
Marley Court North	57	A1
Marley Court South	57	A1
Marley Drive	57	A1
Marley Grove	57	A1
Marley Lawn	57	A1
Marley Rise	57	A1
*Marley Villas (off Marley Walk)	57	A1
Marley Walk	57	A1
Marlfield	59	C3
Marlfield Close	54	F3
Marlfield Court	54	F3
Marlfield Cres	54	F3
Marlfield Green	54	F3
Marlfield Grove	54	F3
Marlfield Lawn	54	F3
Marlfield Mall	54	F3
Marlfield Place	54	F3
Marlfield Row	54	F3
*Marlfield Terrace (Marlfield Place)	54	F3
Marmion Court Flats	70	F3
Marne Villas	70	F2
Marrowbone Lane	74	E2
Marrowbone Lane Close (off Marrowbone Lane)	74	E1
Marrowbone Lane Flats	74	E1
Marrsfield Ave	14	E3
Marshal Court Apts	74	E1
Marshalsea Court (Merchants Quay)	70	F4
*Marshalsea Lane (off Bridgefoot Street)	70	E4
Marsham Court	58	E1
Mart Lane	59	B3
*Martello Ave (off Summerhill Road)	50	D4
Martello Court	4	D4
Martello Mews	48	E1
Martello Terrace	29	B3
*Martello Terrace (off Seafort Parade Booterstown)	48	F3

STREET NAME	PAGE	GRID REF
*Martello Terrace (off Windsor Terrace Dún Laoghaire)	50	E4
*Martello Terrace (Strand Road Bray)	67	C1
*Martello View (off Strand Road)	39	B4
*Martello Wood (off Strand Road)	39	B4
Martin Grove	24	D4
Martin Savage Park	23	C3
Martin Street	75	A3
*Martin White Chalets (off Herbert Road)	39	A4
Martin's Row	36	E2
*Martin's Terrace (off Hanover Street East)	72	D4
*Mary Aikenhead Flats (off Basin Street Lower)	74	D1
Mary Street	71	A3
Mary Street Little	71	A4
*Maryfield Ave (off Ardlea Road)	26	E2
Maryfield Cres	26	E2
Maryfield Drive	26	D2
*Maryland (Shanganagh Road near School)	64	E2
Marymount	12	F2
Mary's Abbey	71	A4
Mary's Lane	71	A4
Maryville Road	26	F3
Mask Ave	26	E2
Mask Cres	26	E2
Mask Drive	26	E2
Mask Green	26	E2
Mask Road	26	E2
Mather Road North	48	E3
Mather Road South	48	D3
Matt Talbot Court	71	C2
Maunsell Place	71	A2
*Maxwell Court (off Maxwell Road)	47	A1
Maxwell Lane	47	A2
Maxwell Road	47	A1
Maxwell Street	74	E2
May Cottages	71	A1
May Lane	70	F4
May Park	26	D3
*May Street (off Fitzroy Ave)	71	A1
Mayberry Park	45	A4
Mayberry Road	44	F4
Mayeston	11	C4
Mayeston Boulevard (Mayeston)	11	C4
Mayeston Close (Mayeston)	11	B3
Mayeston Court (Mayeston)	11	B4
Mayeston Cres (Mayeston)	11	C4
Mayeston Downs (Mayeston)	11	C4
Mayeston Drive (Mayeston)	11	B4
Mayeston Green (Mayeston)	11	C4
Mayeston Lawn (Mayeston)	11	B3
Mayeston Rise (Mayeston)	11	C4
Mayeston Square (Mayeston)	11	B4
Mayeston Walk (Mayeston)	11	C4
Mayfair	3	C2
Mayfield	47	A2
*Mayfield Court (Mayfield Park)	35	B4
Mayfield Park	35	B4
Mayfield Road (Kilmainham)	73	C2
Mayfield Road (Terenure)	46	F1
Mayfield Terrace (Ballinteer)	57	C2
*Mayfield Terrace (Vevay Road, Putland Road)	67	C3
Mayne Bridge	14	F3
Maynetown	14	F3
Maynooth	18	D2
Maynooth Park	18	D4
Maynooth Road (Dunboyne)	7	A3
Maynooth Road (Celbridge)	31	C1
Mayola Court	47	B4
Mayor Square	72	E3
Mayor Street Lower	72	D3
Mayor Street Upper	72	F3
*Mayville Terrace (off Leslie Ave)	60	F1
Maywood Ave	27	B2
Maywood Close	27	B2
Maywood Cres	27	B3
Maywood Drive	27	B2
Maywood Grove	27	B3
Maywood Lawn	27	B3
Maywood Park	27	B2
Maywood Road	27	B2
Mc Cartney Bridge (Grand Canal)	76	D3
*Mc Donagh House (Whitefriar Street)	75	A1
Mc Kee Court (Blackhorse Ave)	69	C2

STREET NAME	PAGE	GRID REF
Mc Kenny Bridge (Grand Canal)	76	E2
McAuley Ave	26	F2
McAuley Drive	26	F2
McAuley Park	26	F2
McAuley Road	26	F2
McCabe Villas	48	E3
McCarthy Terrace	74	D2
McCreadies Lane	3	A3
McDowell Ave	74	D1
*McGovern Corner Apts (off Cork Street)	74	E2
*McGrane Court (off Sandyford Road)	57	C1
McKee Ave	24	E1
McKee Park	69	C1
McKee Road	24	E1
McKelvey Ave	11	A4
McKelvey Road	11	A4
McMahon Street	75	A3
*McMorrough Road (off Terenure Road North)	46	F2
Meade's Terrace	76	D1
*Meadow Ave (off Meadow Grove)	57	B1
Meadow Close (Dundrum)	57	A1
Meadow Close (Newtown Park Ave)	59	A1
Meadow Copse	21	C1
*Meadow Court (off Wyattville Road)	60	D4
*Meadow Dale (off Meadow Green)	21	C1
Meadow Downs	21	C1
Meadow Drive	21	C1
Meadow Green	21	C1
Meadow Grove	57	B1
Meadow Mount	57	A1
Meadow Park	57	A1
Meadow Park Ave	47	A4
Meadow Vale	59	B2
Meadow View (Dunboyne)	7	B2
Meadow View (Nutgrove Ave)	57	A1
*Meadow Villas (off Meadow Grove)	57	A1
Meadow Way	21	C1
Meadowbank	46	F3
Meadowbrook	17	C4
Meadowbrook Ave (Maynooth)	17	C4
Meadowbrook Ave (Sutton)	28	D1
Meadowbrook Close	17	C4
Meadowbrook Court	17	C4
Meadowbrook Cres	17	C4
Meadowbrook Drive	17	C4
Meadowbrook Lawn	28	D1
Meadowbrook Lawns	17	C4
Meadowbrook Park	28	D1
Meadowbrook Road	17	C4
Meadowfield	58	E4
Meadowlands	59	C1
Meadowlands Ave	59	C1
*Meadowlands Court (off Meadowlands Ave)	59	C1
*Meadowlands Mews (off Meadowlands Ave)	59	C1
Meadowview Grove	33	C2
Meagans Lane	53	B4
Meakstown Cottages	11	B3
Meath Place (Meath Street)	74	F1
Meath Place (Bray)	67	C2
Meath Road	68	D2
Meath Square	74	F1
Meath Street	74	F1
*Meath Terrace (on Meath Place)	74	F1
*Meathville Terrace (on Long Lane)	75	A2
*Meenan Square (off Owenstown Park Fosters Ave)	48	D3
*Meeting House Square (on Sycamore Street)	71	B4
Meetinghouse Lane	71	A4
Méile an Rí Cres	34	F3
Méile an Rí Drive	34	F3
Méile an Rí Green	34	F3
Méile an Rí Park	34	F3
Méile an Rí Road	34	F3
Méile an Rí View	34	F3
Mellennium Walkway 71 B3	71	B2
Mellifont Ave	50	D4
Mellowes Ave	24	D1
Mellowes Court	24	D2
*Mellowes Cres (off Mellowes Court)	24	D2
Mellowes Park	24	D1
Mellowes Road	24	D1
Mellows Bridge (River Liffey)	70	F4
*Mellows Quay Apts (adjacent Emmet Place)	70	F4
Melrose Ave (Fairview)	25	C4
Melrose Ave (Clondalkin)	43	C1
*Melrose Court (off Philipsburgh Ave)	25	C4
Melrose Cres	43	C1
Melrose Green	43	C1
Melrose Grove	43	C1
Melrose Lawn	34	F4
Melrose Park (Swords)	2	E3
Melrose Park (Clondalkin)	43	C1
Melrose Park The Ave	2	E3
Melrose Park The Close	2	E3
Melrose Park The Cres	2	E3
Melrose Park The Drive	2	E3
Melrose Park The Green	2	E3
Melrose Park The Grove	2	E3
Melrose Park The Heights	2	E3
Melrose Park The Lawn	2	E3
Melrose Park The Park	2	E3
Melrose Park The Rise	2	E3
Melrose Park The Villa	2	E3
Melrose Park The Walk	2	E3
Melrose Road	34	F4
Melville Close	11	B4
Melville Court	11	B4
Melville Cove	11	B4
Melville Cres	11	B4
Melville Drive	11	B4
Melville Green	11	B4
Melville Grove	11	B4
Melville Lawn	11	B4
Melville Park	11	B4
Melville Rise	11	B4
Melville Square	11	B4
Melville Terrace	11	B4
Melville View	11	B4
Melville Way	11	B4
Melvin Road	46	F2
Memorial Court	69	B4
Memorial Road (Inchicore Road)	73	A1
Memorial Road (Custom House Quay)	71	C3
Mercer House	75	B2
Mercer Street Lower	75	B1
Mercer Street Upper	75	B2
Merchamp	26	F4
Merchants Arch (off Temple Bar)	71	B4
Merchant's Court	70	F4
*Merchant's Hall (Merchants Quay)	70	F4
Merchant's House	70	F4
Merchant's Quay	70	F4
Merchant's Road	39	A1
Merchant's Square	72	F3
*Meretimo Villas (on Edward Road)	68	D3
Merlyn Drive	48	D1
Merlyn Park	48	D1
Merlyn Road	48	D1
Merrion	48	E1
Merrion Close	76	D1
*Merrion Court (Ailesbury Road)	48	E1
*Merrion Cres (off Trimleston Road)	48	E2
*Merrion Gates (off Strand Road)	48	E1
Merrion Grove	48	E3
Merrion Hall	48	E4
Merrion Park	48	E3
Merrion Place	75	C2
Merrion Road	39	A4
Merrion Row	75	C2
Merrion Square East	76	D2
Merrion Square North	76	D1
Merrion Square South	76	D2
Merrion Square West	76	D2
Merrion Strand	48	E1
Merrion Street Lower	76	D1
Merrion Street Upper	75	C2
*Merrion View Ave (off Ailesbury Road)	48	D1
Merrion Village	48	E1
*Merrion Woods (Rear of Belfield Park Apts)	48	E3
*Merry Bush (off Tritonville Ave)	39	A4
Merrycourt	8	E2
Merton Ave	74	F3
*Merton Cres (off Milltown Ave)	47	B2
Merton Drive	47	B1
Merton Park	74	F3
Merton Road	47	B2
Merton Walk	47	B2
Merville Ave (Fairview)	25	C4
Merville Ave (Stillorgan)	58	F1
Merville Court	24	E2
Merville Road	58	F1
Mespil Estate	76	D3
Mespil Lodge	76	D3
Mespil Road	76	D3
Metropolitan Apts	73	A1
Michael Collins Park	35	A4
*Michell House	76	D4
Middle Third	26	E3
Middle Third Terrace	26	E3
Milesian Ave	2	E2
Milesian Court	2	E2
Milesian Grove	2	E2
Milesian Lawn	2	E2
Milestown	19	C1
Milford	3	A2
Military Road (Rathmines)	75	B4
Military Road (Kilmainham)	73	C1
Military Road (Phoenix Park)	36	F2
Military Road (Killiney)	60	E4
*Mill Bank (near Hills Industrial Estate)	34	D1
Mill Bridge (Swords)	2	D2
Mill Brook Apts	35	C1
Mill Court Ave	43	C1
Mill Court Drive	43	C1
Mill Field (Enniskerry)	66	E3
Mill House	62	F3
Mill Lane (Newmarket)	74	F2
Mill Lane	23	B2
Mill Lane (Palmerston)	35	C1
Mill Lane (Leixlip)	33	A1
Mill Lane (Loughlinstown)	64	E2
Mill Park	44	D1
*Mill Race Apts (Martins Row)	36	E2
Mill Road (Blanchardstown)	22	F2
Mill Road (Saggart)	53	A2
Mill Street (The Coombe)	74	F2
*Mill Street (off Cross Ave Dún Laoghaire)	50	D4
Millar's Hall (Bridgefoot Street)	74	F1
Millar's Hall (Cork Street)	74	E2
Millbank	14	F2
Millbourne Ave	25	A4
Millbrook Ave	27	A1
Millbrook Court	73	C1
Millbrook Drive	27	A1
Millbrook Grove	27	A1
Millbrook Lawns	55	A1
Millbrook Road	27	A1
Millbrook Terrace	73	B1
*Millbrook Village (off Milltown Road)	47	C1
Millennium Bridge (River Liffey)	71	B4
Millers Wood	67	B3
Millfarm	7	C2
Millfield (Portmarnock)	14	F2
Millgate Drive	45	C3
Millmount Ave	25	A4
Millmount Grove	47	B3
Millmount Place	25	B4
*Millmount Terrace (Drumcondra)	25	B4
*Millmount Villas (off Millmount Ave)	25	A4
Millrace Ave	53	A2
Millrace Court	53	A2
*Millrace Court (Millrace Road)	23	B3
Millrace Cres	53	A2
Millrace Drive	53	A2
Millrace Garden	53	A2
Millrace Green	53	A2
Millrace Park	53	A2
Millrace Road	23	B3
Millrace View	53	A2
Millrace Walk	53	A2
*Millrose Estate (off Canal Terrace)	36	E4
Millstead	22	F2
Millstream	14	F2
Millstream Road	33	C2
Milltown (Peamount)	42	F2
Milltown (Clonskeagh)	47	C2
Milltown Ave	47	B2
Milltown Bridge Road	47	C2
*Milltown Collonade (on Milltown Road)	47	B2
Milltown Drive	47	A3
Milltown Grove (Churchtown)	47	A3
*Milltown Grove (off Dundrum Road)	47	B2
*Milltown Hill (off Milltown Road)	47	B2
Milltown Park	47	B1
Milltown Path	47	B2
Milltown Road	47	B2
*Milltown Terrace (off Dundrum Road)	47	B3
*Millview (off Ninth Lock Road)	44	E1
Millview Close	3	A3
Millview Cottages	73	A2
Millview Court	3	A2
Millview Lawns	3	A3
Millview Road	3	A3
Millwood Court	27	A1
Millwood Park	27	A1
Millwood Villas	27	A1
Milner's Square	25	B2
Milton Hall	1	C2
Milton Terrace (Swords)	2	D2
*Milton Terrace (north of Galtrim Park)	67	C2
*Milward Terrace (Meath Road, Victoria Ave)	68	D2
Mimosa Hall	58	F3
Mine Hill Lane	63	B3
Minnow Brook	46	F2
*Minnow Brook (opposite Terenure Park)	46	F2
*Minstrel Court (Charles Sheil's Houses)	58	F2
Misery Hill	72	E4
Mitchelstown	10	D2
Moat Lane	1	A2
Moatfield Ave	26	F1
Moatfield Park	26	F1
Moatfield Road	26	F1
Moatview Ave	13	B4
Moatview Court	13	B4
Moatview Drive	13	B4
Moatview Gardens	13	B4
Moatview Terrace	13	B4
*Mobhi Court (off Saint Mobhi Boithirin)	25	A3
Moeran Road	45	C1
Moira Road (off Oxmanstown Road)	70	D3
Moira Villas	74	F1
Moland House	71	C3
Moland Place	71	C3
Molesworth Close	1	A2
Molesworth Place	75	C1
Molesworth Street	75	C1
Mollison Ave	14	D4
Molyneux Yard	74	F1
Monalea Grove	55	C1
Monalea Park	55	C1
Monalea Wood	55	C1
Monaloe Ave	59	C3
*Monaloe Court (off Clonkeen Road)	59	B3
*Monaloe Cres (off Clonkeen Road)	59	B3
Monaloe Drive	59	C3
Monaloe Park	59	C3
Monaloe Park Road	59	C3
Monaloe Way	59	C3
Monasterboice Road	46	D1
Monastery	66	E3
Monastery Cres	44	E1
Monastery Drive	44	E1
Monastery Gate	44	F1
Monastery Gate Ave	44	F1
Monastery Gate Close	44	F1
Monastery Gate Copse	44	F1
Monastery Gate Green	44	F1
Monastery Gate Lawn	44	F1
Monastery Gate Villas	44	F1
Monastery Grove	66	E2
Monastery Heath	44	E1
Monastery Heath Ave	44	E1
Monastery Heath Court	44	E1
Monastery Heath Green	44	E1
Monastery Heath Square	44	E1
*Monastery Heights (off Monastery Road)	44	E1
Monastery Park	44	E1
Monastery Rise	44	E1
Monastery Road	44	E1
Monastery Walk	44	E1
Monck Place	70	F1
Monks Hill	66	E2
Monks Meadow	4	D4

STREET NAME	PAGE	GRID REF	STREET NAME	PAGE	GRID REF	STREET NAME	PAGE	GRID REF	STREET NAME	PAGE	GRID REF
Monksfield	44	F1	Morehampton Square			Mount Garrett Walk	9	A2	Mountpleasant Villas	75	C4
Monksfield Ave	44	F1	(off Serpentine Park)	76	E4	*Mount Harold Terrace			*Mountpleasant Villas		
Monksfield Court	44	F1	Morehampton Terrace	47	C1	(off Leinster Road)	46	F1	(East of Dargle Heights)	67	B2
Monksfield Downs	44	F1	Morgan Place	70	F4	Mount Hybla Court	23	A4	Mountsandel	59	B4
Monksfield Grove	44	F1	Morgans Place	23	A3	Mount Hybla House	23	A4	Mountseskin Road	53	C4
Monksfield Heights	44	F1	Moritz House	55	B2	Mount Merrion	48	E4	Mountshannon Road	73	C2
Monksfield Lawn	44	F1	Morning Star Ave	70	F3	Mount Merrion Ave	48	F3	*Mounttown Cottages		
Monksfield Meadows	44	F1	Morning Star Road	74	D2	*Mount Norris Villas			(off Mounttown Road)	49	C4
Monksfield Walk	44	F1	*Mornington Ave			(South of Hall)	68	D2	*Mounttown Park		
Monkstown	49	B4	(off Sandycove Point)	50	E4	Mount Olive Grove	27	B1	(off Mounttown Lower)	59	C1
Monkstown Ave	59	B1	Mornington Grove	26	E2	Mount Olive Park	27	B1	Mounttown Road Lower	59	C1
Monkstown Cres	49	C4	Mornington Park	26	E2	Mount Olive Road	27	B1	Mounttown Road Upper	49	C4
Monkstown Farm	59	C1	Mornington Road	47	B1	Mount Prospect Ave	26	F4	Mountview Road	22	D2
*Monkstown Gate			*Morrogh Terrace			Mount Prospect Drive	26	F4	Mourne Road (Brickfields Park)	73	A3
(off The Hill Dún Laoghaire)	49	C4	(off Philipsburgh Ave)	25	C3	Mount Prospect Grove	26	F4	Mourne Road (Drimnagh)	36	F4
Monkstown Grove	59	C1	Morrow House	14	F4	Mount Prospect House			Moy Elta Road	72	E2
*Monkstown Manor			Moss Street	71	C4	(off Clontarf Road)	27	A4	Moy Glas Ave	34	E3
(off Monkstown Farm)	59	B1	Mount Albany	59	A1	Mount Prospect Lawn	26	F4	Moy Glas Chase	34	E3
Monkstown Road	49	B4	Mount Albion Road (Dundrum)	57	B1	Mount Prospect Park	26	F4	Moy Glas Close	34	E3
*Monkstown Square			Mount Alton	55	C1	Mount Saint Annes	47	B2	Moy Glas Court	34	E3
(off Monkstown Ave)	59	B1	Mount Alton Court	56	D1	Mount Salus Road	60	F2	Moy Glas Dale	34	E3
Monkstown Valley	49	B4	Mount Andrew	34	F2	*Mount Sandford			Moy Glas Dene	34	E3
Montague Court	75	B2	Mount Andrew Ave	34	F2	(off Milltown Road)	47	C1	Moy Glas Drive	34	E3
Montague Lane	75	B2	Mount Andrew Close	34	F1	Mount Street Cres	76	E2	Moy Glas Glen	34	E3
Montague Place	75	B2	Mount Andrew Court	34	F1	Mount Street Lower	76	D1	Moy Glas Green	34	E3
Montague Street	75	B2	Mount Andrew Cres	34	F1	Mount Street Upper	76	D2	Moy Glas Grove	34	E3
*Monte Vella			Mount Andrew Dale	34	F2	Mount Symon Ave	21	C2	Moy Glas Lawn	34	E3
(off Barnhill Road)	60	F2	Mount Andrew Grove	34	F1	Mount Symon Close	21	C2	Moy Glas Park	34	E3
*Montebello Terrace			Mount Andrew Place	34	F1	Mount Symon Cres	21	B2	Moy Glas Road	34	E3
(at South Esplanade)	68	D2	Mount Andrew Rise	34	F1	Mount Symon Dale	21	B2	Moy Glas Vale	34	E3
*Montgomery Court			*Mount Anthony Estate			Mount Symon Drive	21	C2	Moy Glas View	34	E3
(West ofConnolly Station)	72	D3	(off Ardee Road)	47	A1	Mount Symon Estate	21	B2	Moy Glas Way	34	E3
Montini Road	27	C1	Mount Anville Lawn	48	D4	Mount Symon Green	21	B2	Moy Glas Wood	34	E3
Montpelier Court	70	D3	Mount Anville Park	48	D4	Mount Symon Lawn	21	C2	Moyclare Ave	28	D1
Montpelier Drive	70	D3	Mount Anville Road	48	D4	Mount Symon Park	21	C2	Moyclare Close	28	D1
Montpelier Gardens	70	D3	Mount Anville Wood	48	D4	Mount Symon Rise	21	B2	Moyclare Drive	28	D1
Montpelier Hill	70	D3	Mount Argus Ave	46	F1	Mount Talbot	44	F1	Moyclare Gardens		
*Montpelier Manor			Mount Argus Close	46	F1	Mount Tallant Ave	46	F2	(off Moyclare Road)	28	D1
(off Monkstown Road)	49	B4	Mount Argus Court	46	F1	Mount Temple Road	70	E3	Moyclare Park	28	D1
*Montpelier Mews			Mount Argus Cres	46	F1	Mount Venus Road	56	D4	Moyclare Road	28	D1
(Montpellier Hill)	70	D3	Mount Argus Green	46	F1	Mount Wood	59	C1	Moycullen Road	35	C3
Montpelier Parade	49	B4	Mount Argus Grove	46	F1	Mountain Park	55	A1	Moygaddy	18	D1
Montpelier Parade Mews			Mount Argus Park	46	F1	Mountain View (Jobstown)	54	D2	Moyglare	17	A1
(off Montpelier Parade)	49	B4	Mount Argus Road	46	F1	Mountain View (Shankill)	64	E3	Moyglare Abbey	17	B2
Montpelier Park	70	D3	*Mount Argus Square			*Mountain View Apts (Vevay			Moyglare Hall	17	C2
*Montpelier Place			(Mount Argus Ave)	46	F1	Road, Wolfe Tone Square)	67	C3	Moyglare Meadows	17	C2
(off Monkstown Road)	49	B4	Mount Argus Terrace	46	F1	*Mountain View Ave			Moyglare Road	17	C2
Montpelier Square	70	D3	Mount Argus View	46	F1	(off Shamrock Villas)	46	F1	Moyglare Village	17	C2
Montpelier View	54	D2	Mount Argus Way	46	F1	Mountain View Cottages			Moyle Cres	44	E1
*Montpelier Walk			*Mount Auburn			(Castleknock)	22	D4	Moyle Road	24	E3
(off Kiltalown Road)	54	D2	(off Killiney Hill Road)	60	E3	*Mountain View Cottages			*Moyne Court (off Moyne Road)	47	B1
Montpellier Mews	70	D4	Mount Bellew Cres	34	F2	(off Mountain View Road)	47	B1	Moyne Lodge	14	F3
Montrose Ave	26	D2	Mount Bellew Green	34	F2	Mountain View Court	71	C2	Moyne Park	14	F3
Montrose Close	26	D2	Mount Bellew Rise	34	E2	*Mountain View Court			Moyne Road (Balgriffin)	14	E3
Montrose Court	26	D2	Mount Bellew Way	34	E2	(off Shamrock Villas)	46	F1	Moyne Road (Ranelagh)	47	B1
Montrose Cres	26	D1	Mount Brown	73	C1	Mountain View Drive	57	A1	*Moynihan Court		
Montrose Drive	26	D1	Mount Carmel	71	A3	Mountain View Park			(off Avonmore Road)	55	B1
Montrose Grove	26	D2	Mount Carmel Ave	47	C4	(Churchtown)	47	A4	Moyville	56	E2
Montrose Park	26	D2	Mount Carmel Park	55	C1	Mountain View Road (Ranelagh)	47	B1	Moyville Lawns	56	E1
Moore Lane	71	B3	Mount Carmel Road	47	C4	*Mountain View Road			Muckross Ave	46	D2
Moore Street	71	B3	Mount Dillon Court	26	E2	(off Church Road Ballybrack)	60	E4	Muckross Cres	46	D2
Moorefield	60	E4	Mount Drinan Ave	2	E3	*Mountain Villa (off Dale View)	60	E4	*Muckross Drive		
*Moore's Cottages			Mount Drinan Cres	2	E3	Mountainview Drive	67	C4	(off Muckross Ave)	46	D2
(off Annaville Ave)	59	A1	Mount Drinan Grove	2	E3	*Mountbrook (off Seamount)	48	E3	Muckross Green	46	D2
Mooretown	1	B1	Mount Drinan Lawn	2	E3	Mountdown Ave	45	C3	Muckross Grove	46	D2
Mooretown Ave	1	C1	Mount Drinan Park	2	E3	Mountdown Drive	45	C3	Muckross Parade	71	B1
Mooretown Grove	1	C1	Mount Drinan Walk	2	E3	Mountdown Park	45	C3	Muckross Park	46	D2
Mooretown Park	1	C1	Mount Drummond Ave	74	F4	Mountdown Road	45	C3	*Muirfield Drive		
Moorfield	35	A4	Mount Drummond Court	74	F4	Mountfield	3	B3	(off Naas Road Bluebell)	36	F4
Moorfield Ave	35	A4	Mount Drummond Square	75	A4	Mountfield Lawn	3	C3	Mulally's Lane	52	F2
*Moorfield Close			Mount Eagle Court	58	E3	Mountfield Lodge	3	C3	Mulberry Cres	22	F4
(off Moorefield Drive)	35	A4	Mount Eagle Drive	58	E3	Mountfield Park	3	C4	Mulberry Drive	22	E4
Moorfield Drive	35	A4	Mount Eagle Green	58	E3	Mountgorry Lodge	2	E2	Mulberry Park	22	E4
Moorfield Green	35	A4	Mount Eagle Grove	58	E3	Mountgorry Wood Apts	2	E2	Muldowney Court	3	C3
Moorfield Grove	35	A4	Mount Eagle Lawn	58	E3	Mountjoy Parade	71	C1	Mulgrave Street	50	D4
Moorfield Lawns	35	A4	Mount Eagle Park	58	E3	Mountjoy Place	71	C2	Mulgrave Terrace	50	D4
Moorfield Parade	35	A4	Mount Eagle Rise	58	D3	Mountjoy Square	71	C2	Mulhuddart	9	A4
Moorfield Walk	35	A4	Mount Eagle View	58	E3	Mountjoy Square Apts			Mulhuddart Bridge	9	A4
Moracrete Cottages	73	C4	Mount Eagle Way	58	E3	(Mountjoy Square West)	71	B2	Mulhuddart Wood	9	A4
*Moran's Cottages			Mount Eden Road	47	C1	Mountjoy Square Apts			Mullauns	42	D1
(off Charleston Road)	47	B1	Mount Eustace	9	B2	(Mountjoy Square South)	71	C2	Mullen Bridge	18	D3
Moreen Ave	58	D2	Mount Eustace Ave	9	B2	Mountjoy Square East	71	C2	*Mullinahack		
Moreen Close	58	D2	Mount Eustace Close	9	A2	Mountjoy Square North	71	C2	(Oliver Bond Street)	70	F4
*Moreen Lawn (off Moreen Ave)	58	D2	Mount Eustace Drive	9	B2	Mountjoy Square South	71	C2	Mullinastill Road	64	D2
Moreen Park	58	D2	Mount Eustace Green	9	B2	Mountjoy Square West	71	B2	*Mullingar Terrace		
Moreen Road	58	D2	Mount Eustace Grove	9	A2	Mountjoy Street	71	A2	(off Martin's Row Chapelizod)	36	E2
Moreen Walk	58	D2	Mount Eustace Park	9	B2	Mountjoy Street Middle	71	A2	Mulroy Road	24	E4
*Morehampton Hall			Mount Eustace Rise	9	B2	Mountpleasant Ave Lower	75	B4	Mulvey Park	47	C3
(off Morehampton Terrace)	47	C1	Mount Eustace Walk	9	B2	Mountpleasant Ave Upper	75	B4	Munster Street	24	F4
*Morehampton Hall			Mount Gandon (off Lucan Road)	34	D1	Mountpleasant Parade	75	B4	*Munster Terrace		
(off Morehampton Terrace)	47	C1	Mount Garrett	9	A2	Mountpleasant Place	75	C4	(off Breffni Road)	60	E1
Morehampton Lane	76	E4	Mount Garrett Ave	9	A2	Mountpleasant Square	75	B4	Murphy's Lane	63	B4
Morehampton Mews			Mount Garrett Close	9	A2	Mountpleasant Terrace	75	B4	Murphystown Road	58	E2
(off Sandymount Ave)	76	E4	Mount Garrett Drive	9	A2	*Mountpleasant Terrace Upper			Murphystown Way	58	E3
Morehampton Road	76	E4	Mount Garrett Rise	9	A2	(Mountpleasant Villas)	75	C4	Murragh	14	F2

STREET NAME	PAGE	GRID REF
*Murray's Cottages (off Sarsfield Road)	36	F3
Murrough Road	1	B1
Murtagh Road	70	E3
Muskerry Road	36	E3
Mutton Lane	56	E4
Myra Close	73	A1
Myra Manor	3	A4
*Myrtle Ave (off Royal Terrace East)	60	D1
Myrtle Grove (Stillorgan)	58	F1
*Myrtle Grove (off Beech Road)	67	B1
Myrtle Park	60	D1
Myrtle Square	14	F4
Myrtle Street	71	A2

N

STREET NAME	PAGE	GRID REF
N2 Junction 1 (M50/N2 Finglas)	11	A4
N2/M2 Junction 2 (Saint Margaret's)	10	D1
N4 Junction 1 (N4/M50)	35	B1
N4 Junction 2 (Liffey Valley)	35	A1
N4 Junction 3 (Lucan)	34	E1
N4 Junction 4 (Newcastle)	34	D2
N4 Junction 4a (Dodsboro)	33	C2
N7 Junction 1 (M50/N7 Red Cow)	44	F2
N7 Junction 1A (Newlands Cross)	44	E2
N7 Junction 2 (Kingswood)	43	C3
N7 Junction 3 (Citywest)	43	B4
N7 Junction 4 (Rathcoole)	52	F1
N7 Junction 5 (Athgoe)	51	B3
Naas Road (Walkinstown)	45	A1
Naas Road (Rathcoole)	52	F1
Naas Road (Saggart)	53	B1
Naas Road (Kingswood)	43	C4
Nagle Court	18	D2
*Nangor Cres (off Cherrywood Villas)	44	D1
Nangor Place (off Cherrywood Villas)	43	C1
Nangor Road (Grange Castle)	43	A2
Nangor Road (Clondalkin)	44	D1
Nangor Road (Fox and Geese)	44	F1
Nanikin Ave	27	A3
Nash Street	36	F3
Nashville Park	30	E2
Nashville Road	30	D2
Nassau Street	75	C1
Naul Road (Brackenstown Road)	1	A3
Naul Road (Cloghran)	1	C4
Navan Road (Cabra)	69	C1
Navan Road (Dunboyne)	7	B2
Navan Road (Clonee)	8	E3
Navan Road (Mulhuddart)	8	F4
Navan Road (Blanchardstown)	22	E1
Navan Road (Castleknock)	23	A3
Neagh Road	46	E2
Neilstown Ave	35	A3
*Neilstown Cottages (off Newlands Road)	35	A4
Neilstown Cres	35	A3
Neilstown Drive	35	A3
Neilstown Gardens	35	A3
Neilstown Park	35	A3
Neilstown Road	35	A3
*Neilstown Village Court (off Neilstown Road)	35	A3
Nelson Street	71	A1
Nephin Road	24	D4
*Neptune Terrace (off Breffni Road)	60	E1
Nerano Road	60	G2
Nerney's Court	71	B2
Nethercross Court	2	D1
Neville Road	47	A2
Nevinstown Lane	1	C3
*New Bancroft Hall (off Main Street Tallaght)	55	A1
*New Bancroft Place (off Main Street Tallaght)	55	A1
*New Bancroft Square (off Main Street Tallaght)	55	A1
New Bawn Drive	55	A2
New Bawn Park	55	A2
New Bride Street	75	A2
New Bridge	32	F2
*New Brighton Terrace (Parnell Road)	67	C2
*New Cornelscourt (off Bray Road)	59	B3
*New Court (New Street South)	75	A2
New Grange Road	59	A1
New Grove Estate	14	E4
New Ireland Court	73	C2
New Ireland Road	73	C2
New Lucan Road	35	B1
New Nangor Road	43	C1
*New Park Lodge (off Knocksinna Park)	59	A2
New Park Road	59	A1
*New Rathmore Terrace (Upper Dargle Road)	67	B2
*New Ravenswell Row (near Ardee Street)	67	B2
New River Road	23	A2
New Road (Howth)	30	E3
New Road (Inchicore)	36	F3
New Road (Clondalkin)	44	E2
*New Row (off Martin's Row Chapelizod)	36	E2
New Row Place	75	A2
New Row South	74	F2
New Row Square	74	F2
New Street	3	B2
New Street Gardens (off New Street)	75	A2
New Street North (off Church Street)	70	F3
New Street South	75	A2
New Vale	64	E3
New Vale Cottages	64	D3
New Vale Cres	64	E3
New Wapping Street	72	F3
Newbridge Ave (Irishtown)	39	A3
Newbridge Drive	39	A3
Newbrook Ave	27	B1
Newbrook Road	27	B1
Newbury Ave	13	A4
Newbury Drive	13	A4
Newbury Grove	13	A4
*Newbury Heights (on Clonshaugh Road)	13	A4
Newbury Lawns	13	B4
Newbury Park	13	A4
*Newbury Terrace (on Clonshaugh Road)	13	A4
Newbury Wood	13	A4
Newcastle	41	C4
Newcastle Apts	20	D4
Newcastle Boulevard	42	D4
Newcastle Demesne	41	B4
Newcastle Farm	41	B4
Newcastle Lyons	42	D4
Newcastle Manor	42	D4
Newcastle Manor (The Square)	42	D4
Newcastle Manor Green	42	D4
Newcastle Manor Heights	42	D4
Newcastle Manor Park	42	D4
*Newcastle Manor Place (Newcastle Manor)	42	D4
Newcastle Manor Square	42	D4
Newcastle Manor: The Close	42	D4
Newcastle Manor: The Court	42	D4
Newcastle Manor: The Cres	42	D4
Newcastle Manor: The Green	42	D4
Newcastle Manor: The Heights	42	D4
Newcastle Manor: The Park	42	D4
*Newcastle Manor: The Place (Newcastle Manor)	42	D4
Newcastle Manor: The Rise	42	D4
Newcastle Road (Lucan)	34	D2
Newcastle Road (Rathcoole)	52	E1
Newcomen Ave	72	D1
Newcomen Bridge (Royal Canal)	72	D2
Newcomen Court	72	D1
Newcourt (Bray)	68	D4
Newcourt Ave	68	D3
Newcourt Mews	2	D1
Newcourt Road	68	D3
*Newcourt Villas (start of Putland Road)	67	C3
Newgrange Road	24	F4
Newgrove Ave	39	B4
Newhall Court	54	D2
*Newington Terrace (off Castlewood Ave)	47	A1
Newlands Ave	44	E2
Newlands Court	26	D2
Newlands Drive	44	E2
Newlands Manor	44	D3
Newlands Manor Court	44	D3
Newlands Manor Drive	44	D3
Newlands Manor Fairway	44	D3
Newlands Manor Green	44	D3
Newlands Manor Park	44	D3
Newlands Park	44	E2
Newlands Road (Ronanstown)	34	F3
Newlands Road (Clondalkin)	44	E2
Newman Place	18	D3
Newmarket	74	F2
*Newmarket Hall (off Newmarket)	74	F2
*Newmarket Square (off Ward's Hill)	74	F2
*Newmarket Street	74	F2
Newpark	59	A2
Newport Street	74	E1
Newtown (Dunboyne)	7	A3
Newtown (Rathfarnham)	56	F3
Newtown (Glencullen)	62	E3
Newtown (Tinnehinch)	66	E4
Newtown Ave (Coolock)	26	F1
Newtown Ave (Blackrock)	49	A3
Newtown Bridge	7	A2
Newtown Close	13	C4
Newtown Cottages (Saint Margaret's)	11	A1
Newtown Cottages (Coolock)	26	F1
Newtown Court (Coolock)	13	C4
Newtown Court (Maynooth)	17	B4
*Newtown Court (off Eaton Brae Rathgar)	47	A3
Newtown Drive	26	F1
Newtown Glendale	20	D4
Newtown Grove	17	C3
Newtown Hall	17	B3
*Newtown House (off Eaton Brae Rathgar)	47	A3
Newtown Lower	51	C4
Newtown Park (Leixlip)	20	D4
Newtown Park (Coolock)	26	F1
Newtown Park (Tallaght)	55	B1
Newtown Park (Blackrock)	59	A1
*Newtown Park Court (off Mount Albany)	59	A1
Newtown Road (Coolock)	13	C4
Newtown Road (Maynooth)	17	B4
Newtown Road (Celbridge)	32	D4
Newtown Upper	52	D4
*Newtown Villas (off Braemor Road)	47	A3
*Newtown Villas (off Newtown Ave Blackrock)	49	A3
Newtown Way	13	C4
Newtownpark Ave	49	A4
*Newtownpark House (off Mount Albany)	59	A1
Newtownsmith	50	E4
Niall Street	70	D2
Nicholas Ave	70	F3
Nicholas Street	75	A1
Ninth Lock Road	44	D1
No2 Nth. Road Extension	39	A2
Noel Purcell Park	75	B1
Nore Road	24	E3
Norfolk Road	24	F4
Norseman Court (off Norseman Place)	70	E3
Norseman Place	70	E3
North Ave	48	E3
North Bull Island	27	B4
North Circular Road (Phibsborough)	71	C1
North Circular Road (Phoenix Park)	70	D2
North Circular Road Gate (Phoenix Park)	69	C3
North Clarence Street Flats	72	D2
North Great George's Street	71	B2
North Lotts	71	B4
North Quay Extension	39	A2
North Road (Phoenix Park North Circular)	69	B1
North Road (Finglas)	24	D1
North Road (Phoenix Park Ashtown)	23	B4
North Road (Kilshane)	10	F2
North Strand Road	72	E1
North Street	2	D1
North Street	21	A1
North Wall	72	E3
North Wall Quay	72	E4
*Northbank Apts (Alexander Terrace)	72	F3
Northbrook Ave (Ranelagh)	75	C4
Northbrook Ave Lower	72	E1
Northbrook Ave Upper	72	E1
Northbrook Lane	75	C4
Northbrook Road	75	C4
Northbrook Terrace	72	E1
Northbrook Villas	75	C4
Northbrook Walk	75	C4
Northcote Ave	49	C4
*Northcote Place (off North Cote Ave)	49	C4
*Northcote Terrace (off North Cote Ave)	49	C4
Northern Close	13	B3
Northern Cross Route (Poppintree)	11	B3
Northern Cross Route (Abbotstown)	23	A2
Northland Drive (off Tolka Estate)	24	F3
Northland Grove (off Tolka Estate)	24	F3
Northumberland Ave	50	D4
Northumberland Court	76	E2
*Northumberland Park (off Northumberland Ave Dún Laoghaire)	50	D4
Northumberland Place (Grand Canal Street Upper)	76	E2
*Northumberland Place (off Northumberland Ave Dún Laoghaire)	50	D4
Northumberland Road	76	E2
Northumberland Square	71	C3
Northway Estate	11	A4
Northwood	12	E4
Northwood Ave	12	E4
Northwood Road	12	D4
Norton's Ave	70	F1
Norwood	64	E1
*Norwood Park (off Sandford Road)	47	C1
Nottingham Street	72	E1
Novara Ave	67	C2
*Novara Mews (Novara Ave)	67	C2
*Novara Park (Novara Ave)	67	C2
*Novara Terrace (Novara Ave)	67	C2
Nugent Road	47	A4
Nunciature Road (Phoenix Park)	23	C4
Nun's Lane	26	E3
Nuns Walk	26	E3
Nurney Lawn	14	D4
Nutgrove Ave	47	A4
*Nutgrove Ave (off Nutgrove Ave)	47	B4
*Nutgrove Court (off Nutgrove Ave)	47	A4
Nutgrove Cres	57	A1
Nutgrove Park (Clonskeagh)	47	C2
Nutgrove Way	57	A1
Nutley Ave	48	D1
Nutley Lane	48	D2
Nutley Park	48	D2
Nutley Road	48	D1
*Nutley Square (off Greenfield Park U.C.D.)	48	D2

O

STREET NAME	PAGE	GRID REF
O Neill's Park	18	D3
Oak Apple Green	47	A2
Oak Ave	12	F4
Oak Close	44	F1
Oak Court	12	F4
Oak Cres	12	F4
Oak Dene	60	E3
Oak Downs	44	D2
Oak Drive (Santry)	12	F4
Oak Drive (Fox and Geese)	44	F1
Oak Glen Park	67	C4
Oak Glen View	67	C4
Oak Green	12	F4
Oak Grove	12	F4
Oak Hall	3	B3
Oak House (Sussex Road)	76	D3
Oak House (Swords)	1	Inset
Oak Lawn (Santry)	12	F4
Oak Lawn (Castleknock)	22	F3
Oak Lodge	23	A4
Oak Rise (Santry)	12	F4
Oak Rise (Clondalkin)	44	D2
Oak Road (Donnycarney)	26	D3
Oak Road (Fox and Geese)	44	F1

STREET NAME	PAGE	GRID REF
Oak View	12	E4
Oak Way	44	D2
*Oakbury Court (off Serpentine Ave)	39	A4
Oakcourt Ave	35	C2
Oakcourt Close	35	C2
Oakcourt Drive	35	C2
Oakcourt Grove	35	C2
Oakcourt Lawn	35	C2
Oakcourt Park	35	C2
Oakdale Close	55	B3
Oakdale Cres	55	B3
Oakdale Drive (Firhouse)	55	B3
Oakdale Drive (Sallynoggin)	59	C2
Oakdale Grove	55	B3
Oakdale Park	55	B3
Oakdale Road	55	B3
Oakdown Road	47	A4
Oakfield Place	75	A3
Oaklands Ave	2	D2
*Oaklands Court (off Claremont Road)	39	A4
Oaklands Cres	47	A2
Oaklands Drive (Sandymount)	39	A4
Oaklands Drive (Rathgar)	47	A2
Oaklands Park (Swords)	2	D2
Oaklands Park (Sandymount)	39	A4
Oaklands Terrace	46	F2
Oaklawn	19	C4
Oaklawn Close	19	C4
Oaklawn West	19	C4
Oakleigh	31	C4
Oakleigh Court	3	A3
*Oakley Court (off Oakley Road)	47	B1
Oakley Grove	49	A4
Oakley Park (Clontarf)	26	F4
*Oakley Park (off Oakley Road)	47	B1
Oakley Park (Blackrock)	49	A4
Oakley Road	47	B1
*Oakley Square (off Oakley Road)	47	B1
Oakpark Ave	25	C1
Oakpark Close	25	C1
Oakpark Drive	25	C1
Oakpark Grove	25	C1
Oaks (opposite Knockmaroon Gate)	36	D1
*Oakton Court (off Oakton Park)	60	E4
Oakton Drive	60	D4
*Oakton Green (off Oakton Park)	60	D4
Oakton Park	60	D1
Oaktree Ave	22	E3
Oaktree Drive	22	E3
Oaktree Green	22	E3
Oaktree Grove	22	E3
Oaktree Lawn	22	E3
Oaktree Road	58	F1
Oakview	66	D3
Oakview Ave	21	C1
Oakview Close	21	C1
Oakview Court	21	C1
Oakview Drive	21	C1
*Oakview Grove (off Oakview Ave)	21	C1
Oakview Lawn	21	C1
Oakview Park	21	C1
Oakview Rise	21	C1
Oakview Walk	21	C1
Oakview Way	21	C1
*Oakwood (off Tivoli Road)	49	C4
*Oakwood Apts (off The Glen Raheny)	27	B3
Oakwood Ave (Swords)	1	C2
Oakwood Ave (Glasnevin)	24	E1
Oakwood Close	24	E1
Oakwood Grove Estate	35	A4
Oakwood Park	24	E1
Oakwood Road	24	E1
Oatfield Ave	35	B3
Oatfield Close	35	B3
*Oatfield Cres (off Oatfield Drive)	35	B2
Oatfield Drive	35	B3
Oatfield Grove	35	B3
Oatfield Lawn	35	B3
Oatfield Park	35	B3
*Obelisk Ave (off Obelisk Grove)	59	A1
Obelisk Court	3	C2
Obelisk Court (Stillorgan)	59	A1
Obelisk Grove	59	A1
Obelisk Lane	18	E4
Obelisk Rise	59	A1
Obelisk Walk	59	A1
*Oblate Drive (off Nash Street)	36	F3
*Oblate View Apts (Tyrconnell Road opposite Church)	36	F3
O'Brien Road	45	C1
*O'Brien's Place North (off Joyce Road)	25	A3
Observatory Court	75	B4
*Observatory Lane (off Rathmines Road Lower)	47	A1
O'Byrne Road	67	C3
*O'Byrne Villas (O'Byrne Road)	67	C3
*O'Callaghan Court	76	D1
O'Carolan Road	74	F2
O'Casey Ave	35	C4
O'Connell Ave	71	A1
O'Connell Bridge (River Liffey)	71	B4
O'Connell Gardens	39	A3
O'Connell Street	71	B3
O'Curry Ave (off O'Curry Road)	74	F2
O'Curry Road	74	F2
O'Daly Road	25	A3
Odd Lamp Road (Phoenix Park)	36	F1
O'Devaney Gardens	70	D3
*O'Donnell Gardens (off Eden Road Lower)	60	D1
O'Donoghue Street	36	F3
O'Donovan Road	74	F3
O'Donovan Rossa Bridge (River Liffey)	71	A4
*O'Dwyer Road (off O'Brien Road)	45	C1
Offaly Bridge	18	E1
Offaly Road	24	F4
Offington Ave	29	B2
Offington Court	29	B2
Offington Drive	29	B2
Offington Lawn	29	B2
Offington Manor Apts	29	B1
Offington Park	29	B1
Ogham	60	D3
O'Hanlon's Lane	3	B2
O'Hara Ave	75	A4
*O'Hogan Close (off O'Hogan Road)	36	E3
O'Hogan Road	36	E3
*Oisin Court (off Claremont Road)	39	A4
*Olaf Hall (off Balally Hill)	58	D2
*Olaf House Apts (Ushers Quay)	70	F4
Olaf Road	70	E3
Olcovar	64	E3
Old Bawn Ave	55	A2
Old Bawn Bridge	55	A2
Old Bawn Close	55	A2
*Old Bawn Court (off Old Bawn Road)	55	A1
Old Bawn Drive	55	A2
Old Bawn Park	55	A2
Old Bawn Road	55	A1
Old Bawn Terrace	55	A2
Old Bawn Way	55	A2
Old Belgard Road	44	F4
Old Blessington Road	55	A1
Old Brazil Way	1	A2
Old Bridge Road	46	D4
*Old Brighton Terrace (Parnell Road)	67	C2
Old Cabra Road	70	D1
Old Camac Bridge (Camac River)	73	B1
Old Carrickbrack Road	30	D4
Old Connaught	67	A1
Old Connaught Ave	67	B1
Old Connaught Grove	67	B2
Old Connaught View	67	B2
Old Corduff Road	22	E1
Old Cornmill Road	33	C2
Old County Glen	73	C4
Old County Road	73	B4
Old Dublin Road (Stillorgan)	48	E4
Old Dunleary	49	C4
Old Estuary Mill	2	F2
Old Fairgreen	7	B2
Old Fort Road	1	A2
Old Glenamuck Road	63	A1
Old Greenfield	17	C4
Old Hill	20	D4
Old Kilmainham	73	C1
Old Kilmainham Village	74	D1
Old Mill Court	74	F2
Old Mountpleasant	75	C4
Old Naas Road (Bluebell)	36	E4
Old Naas Road (Brownsbarn)	43	C4
*Old Naas Road Cottages (off Old Naas Road)	36	E4
Old Navan Road	22	F2
Old Orchard	46	E4
*Old Orchard Terrace (near Owendore Ave)	46	F4
Old Quarry (Kilshane)	10	D2
Old Quarry (Dalkey)	60	F2
Old Quay	29	B2
Old Quay Mews	29	B2
Old Quay Terrace	29	B2
Old Rathmichael	64	D3
*Old Rathmore Terrace (Upper Dargle Road)	67	B2
*Old Ravenswell Row (Upper Dargle Road)	67	B2
*Old Rectory (off Chapel Hill)	34	D1
Old Rectory Park	47	C4
Old Road	14	E2
Old Street	3	B2
Old Yellow Walls Road	3	A2
Oldbawn	55	A2
Oldbridge	34	E3
Oldbridge Close	34	E3
Oldbridge Court	34	E3
Oldbridge Glen	34	E3
Oldbridge Green	34	E3
Oldbridge Grove	34	E3
Oldbridge Park	34	E3
Oldbridge View	34	E3
Oldbridge Walk	34	E3
Oldbridge Way	34	E3
Oldcarton	18	F1
Oldcastle Ave	29	B2
Oldcastle Drive	43	B1
Oldcastlepark	43	B1
Oldcastlepark Close	43	B1
Oldcastlepark Green	43	B1
Oldcastlepark Grove	43	B1
Oldcastlepark Lawn	43	B1
Oldcastlepark View	43	B1
Oldchurch Ave	43	C1
Oldchurch Close	43	C1
Oldchurch Court	43	C1
Oldchurch Cres	43	C1
Oldchurch Drive	43	C1
Oldchurch Grove	43	C1
Oldchurch Lawn	43	C1
Oldchurch Park	43	C1
Oldchurch Way	43	C1
Oldcourt	67	B3
Oldcourt Ave (Bohernabreena)	55	B2
Oldcourt Ave (Boghall Road)	67	B3
Oldcourt Close	55	B2
Oldcourt Cottages	55	B3
Oldcourt Drive	67	B3
Oldcourt Farm	55	B2
Oldcourt Grove	67	B4
*Oldcourt Lawn (off Oldcourt Ave)	55	B2
Oldcourt Lodge	55	B2
Oldcourt Manor	55	B3
*Oldcourt Mill (off Oldcourt Road)	55	B3
Oldcourt Park	67	B3
Oldcourt Road	55	B3
*Oldcourt Terrace (Vevay Road, Lauderdale Estate)	67	C3
Oldcourt View	55	B2
Oldfarm	22	E3
Oldfield Hall	57	C3
Oldtower Cres	35	A2
Oldtown Ave	25	A1
Oldtown Cottages	31	C3
Oldtown Mill	31	C3
Oldtown Mill Road	31	C3
*Oldtown Park (off Shanliss Road)	25	A1
Oldtown Road	25	A1
Oldtown Road	31	B3
O'Leary Road	73	B2
*Olivemount Grove (off Olivemount Road)	47	C3
Olivemount Road	47	C3
*Olivemount Terrace (off Olivemount Road)	47	C3
Oliver Bond House Flats	70	F4
Oliver Bond Street	70	F4
Oliver Plunkett Ave (Ringsend)	39	A3
Oliver Plunkett Ave (Dún Laoghaire)	59	C1
Oliver Plunkett Road	59	C1
*Oliver Plunkett Square (off Oliver Plunkett Road)	59	C1
*Oliver Plunkett Terrace (off Oliver Plunkett Road)	59	C1
*Oliver Plunkett Villas (off Oliver Plunkett Ave)	59	B1
*Oliver's Alley (off Wood Street)	75	A1
Olney Cres	46	F2
*Olney Grove (off Olney Cres)	46	F2
*Olympic Apts (Pleasants Street)	75	A2
Omni Park	25	B1
O'Moore Road	36	E3
*O'Neachtain Road (off Ferguson Road)	25	A3
O'Neill's Buildings	75	A1
Ongar Chase Estate	21	A1
Ongar Green	21	A1
Ongar Green Ave	21	A1
Ongar Green Cres	21	A1
Ongar Green Drive	21	A1
Ongar Green Green	21	A1
Ongar Green Place	21	A1
Ongar Park Estate	21	B1
Ongar Road	21	B2
Ongar Square	21	A1
Ongar Village	21	A1
Ongar-Hartstown Relief Road	21	C2
Ontario Terrace	75	B4
Onward Close	3	C4
Onward Walk	3	C4
Ophaly Court	47	C4
*O'Rahilly House Flats (off Thorncastle Street)	39	A3
O'Rahilly Parade	71	B3
Oranmore Road	35	C3
*Oratory Mews Court (off Library Road)	50	D4
Orby Ave	58	E3
Orby Close	58	F3
Orby Court	58	F3
Orby Lawn	58	E3
Orby Park	58	F3
Orby View	58	E3
Orby Village	58	E3
Orby Way	58	E3
Orchard Ave (Clonsilla)	21	C2
Orchard Ave (Citywest)	53	B1
Orchard Close	22	D2
*Orchard Cottages (off Newtown Park)	59	A1
Orchard Court	22	E2
Orchard Green	22	E2
Orchard Grove (Blanchardstown)	22	E2
Orchard Grove (Newcastle)	42	D4
Orchard Lane (Ranelagh)	75	C4
Orchard Lane (Clondalkin)	44	E1
Orchard Lane (Blackrock)	59	A1
Orchard Lawns	35	C3
Orchard Lodge	44	E1
Orchard Road (Ballybough)	25	B4
Orchard Road (Raheny)	27	B2
Orchard Road South	47	B2
Orchard Square	47	C3
*Orchard Terrace (Grangegorman Upper)	70	F1
*Orchard Terrace (Vevay Road, Putland Road)	67	C3
*Orchard View (Near Marne Villas)	70	F2
Orchardstown Ave	46	E4
Orchardstown Drive	46	E4
Orchardstown Park	46	E4
Orchardstown Villas	56	E1
*Orchardton (off Willow Bank Drive)	56	E1
Ordnance Survey Road (Phoenix Park)	36	E1
O'Reilly Ave	73	C1
O'Reilly's Cottages	74	F4
Oriel Hall	72	D3
Oriel Street Lower	72	E2
Oriel Street Upper	72	E2
Orlagh Ave	56	D2
Orlagh Close	56	D2
Orlagh Court	56	D2
Orlagh Cres	56	D2
Orlagh Downs	56	D2
Orlagh Grange	56	D2
Orlagh Green	56	D2
Orlagh Grove	56	D2
Orlagh Lawn	56	D2
Orlagh Lodge	56	D2
Orlagh Meadows	56	D2
Orlagh Park	56	D2
Orlagh Pines	56	D2
Orlagh Rise	56	D2
Orlagh View	56	D2
Orlagh Way	56	D2
Orlagh Wood	56	D2

STREET NAME	PAGE	GRID REF
*Ormeau Drive (off Carysfort Road)	60	F1
Ormeau Street	76	F1
Ormond Ave	1	B1
Ormond Close	1	B1
Ormond Cres	1	B1
Ormond Drive	1	B1
Ormond Grove	1	B1
Ormond Lawn	1	B1
Ormond Market (off Ormond Quay Upper)	71	A4
Ormond Place	71	A4
Ormond Quay Lower	71	B4
Ormond Quay Upper	71	A4
Ormond Road	25	B4
Ormond Road South	47	B1
Ormond Square	71	A4
Ormond Street	74	F2
*Ormond Terrace (off Sorrento Road)	60	F2
Ormond View	1	B1
Ormond Way	1	B1
O'Rourke Park	59	C2
Orpen	58	F1
Orpen Close	48	F4
*Orpen Dale (off Stillorgan Grove)	48	F4
Orpen Green	58	F1
Orpen Hill	58	F1
Orpen Rise	58	F1
Orr's Terrace	74	F4
*Orwell Bank (off Orwell Park)	47	A3
*Orwell Court (off Braemor Road)	47	A3
Orwell Gardens	47	A3
*Orwell Mews (off Orwell Road Rathgar)	47	A2
Orwell Park (Templeogue)	45	C4
Orwell Park (Rathgar)	47	A3
Orwell Park Ave	46	D3
Orwell Park Close	46	D3
Orwell Park Cres	46	D3
Orwell Park Dale	45	C4
Orwell Park Drive	46	D3
Orwell Park Glade	45	C3
Orwell Park Glen	46	D3
Orwell Park Green	46	D3
Orwell Park Grove	45	C3
Orwell Park Heights	45	C4
Orwell Park Lawns	45	C3
Orwell Park Rise	45	C4
Orwell Park View	45	C4
Orwell Park Way	46	D3
Orwell Road	47	A2
Orwell Walk	47	A3
Orwell Woods	47	A2
*Osborne Court (off Seapoint Ave)	49	B3
*Osborne Terrace (Northbrook Road)	75	C4
Oscar Square	74	F2
Oscar Traynor Road (Kilmore)	13	A4
Oscar Traynor Road (Coolock)	26	E1
*O'Shea's Cottages (off Bray Road Cabinteely)	59	C3
Osprey Ave	45	C3
*Osprey Court (beside Telephone Exchange)	64	E3
Osprey Drive	45	C3
Osprey Lawn	45	C3
Osprey Park	45	C3
Osprey Road	45	C3
Ossory Road	72	E2
*Ossory Road Apts (near Ossory Industrial Estate)	72	E2
Ostman Place	70	E3
O'Sullivan Ave	72	D1
Oswald Road	39	A3
Otranto Place	60	E1
*Otterbrook (off Willbrook Road)	46	F4
Oulart	1	C3
Oulton Road	26	E4
Ounavarra	33	C1
Our Lady's Close (off Our Lady's Road)	74	E2
Our Lady's Road	74	E2
Outer Ring Road	43	B2
Outfarm Lane	22	E3
Outlands	1	B1
*Ovenden House (off Dean Street)	75	A2
Overend Way	57	C1
Ovoca Road	75	A3
Owendoher Haven	56	E1

STREET NAME	PAGE	GRID REF
Owendoher Lodge	56	E1
Owendore Ave	46	F4
Owendore Cres	46	F4
Owen's Ave	73	C1
Owensilla	24	F1
Owenstown Park	48	D3
*Oxford Grove (off Oxford Road)	47	B1
Oxford Lane	75	C4
Oxford Road	47	B1
Oxford Terrace (on Hawthorn Terrace)	72	E2
Oxmantown Lane	70	F4
Oxmantown Road	70	D2

P

STREET NAME	PAGE	GRID REF
Pace Ave	8	E4
Pace Cres	8	E4
Pace Road	8	E4
Pace View	8	E4
Pacelli Ave	27	C1
Pairc Gleann Trasna	55	A3
Páirc Mhuire	53	A2
Páirc View	53	A2
*Pakenham (off Sloperton)	49	C4
Pakenham Bridge	21	C4
Pakenham Road	49	C4
*Palace Garden Apts (Palace Street)	71	B4
Palace Street (off Dame Street)	71	B4
Palmer Park	56	F2
Palmers Ave	35	B2
Palmers Close	35	B2
Palmers Copse	35	B2
Palmers Court	35	B2
Palmers Cres	35	B2
Palmers Drive	35	B2
Palmers Glade	35	B2
Palmers Grove	35	B2
Palmers Lawn	35	B2
Palmers Park	35	B2
Palmers Road	35	B2
Palmers Walk	35	B2
Palmerston	35	C1
*Palmerston Close (off Windsor Road)	47	B1
Palmerston Court	47	A1
Palmerston Gardens	47	B2
*Palmerston Grove (off Milltown Road)	47	C2
*Palmerston Hall Apts (Palmerston Place)	71	A2
Palmerston Lane	47	B2
Palmerston Park (Rathgar)	47	B2
Palmerston Place	71	A2
Palmerston Road	47	B1
Palmerston Villas	47	A2
Palmerstown Ave	35	C2
Palmerstown Close	35	B2
Palmerstown Court	35	C2
Palmerstown Drive	35	C2
Palmerstown Green	35	B2
Palmerstown Heights	35	B2
Palmerstown Lawn	35	B2
Palmerstown Manor	35	B2
Palmerstown Park (Kennelsfort Road)	35	B2
Palmerstown Woods	35	B4
Paradise Place	71	A2
*Paramount Court Apts (off Corrig Road)	58	E2
Park Ave (Brackenstown Road)	1	B2
Park Ave (Castleknock)	22	F3
Park Ave (Sandymount)	39	B4
Park Ave (Willbrook)	56	F1
Park Ave (Deans Grange)	59	A1
Park Ave West	70	D3
Park Boulevard	9	B2
Park Close (Sallynoggin)	60	D2
*Park Court (off Park Lane Sandymount)	39	A4
Park Court Apts	23	A3
Park Cres (Blackhorse Ave)	69	A1
Park Cres (Kimmage)	46	D2
*Park Cres House (adjacent Lydon Gate)	24	D4
Park Drive (Ranelagh)	47	B1
Park Drive (Cabinteely)	59	B3
Park Drive Ave	22	F3
Park Drive Close	22	F3

STREET NAME	PAGE	GRID REF
Park Drive Court	22	F3
Park Drive Cres	22	F3
Park Drive Green	22	F3
Park Drive Grove	22	F3
Park Drive Lawn	22	F3
*Park Hall (off Merton Walk)	47	B2
*Park Lane (off Martin's Row Chapelizod)	36	E2
Park Lane (Sandymount)	39	A4
*Park Lane (off Park Road Dún Laoghaire)	50	D4
Park Lane 72 E4	72	E4
Park Lawn	27	A4
Park Lodge	69	C3
Park Lodge	22	F3
Park Manor	22	E3
Park Place	69	B4
Park Road (off Navan Road)	23	C3
Park Road (Dún Laoghaire)	50	D4
Park Road (Sallynoggin)	60	D2
*Park Spring's (off Nephin Road)	24	D4
*Park Street (off Hanover Street West)	74	F1
*Park Street (off First Ave)	36	F3
Park Terrace (Coombe)	74	F1
Park View	75	C4
Park View (Cabra)	69	C1
Park View (Portmarnock)	15	A1
Park View (Castleknock)	23	B4
*Park View (Mount Prospect Lawns off Kincora Court)	26	F4
*Park View (off Orwell Road Rathgar)	47	A3
Park View (Enniskerry Road)	58	D4
*Park View Apts (off Old Bawn Road)	55	A1
Park View House	9	B2
Park View Lawns	44	D2
Park View Manor	9	B2
Park Villas (Castleknock)	23	A3
*Park Villas (off Stillorgan Grove)	48	F4
Park West Ave	35	C4
Park West Pointe	35	C4
Park West Road	36	D4
*Parker Hill (off Rathmines Road Lower)	47	A1
Parker House	14	F4
Parkgate Place (off Parkgate Street)	70	D4
Parkgate Street	70	D4
Parkgate Street Gate 70 D4	70	D4
Parkhill Ave	44	F3
Parkhill Close	45	A3
Parkhill Court	44	F3
Parkhill Drive	44	F3
Parkhill Green	44	F3
*Parkhill Heights (off Greenhills Road Kilnamanagh)	45	A3
Parkhill Lawn	44	F3
Parkhill Rise	44	F3
Parkhill Road	44	F3
Parkhill Way	45	A3
Parkhill West	44	F4
*Parkhouse Apts (Benson Street)	72	F4
Parklands (Santry)	12	E4
Parklands (Maynooth)	18	D3
Parklands (Castleknock)	22	F3
Parklands Ave	55	B2
Parklands Close	18	D3
Parklands Court (Maynooth)	18	D3
Parklands Court (Scholarstown Link Road)	55	B2
Parklands Cres	18	D3
Parklands Drive	55	B2
Parklands Grove	18	D3
Parklands Lawns	18	D3
Parklands Lodge	18	D3
Parklands Rise	18	D3
Parklands Road	55	B2
Parklands Square	18	D3
Parklands View	55	B2
Parklands Way	18	D3
Parkmore	23	A3
Parkmore Drive	46	E2
Parknasilla Ave	64	D2
Parknasilla Close	64	D2
Parknasilla Lane	64	D2
Parknasilla Rise	64	D2
Parknasillog	65	C2
*Parkside View (off Nephin Road)	24	D4
Parkvale (Sutton)	28	D1

STREET NAME	PAGE	GRID REF
Parkvale (Dundrum)	57	C1
Parkview (Swords)	1	B2
Parkview (Ashtown)	23	C3
*Parkview (off Greenhills Road Kilnamanagh)	45	A3
*Parkview (Robswall)	3	C3
Parkview Ave (Harold's Cross)	46	F1
Parkview Court (Blackhorse Ave)	69	B1
*Parkview Court (off Harold's Cross Road)	46	F1
*Parkview Place (off Bridge Street)	39	A3
*Parkview Road	24	E1
*Parkview Terrace (north of River Lane)	67	B2
Parkwood Ave	55	A2
Parkwood Grove	55	A2
Parkwood Lawn	55	A2
Parkwood Road	55	A2
Parliament Street	71	A4
Parnell Ave	74	F4
Parnell Bridge (Grand Canal)	74	E4
Parnell Cottages	3	B3
Parnell Court	74	F4
Parnell Drive	9	A4
Parnell Green	9	A4
*Parnell Hall	74	E4
Parnell Lane	9	A4
Parnell Place	71	B2
Parnell Road (Harold's Cross)	74	E3
Parnell Road (Bray)	67	C2
Parnell Square East	71	B2
Parnell Square North	71	B2
Parnell Square West	71	B2
Parnell Street (O'Connell Street)	71	B3
Parnell Street (Sallynoggin)	60	D1
*Parochial Ave (Between College Street and Main Street Baldoyle)	15	A4
Parslickstown Ave	9	A4
Parslickstown Close	9	A4
Parslickstown Court	9	A4
Parslickstown Drive	9	A4
Parslickstown Gardens	9	A3
Parslickstown Green	9	A4
Parson Court	17	C3
Parson Lodge	17	C3
Parson Street	17	C3
Parsons Court	42	D4
*Parson's Court (opposite Newcastle Manor)	42	D4
Parsons Hall	17	B3
*Partridge Terrace (off Nash Street)	36	F3
Pass If You Can	11	A1
*Patrician Park (off Kill Ave)	59	C1
Patrician Villas	48	F4
Patrick Doyle Road	47	B2
*Patrick Heeney House (Summerhill)	71	C2
Patrick Street (Kevin Street Upper.)	75	A1
Patrick Street (Dún Laoghaire)	50	D4
*Patrick's Row (off George's Ave)	49	A3
*Patricks Terrace	71	A2
*Patrickswell Court (off Patrickswell Place)	24	D2
Patrickswell Place	24	D2
Paul Street	70	F3
Pavillion Gate	59	A4
*Pavillion View Apts. (off Rathmines Road Lower)	47	A1
Pea Field	48	F3
Peamount	42	D2
Peamount Road (Newcastle)	42	D3
Peamount Road (Peamount)	42	D2
*Pear Tree Field (off Carysfort Downs)	58	F1
Pearse Ave	60	D2
Pearse Brothers Park	56	F2
*Pearse Close (off Pearse Street Sallynoggin)	60	D2
Pearse Drive	60	D2
Pearse Gardens	59	C2
Pearse Green	60	D2
Pearse Grove	76	E1
Pearse House	72	D4
Pearse Park	60	D2
Pearse Road (Sallynoggin)	60	D2
*Pearse Road (near Ardee Street)	67	B2
Pearse Square (Pearse Street)	76	E1
Pearse Square (Bray)	67	B2

STREET NAME	PAGE	GRID REF
Pearse Street (Westland Row)	71	C4
Pearse Street (Sallynoggin)	60	D2
Pearse Villas	60	D2
Pebble Hill	18	D2
Pebble Hill Lodge	18	D2
Peck's Lane	23	A3
Pelletstown Ave	23	C3
Pelletstown Manor	23	C3
Pemberton	67	A3
Pembroke Cottages (Ringsend)	39	A2
*Pembroke Cottages (off Donnybrook Mews)	47	C1
*Pembroke Cottages (off Main Street Dundrum)	47	C4
*Pembroke Cottages (off Rosemount Terrace Booterstown)	48	F3
Pembroke Court (off Pembroke Road)	76	F3
Pembroke Gardens	76	E3
Pembroke Lane (Lower Baggot Street)	76	D2
Pembroke Lane (Pembroke Road)	76	E3
Pembroke Park	76	E4
Pembroke Place (off Sandymount Ave)	76	F4
Pembroke Place (Pembroke Street Upper)	75	C3
Pembroke Road	76	E3
Pembroke Row	76	D2
Pembroke Square	76	E2
Pembroke Street	39	A3
Pembroke Street Lower	75	C2
Pembroke Street Upper	75	C2
*Pembroke Terrace (off Main Street Dundrum)	47	C4
Penrose Street	76	F1
*Percy Close (off Haddington Road)	76	E2
*Percy French Road (off Balfe Ave)	45	C1
Percy Lane	76	E2
Percy Place	76	E2
Peter Place	75	B3
Peter Row	75	A2
Peter Street	75	A2
Peterson's Court	72	D4
Petrie Road	74	F3
Peyton	52	F4
Peyton Ave	52	F2
Peyton Court	52	F2
Peyton Drive	52	F2
Pheasant Run	8	F4
Pheasant Run The Drive	8	F4
Pheasant Run The Green	8	F4
Pheasant Run The Grove	8	F4
Pheasant Run The Park	8	F4
Phelan Ave	24	D3
Phibblestown Ave	21	A1
Phibblestown House Apts	21	B1
Phibblestown Wood	21	A1
Phibsborough	71	A1
Phibsborough Ave	70	F1
Phibsborough Place	71	A2
Phibsborough Road	71	A1
Philipsburgh Ave	25	C4
Philipsburgh Terrace	25	C4
*Philomena Terrace (off Oliver Plunkett Ave)	39	A3
Phoenix Ave	23	A3
Phoenix Court (North Circular Road)	70	D2
Phoenix Court (Arbour Hill)	70	D3
Phoenix Court (Castleknock)	23	A3
Phoenix Court Apts	69	C3
Phoenix Drive	23	A3
Phoenix Gardens	23	A3
*Phoenix House (Leinster Street South)	75	C1
Phoenix Manor	70	D2
Phoenix Park	69	A2
Phoenix Park Way	23	B3
Phoenix Place	23	A3
*Phoenix Street (off First Ave)	36	F3
Phoenix Street North	70	F4
*Phoenix Street West (off Phoenix Street North)	70	F4
Phoenix Terrace	48	F3
Phoenix View	74	D1
Phrompstown	66	F1
Pickford's Terrace	72	F3
*Pier 19 Apts (Bridgefoot Street)	70	F4
Pig Lane	71	C2
Pigeon House Road (Ringsend)	39	B3
Pike Bridge	18	F3
*Pile's Terrace (Sandwith Street Upper)	76	D1
*Pilot View (off Harbour Road)	60	F1
Pim Street	74	E1
Pimlico	74	F1
Pimlico Cottages	74	E1
Pimlico Terrace	74	F1
Pine Ave	59	A2
Pine Copse Road	57	B1
Pine Court (Portmarnock)	15	A1
Pine Court (Deans Grange)	59	A1
*Pine Grove (off Firhouse Road)	56	D1
Pine Grove Park	1	C1
Pine Grove Road	1	C1
Pine Haven	48	F3
Pine Hurst	24	E4
Pine Lawn (Tallaght)	55	A2
Pine Lawn (Deans Grange)	59	A1
Pine Road	39	A3
Pine Valley Ave	57	B2
Pine Valley Drive	57	B3
Pine Valley Grove	57	B3
Pine Valley Park	57	B3
Pine Valley Way	57	B3
Pinebrook Ave	26	D2
Pinebrook Close	21	C1
Pinebrook Cres	26	D2
Pinebrook Downs	21	C1
Pinebrook Drive	26	D2
Pinebrook Glen	21	C1
Pinebrook Grove	26	E2
Pinebrook Heights	21	C1
Pinebrook Lawn	21	C1
Pinebrook Rise	26	D2
Pinebrook Road	26	D2
Pinebrook Vale	21	C1
Pinebrook View	21	C1
Pinebrook Way	21	C1
Pinecroft	62	F1
Pines (opposite Knockmaroon Gate)	36	D1
*Pinetree Cres (off Parkhill Road)	44	F4
*Pinetree Grove (off Parkhill Road)	44	F3
Pineview Ave	55	A2
Pineview Drive	55	A2
Pineview Grove	55	A2
Pineview Lawn	55	A2
Pineview Park	55	A2
Pineview Rise	55	A2
Pineview Road	55	A2
Pinewood	60	D4
Pinewood Ave	24	F1
Pinewood Close	67	C4
Pinewood Court	8	F4
Pinewood Cres	24	F1
Pinewood Drive	24	F1
Pinewood Green	24	F1
*Pinewood Grove (off Pinewood Drive)	25	A1
Pinewood Park	56	E1
Pinewood Villas	24	F1
Pinewoods	44	D2
Pinnockhill Roundabout	1	C3
Pipe Hill	1	C2
Plaza Apts.	25	A1
Pleasants Lane	75	B2
Pleasants Place	75	B2
Pleasants Street	75	A2
Pluckstown	51	A2
Plums Road	58	D1
Plunket Hall	2	E2
Plunkett Ave (Finglas)	24	D1
Plunkett Ave (Foxrock)	59	A3
Plunkett Cres	11	A4
Plunkett Drive	24	D1
Plunkett Green	24	D1
Plunkett Grove	24	D1
Plunkett Hall	7	A2
Plunkett Road	24	D1
Poddle Close	46	E1
*Poddle Green (off Poddle Park)	46	E1
Poddle Park	46	E2
Polo Road (Phoenix Park)	69	B2
Poolbeg Quay	39	A3
Poolbeg Street	71	C4
Poole Street	74	F2
Poplar Row	72	E1
Poplar Row Flats	72	E1
Poppintree	11	C4
Poppintree Lane	11	C4
Poppintree Parade	11	C4
Poppintree Park Lane West	11	C4
Poppintree Terrace	11	C4
Port Tunnel (East Wall Entrance)	72	F1
Port Tunnel (Santry Entrance)	25	C1
Port View House	39	A2
Porters Ave	22	D2
Porters Gate	21	B2
Porters Gate Ave	21	C2
Porters Gate Close	21	B2
Porters Gate Court	21	B2
Porters Gate Drive	21	B2
Porters Gate Green	21	B2
Porters Gate Grove	21	B2
Porters Gate Heights	21	C2
Porters Gate Lawn	21	B2
Porters Gate Rise	21	C2
Porters Gate View	21	B2
Porters Gate Way	21	B2
Porters Road	22	D2
Portersfield Apts	22	D2
Porterstown	5	A3
Porterstown Link Road	22	D3
Porterstown Road	22	D2
Portland Close	72	D2
Portland Court (off Portland Place)	71	C1
*Portland Lock (off Portland Place)	71	C1
Portland Lock Apts	71	C1
Portland Place	71	B1
Portland Row	72	D2
Portland Square	71	C1
Portland Street North	71	C1
Portland Street West	74	E1
Portmahon Drive	73	C2
Portmarnock	15	A1
Portmarnock Ave	4	D4
Portmarnock Cres	4	D4
Portmarnock Drive	4	D4
Portmarnock Grove	4	D4
Portmarnock Park	4	D4
Portmarnock Rise	15	A1
Portmarnock Walk	4	D4
*Portobello Dock (Lennox Street)	75	B3
Portobello Harbour	75	B3
Portobello Harbour Apts	75	B4
Portobello Place	75	B3
Portobello Road	75	A4
*Portobello Wharf Apts (off Windsor Terrace)	74	F4
Portside Court	72	E1
Pottery Road	59	C2
Pound Hill	17	C1
Pound Lane	17	C3
Pound Park	17	C3
Pound Street	33	A1
Power's Court	76	E2
Power's Square (off John Dillon Street)	75	A1
Powerstown Road	9	A3
Prebend Street	70	F3
Premier Business Park	23	B1
Premier Square	24	E2
Preston Street	72	D2
*Price's Lane (Aston Quay)	71	B4
Price's Place (Ranelagh)	75	B4
Priestfield Cottages	74	E3
Priestfield Drive	74	E3
Primeside Park	10	D3
Primrose Ave	71	A2
Primrose Forge	32	D4
Primrose Gate	32	E4
Primrose Grove	13	C4
Primrose Hill (Celbridge)	32	D4
*Primrose Hill (off Tivoli Road)	49	C4
Primrose Lane	34	D1
Primrose Street (off Wellington Street Upper)	71	A2
*Prince Arthur Terrace (Leinster Road)	47	A1
*Prince Edward Terrace Lower (off Carysfort Ave Blackrock)	49	A4
*Prince Edward Terrace Upper (off Carysfort Ave Blackrock)	49	A4
*Prince of Wales Terrace (off Sandymount Ave)	39	A4
*Prince of Wales Terrace (off Quinnsborough Road)	67	C2
Prince's Street North	71	B3
Prince's Street South	72	D4
Princeton	48	D3
Prior Hall	74	D1
*Prior's Gate (off Main Road Tallaght)	55	A1
Priorswood Road	13	C4
Priory Ave	48	F4
Priory Chase	31	C4
Priory Close	31	C4
Priory Court (Celbridge)	31	C4
*Priory Court (off Grange Road)	57	A2
Priory Cres	31	C4
Priory Drive (Celbridge)	31	C4
Priory Drive (Stillorgan)	48	F4
Priory East	24	D4
Priory Green	31	C4
Priory Grove (Celbridge)	31	C4
Priory Grove (Stillorgan)	48	F4
Priory Hall (Donaghmede)	14	E4
Priory Hall (Kimmage)	46	D2
Priory Hall (Stillorgan)	48	F4
Priory Lodge	31	C4
Priory North	24	D3
Priory Road	46	F1
Priory Square	31	C4
Priory View	31	C3
Priory Walk (Celbridge)	31	C4
Priory Walk (Kimmage)	46	D2
Priory Way (Celbridge)	31	C3
Priory Way (Kimmage)	46	D2
Priory West	24	D4
Proby Garden	49	A4
Proby Hall	60	E2
Proby Park	60	E2
Proby Square	49	A4
Proby's Lane	71	B3
Promenade Road	39	A1
Prospect Ave (Finglas Road)	25	A4
Prospect Ave (Stocking Lane)	56	E2
*Prospect Court (off Prospect Ave)	25	A4
Prospect Court (Edmondstown)	56	E2
Prospect Drive	56	E2
Prospect Glen	56	E2
Prospect Grove	56	E2
Prospect Heath	56	E2
Prospect Heights	56	E2
Prospect Hill	24	E2
*Prospect Lane (off Milltown Road)	47	C2
Prospect Lawn	59	B3
*Prospect Lodge (off Knocklyon Road)	55	C1
Prospect Meadows	56	E2
Prospect Road	25	A4
*Prospect Square (off Prospect Ave)	25	A4
*Prospect Square (beside Premier Square)	24	E2
Prospect Terrace (Kilmainham)	73	B1
*Prospect Terrace (off Marine Drive Sandymount)	39	B3
Prospect View	56	E2
Prospect Way	25	A4
Protestant Row	75	B2
Proud's Lane	75	B2
Provost Row	70	E3
Prussia Street	70	E2
Pucks Castle Lane	63	C3
*Purcell Lane (Saint Kevin's Square)	67	C2
Purley Park	3	C4
*Purser Gardens (off Summerville Park)	47	A1
Putland Road	67	C3
*Putland Villas (Vevay Road, Wolfe Tone Square)	67	C3
Pyro Villas	74	E2
*Quarry Cottages (off Killester Ave Middle)	26	E3

Q

Quarry Drive	45	C2
Quarry Road (Cabra)	24	E4
Quarry Road (Ferndale Road)	64	D4
Quarryfield Court	44	E2
Quarryvale	35	A1
Quarryvale Park	35	A2
Quartiere Bloom	71	B4
Queen's Park	49	B4
Queen's Road	50	D4
Queen's Street	70	F4
Quinn Ave	74	D1
Quinn's Lane	75	C2

STREET NAME / PAGE / GRID REF

Quinn's Road 64 E3
Quinsborough 51 A4
Quinsborough Road 67 C2

R

*Radcliff Hall
(off Saint John's Road East) 39 B4
*Radcliffe
(adjacent Binn Eadair View) 29 A1
Radharc na hAbhann 55 A2
Radlett Grove 4 D4
Rafter's Ave 73 A4
Rafter's Lane 73 A4
Rafter's Road 73 A4
Raglan Hall Apts
(off Seafort Ave) 76 E4
*Raglan House
(off Serpentine Ave) 39 A4
Raglan Lane 76 E4
Raglan Road 76 E4
Raheen Ave 54 E1
Raheen Close 54 E1
Raheen Court 54 E1
Raheen Cres 54 E1
Raheen Drive (Ballyfermot) 36 D3
Raheen Drive (Tallaght) 54 E1
Raheen Green 54 E1
Raheen Park (Ballyfermot) 36 D3
Raheen Park (Tallaght) 54 E1
Raheen Park (Bray) 68 D3
Raheen Park Ave 68 D3
Raheen Road 54 E1
Raheny 27 A2
Raheny Park 27 A3
Raheny Road 27 A1
Rail Park 18 D4
Railway Ave (Malahide) 3 B2
Railway Ave (Baldoyle) 28 D1
Railway Ave (Inchicore) 36 F3
Railway Close 14 F4
*Railway Cottages
(off Serpentine Park) 39 A4
*Railway Court
(off Railway Ave Malahide) 3 B2
Railway Mews 14 F4
Railway Road 14 F4
*Railway Road
(off Castle Street Dalkey) 60 F2
Railway Street 71 C2
Railway Terrace
(off Macken Street) 76 E1
Rainsford Ave 74 E1
*Rainsford Lane
(off Military Road Ballybrack) 60 E4
Rainsford Street 74 E1
Ralahine 60 D4
Raleigh Square 73 B4
*Ralph Mews
(off Newtownpark Ave) 59 A1
*Ralph Square
(off Main Street Leixlip) 33 A1
Ramillies Road 36 E3
Ramleh Close 47 C2
Ramleh Park 47 C2
Ramor Park 22 E2
Ranelagh 75 C4
Ranelagh Ave 75 C4
*Ranelagh Close
(opposite Manders Terrace) 75 C4
*Ranelagh Mews
(near Mountpleasant Parade) 75 B4
Ranelagh Road 75 C4
Raphoe Road 46 D1
Rath Geal 43 C1
Rathbeale Court 1 C1
Rathbeale Cres 1 C1
Rathbeale Rise 1 C2
Rathbeale Road 1 C1
Rathborne
(opposite Knockmaroon Gate) 36 D1
Rathborne Ave 23 C3
Rathborne Close 23 C3
Rathborne Drive 23 C3
Rathborne Place 23 C3
Rathborne Way 23 C3
*Rathbourne Court
(adjacent Courtview Apts) 23 C3
*Rathclaren (near Glenlucan) 67 B3
Rathcoole Interchange (N7) 52 F1

Rathcoole Park 52 F2
Rathcreedan 52 D1
Rathdown Ave 46 F3
*Rathdown Court
(off Corrib Road) 46 F2
Rathdown Cres 46 F3
Rathdown Drive 46 E3
*Rathdown Grove
(off Sandyford Road) 58 D2
Rathdown Park 46 F3
Rathdown Road 70 F1
Rathdown Square 70 E2
*Rathdown Terrace
(off Sandyford Road) 58 D2
Rathdown Villas 46 F3
Rathdrum Road 74 D4
Rathelawns 52 F2
Rathfarnham 46 F3
*Rathfarnham Mill
(off Main Street Rathfarnham) 46 F4
Rathfarnham Park 46 F3
Rathfarnham Road 46 F3
Rathfarnham Wood 46 F4
Rathgar 47 A2
Rathgar Ave 46 F2
*Rathgar Court
(off Rathgar Road) 47 A1
*Rathgar Park
(off Terenure Road East) 46 F2
*Rathgar Park
(off Orwell Road Rathgar) 47 A2
Rathgar Place 47 A1
Rathgar Road 47 A1
*Rathgar Villas
(off Rathgar Ave) 46 F2
Rathingle Road 1 B3
*Rathland Drive
(off Ravensdale Drive) 46 E2
Rathland Road 46 E2
Rathlin House 22 F1
Rathlin Road 25 A3
Rathlyon Grove 55 C2
Rathlyon Park 55 C2
Rathmichael 63 C3
Rathmichael Dales 64 D3
Rathmichael Haven 64 D3
Rathmichael Hill 63 C2
Rathmichael Lane 63 C2
Rathmichael Manor 64 D2
Rathmichael Park 64 E2
Rathmichael Road 63 C2
Rathmichael Woods 64 E2
Rathmines 75 A4
Rathmines Ave 47 A1
*Rathmines Ave Court
(off Rathmines Road Upper) 47 A1
Rathmines Close 47 A1
*Rathmines Park
(off Rathmines Road Upper) 47 A1
Rathmines Road Lower 75 B4
Rathmines Road Upper 47 A1
*Rathmines Square Apts
(off William's Park) 47 A1
*Rathmines Wood
(off William's Park) 47 A1
Rathmintan Close 54 D2
Rathmintan Court 54 D2
Rathmintan Cres 54 D2
Rathmintan Drive 54 D2
Rathmore 14 F2
Rathmore Ave 9 B2
Rathmore Ave 58 D1
Rathmore Cres 9 B2
Rathmore Drive 9 B2
Rathmore Grove 9 B2
Rathmore Park 27 A2
Rathmore Villas 46 F2
Rathsallagh Ave 64 E2
Rathsallagh Bridge 64 E2
Rathsallagh Drive 64 E2
Rathsallagh Grove 64 E2
Rathsallagh Park 64 E2
Rathvale Ave 26 F1
Rathvale Drive 26 F1
Rathvale Grove 26 F1
Rathvale Park 26 F1
Rathvilly Drive 24 D2
Rathvilly Park 24 D2
Ratoath Ave 24 D2
Ratoath Drive 23 C1
Ratoath Estate 24 D3
Ratoath Road (Hollystown) 9 B1
Ratoath Road (Cabra) 24 E4
Ratoath Road (Finglas) 23 C2
Ratra Park 23 C4

Ratra Road 23 C4
*Ravens Court
(off Cardiff Castle Road) 24 D2
Ravens Rock Road 58 E2
*Ravensdale Drive
(off Ravensdale Park) 46 E2
Ravensdale Park 46 E2
Ravensdale Road 72 F2
Ravenswell Road 67 C2
*Ravenswood
(adjacent to Lawson Spinney) 3 A3
Ravenwood Ave 21 B1
Ravenwood Cres 21 B1
Ravenwood Drive 21 B1
Ravenwood Estate 21 B1
Ravenwood Green 21 B1
Ravenwood Lawn 21 B1
Ravenwood Rise 21 B1
Ravenwood Road 21 B1
Ravenwood View 21 B1
*Raverty Villas (off Beech Road) 67 B1
Rawson Court 76 E2
Raymond Street 74 F3
Rectory Slopes 67 B3
Rectory Way 67 A3
*Red Arches Ave
(Red Arches Estate) 14 F4
*Red Arches Close
(Red Arches Estate) 14 F4
*Red Arches Drive
(Red Arches Estate) 14 F4
*Red Arches Park
(Red Arches Estate) 14 F4
Red Arches Road 14 F4
*Red Brick Terrace
(off Annaville Ave) 59 A1
*Red Cow Cottages
(off Lucan Road Palmerston) 35 C1
Red Cow Interchange 44 F1
Red Cow Lane 70 F3
Redberry 34 D3
Redesdale Cres 48 D4
Redesdale Road 48 D4
Redfern Ave 3 C4
Redgap 52 E3
Redmond's Court
(off Kilbarrack Road) 27 B1
Redmond's Hill 75 B2
Redwood 9 B1
Redwood Ave 45 A4
Redwood Close 45 A4
Redwood Court (Tallaght) 44 F4
Redwood Court (Churchtown) 47 A3
Redwood Drive 44 F4
Redwood Grove 48 F3
Redwood Heights 45 A4
Redwood Lawn 44 F4
Redwood Park 45 A4
Redwood Rise 45 A4
Redwood View 45 A4
Redwood Walk 44 F4
Regal Park 69 B1
Reginald Square 74 F1
Reginald Street 74 F1
Rehoboth Ave 74 E3
Rehoboth Place 74 D3
Reilly's Ave 74 D3
*Renoir Apts
(off Serpentine Ave) 39 A4
Reuben Ave 74 D2
Reuben Square Apts
(Reuben Street) 74 D3
Reuben Street 74 D2
Reuben Walk 74 D2
*Rexton Court (Merrion Road,
Sandymount Ave) 39 A4
*Rhodaville
(off Mountpleasant Ave) 75 B4
*Riachville (off Collinswood) 25 C2
Rialto Bridge 73 C2
Rialto Buildings 74 D2
Rialto Cottages 73 C2
*Rialto Court
(off Rialto Buildings) 74 D2
Rialto Drive 73 C3
Rialto Park 73 C2
Rialto Street 74 D2
Ribh Ave 26 F2
Ribh Road 26 F2
Richelieu Park 48 E1
Richmond 59 A1
*Richmond Apts 70 F3
Richmond Ave (Fairview) 25 B4
Richmond Ave (Monkstown) 49 C4
Richmond Ave South 47 B2

Richmond Cottages
(Summerhill) 72 D1
Richmond Cottages North 72 D1
Richmond Court (Marino) 25 C4
Richmond Court (Milltown) 47 B2
Richmond Cres 72 D1
Richmond Estate 25 C4
*Richmond Gardens
(Richmond Ave) 25 C4
*Richmond Green
(off Carrickbrennan Road) 49 C4
Richmond Grove 49 C4
*Richmond Hall
(off Richmond Road) 25 B4
Richmond Hill (Rathmines) 75 B4
Richmond Hill (Monkstown) 49 C4
*Richmond House
(off Richmond Road) 25 B4
Richmond Lane 71 C1
Richmond Lodge 25 B4
*Richmond Manor
(Richmond Hill) 75 B4
*Richmond Manor
(Richmond Hill) 75 B4
Richmond Mews 75 B4
Richmond Parade 72 D1
Richmond Park (Monkstown) 49 B4
Richmond Park (Herbert Road) 67 A4
Richmond Place (Rathmines) 75 B4
Richmond Place South
(South Richmond Street) 75 B3
Richmond Road 25 B4
Richmond Row 75 B3
Richmond Street North 72 D1
Richmond Street South 75 B3
*Richmond Terrace
(west side of text Meath) 68 D2
Richmond Villas 75 B3
Richview 47 C2
Richview Park 47 B2
*Richview Villas
(off Whitethorn Road) 47 C2
Riddlesford 67 C4
Ridge Hall 64 E1
Ridge Hill 64 E1
Ridgeford Apts 57 C1
*Ridgeway Villas
(on Rowserstown Lane) 73 B1
Ridgewood Ave 1 B3
Ridgewood Close 1 B3
Ridgewood Court 1 B3
Ridgewood Green 1 B3
Ridgewood Grove 1 B3
Ridgewood Park 1 B3
Ridgewood Place 1 B3
Ridgewood Square 1 B3
Rinawade Ave 32 E1
Rinawade Close 32 E1
Rinawade Cres 32 E1
Rinawade Downs 32 E1
Rinawade Glade 32 E1
Rinawade Green 32 E1
Rinawade Grove 32 E1
Rinawade Lawns 32 E1
Rinawade Park 32 F1
Rinawade Rise 32 E1
Rinawade Vale 32 E1
Rinawade View 32 E1
*Ring Street (off Ring Terrace) 36 F3
Ring Terrace 36 F3
Ringsend 39 A3
Ringsend Park 39 A2
Ringsend Road 76 F1
*Rinn na Mara (off Doyles Lane) 27 A4
Ripley Court 67 B3
Ripley Hills 67 B3
*River Close (near Brookdene) 64 E1
River Court 7 B3
*River Court Apts
(off Camac Close) 73 A1
River Drive 24 D3
River Forest 20 D4
River Forest View (Leixlip) 19 C3
*River Gardens
(off Glasnevin Hill) 25 A3
*River Lane (at Clifton Park) 64 E2
River Lane (Bray) 67 B2
*River Lane Grove
(at Clifton Park) 64 E2
River Lawns 31 C4
River Mall 2 D2
River Road (Blanchardstown) 22 F2
River Road (Ashtown) 23 C3
River Road Cottages 23 A2
River Valley Ave 1 C2

STREET NAME	PAGE	GRID REF
River Valley Close	1	B2
River Valley Court	1	B2
River Valley Drive	1	C2
River Valley Grove	1	C3
River Valley Heights	1	C2
River Valley Lawn	1	C2
River Valley Park	1	C2
River Valley Rise	1	C3
River Valley Road	1	C2
River Valley View	1	B2
River Valley Way	1	B2
River View	31	C4
Riverbank (Braemor Road)	47	A3
*Riverbank (off Overend Way Dundrum)	57	C1
Riverbank Hall	24	F3
*Riverbank House	69	B4
Riverdale	20	D4
Riverpark Apts	69	C4
Riverpark View	9	A4
Riverrun Apts	74	D1
Riversdale (Palmerstown)	35	C1
*Riversdale (off Overend Way Dundrum)	57	C1
Riversdale Ave (Palmerston)	35	C1
Riversdale Ave (Clondalkin)	44	E1
Riversdale Ave (Terenure)	46	F3
Riversdale Court	35	C1
Riversdale Cres	44	E1
Riversdale Drive	44	E1
Riversdale Green	35	B4
Riversdale Grove (Palmerstown)	35	B1
*Riversdale Grove (off Kimmage Road Lower)	46	E2
Riversdale Park (Palmerstown)	35	C1
Riversdale Park (Clondalkin)	44	E1
Riversdale Road	44	E1
*Riversdale View (off Boden Wood)	46	F4
Riverside	9	A4
*Riverside (off Watery Lane)	44	E1
*Riverside (off Poddle Park Kimmage)	46	E2
*Riverside Apts (off Milltown Road)	47	B2
Riverside Ave	13	A4
Riverside Cottages	46	E4
Riverside Cres	13	A4
Riverside Drive (Coolock)	13	B4
Riverside Drive (Palmerston)	35	C1
Riverside Drive (Rathfarnham)	47	A3
Riverside Grove	13	A4
Riverside Park	13	A4
Riverside Road	13	A4
*Riverside Walk (off Clonskeagh Road)	47	C1
Riverston Abbey	24	D4
*Riverstown Gardens (beside Ashington Gardens)	24	D3
Rivervale	23	C3
*Rivervale Apts (off Upper Dargle Road)	67	B2
*Riverview (Grand Canal Docks)	76	E1
Riverview (Palmerstown)	35	C1
Riverview (Oldbawn)	55	A2
Riverview (opposite Knockmaroon Gate)	36	D1
Riverview Apts	32	D4
*Riverview Court (off Lucan Road Chapelizod)	36	E2
Riverwood Chase	22	D3
Riverwood Close	22	D3
Riverwood Copse	22	D3
Riverwood Court	22	D3
Riverwood Cres	22	D3
Riverwood Dale	22	D3
Riverwood Dene	22	D3
Riverwood Drive	22	D3
Riverwood Gardens	22	D3
Riverwood Glebe	22	D3
Riverwood Glen	22	D3
Riverwood Green	22	D3
Riverwood Grove	22	D3
Riverwood Hall	22	D3
Riverwood Heath	22	D3
Riverwood Lawn	22	D3
Riverwood Park	22	D3
Riverwood Place	22	D3
Riverwood Road	22	D3
Riverwood Terrace	22	D3
Riverwood Vale	22	D3
Riverwood View	22	D3
Riverwood Way	22	D3
Robert Emmet Bridge (Grand Canal)	74	F4
Robert Emmet Walk	70	E4
Robert Emmett Close	74	E1
*Robert Place (off Mabel Street)	25	B4
Robert Street	74	E1
*Robert Street (Jones's Road off Mabel Street)	25	B4
*Robin Hill Apts (on Blackthorn Drive)	58	D2
Robin Villas	35	C1
Robinhood Park	45	B1
Robinhood Road	45	A1
Robinsons Court	74	F2
Robswall	3	C3
Robswall Path	4	D3
Robswall Walk	4	D3
Rochestown Ave	59	C2
*Rochestown House (off Rochestown Ave)	59	C2
*Rochestown House Apts (off Rochestown Ave)	59	C2
Rochestown Park	60	D2
Rochfort Ave	34	F2
Rochfort Close	34	F2
Rochfort Cres	34	F3
Rochfort Downs	34	F2
Rochfort Green	34	F2
Rochfort Park	34	F2
Rochfort Way	34	F3
Rock Bridge	32	D4
Rock Hall	49	A3
Rock Hill	49	A3
*Rock Lane (Baggot Street Lower)	76	D2
Rock Lodge	60	E3
Rock Road	49	A3
Rockbrae Hall	57	C3
Rockbrook	56	E4
Rockfield (Maynooth)	18	D4
Rockfield (Lucan)	34	D3
Rockfield (Dundrum)	57	C1
Rockfield Ave (Maynooth)	18	D4
Rockfield Ave (Kimmage)	46	D2
Rockfield Close	22	D3
Rockfield Drive (Coolmine)	22	D3
Rockfield Drive (Clondalkin)	44	D2
Rockfield Drive (Kimmage)	46	D2
Rockfield Gardens	18	D3
Rockfield Green	18	D3
Rockfield Lodge	18	D4
Rockfield Manor	18	D4
Rockfield Park (Maynooth)	18	D4
Rockfield Park (Coolmine)	22	D2
Rockfield Rise	18	D3
Rockfield Square	18	D3
Rockfield Walk	18	D3
Rockford Manor	59	B1
Rockford Park	59	B1
*Rockford Terrace (off Rowan Park)	49	B4
Rockfort Ave	60	F2
Rockingham Ave	19	C4
Rockingham Green	19	C4
Rockingham Grove	19	C4
Rockingham Park	19	C4
Rockingham Terrace	2	D2
*Rocklands (off Harbour Road)	60	F1
*Rockmeade Court (off Windmill Road Crumlin)	46	D1
Rockstown	30	E2
Rockview	57	C3
Rockville	62	F2
Rockville Cres	49	B4
Rockville Drive (Monkstown)	49	B4
Rockville Drive (Carrickmines)	63	A1
*Rockville Estate (off Rockville Road)	49	A4
Rockville Park	49	B4
Rockville Road	49	A4
*Rockwell Cove Apts (off Idrone Terrace)	49	A3
Rockwood	34	D3
Rocwood	58	F2
Roebuck Ave	48	E3
Roebuck Castle	48	D3
*Roebuck Cres (off Roebuck Road)	47	C3
Roebuck Downs	47	C3
Roebuck Drive	46	D2
Roebuck Hill	48	D3
*Roebuck Lawn (off Beechmount Drive)	47	C3
Roebuck Park	47	C4
Roebuck Road	48	D3
Roger Casement Park	67	B2
Roger's Lane	75	C2
*Roland Court (off Rathgar Road)	47	A1
*Rollins Court (off Rollins Villas)	60	D1
Rollins Villas	60	D1
Ronanstown	35	A4
Roncalli Road	27	C1
Rookwood View	56	E2
Roosevelt Cottages	24	D4
Rooske Road	7	B3
*Ropewalk Place (off Cambridge Park)	39	A3
Rory O'Connor Park	59	B1
Rory O'More Bridge (River Liffey)	70	E4
Ros Mór View	56	D2
*Rosary Gardens East (off Library Road)	50	D4
*Rosary Gardens West (off Library Road)	49	C4
Rosary Road	74	D2
Rosary Terrace (Ringsend)	39	A3
*Rosary Terrace (off Library Road)	50	D4
Rosbeg Court	27	C2
Rosberry	34	E3
Rosberry Ave	34	E3
Rosberry Court	34	E3
Rosberry Lane	34	E3
Rosberry Park	34	E3
Rosberry Place	34	E3
Rose Park	59	C1
Rose Vale Court	22	D1
Roseacre	58	E3
Rosebank	55	A2
*Rosebank Court (off Nangor Road)	35	B4
*Rosebank Hall (off Nangor Road)	35	A4
*Rosebank Place (off Nangor Road)	35	A4
*Rosebank View (off Nangor Road)	35	B4
Rosedale (Dunboyne)	7	B2
Rosedale (Clonsilla)	21	B1
*Rosedale Apts (off Tyrconnell Road)	36	F3
*Rosedale Apts (off Tyrconnell Road)	36	F3
Rosedale Close	21	B1
Rosedale Cres	21	B1
Rosedale Terrace (Lower Clanbrassil Street)	74	F3
Roseglen Ave	27	B2
*Roseglen Manor (off Roseglen Ave)	27	B2
Roseglen Road	27	B2
Rosehall	46	E4
Rosehaven	22	E3
*Rosehill (off Carysfort Ave)	59	A1
Roselawn	34	E1
Roselawn Ave	22	E2
Roselawn Close	22	F2
Roselawn Court	22	F2
Roselawn Cres	22	E2
Roselawn Drive (Blanchardstown)	22	E2
Roselawn Drive (Oldcourt)	67	C3
Roselawn Glade	22	E2
Roselawn Grove	22	E2
*Roselawn Park (off Boghall Road)	67	C3
Roselawn Road	22	E2
Roselawn View	22	E2
Roselawn Walk	22	E2
Roselawn Way	22	F2
*Rosemount (off Charlemont)	25	C3
Rosemount (Malahide Road Donnycarney)	26	D3
Rosemount (Churchtown)	47	C4
Rosemount Ave	26	E2
Rosemount Court (Inchicore Road)	73	B1
Rosemount Court (Dundrum)	47	C4
Rosemount Court (Booterstown)	48	F3
Rosemount Cres (Roebuck Road)	47	C3
Rosemount Glade	47	C4
Rosemount Hall	47	C4
Rosemount Park	47	C4
Rosemount Park Drive	10	D4
Rosemount Park Road	10	D4
Rosemount Road	70	F1
Rosemount Terrace (Arbour Hill)	70	E3
*Rosemount Terrace (off Dundrum Road)	47	B4
Rosemount Terrace (Booterstown)	48	E3
Rosevale Court	26	F3
Rosevale Mansions	26	F3
*Roseville Court (near Church)	67	B1
*Roseville Terrace (off Dundrum Road)	47	C4
Rosewood Grove	34	F3
Rosie Hackett Bridge	71	C4
Rosmeen Gardens	50	D4
Rosmeen Park	60	D1
*Ross Cottages (adjacent Townyard Lane)	3	B2
Ross Road	75	A1
Ross Street	70	D2
Ross View	35	C1
*Rossaveal Court (off Drumfinn Road)	36	D2
Rossberry Terrace	34	E4
Rossecourt Ave	34	F3
Rossecourt Green	34	F3
Rossecourt Grove	34	F3
Rossecourt Heights	34	F3
Rossecourt Lane	34	F3
Rossecourt Rise	34	F3
Rossecourt Square	34	F3
Rossecourt Terrace	34	F3
Rossecourt Way	34	F3
Rossfield Ave	54	D1
*Rossfield Close (off Glenshane Cres)	54	D1
*Rossfield Court (off Rossfield Gardens)	54	D1
Rossfield Cres	54	D1
Rossfield Drive	54	D1
Rossfield Gardens	54	D1
Rossfield Green	54	D1
Rossfield Grove	54	D1
Rossfield Park	54	D1
Rossfield Way	54	D1
*Rosslyn (Rosslyn Court)	67	C2
Rosslyn Court	67	C2
*Rosslyn Grove (Rosslyn Court)	67	C2
Rossmeen Park (off Sumerhill Road)	50	E4
Rossmore Ave (Ballyfermot)	36	D3
Rossmore Ave (Templeogue)	45	C4
Rossmore Close	46	D4
Rossmore Cres	46	D4
Rossmore Drive (Ballyfermot)	36	D2
Rossmore Drive (Templeogue)	45	C4
Rossmore Grove	45	C4
Rossmore Lawns	46	D4
Rossmore Park	46	D4
Rossmore Road (Ballyfermot)	36	D2
Rossmore Road (Templeogue)	46	D4
Rostrevor Court	76	E1
Rostrevor Road	47	A3
Rostrevor Terrace (Lower Grand Canal Street)	76	E1
Rostrevor Terrace (Orwell Road)	47	A2
*Roth Abbey Court (off Roth Abbey)	73	B2
Rothe Abbey	73	B2
Round Gardens	53	B1
Rowan Ave	58	D2
Rowan Close	32	D3
Rowan Grove	67	B2
*Rowan Hall (off Milltown Road)	47	C1
Rowan Hamilton Court	24	E4
Rowan House	76	D3
Rowan Park	49	B4
Rowan Park Ave	49	B4
Rowanbyrn	59	B1
Rowans Road	58	D2
Rowlagh Ave	35	A3
Rowlagh Cres	35	A3
Rowlagh Gardens	35	A3
Rowlagh Green	35	A3
Rowlagh Park	35	A3
Rowserstown Lane	73	B1
Royal Canal Ave	23	C3
Royal Canal Bank (Phibsborough)	71	A1
Royal Canal Bank (Phibsborough)	25	A4
*Royal Canal Court (Saint Peters Close)	71	A1
Royal Canal Terrace	70	F2

STREET NAME	PAGE	GRID REF
*Royal Canal View (Weaver Lane)	71	A1
Royal Hibernian Way	75	C1
*Royal Marine Terrace (at Strand Road)	67	C2
Royal Oak	12	F4
Royal Terrace East	60	D1
*Royal Terrace Lane (off Royal Terrace West)	60	D1
*Royal Terrace North (off Royal Terrace East)	60	D1
Royal Terrace West	60	D1
Royse Road	25	A4
Royston	46	D2
Royston Village	46	D2
Ruben Square	74	D3
Ruby Hall	59	C2
Rugby Road	47	B1
Rugged Lane	21	C4
*Rugby Villas (off Oxford Road)	47	B1
Rushbrook	22	E2
Rushbrook Ave	45	C3
Rushbrook Court	45	C4
Rushbrook Cres	45	C3
Rushbrook Drive	45	C3
Rushbrook Grove	45	C3
Rushbrook Park	45	C3
Rushbrook Road	45	C3
Rushbrook View	45	C3
Rushbrook Way	45	C4
Rusheeney	21	B1
Rusheeney Ave	21	B1
Rusheeney Close	21	B1
Rusheeney Court	21	C1
Rusheeney Cres	8	F4
Rusheeney Green	21	C1
Rusheeney Grove	21	B1
Rusheeney Manor	21	B1
Rusheeney Park	21	B1
Rusheeney View	21	C1
Rusheeney Way	21	B1
*Rus-in-Urbe Terrace (off Glenageary Road Lower)	60	D1
Russel Street Bridge (Royal Canal)	71	C1
Russell Ave (Jones's Road)	71	C1
Russell Ave (Fortunestown Way)	54	D1
Russell Ave East	72	E2
Russell Close	54	D2
Russell Court	54	D2
*Russell Court Apts (Little Britain Street)	71	A3
Russell Cres	54	D1
Russell Downs	54	D1
Russell Drive	54	D2
Russell Green	54	D2
Russell Grove	54	D2
Russell House	2	E2
Russell Lane	54	D1
Russell Lawns	54	D2
Russell Meadows	54	D1
Russell Place	54	D1
Russell Rise	54	D1
Russell Street	71	C1
Russell View	54	D2
Russell Walk	54	D1
Russell's Mews	2	E3
Russell's Place	2	E3
Russell's Terrace	2	E4
Rutland Ave (Crumlin Road)	74	D4
Rutland Ave (Clogher Road)	46	E1
Rutland Cottages	71	C2
Rutland Court	71	C2
Rutland Grove	46	F1
Rutland Place North	71	C2
Rutland Place West	71	B2
Rutland Street	71	C2
Rutland Street Lower	71	C2
Rutledge Terrace	74	E3
*Ryan's Cottages (off Harold's Cross Road)	46	F1
Ryder's Row	71	A3
Rye Bridge	33	A1
Rye River Ave	20	D4
Rye River Close	20	D4
Rye River Court	20	D4
Rye River Cres	20	D4
Rye River Gardens	20	D4
Rye River Grove	20	D4
Rye River Mall	20	D4
Rye River Park	20	D4
Ryecroft	67	C3
Ryemont Abbey	20	D4
Ryevale Lawns	20	D4
Rynville Manor	67	B4

S

STREET NAME	PAGE	GRID REF
Sackville Ave	72	D1
Sackville Court Apts	71	B2
Sackville Gardens	72	D1
Sackville Place	71	B3
Saddlers Ave	9	A4
Saddlers Close	9	A4
Saddlers Court	75	B4
Saddlers Cres	9	A4
Saddlers Drive	9	A4
Saddlers Glade	9	A4
Saddlers Grove	9	A4
Saddlers Lawn	9	A4
*Saddlers Place (off Military Road)	75	A4
Sadleir Hall	7	A2
Saggart	53	B2
Saggart Abbey	53	C2
Saggart Lakes	53	B2
Saggart Lodge Court	53	B2
Saint Agatha Court (off William Street North)	72	D2
St. Agnes Park	46	D1
St. Agnes Road	46	D1
*St. Agnes Terrace (off St. Agnes Road Crumlin)	46	D1
*St. Agnes Terrace (on St. Agnes Road)	46	D1
*St. Agnes Terrace (off Dodder Road Lower Rathfarnham)	46	F3
St. Aidan's Drive	48	D4
*St. Aidan's Park (off St. Aidan's Park Road)	25	C4
St. Aidan's Park Ave	25	C4
St. Aidan's Park Road	25	C4
*St. Aidan's Terrace (near Duncairn Ave)	67	C2
St. Alban's Park	48	E1
St. Alban's Road	74	F3
*St. Alphonsus Ave (off St. Joseph's Ave)	25	A4
St. Alphonsus Road	25	A4
St. Andrew Street	75	B1
St. Andrews	34	F2
*St. Andrews Court (off Main Street Lucan)	34	D1
St. Andrews Drive	34	F2
St. Andrews Fairway	34	F2
St. Andrews Green	34	F2
St. Andrew's Grove	03	B3
St. Andrew's Lane (off Exchequer Street)	75	B1
St. Andrews Park	1	C1
St. Andrews Wood	34	F2
*St. Anne's Court (beside All St.'s Close)	27	A3
St. Anne's (Ranelagh)	75	C4
St. Anne's (Kimmage)	46	E2
St. Anne's Ave	27	A3
St. Anne's Drive	27	A3
St. Anne's Park	64	E3
St. Anne's Road North	25	A4
St. Anne's Road South	74	E3
*St. Anne's Square (off St. Marnock's Ave)	14	F2
*St. Anne's Square (off Frascati Road Blackrock)	49	A3
St. Anne's Terrace (Ranelagh)	75	C4
St. Anne's Terrace (Raheny)	27	A3
St. Anne's Terrace (Rathcoole)	52	E2
*St. Anns Close (off Temple Road)	49	A3
St. Anns Court	71	B2
*St. Ann's Square Lower (off St. Marnock's Ave)	14	F2
St. Anthony's Ave	44	E2
St. Anthony's Cres	74	D2
St. Anthony's Cres	45	C2
St. Anthony's Place	71	B2
St. Anthony's Road	74	D2
St. Aongus Court	45	B4
St. Aongus Cres	45	B4
St. Aongus Green	45	B4
St. Aongus Grove	45	B4
St. Aongus Lawn	45	B4
*St. Aongus Mews (St. Aongus Road)	45	B4
St. Aongus Park	45	B4

STREET NAME	PAGE	GRID REF
St. Aongus Road	45	B4
*St. Aongus Yard (St. Aongus Road)	45	B4
St. Assam's Ave	27	A2
St. Assam's Drive	27	A2
St. Assam's Park	27	A2
St. Assam's Road East	27	B2
St. Assam's Road West	27	A2
St. Attracta Road	24	F4
*St. Aubyn's Court (opposite Arran Drive)	64	E1
St. Audoen's House Flats	70	F4
St. Audoen's Terrace (off High Street)	75	A1
St. Augustine Street	70	F4
St. Augustine's Park	59	A1
St. Barnabas Gardens	72	E2
St. Begnet's Villas	60	E1
St. Benedicts Gardens	71	B1
St. Berach's Place	27	B1
*St. Bernadette's Hall (Richmond Hill)	75	B4
St. Brendan's Ave	26	E2
*St. Brendan's Cottages (off Irishtown Road)	39	A3
St. Brendan's Cres	45	B2
St. Brendan's Drive	26	E2
St. Brendan's Park	26	F2
*St. Brendan's Road (off St. Anne's Road North)	25	A4
St. Brendan's Terrace (Coolock)	26	E1
*St. Brendan's Terrace (off North Cote Ave)	49	C4
St. Brendan's Terrace (Rockbrook)	56	E4
St. Bricin's Park	70	D3
St. Bridget's Ave (North Strand)	72	E1
St. Bridget's Drive	45	B2
*St. Bridget's Flats (off Embassy Lawn)	47	C2
St. Brigid's Close	26	E2
St. Brigid's Green	26	E2
St. Brigid's Grove	26	E2
St. Brigid's Ave	14	F2
St. Brigid's Church Road	58	F1
St. Brigid's Cottages (North Strand)	72	E1
St. Brigid's Cottages (Blanchardstown)	22	F2
St. Brigid's Cottages (Clondalkin)	44	F2
*St. Brigid's Court (off Killester Park)	26	E3
St. Brigid's Cres	26	E2
*St. Brigid's Drive (off Killester Park)	26	E3
St. Brigid's Drive (Clondalkin)	44	E2
St. Brigid's Lawn	26	E2
St. Brigid's Park (Blanchardstown)	22	F2
*St. Brigid's Park (St. Brigid's Road)	44	E2
St. Brigid's Park (Cornelscourt)	59	B3
St. Brigid's Road (Artane)	26	E2
St. Brigid's Road (Clondalkin)	44	E2
St. Brigid's Road Lower	25	A4
St. Brigid's Road Upper	25	A4
*St. Brigid's Terrace (near Adelaide Villas)	67	C2
*St. Broc's Cottages (off Victoria Ave)	47	C1
St. Canice's Court	23	C1
St. Canice's Park	24	F2
St. Canice's Road	25	A2
St. Canice's Square	24	E2
St. Catherine's Ave	74	E3
*St. Catherine's Court (off Oliver Bond Street)	74	F1
St. Catherines Grove (off St. Cutberth's Road)	43	C1
St. Catherine's Lane West	74	F1
St. Catherine's Park	60	E1
St. Catherine's Road	60	E1
St. Catherine's Terrace	29	A1
St. Catherine's View	20	E4
St. Catherines West	74	E3
*St. Catheryn's Court (off Durham Road)	39	B4
*St. Cathryn's Court (Newgrove Ave)	39	B4
St. Clair's Lawn	67	B3
*St. Clair's Terrace (Oldcourt Park)	67	B3
*St. Clare's Ave (off Harold's Cross Road)	74	F4

STREET NAME	PAGE	GRID REF
*St. Clare's Terrace (Greenfield Place)	75	A4
*St. Clement's Road (off St. Anne's Road North)	25	A4
St. Colmcille's Way	55	C2
St. Columbanus Ave	47	B3
*St. Columbanus Place (off St. Columbanus Road)	47	B3
St. Columbanus Road	47	B3
St. Columbas Heights	1	C2
St. Columbas Rise	1	C2
St. Columba's Road	45	B2
St. Columba's Road Lower	25	A4
St. Columba's Road Upper	25	A4
*St. Columcille's Cres (on Chapel Lane)	2	D2
St. Columcille's Drive	2	D2
*St. Columcille's Terrace (at Ashbrook)	67	C2
St. Columcills Park	2	D2
St. Conleth's Road	45	C2
St. Cronan`s Cottages	1	C2
St. Cronan's Close	1	B2
St. Cronan's Court	1	B1
St. Cronan's Grove	1	C1
St. Cronan's Lawn	1	B1
*St. Cronan's Road (at Ashbrook)	67	C2
St. Cronan's View	1	B2
St. Cronan's Way	1	C2
St. Cuthberts Court	43	C1
St. Cuthbert's Road	43	B1
St. David's	26	D2
*St. David's Court (off Castle Ave Clontarf)	26	E4
St. David's Park	26	D2
St. David's Terrace (Blackhorse Ave)	70	D2
*St. David's Terrace (off Glasnevin Hill)	25	A3
St. Davids Wood	26	D2
St. Declan's Road	25	C4
*St. Declan's Terrace (off St. Declan's Road)	25	C4
St. Domhnach's Well Street (off Baldoyle Road)	28	D1
St. Dominic's Ave	55	A1
*St. Dominic's Court (off St. Dominic's Terrace)	55	A1
St. Dominic's Road	55	A1
St. Dominic's Terrace	55	A1
St. Donagh's Cres	27	B1
St. Donagh's Park	27	B1
St. Donagh's Road	27	B1
St. Edmunds	35	A1
St. Eithne Road	24	F4
St. Elizabeth's Court	70	E1
St. Enda's Drive	56	F1
St. Enda's Park	56	F1
St. Enda's Road	46	F2
*St. Finbarr's Court (on St. Finbarrs Road)	24	E4
St. Finbarr's Close	45	B3
St. Finbarr's Road	24	E4
St. Finian's Green	34	D2
St. Finian's Grove	34	D2
St. Finian's Ave	34	D2
St. Finian's Close	34	D2
St. Finian's Cres	34	D2
St. Fintan Road	24	F4
St. Fintan Terrace	24	F4
St. Fintan's Cres	29	B3
St. Fintan's Grove	29	B3
St. Fintan's Park (Sutton)	29	B2
St. Fintan's Park (Deans Grange)	59	B1
St. Fintan's Road	29	B3
*St. Fintan's Terrace (off Lucan Road Palmerston)	35	C1
St. Fintan's Villas	59	B1
St. Francis Square	75	A1
St. Gabriel's	59	C3
St. Gabriel's Court (off St. Gabriel's Road)	27	A4
St. Gabriel's Road	26	F4
*St. Gall Gardens North (off St. Columbanus Road)	47	B3
*St. Gall Gardens South (off St. Columbanus Road)	47	B3
*St. Gatien Road (off Whitechurch Road)	56	F1
St. George's Ave (Clonliffe Road)	25	B4
St. George's Ave (Killiney)	60	E3

STREET NAME	PAGE	GRID REF
*St. George's Villas (off Inchicore Terrace South)	36	F3
St. Georges Road (off Mckee Ave)	24	E1
St. Gerard's Road	45	C2
*St. Helena's Court (off St. Helena's Drive)	24	E2
St. Helena's Drive	24	E2
St. Helena's Road	24	E2
*St. Helen's (off Marine Parade)	60	E1
St. Helen's Road	48	E2
St. Helen's Terrace	73	A2
*St. Helen's Villas (off St. Helen's Road)	48	F2
St. Helen's Wood	48	E3
*St. Helier's Copse (off Coppinger Wood)	48	F4
St. Ignatius Ave	71	B1
St. Ignatius Road	71	B1
*St. Ita's Road (off Botanic Ave)	25	A3
St. Ives	3	B2
St. James Ave (Clonliffe Road)	72	D1
*St. James Court (off Mount Brown)	73	C1
*St. James Court (off Serpentine Ave)	39	A4
*St. James Place (Sandymount Road)	39	A3
*St. James Place (off Sandymount Road)	39	A4
*St. James Terrace (off Sandymount Road)	39	A3
St. Jame's Wood	73	B2
St. James's	26	D4
St. James's Ave (James's Street)	74	D1
St. James's Court Apts	74	E1
*St. James's Place (off Tyrconnell Road)	36	F3
St. James's Road	45	B2
St. James's Terrace (Dolphin's Barn)	74	D3
St. James's Walk	74	D2
St. James's Walk	74	D2
St. Jarlath Road	24	F4
St. John Street	74	F2
*St. John's Close (off Mounttown Road. Lower)	59	C1
St. John's Court (Donnycarney)	26	D3
*St. John's Wood (off Orwell Road)	47	A2
St. John's	48	E1
St. John's Ave (The Coombe)	74	F2
St. John's Ave (Clondalkin)	44	D2
*St. Johns Close (opposite Glandore Park)	59	C1
St. John's Close	44	D2
St. John's Cottages	73	C1
St. John's Court	25	B1
St. John's Court (Beaumont)	26	D1
St. John's Court (Clondalkin)	44	D2
St. John's Cres	44	D2
St. John's Drive	44	D2
St. John's Gate	44	D2
St. John's Green	44	D2
St. John's Grove	44	D2
*St. John's Lane (off Strand Road)	48	E1
St. John's Lawn	44	D2
St. John's Park (Dún Laoghaire)	49	C4
St. John's Park East	44	D2
St. Johns Park West	44	D2
St. John's Road	44	D2
St. John's Road East	48	E1
St. John's Road West (Islandbridge)	69	C4
St. John's Road West (Clondalkin)	44	D2
*St. Johns Terrace (Donnellan Ave)	73	C1
*St. John's Terrace (Mount Brown)	73	C1
St. John's Well Way	73	C1
*St. John's Wood (off Castle Ave Clontarf)	26	E4
St. John's Wood (Clondalkin)	44	D2
St. John's Wood West	44	D2
St. Joseph Street (off Leo Street)	71	B1
St. Joseph's	23	C2
St. Joseph's Ave (Drumcondra)	25	A4
*St. Joseph's Ave (off Clonliffe Road)	25	B4
St. Joseph's Cottages	23	C4
St. Joseph's Court	70	E2
*St. Joseph's Grove (off Rosemount Park)	47	C4

STREET NAME	PAGE	GRID REF
*St. Joseph's Mansions	72	D2
St. Joseph's Parade	71	A1
St. Joseph's Place (Dorset Street Lower)	71	B2
St. Joseph's Place (Prussia Street)	70	E2
St. Joseph's Road (Aughrim Street)	70	E2
St. Joseph's Road (Walkinstown)	45	C2
*St. Joseph's Square (off Vernon Ave)	39	C1
*St. Joseph's Terrace (off Dolphin's Barn)	74	D3
St. Joseph's Terrace (North Circular Road)	71	C1
St. Joseph's Terrace	71	A2
*St. Joseph's Terrace (off Philipsburgh Ave)	25	C4
*St. Joseph's Terrace (off Pembroke Street)	39	A3
*St. Joseph's Terrace (on Tivoli Road)	50	D4
St. Joseph's Villas (Summerhill)	72	D1
*St. Judes Apts (adjacent to The Close)	31	C3
St. Kevin's Ave (off Blackpitts)	74	F2
St. Kevins Church Apts	75	A3
St. Kevin's Cottages	75	A3
St. Kevin's Court	47	A2
St. Kevin's Gardens	47	A2
St. Kevin's Parade	75	A3
St. Kevin's Park (Rathgar)	47	A2
St. Kevin's Park (Stillorgan)	58	D1
St. Kevin's Road	75	A4
St. Kevin's Square	67	C2
*St. Kevin's Terrace (New Bride Street)	75	A2
*St. Kevin's Terrace (St. Kevin's Square)	67	C2
St. Kevin's Villas	60	D1
St. Killian's Ave	45	B2
St. Killians Cres	67	B4
*St. Killian's Park (off Watery Lane)	44	E1
St. Laurence Court	36	E3
*St. Laurence Grove (off St. Laurence Road)	36	E2
*St. Laurence O'Toole Court (off Oriel Street Upper)	72	D3
St. Laurence Park	48	F4
St. Laurence Place (Western Way)	71	A2
St. Laurence Place East (Lower Sheriff Street)	72	E3
St. Laurence Road	36	E2
*St. Laurence Terrace (off Lucan Road Chapelizod)	36	E2
*St. Laurence's Terrace (near Adelaide Villas)	67	C2
*St. Lawrence Building Apts (off Harbour Road, opposite west pier)	30	D1
*St. Lawrence Glen (off St. Lawrence Road)	36	E3
St. Lawrence O'Toole Ave	14	F2
*St. Lawrence Quay (off Harbour Road, close to Post Office)	30	D1
St. Lawrence Road (Clontarf)	26	D4
St. Lawrence Road (Howth)	30	D1
St. Lawrence's Court	26	D4
St. Lawrence's Terrace	30	D2
St. Loman's Road	34	F2
St. Luke's Ave	74	F2
*St. Luke's Court (off Cromcastle Green)	26	D1
*St. Luke's Cres (off Dundrum Road)	47	B2
St. Luke's Gate	74	F2
*St. Maelruans Courtyard (off St. Maelruans Park)	55	A1
St. Maelruans Park	55	A1
St. Maignenn's Terrace	73	C1
St. Malachy's Drive	45	C2
*St. Malachy's Road (off Botanic Ave)	25	A3
*St. Margaret's Close (off Castlepark Road)	60	E1
St. Margaret's (North Road)	11	B1
St. Margaret's (Booterstown)	48	F3
St. Margaret's Ave (off Pimlico)	74	F1
St. Margaret's Ave (Malahide)	3	B3
St. Margaret's Ave (Kilbarrack)	27	C2

STREET NAME	PAGE	GRID REF
*St. Margaret's Ave North (Richmond Lane)	71	C1
St. Margaret's Court	11	A4
St. Margaret's Park	3	B3
St. Margaret's Road (Poppintree)	11	C4
St. Margaret's Road (Malahide)	3	B3
St. Margaret's Road (Finglas)	11	A4
St. Margaret's Road (Ballymun)	12	D4
St. Margaret's Terrace	74	E2
St. Mark's Ave	35	A2
St. Mark's Cres	35	A3
St. Mark's Drive	35	A3
St. Mark's Gardens	35	A3
St. Mark's Green	35	A3
St. Mark's Grove	35	A3
St. Marnock's Ave	14	F2
St. Martin's Drive	46	E2
St. Martin's Park	46	E1
St. Mary's Ave (Rathfarnham)	46	F4
St. Mary's Ave North (Mountjoy Street)	71	A2
St. Mary's Ave West	36	F3
*St. Mary's Court (on Church Road)	72	F2
St. Mary's Cres	45	C1
St. Mary's Drive	45	C1
St. Mary's Lane	76	E2
St. Mary's Mansions	71	C2
St. Mary's Park (Leixlip)	20	D4
St. Mary's Park (Finglas)	23	C2
St. Mary's Park (Crumlin)	45	C1
*St. Mary's Place (south of Church on Main Street Howth)	30	D2
St. Mary's Place North	71	A2
*St. Mary's Road (south of Church on Main Street Howth)	30	D2
St. Mary's Road (Crumlin)	46	D1
St. Mary's Road North (East Wall)	72	E2
St. Mary's Road South (Ballsbridge)	76	E3
*St. Mary's Street (off North Cote Ave)	49	C4
*St. Marys Terrace (South of Hall)	68	D2
St. Mary's Terrace (Mountjoy Street)	71	A2
St. Mary's Terrace (Arbour Hill)	70	E3
St. Mary's Terrace (Dunboyne)	7	B2
*St. Mary's Terrace (off Martin's Row Chapelizod)	36	E2
*St. Mary's Terrace (Bath Street)	39	A3
*St. Mary's Terrace (off Grange Road Rathfarnham)	46	F4
*St. Mary's Terrace (entrance to Bentley Road)	67	C4
St. Mathias Wood	60	D4
St. Mel's Ave	45	B3
*St. Michael's Villas (Sarsfield Road)	36	E3
St. Michael's Close (off High Street)	75	A1
St. Michael's Estate	73	A2
St. Michael's Hill (off High Street)	75	A1
St. Michael's House	47	C4
St. Michael's Place	71	A2
*St. Michael's Road (off Botanic Ave)	25	A3
St. Michael's Terrace (Blackpitts)	74	F2
*St. Michael's Terrace (off York Road Dún Laoghaire)	49	C4
St. Michan's House Flats	71	A4
St. Michan's Park	71	A3
St. Michan's Place (off Chancery Street)	71	A4
St. Michan's Street	71	A4
*St. Mobhi Ave (on St. Mobhi Road)	25	A3
St. Mobhi Boithirin	25	A3
St. Mobhi Drive	25	A3
*St. Mobhi Grove (off Botanic Road)	25	A3
*St. Mobhi Mews (St. Mobhi Boithrin)	25	A3
St. Mobhi Road	25	A3
St. Mochtas Ave	22	D3
St. Mochtas Chase	22	D2
St. Mochtas Close	22	D3
St. Mochtas Drive	22	D3
St. Mochtas Green	22	D3
St. Mochtas Grove	22	D3

STREET NAME	PAGE	GRID REF
St. Mochtas Lawn	22	D2
St. Mochtas Road	22	D3
St. Mochtas Vale	22	D3
St. Mura's Terrace	72	F2
*St. Nathy's House (off Churchtown Road)	47	B4
*St. Nathy's Villas (off Nutgrove Ave)	47	B4
St. Nessan's Apts	30	E2
*St. Nessan's Close (streets between Tuckett's Lane and Main Street)	30	D2
*St. Nessans Court (streets between Tuckett's Lane and Main Street)	30	D2
*St. Nessan's Terrace (streets between Tuckett's Lane and Main Street)	30	D2
St. Nicholas Place	75	A1
St. Oliver's Park	35	B3
St. Pappin's Green	24	D4
St. Pappin's Road	25	A2
*St. Pappin's Street (adjacent Santry Cross Junction)	12	D4
St. Patrick's Ave (Fairview)	72	E1
St. Patrick's Ave (Portmarnock)	14	F2
*St. Patrick's Ave (St. Patrick's Park)	44	D1
*St. Patrick's Ave (off Castle Street Dalkey)	60	F2
St. Patrick's Close (Kevin Street Upper)	75	A2
*St. Patrick's Close (off St. Patrick's Cres)	59	C1
St. Patrick's Cottages	46	F4
St. Patrick's Court	74	F3
St. Patrick's Cres (Rathcoole)	52	E2
St. Patrick's Cres (Kill O'The Grange)	59	C1
St. Patrick's Parade	25	A4
St. Patrick's Park (Dunboyne)	7	B2
St. Patrick's Park (Blanchardstown)	22	E2
St. Patrick's Park (Celbridge)	31	C3
St. Patrick's Park (Celbridge)	32	D3
St. Patrick's Park (Clondalkin)	44	D1
St. Patrick's Park (Stepaside)	58	E4
St. Patrick's Place	71	A2
*St. Patrick's Place (off Royal Canal Bank)	25	A4
St. Patrick's Road (Drumcondra)	25	A4
St. Patrick's Road (Clondalkin)	35	A4
St. Patrick's Road (Walkinstown)	45	C2
*St. Patrick's Road (off Castle Street Dalkey)	60	F2
*St. Patrick's Square (off Castle Street Dalkey)	60	F2
*St. Patrick's Square (off Castle Street Bray)	67	C1
*St. Patrick's Terrace (Russell Street)	71	C1
*St. Patrick's Terrace (North Brunswick Street)	70	F3
*St. Patrick's Terrace (off Fitzroy Ave)	25	B4
*St. Patrick's Terrace (off Inchicore Terrace South)	36	F3
*St. Patrick's Terrace (off Oliver Plunkett Road)	59	C1
*St. Patrick's Villas (off Thorncastle Street)	39	A3
*St. Paul's Court (Slademore Ave)	26	F1
*St. Pauls Drive (Limekiln Lane)	45	C2
*St. Paul's Terrace (off Adelaide Road)	60	E1
St. Peter's Ave	70	F1
St. Peter's Close	71	A1
St. Peter's Court	71	A1
St. Peter's Cres	45	C2
St. Peter's Drive	45	C2
St. Peter's Park	7	B2
St. Peter's Road (Phibsborough)	24	F4
St. Peter's Road (Walkinstown)	45	C2
St. Peter's Road (Bray)	67	B1
St. Peter's Square	71	A1
St. Peter's Terrace (Howth)	30	D2
*St. Peter's Terrace (off St. Peter's Drive Walkinstown)	45	C2
*St. Peter's Terrace (off Adelaide Road)	60	E1
*St. Peter's Terrace (St. Peters Road)	67	B1

STREET NAME	PAGE	GRID REF
St. Philomenas	9	C4
St. Philomena's Court	9	C4
St. Philomena's Park	9	C3
*St. Philomena's Road (off Dalcassian Downs)	24	F4
St. Raphaels Ave	31	C4
St. Ronan's Ave	35	A3
St. Ronan's Close	35	A3
St. Ronan's Cres	35	A3
St. Ronan's Drive	35	A3
St. Ronan's Gardens	35	A3
St. Ronan's Green	35	A3
St. Ronan's Grove	35	A3
St. Ronan's Park	35	A3
St. Ronan's Way	35	A3
St. Samson Court	14	D3
St. Samson Square	14	D3
St. Stephen's Green East	75	C2
St. Stephen's Green North	75	C2
St. Stephen's Green South	75	B2
St. Stephen's Green West	75	B2
St. Sylvester Villas	3	B3
St. Teresa's Gardens	74	E2
*St. Teresa's Place (off Prospect Ave)	25	A4
*St. Teresa's Road (off Botanic Road Glasnevin)	25	A4
St. Teresa's Road (Crumlin)	46	D2
St. Thomas Mead	48	E3
St. Thomas Road (Ardee Street)	74	F2
*St. Thomas Wood (opposite Belfield Park Apts)	48	E3
St. Thomas's Road (Mount Merrion)	48	E3
St. Ultan's Flats	75	B3
St. Vincent Street North	71	A1
St. Vincent Street South	75	A3
St. Vincent Street West	73	A2
St. Vincent's Cottages	23	C4
*St. Vincent's Court (off Collins Ave)	25	C3
St. Vincent's Court	26	D3
St. Vincent's Park	49	A4
St. Werburghs	2	E2
St. Wolstan's Abbey	32	E3
St. Wolston's Abbey	32	D4
St.doolaghs	14	D3
St.sbury Ave	60	E4
Salamanca	48	D4
*Salem Court (off Maxwell Road)	47	A1
Salestown	6	D4
*Salisbury Court Apts (off Dufferin Ave)	74	F3
Sallowood View	12	E4
Sally Park	55	C1
Sally Park Close	55	C1
Sallyglen Road	60	D2
Sallymount Ave	47	B1
*Sallymount Gardens (off Sallymount Ave)	47	B1
*Sallymount Terrace (off Sallymount Ave)	47	B1
Sallynoggin	60	D2
Sallynoggin Park	59	C2
Sallynoggin Road	59	C2
Salmon Pool Apts	69	A4
Salthill	49	C4
*Salthill Place (off Crofton Road)	50	D4
Saltzburg	48	D4
Sampson's Lane	71	B3
Samuel Beckett Bridge	72	E4
Sanderling Apts	48	E3
Sandford Ave (Donore Ave)	74	E3
Sandford Ave (Donnybrook)	47	C1
Sandford Close	47	B1
Sandford Gardens	74	F3
*Sandford Gardens (off Sandford Ave)	47	C1
Sandford Lodge	47	B1
Sandford Park (Sandford Gardens)	74	F3
Sandford Road	47	B1
Sandford Row	47	B1
Sandford Square	47	B1
Sandford Terrace	47	B1
Sandford Wood	1	C1
Sandon Cove	26	E4
Sandsfords Bridge	19	A3
Sandwith Street Lower	72	D4
Sandwith Street Upper	76	D1
Sandycove Ave East	60	E1
Sandycove Ave North	50	E4
Sandycove Ave West	60	E1

STREET NAME	PAGE	GRID REF
Sandycove Lane East	60	E1
Sandycove Point	50	E4
Sandycove Road	60	E1
Sandyford	58	D2
Sandyford Downs	58	D3
Sandyford Hall	58	E3
Sandyford Hall Ave	58	E3
Sandyford Hall Close	58	E4
Sandyford Hall Court	58	E3
Sandyford Hall Cres	58	E3
Sandyford Hall Drive	58	E4
Sandyford Hall Green	58	E3
Sandyford Hall Grove	58	E4
Sandyford Hall Lawn	58	E3
Sandyford Hall Park	58	E3
Sandyford Hall Place	58	E3
Sandyford Hall Rise	58	E3
Sandyford Hall View	58	E4
Sandyford Hall Walk	58	E3
Sandyford Park	58	D3
Sandyford Road	57	C1
Sandyford View	57	C3
Sandyford Village	58	D3
Sandyhill Ave	24	F1
Sandyhill Court	11	C4
Sandyhill Gardens	24	F1
Sandyhill Terrace	11	C4
Sandyhill Way	11	C4
Sandymount	39	A4
Sandymount Ave	39	A4
*Sandymount Castle (off Gilford Road)	39	A4
*Sandymount Castle Drive (off Gilford Road)	39	A4
*Sandymount Castle Park (off Gilford Road)	39	B4
*Sandymount Castle Road (off Gilford Road)	39	A4
*Sandymount Court (off Beach Road)	39	A3
*Sandymount Green (off Gilford Road)	39	A4
Sandymount Road	39	A3
Sans Souci Park	48	F3
Sans Souci wood	67	C3
Santa Sabina Manor	29	B2
Santry	25	B1
Santry Ave	12	E4
Santry Close	12	F4
Santry Court	12	F4
Santry Cross (Ballymun)	12	D4
Santry Villas	12	E4
Sarah Bridge (River Liffey)	69	B4
Sarah Curran Ave	56	F1
*Sarah Curran Road (off Sarah Curran Ave)	56	F1
Sarah Place	69	B4
Saran Wood	67	B4
Sarney	6	E2
*Sarsfield Court (off Main Street Lucan)	34	D1
Sarsfield Court (Inchicore)	36	F3
Sarsfield Park	34	D1
Sarsfield Quay	70	E4
Sarsfield Road	36	F3
Sarsfield Street (Phibsborough)	71	A1
Sarsfield Street (Sallynoggin)	60	D1
*Sarsfield Terrace (off Main Street Lucan)	34	D1
Sarto Lawn	27	C1
Sarto Park	27	C1
Sarto Rise	27	C1
Sarto Road	27	C2
Saul Road	46	E1
Saval Grove	60	E2
Saval Park Cres	60	E2
Saval Park Gardens	60	E2
Saval Park Road	60	E2
Scariff House	22	F1
Scholarstown Park	56	D2
Scholarstown Road	56	D2
School Ave	26	E2
School Lane	28	D1
School Street	74	E1
*School Street Flats (off Marrowbone Lane)	74	E1
School Walk	52	E2
Schoolhouse Court	25	B1
Schoolhouse Lane (Kildare Street)	75	C1
Schoolhouse Lane (Santry)	25	B1
Schoolhouse Lane West (off High Street)	75	A1
*Schoolhouse Mews (off Schoolhouse Lane)	25	B1

STREET NAME	PAGE	GRID REF
Schools Road	67	B4
Scotchstone Bridge	2	D1
Scott Park	67	C3
Scribblestown	23	C3
Scribblestown Ave	23	C3
Scribblestown Close	23	C3
Scribblestown Grove	23	C3
Scribblestown Park	24	D3
Scribblestown Place	23	C3
Scribblestown Road	23	C3
Sea Road	3	A2
Seabank Court (Malahide)	3	C2
*Seabank Court (off Marine Parade)	60	E1
Seabrook Manor	14	E2
Seabury	48	E1
Seabury Ave	2	F2
Seabury Close	2	F2
Seabury Court	2	F2
Seabury Cres	2	F2
Seabury Dale	2	F2
Seabury Downs	2	F2
Seabury Drive	3	A2
Seabury Gardens	2	F2
Seabury Glen	2	F2
Seabury Green	2	F2
Seabury Grove	2	F2
Seabury Heights	2	F2
Seabury Lane	2	F2
Seabury Lawns	2	F2
Seabury Meadows	2	F2
Seabury Orchard	2	F2
Seabury Parade	2	F2
Seabury Park	2	F2
Seabury Place	2	F2
Seabury Road	2	F2
Seabury Vale	2	F2
Seabury View	2	F2
Seabury Walk	2	F2
Seabury Wood	2	F2
Seacliff Ave	27	C1
Seacliff Drive	27	C1
Seacliff Road	27	C1
Seacourt	26	F4
Seacrest	67	C3
Seafield (off Baldoyle Road)	28	D1
Seafield (Shankill)	64	F2
Seafield Ave (Clontarf)	26	F4
Seafield Ave (Monkstown)	49	B4
Seafield Close	48	E3
Seafield Close	26	F4
Seafield Court (Malahide)	3	B2
Seafield Court (Loughlinstown)	64	E1
Seafield Cres	48	E3
Seafield Downs (off Kincora Road Clontarf)	26	F4
Seafield Drive	48	F2
Seafield Grove (off St. Gabriel's Road)	27	A4
*Seafield Park (off Seafield Road)	48	E2
Seafield Road (Booterstown)	48	E2
Seafield Road (Killiney)	60	E4
Seafield Road (Ballybrack)	64	E1
Seafield Road East	26	F4
Seafield Road West	26	E4
*Seafield Terrace (off Coliemore Road)	60	F2
Seafort Ave	39	A4
*Seafort Cottages (off Seafort Ave)	39	A4
*Seafort Gardens (off Sandymount Road)	39	A3
Seafort Parade	48	F3
*Seafort Terrace (off Seafort Ave)	39	A4
*Seafort Villas (off Seafort Ave)	39	A4
Seagrange Ave	14	F4
Seagrange Drive	27	C1
Seagrange Road	27	C1
Seagrave	14	F2
Seagrave Close	11	B4
Seagrave Court	11	B4
Seagrave Drive	11	B4
Seagrave Rise	11	B4
Seagrave Terrace	11	B4
Seagrave Way	11	B4
Seamount	3	C3
Seamount	48	E3
Seamount Drive	3	C3
Seamount Grove	3	C3
Seamount Heights	3	C3
Seamount Park	3	C3
Seamount Road	3	C3
Seamount View	2	E2

STREET NAME	PAGE	GRID REF
Seamus Ennis Road	24	E1
Seán Heuston Bridge (River Liffey)	70	D4
Sean MacDermott Street Lower	71	C2
Sean MacDermott Street Upper	71	C3
Sean Moore Road	39	A3
Sean O'Casey Ave	71	C2
Seán O'Casey Bridge (River Liffey)	72	D4
Sean Tracey House	72	D2
*Seanchlos Apts (Johnstown Road Rathcoole)	52	E2
Seapark (Malahide)	3	C3
Seapark (Dollymount)	26	F4
Seapark Drive	26	F4
Seapark Hill	3	C3
Seapark Road	26	F4
*Seapoint Ave (Between College Street and Main Street Baldoyle)	15	A4
Seapoint Ave (Blackrock)	49	B3
*Seapoint Court (Between College Street and Main Street Baldoyle)	15	A4
Seapoint Court (Bray)	67	C1
Seapoint Road	67	C2
*Seapoint Terrace (off Strand Street Ringsend)	39	A3
*Seapoint Terrace (off Belgrave Road)	49	B3
*Seapoint Terrace (near Duncairn Ave)	67	C2
*Seapoint Villas (near Duncairn Ave)	67	C2
Seascout Den	40	D1
Seatown Park	2	D1
Seatown Park The Ave	2	D1
Seatown Park The Court	2	D1
Seatown Park The Cres	2	D1
Seatown Park The Drive	2	D1
Seatown Park The Green	2	D1
Seatown Park The Grove	2	D1
Seatown Road	2	D1
Seatown Roundabout (Swords)	2	D1
Seatown Terrace	2	D2
Seatown Villas	2	D1
Seatown Walk	2	D2
Seatown West	2	D1
Seaview Ave East	72	E1
Seaview Ave North	26	D4
Seaview Cottages	63	C4
Seaview Lawn	64	E2
Seaview Park	64	E2
*Seaview Terrace (streets between Tuckett's Lane and Main Street)	30	D2
Seaview Terrace (Donnybrook)	48	D1
*Seaview Terrace (off Clarence Street Dún Laoghaire)	49	C4
Seaview Wood	64	E2
Second Ave (Seville Place)	72	E3
Second Ave (Tallaght)	44	F4
Sefton	59	C2
Sefton Green	59	C2
*Sefton Hall (off Kelston Ave)	59	A2
*Selskar Terrace (Old Mountpleasant)	75	C4
Serpentine Ave	39	A4
Serpentine Park	39	A4
Serpentine Road	39	A4
Serpentine Terrace	39	A4
Seskin View Ave	55	A2
Seskin View Drive	55	A2
Seskin View Park	55	A2
Seskin View Road	55	A2
Setanta Place	75	C1
*Seven Houses (off Glenageary Road Lower)	60	D1
Seven Oaks (Whitehall)	25	B3
Seven Oaks (Inchicore)	36	F3
*Seven Oaks (off Belgrave Road)	47	A1
Seventh Lock Cottages	36	D4
Seventh Lock Place	36	D4
Seville Place	72	D2
Seville Terrace	72	D2
Seymour Road	67	C2
Shackelton	8	F4
Shackelton Road	31	C3
Shaldon Grange	62	F2
*Shalimar Apts (off Monastery Road)	44	F1
Shamrock Cottages	72	D2
*Shamrock Hill Mews (off Stillorgan Road)	47	C1
Shamrock Place	72	D2

STREET NAME	PAGE	GRID REF
Shamrock Street	71	A2
Shamrock Terrace	72	D2
Shamrock Villas	46	F1
*Shanagarry (off Milltown Road)	47	B2
Shanard Ave	25	A1
Shanard Road	25	A1
Shanboley Road	25	C1
Shancastle Ave	35	A2
Shancastle Close	35	A2
Shancastle Cres	35	A2
Shancastle Drive	35	A2
Shancastle Lawns	35	A2
Shancastle Park	35	A2
Shandon Cres	24	F4
Shandon Drive	24	F4
Shandon Gardens	24	F4
*Shandon Green (off Shandon Cres)	24	F4
Shandon Mill (off Shandon Park)	24	F4
Shandon Park (Phibsborough)	24	F4
Shandon Park (Monkstown)	49	B4
Shandon Road	24	F4
Shangan Ave	25	B1
Shangan Court	25	A1
Shangan Cres	25	A1
Shangan Drive	25	B1
Shangan Gardens	25	B1
Shangan Green	25	B1
*Shangan Hall Apts (off Shangan Road)	25	A1
Shangan Park	25	B1
Shangan Road	25	A1
Shanganagh Cliffs	64	E2
Shanganagh Grove	64	E3
Shanganagh Road	64	E1
Shanganagh Terrace	60	E4
Shanganagh Vale	60	D4
*Shanganagh Wood (west off Railway Station)	64	E2
Shanglas Road	25	C1
Shanid Road	46	F2
Shankill	64	E3
*Shankill View (near Bray Bridge)	67	C2
Shanliss Ave	25	B1
Shanliss Drive	25	B1
*Shanliss Gardens (off Shanliss Road)	25	A1
Shanliss Grove	25	B1
Shanliss Park	25	B1
Shanliss Road	25	A1
Shanliss Walk	25	B1
Shanliss Way	25	B1
Shannon Terrace	73	C1
Shanowen Ave	25	A1
Shanowen Cres	25	B1
Shanowen Drive	25	B1
Shanowen Grove	25	A1
Shanowen Hall	25	B2
Shanowen Park	25	A1
Shanowen Road	25	B1
Shanowen Square	25	B2
Shanrath Road	25	B1
Shantalla Ave	25	C1
Shantalla Drive	25	C2
Shantalla Park	25	C2
Shantalla Road	25	C2
Shanvarna Road	25	B1
Sharavogue	60	E2
Shaw Court Apts	75	B3
Shaw Street	71	C4
Shaw's Lane	76	F2
Shea's Court	70	E2
Shea's Lane	70	E2
Sheelin Ave	64	E1
Sheelin Drive	64	E1
*Sheelin Grove (off Sheelin Ave)	64	E1
*Sheelin Hill (off Ridge Hill)	64	E1
*Sheelin Walk (off Sheelin Ave)	64	E1
Sheephill Ave	9	C4
Sheephill Green	9	C4
Sheephill Park	9	C4
Sheepmoor Ave	22	D1
Sheepmoor Close	22	D1
Sheepmoor Cres	22	D1
Sheepmoor Gardens	22	D1
Sheepmoor Green	22	D1
Sheepmoor Grove	22	D1
Sheepmoor Lawn	22	D1
Sheepmoor Way	22	D1
Shelbourne Ave (off Gilford Road)	76	F3
Shelbourne Lane (off Gilford Road)	76	F3
*Shelbourne Park Apts	76	F1
Shelbourne Park Mews	76	F1
Shelbourne Place	76	F2
Shelbourne Road	76	F2
Shelbourne Village	76	F1
Shelerin Road	21	C2
Shellys Banks Road	39	B3
Shelmalier Road	72	F2
Shelmartin Ave	25	C4
*Shelmartin Terrace (off Shelmartin Ave)	25	C4
Shelton Drive	46	D2
Shelton Gardens	46	D2
Shelton Grove	46	D2
Shelton Park	46	D2
Sherborne	47	A2
Sheridan Court	71	B2
Sheridan Place	71	B2
Sheriff Street Lower	72	D3
Sheriff Street Upper	72	E3
Sherkin Court	25	B3
Sherkin Gardens	25	B3
Sherrard Ave	71	B1
*Sherrard Court (off Portland Place)	71	B1
Sherrard Street Lower	71	C1
Sherrard Street Upper	71	B1
Sherrards Court	71	B1
Shieling Square	27	B2
Shielmartin Drive	29	B3
*Shielmartin Park (off Shielmartin Road)	29	B3
Shielmartin Road	29	B3
Shinkeen Bridge	32	E3
Ship Street Great	75	A1
Ship Street Little	75	A1
Shrewsbury	39	A4
Shrewsbury Court	59	C3
Shrewsbury Hall	64	E3
Shrewsbury House	59	C4
Shrewsbury Lawn	59	C4
Shrewsbury Lodge	59	C3
Shrewsbury Park	48	D1
Shrewsbury Road (Ailesbury Road)	48	D1
Shrewsbury Road (Shankill)	64	E3
*Shrewsbury Square (off Sandymount Ave)	39	A4
Shrewsbury Woods	59	C4
Sibthorpe Lane	76	D4
*Sidbury Court (between Sidmonton and Albert Ave)	68	D2
Sidmonton Ave	67	C2
*Sidmonton Court (west side of Meath Road)	68	D3
Sidmonton Gardens	67	C2
Sidmonton Park	68	D2
*Sidmonton Place (Kingsmill Road)	67	C2
Sidmonton Road	67	C2
*Sidmonton Square (Sidmonton Ave)	67	C2
Sigurd Road	70	E3
Silchester Court	60	D1
Silchester Cres	60	D1
Silchester Park	60	D1
Silchester Road	60	D1
*Silchester Wood (off Adelaide Road)	60	D1
Silken Park	43	C4
Silken Park Ave	43	C4
Silken Vale	17	C3
Silleachain Lane	20	D4
Silloge Ave	25	A1
Silloge Cres	25	A1
Silloge Gardens	25	A1
Silloge Road	25	A1
Silver Birches (Dunboyne)	7	B2
Silver Birches (Dundrum)	47	C4
Silver Birches Close	7	B2
Silver Birches Cres	7	B2
*Silver Pines (off Brewery Road)	58	F2
Silveracre Avenue	56	F1
Silverberry	34	D3
Silverdale	34	D3
Silverdale Court	67	B3
Silverpine	67	B3
Silverwood	34	D3
Silverwood Drive	46	E4
Silverwood Road	46	E4
Simmon's Place (off Thompson's Cottages)	71	C2
*Simmonscourt Ave (off Simmonscourt Road)	48	D1
Simmonscourt Castle	48	D1
Simmonscourt Road	39	A4
*Simmonscourt Square (off Simmonscourt Road)	48	D1
*Simmonscourt Terrace (off Beaver Row)	47	C1
*Simmonscourt View (off Simmonscourt Road)	48	D1
Simmonstown	41	A1
Simmonstown Manor	32	D4
Simmonstown Park	32	D4
Simons Ridge	57	C3
*Simpsons Lane (off Bath Street)	39	A3
Sion Hill Ave	46	F1
*Sion Hill Court (off Sion Hill Road)	25	C3
Sion Hill Road	25	C3
*Sion House (off Thomas Davis Street West)	36	F3
Sion Road	60	D2
Sionhill	48	F3
*Sir Ivor Mall (off Leopardstown Road)	58	F2
Sir John Rogerson's Quay	72	E4
Sitric Place (off Sitric Road)	70	E3
Sitric Road	70	E3
Skeagh	41	A3
Skelligs Court	22	F1
Skelly's Lane	26	D2
Skreen Road	69	B1
Slade	53	A3
Slade Castle Ave	53	A2
Slade Castle Close	53	A2
Slade Castle Heights	53	A2
Slade Castle View	53	A2
Slade Road	53	A3
Slade Row	70	D3
Slademore Ave	26	F1
Slademore Close	26	F1
Slademore Court	13	C4
Slademore Drive	26	F1
Slane Road	73	C4
Slaney Close	24	E3
Slaney Road	24	E3
Slate Cabin Lane	57	C3
Slemish Road	69	B1
Slieve Rua Drive	58	D1
Slievebloom Park	45	C1
Slievebloom Road	45	C1
Slievemore Road	73	A4
Slievenamon Road	73	B3
*Sloan Terrace (east side of text Meath)	68	D2
Sloperton	49	C4
Smithfield	70	F4
*Smithfield Apts (Near Ellis Quay Apts)	70	F4
Smithfield Gate Apts	70	F3
*Smithfield Market Square Apts (Smithfield)	70	F4
*Smithfield Terrace (Smithfield)	70	F4
*Smith's Cottages (off Bushfield Terrace)	47	B1
*Smith's Lane (off Harold's Cross Road)	46	F1
*Smith's Villas (off York Road Dún Laoghaire)	49	C4
*Smyth Gardens (off York Road Dún Laoghaire)	49	C4
Snowdrop Walk	13	C4
Snugborough	14	E3
Snugborough Road	22	F1
Snugborough Road Extension	22	D2
Somerset Street	76	F1
Somerton	59	C2
*Somerton Mews	59	C2
Somerton Road	22	E4
Somerville Ave	45	C1
*Somerville Court (off St. Agnes Road Crumlin)	46	D1
Somerville Drive	46	D1
*Somerville Park (off Somerville Ave)	45	C1
Sommerville	47	C4
Sonesta	3	A2
*Sophie Baret Residence (off Lower Kilmacud Road)	48	D4
Sorbonne	48	D4
Sorrel Dale	22	D2
Sorrel Drive	21	C2
Sorrel Heath	21	C2
Sorrel Park	21	C2
Sorrell Hall	57	C3
*Sorrento Close (off Sorrento Road)	60	F2
*Sorrento Court (off Sorrento Road)	60	F2
*Sorrento Drive (off Sorrento Road)	60	F2
*Sorrento Heights (off Sorrento Road)	60	F2
*Sorrento Lawn (off Sorrento Road)	60	F2
*Sorrento Mews (off Sorrento Road)	60	F2
*Sorrento Park (on Sorrento Road)	60	F2
Sorrento Road	60	F2
Sorrento Terrace	60	G2
South Ave	48	E4
South Bank	2	D1
South Bank (Swords)	1	C1
South Bank Road	39	B3
South Circular Road (Dolphin's Barn)	74	D3
South Circular Road (Portobello)	74	E3
South Circular Road (Kilmainham)	73	C2
South Circular Road (Islandbridge)	69	B4
South City Market (on South Great Georges Street)	75	B1
*South Dock Apts	76	F1
South Dock Place	76	F1
South Dock Road	76	F1
South Dock Street	76	F1
South Esplanade	68	D2
*South Gate Apts (off Ardee Street)	74	F2
South Great George's Street	75	B1
South Hill (Howth)	29	C3
South Hill (Milltown)	47	C2
South Hill Ave	48	F3
South Hill Park	48	E3
South Lotts Road	76	F1
South Park (Cornelscourt)	59	B3
South Park Drive	59	B2
South Richmond View	75	B3
*South Winds (off Ulverton Road Dalkey)	60	F1
South Wood Park	48	F3
*Southdene (off Monkstown Valley)	49	B4
Southern Cross Ave	73	A2
Southern Cross Route	57	B3
Southfield	74	E4
Southlands	64	E4
Southmede	57	C1
Southview Terrace	74	D1
Spa Road	73	A2
Spa Road (Phoenix Park)	69	B2
Spa Road (Inchicore)	36	F3
*Spafield Terrace (off Sandymount Ave)	39	A4
*Spawell Cottages (off Tallaght Road)	45	C4
Spawell Roundabout	46	D4
Spencer Dock	72	E3
Spencer Place (off Spencer Street North)	72	E1
Spencer Row	71	C3
Spencer Street North	72	E1
Spencer Street South	75	A3
Spencer Villas	60	E1
Spences Terrace	74	E2
Sperrin Road	73	A4
Spiddal Park	35	C3
Spiddal Road	35	C3
Spire View	70	F1
Spire View	24	D4
*Spire View Court (off Spire View Lane)	47	A1
Spire View Lane	47	A1
Spitalfields	74	F1
Spring Garden Lane	71	C4
Spring Garden Street	72	D1
Springbank Cottages	53	A2
Springdale Court Apts	26	F2
Springdale Road	26	F2
Springfield (Cabra)	69	B1
Springfield (Tallaght)	54	F1
Springfield Ave	46	E4
Springfield Close	31	C4

STREET NAME	PAGE	GRID REF	STREET NAME	PAGE	GRID REF	STREET NAME	PAGE	GRID REF	STREET NAME	PAGE	GRID REF
Springfield Cres	46	E4	*Stillorgan Court			Straffan Way	17	C4	Summerville	39	B1
Springfield Drive	46	E4	(off Upper Kilmacud Road			Straffan Wood	17	C4	Summerville Park	47	A1
Springfield Drive	31	C4	Extension)	58	E1	Straleek	41	B1	*Summerville Terrace		
Springfield Lane	63	A1	Stillorgan Grove	48	F4	Stralem Court	21	B1	(on Dalkey Ave)	60	F2
Springfield Park (Templeogue)	46	E4	Stillorgan Heath	58	F1	Stralem Cres	21	B1	Sunbury Court	47	A2
Springfield Park (Deans Grange)	59	A2	Stillorgan Park	48	F4	Stralem Grove	21	B1	Sunbury Gardens	47	A2
Springfield Road	46	E3	Stillorgan Park	49	A4	Stralem Mews	21	B1	*Sunbury Park		
Springhill Ave	59	A1	Stillorgan Park Ave	58	F1	Stralem Terrace	21	B1	(off Sunbury Gardens)	47	A2
*Springhill Cottages			Stillorgan Road (Donnybrook)	48	D1	*Strand Court			Suncroft Ave	14	F2
(off Brookville Park)	59	B1	Stillorgan Road			(on Strand Street Malahide)	3	B2	Suncroft Drive	54	D2
Springhill Park (Deans Grange)	59	B1	(Mount Merrion)	48	E3	*Strand Lane			Suncroft Park	54	D2
Springhill Park (Dalkey)	60	E2	Stillorgan Road (Stillorgan)	58	F1	(off St. John's Road East)	48	E1	Sundale Ave	54	D2
Springlawn	22	E2	Stillorgan Road (Foxrock)	59	A2	*Strand Mews (Strand Road)	39	B4	Sundale Close	54	D2
Springlawn Close	22	E2	Stillorgan Wood	58	E1	Strand Road (Portmarnock)	4	D4	Sundale Cres	54	D1
Springlawn Court	22	E2	*Stirling Park (off Orwell Road)	47	A3	Strand Road (Portmarnock)	14	F2	Sundale Green	54	D1
Springlawn Drive	22	E2	Stirrup Lane (off Church Street)	70	F3	Strand Road (Portmarnock)	15	A1	Sundale Grove	54	D2
Springlawn Heights	22	E2	Stockhole	13	A2	Strand Road (Baldoyle)	15	A4	Sundale Heights	54	D1
Springlawn Park	22	E2	Stockhole Lane	12	F1	Strand Road (Sutton)	29	B2	Sundale Lawn	54	D1
Springlawn Road	22	E2	Stocking Ave	56	D2	Strand Road (Sandymount)	39	B4	Sundale Meadows	54	D1
Springmount Apts	24	D2	Stocking Hill	56	D2	Strand Road (Merrion)	48	E1	Sundale Parade	54	D1
Springvale	56	E2	Stocking Lane	56	D3	Strand Road (Ballybrack)	64	E1	Sundale Park	54	D2
Springvale Hall	57	C3	Stocking Well Row	56	D2	Strand Road (Bray)	68	D2	Sundale Road	54	D2
Spruce Ave	58	D2	Stocking Well Wood	56	D2	Strand Street (Malahide)	3	B2	Sundale Villas	54	D1
*St Andrews Court	76	D1	Stocking Wood	56	D3	Strand Street (Ringsend)	39	A3	Sundale Walk	54	D1
*St Augustine Apts			Stocking Wood Copse	56	D3	Strand Street Great	71	A4	Sundrive Park	46	E1
(Oliver Bond Street)	70	F4	Stocking Wood Drive	56	D3	Strand Street Little	71	A4	Sundrive Road	73	C4
St Josephs Terrace	71	A2	Stocking Wood Green	56	D3	*Strand Terrace			Sunnybank Apts	69	B4
Stable Lane (Harcourt Street)	75	B2	Stocking Wood Hall	56	D3	(off Milltown Road)	47	B2	*Sunnybank Court		
Stable Lane			Stocking Wood Heath	56	D3	Strandmill Ave	14	F2	(off Dundrum Road)	47	C4
(Leeson Street Lower)	75	C2	Stocking Wood Manor	56	D3	Strandmill Park	15	A2	*Sunnybank Court		
Stable Lane (Smithfield)	70	F4	Stocking Wood Rise	56	D3	Strandmill Road	15	A2	(off Upper Dargle Road)	67	B1
Stackstown	61	B1	Stocking Wood Walk	56	D3	Strandville Ave (North Strand)	72	E1	Sunnyside	62	F3
Stacummy Bridge	32	F4	Stocking Wood Way	56	D3	Strandville Ave East (Clontarf)	26	D4	*Sunnyside Apts		
Staffordstown	5	C2	Stockton Court	23	A3	*Strandville House			(Malahide Road)	26	E2
Staffordstown Little	5	C1	Stockton Drive	23	A3	(off Strandville Ave East)	26	D4	*Sunville Green		
Stamer Street	75	A3	Stockton Green	23	A3	Strandville Place	72	E1	(off Summerville Drive)	46	D1
*Stanford (Harlech Vale)	48	D3	Stockton Grove	23	A3	Strangford Gardens	72	E2	Susan Terrace	74	F2
Stanford Green	45	C1	Stockton Lawn	23	A3	Strangford Road	72	E2	Susanville Road	25	B4
Stanhope Street	70	F3	Stockton Park	23	A3	*Strasburg Terrace			Sussex Road	76	D3
Stanley Street	70	F3	Stokes Place	75	B2	(off Strand Street Ringsend)	39	A3	*Sussex Street (off Eblana Ave)	50	D4
Stannaway Ave	46	D1	*Stone Mews (off Rathgar Road)	47	A1	*Stratford			Sussex Terrace	76	D3
*Stannaway Court			Stonebridge	21	B2	(off Orwell Road Rathgar)	47	A2	Sutton	29	A1
(off Stannaway Ave)	46	D2	Stonebridge Ave	21	B2	Strathmore Road	60	E4	Sutton Castle Apts	29	B3
Stannaway Drive	46	E1	*Stonebridge Close			Stratton Grove	33	C3	Sutton Court (off Sutton Downs)	28	D1
Stannaway Road	46	E1	(beside Post Office)	64	E3	Stratton Walk	33	C3	Sutton Downs	28	D1
Stapolin	14	F4	Stonebridge Court	64	D3	Streamstown Lane	2	F4	Sutton Grove	28	D1
Stapolin Ave	14	F4	Stonebridge Drive	21	B2	Streamstown Wood	2	F4	Sutton Lane	63	A3
Stapolin House	14	F4	Stonebridge Grove	64	D3	*Streamville Court (Abberley)	64	E1	Sutton Lawns	28	D1
Stapolin Lawns	14	F4	*Stonebridge Lane			Streamville Road	27	A1	Sutton Park	28	D1
Station Close	35	A4	(off Stonebridge Road)	64	D2	Strong's Court	71	B2	*Sutton Road		
Station Hill	14	F4	Stonebridge Road (Clonsilla)	21	B2	Suffolk Street	75	B1	(Pearse Square, Bray)	67	B2
Station Road (Dunboyne)	7	B3	Stonebridge Road (Shankill)	64	D2	Sugarloaf Cres	67	C3	*Sutton Villas		
Station Road (Portmarnock)	14	E2	*Stonemasons Green			*Sugarloaf Terrace			(Pearse Square, Bray)	67	B2
Station Road (Leixlip)	19	C4	(Broadford Cres)	57	A2	(Vevay Road, Putland Road)	67	C3	Swallowbrook	8	F4
*Station Road			Stonemasons Way	57	A2	Suir Road	73	B2	Swallowbrook Cres	8	F4
(off Clover Hill Road)	35	A4	Stonepark Abbey	46	F4	Sullivan Street	69	C3	Swallowbrook Park	8	F4
Station Road (Raheny)	27	A2	Stonepark Court	46	F4	Summer Arch	71	C1	Swallowbrook View	8	F4
Station Road (Sutton)	29	A1	*Stonepark Orchard			Summer Place	71	C2	Swan Alley	74	F1
Station Road (Glenageary)	60	E1	(off Stonepark Abbey)	46	F4	*Summer Row			Swan Grove	75	C4
Station Road (Killiney)	60	E4	*Stoneview Place			(off Summer Street North)	71	C1	*Swan Hall		
*Station Road			(off George's Street Upper)	50	D4	Summer Street North	71	C2	(off Belgard Square West)	54	F1
(east of Library Road)	64	E2	*Stoney Court			Summer Street South	74	E1	Swan Place	76	D4
*Station View Apts			(near James Street North)	72	E1	Summerfield (Blanchardstown)	22	E2	Swan Yard (off Harry Street)	75	B1
(adjacent Oldfarm off			Stoney Park	52	F2	*Summerfield			Swanbrook	67	C4
Carpenterstown Road)	22	E3	Stoney Road (East Wall)	72	E2	(off Irishtown Road)	39	A3	Swan's Nest Ave	27	B1
Station Way	14	E4	Stoney Road (Dundrum)	47	C4	*Summerfield (off			Swan's Nest Court		
Stationcourt	22	D3	Stoneybatter	70	E3	Watermeadow Park Tallaght)	55	A2	(Swan's Nest Ave)	27	B1
Stationcourt Hall	22	D3	*Stoneylea Terrace (Vevay			Summerfield Ave	22	E2	Swan's Nest Road	27	B1
Stationcourt Park	22	D3	Road, Wolfe Tone Square)	67	C3	Summerfield Close	22	E2	*Swanville Place		
Stationcourt View	22	D3	Store Street	71	C1	*Summerfield Close			(off Rathmines Road Lower)	47	A1
Stationcourt Way	22	D3	Stormanstown Road	25	A2	(off Dalkey Ave)	60	F2	Swanward Court	74	E4
Steamstown Wood	2	F4	Stradbrook Close	59	B1	Summerfield Green	22	E2	Sweeney's Terrace	74	F2
Steelstown	51	C3	*Stradbrook Cottages			Summerfield Lawns	22	E2	Sweetbriar Lane	58	D1
Steelstown Interchange (N7)	51	B3	(on Stradbrook Road)	49	B4	Summerfield Meadows	22	E2	Sweetman House	14	F4
*Steeple Gate			*Stradbrook Gardens			Summerfield Rise	22	E2	*Sweetman's Ave		
(off Sandymount Road)	39	A3	(off Stradbrook Road)	49	B4	Summerhill	71	C2	(off Frascati Road Blackrock)	49	A3
Steeven's Gate Apts	74	D1	Stradbrook Grove	49	B4	*Summerhill Court			Sweetman's Ave	49	A3
Steeven's Lane	70	D4	*Stradbrook Hall			(Summerhill)	71	C2	Sweetmount Ave	47	B4
Stella Ave	25	A3	(off Stradbrook Road)	49	B4	*Summerhill Court			Sweetmount Drive	57	B1
Stella Gardens	39	A3	*Stradbrook Hill			(off Islington Ave)	50	E4	*Sweetmount House		
Stella Maris Apts	17	C4	(off Abbey Road Monkstown)	59	B1	Summerhill Parade			(off Beaumont Ave)	47	B4
Stepaside	58	E4	Stradbrook Lawn	49	B4	(Summerhill)	72	D1	Sweetmount Park	47	B4
Stepaside	62	E1	Stradbrook Park	49	B4	*Summerhill Parade			Sweetmount Park	57	B1
Stepaside Lane	62	E1	Stradbrook Road	49	B4	(off Summerhill Road)	50	D4	Swift Hall	59	B4
Stepaside Park	58	E4	Straffan Ave	17	C4	Summerhill Place	71	C2	Swiftbrook (Tallaght)	54	D1
Stepaside Park	62	E1	Straffan Close	17	C4	Summerhill Road (Dunboyne)	7	A2	Swiftbrook Ave	54	D1
Stepaside Village	58	E4	Straffan Court	17	C4	Summerhill Road			Swiftbrook Close	54	D1
Stephen Street Lower	75	B1	Straffan Cres	17	C4	(Dún Laoghaire)	50	D4	Swiftbrook Drive	54	D1
Stephen Street Upper	75	B1	Straffan Drive	17	C4	Summerseat	8	D4	Swiftbrook Park	54	D1
Stephen's Lane	76	D2	Straffan Green	17	C4	Summerseat Cottage	8	D4	Swift's Alley	74	F1
Stephen's Place	76	D2	Straffan Grove	17	C4	Summerseat Court	8	D4	Swift's Grove	13	A3
Stephen's Road	73	B2	Straffan Lawn	17	C4	Summerseat Cres	8	D4	Swift's Row (off Ormond Quay)	71	B4
Sterling Square Apts	8	D3	Straffan Park	17	C4	Summerseat Drive	8	D4	Swiftwood	53	B1
Stewart Hall	71	A3	Straffan Place	17	C4	Summerseat Estate	8	D4	Swilly Road	24	E4
Stillorgan	58	F1	Straffan Road	17	C4	Summerseat Walk	8	D4	Swords	2	E2

STREET NAME	PAGE	GRID REF
Swords Manor Ave	1	B2
Swords Manor Court	1	B1
Swords Manor Cres	1	B1
Swords Manor Drive	1	B1
Swords Manor Grove	1	B2
Swords Manor View	1	B1
Swords Manor Way	1	B1
Swords Road (Santry)	12	F4
Swords Road (Malahide)	3	A3
Swords Road (Collinstown)	12	F2
Swords Road (Santry)	25	B1
Swords Street	70	D3
Sybil Hill Ave	26	F3
Sybil Hill Road	26	F3
Sycamore Ave (Castleknock)	22	E3
Sycamore Ave (Tallaght)	45	A3
Sycamore Ave (Cabinteely)	59	B3
Sycamore Close (Kilnamanagh)	44	F3
Sycamore Close (Cornelscourt)	59	B3
*Sycamore Court (off Carriglea Ave Kill O'The Grange)	59	C2
Sycamore Cres (Mount Merrion)	48	E4
Sycamore Cres (Cabinteely)	59	B3
Sycamore Drive (Castleknock)	22	E3
Sycamore Drive (Tallaght)	45	A3
*Sycamore Drive (off Sycamore Road Dundrum)	57	B1
Sycamore Drive (Cabinteely)	59	B3
Sycamore Green (Cabinteely)	59	B3
*Sycamore Grove (off Pine Ave Foxrock)	59	A2
Sycamore Grove (Cabinteely)	59	B4
Sycamore House	76	D3
Sycamore House (Swords)	1	Inset
Sycamore House (Sutton)	28	D1
*Sycamore House (at Eaton Wood Square)	64	E2
Sycamore Lawn (Castleknock)	22	E3
Sycamore Lawn (Cabinteely)	59	B3
Sycamore Park (Castleknock)	22	E3
Sycamore Park (Finglas)	24	E1
Sycamore Park (Tallaght)	45	A3
Sycamore Road (Finglas)	24	E1
Sycamore Road (Fox and Geese)	45	A1
Sycamore Road (Mount Merrion)	48	E4
Sycamore Road (Dundrum)	57	B1
Sycamore Street	71	B4
Sycamore View	22	E3
Sycamore Walk	59	B4
*Sydenham (off Corrig Ave)	50	D4
*Sydenham Court (off Sandymount Ave)	39	A4
Sydenham Mews	68	D3
*Sydenham Place (on Kilmacud Rd Upr)	47	C4
*Sydenham Road (off Merrion Road)	39	A4
Sydenham Road (Dundrum)	47	C4
Sydenham Villas (Dundrum)	57	C1
*Sydenham Villas (near Sydenham Mews)	68	D3
Sydney Ave	49	A3
Sydney Parade Ave	48	E1
Sydney Terrace	49	A3
Sylvan Ave	45	A3
Sylvan Close	44	F3
Sylvan Drive	44	F3
Symphony House	75	C3
Synge House	47	A3
Synge Lane	75	A3
Synge Place	75	B3
Synge Street	75	B3
Synge Way	35	C4
Synnott Lane	71	B1
Synnott Place	71	B1
Synnott Row	71	B1
*Synnott Terrace (off Dunleary Road)	49	C4
Synod Hall	75	A1

T

Taaffe's Place	72	E1
Tailors Court	75	A1
Tailor's Hall	75	A1
Talbot	2	F3
Talbot Ave	2	F3
Talbot Court (Malahide)	3	A2
Talbot Court (Blanchardstown)	22	F2

STREET NAME	PAGE	GRID REF
Talbot Downs	22	F2
Talbot Hall (Swords)	1	Inset
*Talbot House (Granby Lane)	71	A2
*Talbot Lane (Talbot Street)	71	C3
*Talbot Lane (off Ballinclea Road)	60	E3
Talbot Lodge	48	F4
Talbot Memorial Bridge (River Liffey)	71	C4
Talbot Park	2	F3
Talbot Place	71	C3
Talbot Road (Swords)	2	F3
*Talbot Road (off Killiney Hill Road)	60	E3
Talbot Street	71	C3
Tallaght	55	A1
Tallaght Bypass	54	F1
Tallaght Bypass	55	A1
Tallaght Road	55	B1
*Tallow Hall (off Belgard Square West)	54	F1
Tamarisk Ave	45	A3
Tamarisk Close	45	A3
Tamarisk Court	45	A3
Tamarisk Dale	45	A3
Tamarisk Drive	45	A3
Tamarisk Grove	45	A3
Tamarisk Heights	45	A3
Tamarisk Lawn	45	A3
Tamarisk Park	45	A3
Tamarisk View	45	A3
Tamarisk Walk	45	A3
Tamarisk Way	45	A3
*Tandy Court Apts (off Spitalfields)	74	F1
Tandys Lane	33	C3
Tandys Lane	34	D3
Taney Ave	47	C4
Taney Court	47	C4
Taney Cres	47	C4
Taney Drive	47	C4
Taney Grove	47	C4
*Taney Hall (off Eglinton Terrace)	47	C4
Taney Lawn	47	C4
Taney Manor	47	C4
Taney Park	47	C4
Taney Rise	47	C4
Taney Road	47	C4
Tangier Lane (off Grafton Street)	75	B1
*Tara Cres (off Kilakee Green)	55	B2
Tara Hill Cres	46	F4
*Tara Hill Grove (off St. Patrick's Cottages)	46	F4
Tara Hill Road	46	F4
Tara Lawn	27	A1
Tara Street	71	C4
Tassagard Greens	53	B2
Tassagart Drive	53	A2
*Tathony House Apts (off Mount Brown)	74	D1
Tay Lane	52	E2
Taylors Court	56	E1
Taylor's Hill	57	A3
Taylor's Lane (Pimlico)	74	E1
Taylor's Lane (Ballyboden)	56	E1
Teeling Way	72	F2
Temple Bar	71	B4
Temple Buildings	71	A2
Temple Cottages	71	A2
Temple Court (off Hogan Place)	76	E1
Temple Court (Arbour Hill)	70	D3
*Temple Court (off Temple Road)	49	A3
Temple Court Apts	12	E4
Temple Cres	49	B4
Temple Gardens (Santry)	12	E4
Temple Gardens (Milltown)	47	B2
Temple Grove	32	D3
*Temple Hall Apts. (off Milltown Road)	47	B2
*Temple Hill (on Terenure Road West)	46	E2
Temple Hill	49	B4
Temple Lane North	71	B2
Temple Lane South	71	B4
*Temple Lawns (at Temple Gardens Santry)	12	E4
Temple Lawns (Celbridge)	32	D4
Temple Manor (Dunboyne)	7	B2
Temple Manor (Celbridge)	31	C4
Temple Manor (Greenhills)	45	C3
Temple Manor Ave	45	C3
Temple Manor Close	45	C3

STREET NAME	PAGE	GRID REF
Temple Manor Court	45	C3
Temple Manor Drive	45	C3
Temple Manor Grove	45	C3
Temple Manor Way	45	C3
Temple Park	47	B2
*Temple Park Apts	12	E4
Temple Park Ave	49	B4
Temple Place	75	C4
Temple Place	71	B2
Temple Road (Rathgar)	47	B2
Temple Road (Blackrock)	49	A3
*Temple Square (off Orchard Road South)	47	B2
Temple Street North	71	B2
Temple Street West	70	D4
*Temple Terrace (off Coliemore Road)	60	F2
*Temple Villas (Arbour Hill)	70	D3
*Temple Villas (on Palmerston Road)	47	B1
*Temple Villas (off Cowper Road)	47	B2
Templemore Ave	47	A2
Templeogue	46	D4
Templeogue Lodge	46	D4
Templeogue Road	46	E3
Templeogue Wood	46	D4
Templeroan	56	D1
Templeroan Ave	56	D1
Templeroan Close	56	E1
Templeroan Court	56	D1
Templeroan Cres	56	D1
Templeroan Downs	56	E1
Templeroan Drive	56	D1
Templeroan Green	56	D2
Templeroan Grove	56	D1
Templeroan Lodge	56	D2
Templeroan Meadows	56	E1
Templeroan Mews	56	D1
Templeroan Park	56	D1
Templeroan View	56	D1
Templeroan Way	56	D1
Templeview Ave	14	D4
Templeview Close	14	D4
Templeview Copse	14	D4
Templeview Court	14	D4
Templeview Cres	14	D4
Templeview Downs	14	D4
Templeview Drive	14	D4
Templeview Green	14	D4
Templeview Grove	14	D4
Templeview Lawn	14	D4
Templeview Park	14	D4
Templeview Place	14	D4
Templeview Rise	14	D4
Templeview Row	14	D4
Templeview Square	14	D4
Templeview Vale	14	D4
Templeview View	14	D4
Templeview Walk	14	D4
Templeview Way	14	D4
Templeville Ave	46	D3
Templeville Drive	46	D3
*Templeville Park (off Templeville Road)	46	E3
Templeville Road	46	D3
Tenterfields	74	E2
Terenure	46	F2
Terenure Park	46	F2
*Terenure Place (off Hannaville Park)	46	F2
Terenure Road East	46	F2
Terenure Road North	46	F2
Terenure Road West	46	E2
Terminal Road North	39	C2
Terminal Road South	39	C2
Termon	60	F2
*Termon Court (off Gallaun Road)	11	C4
Terrace Place (off Bella Street)	71	C2
Tetrarch Grove	7	C1
Texas Lane	3	A2
*The Alders (off Monkstown Valley)	49	B4
*The Alders (off Northwood Ave)	12	E4
*The Alders (Carrington)	12	E4
*The Anchora Apts (adjacent Townyard Lane)	3	B2
*The Anchorage (off Clarence Street Dún Laoghaire)	49	C4
The Anchorage (Robswall)	4	D3
*The Anchorage Apts	76	F1
The Appian Way	76	D4
The Arches	17	C3

STREET NAME	PAGE	GRID REF
*The Atrium Apts (Island Street)	70	E4
The Ave (Plunkett Hall)	7	A2
The Ave (Lutterell Hall)	7	B2
The Ave (Dunboyne Castle)	7	B3
The Ave (Mulhuddart Wood)	9	A4
The Ave (Louisa Valley)	19	C4
The Ave (Manorfields)	21	B1
The Ave (Celbridge)	32	D3
The Ave (St. Wolston's Abbey)	32	D4
The Ave (Grange Manor)	34	D3
The Ave (Tallaght)	44	F3
The Ave (Templeogue)	46	D3
The Ave (Ballyboden)	56	E2
The Ave (Ballinteer)	57	C2
The Ave (Carrickmines)	63	A1
The Ave (Ongar)	21	A1
*The Barley Store Apts (off Portland Street North)	71	C1
The Bawn	3	B3
The Bawn Grove	3	B3
The Bay Apts (Merrion Road)	48	E2
*The Beaches (off Northwood Ave)	12	E4
*The Beaches (at The Gallops)	58	E4
The Beaches (Donaghmede)	27	A1
*The Beeches (off Monkstown Valley)	49	B4
*The Beeches (off Barton Drive Willbrook)	56	F1
The Beeches (Kilmacud)	58	D1
*The Beeches (Abberley)	64	E1
*The Beeches (Carrington)	12	E4
The Belfry (Inchicore)	73	A1
The Belfry (Kilbarrack)	27	B1
The Belfry (Citywest Road)	53	C2
*The Belfry Apts (off Collins Ave West)	25	C2
*The Birch (off Overend Way Dundrum)	57	C1
The Birches	59	A3
*The Birches Apts (adjacent Courtview Apts)	23	C3
The Black Ave	33	B1
*The Blackthorn (off Overend Way Dundrum)	57	C1
The Boulevard	9	A2
The Bramblings	26	E3
The Briars	35	C1
The Bridge	64	E3
The Brokerage Apts	71	C4
The Burgage	60	F2
*The Castlelands (off The Courtyard)	46	F4
*The Cedars (off Monkstown Valley)	49	B4
*The Cedars (Abberley)	64	E1
*The Cedars (off Northwood Ave)	12	E4
*The Cedars (Carrington)	12	E4
*The Cedars Apts	76	F4
The Chandler Apts	23	B3
*The Charter (adjacent Santry Cross Junction)	12	D4
The Chase	58	F2
*The Cherries (off Grange Wood)	57	A2
*The Claremont (adjacent Santry Cross Junction)	12	D4
*The Cloisters (off Grace Park Road)	25	B3
The Cloisters (Mount Tallant Ave)	46	F2
The Close (Plunkett Hall)	7	A2
The Close (Dunboyne Castle)	7	A3
The Close (Lutterell Hall)	7	B2
The Close (Manorfields)	21	B1
The Close (Beaumont)	25	C1
The Close (Oldtown Mill)	31	C3
The Close (Celbridge)	31	C3
The Close (Temple Manor)	31	C4
The Close (Grange Manor)	34	D3
The Close (Tallaght)	44	F3
The Close (Templeogue)	46	D3
The Close (Mount Merrion)	48	E3
*The Close (off The Wood Tallaght)	55	A2
The Close (Ballyboden)	56	E2
The Close (Ballinteer)	57	C2
*The Close (Robswall)	3	C3
The Close (Moyglare Hall)	17	C1
The Clovers	23	A3
The Coachworks	75	A3
The Coombe	74	F1
The Coppice (Palmerstown)	35	C3

STREET NAME	PAGE	GRID REF
The Coppins (Celbridge)	32	D3
The Coppins (Foxrock)	59	A3
The Copse (Drumcondra)	25	B3
The Copse (Weston)	33	B2
*The Copse (off The Heights Ballinteer)	57	B2
The Court (Lutterell Hall)	7	B2
The Court (Plunkett Hall)	7	A2
The Court (Sadleir Hall)	7	A2
The Court (Dunboyne Castle)	7	B3
The Court (Mulhuddart Wood)	9	A4
The Court (Larch Hill)	12	F4
The Court (Whitehall)	25	C2
The Court (Clontarf)	26	D4
The Court (off The Village Raheny)	27	B3
The Court (Celbridge)	31	C3
The Court (Oldtown Mill)	31	C3
The Court (Temple Manor)	31	C4
The Court (Tallaght)	44	F3
The Court (Tallaght)	44	F4
The Court (Templeogue)	46	D3
The Court (Donnybrook)	47	C2
The Court (Ballinteer)	57	B2
The Court (Carrickmines)	59	B4
The Court (Ballybrack)	60	E4
The Court (Glenamuck Road)	63	A1
The Court (Shankill)	64	E3
*The Court (Glasnevin)	25	A4
*The Court (Robswall)	4	D3
The Court (Moyglare Hall)	17	C2
The Court (Blanchardstown)	22	F2
*The Court Apts (adjacent Emmet Place)	70	F4
The Courthouse	52	F2
The Courtyard (Grants Row)	76	D1
The Courtyard (Hill Street)	71	B2
The Courtyard (in Parkview Estate)	1	A2
The Courtyard (Clonsilla)	22	D3
The Courtyard (Celbridge)	31	C4
The Courtyard (Templeogue)	46	E3
The Courtyard (Rathfarnham)	46	F4
The Courtyard (Leopardstown)	58	E2
The Courtyard (Bray)	67	B2
*The Courtyard (Robswall)	3	C3
*The Coutryard (off Foxrock Park)	59	A2
The Cove	3	A2
*The Covert (off The Coppice)	35	C1
*The Cres (on Foster Way)	2	D2
The Cres (Malahide)	4	D3
The Cres (Plunkett Hall)	7	A2
The Cres (Lutterell Hall)	7	A2
The Cres (Dunboyne Castle)	7	B3
The Cres (Mulhuddart)	9	A4
The Cres (Larch Hill)	12	F4
The Cres (College Grove)	22	F3
The Cres (Whitehall)	25	B3
*The Cres (off Beaumont Road)	25	C2
The Cres (Oldtown Mill)	31	C3
The Cres (Abbeyfarm)	31	C4
The Cres (Temple Manor)	31	C4
The Cres (St. Wolston's Abbey)	32	D4
The Cres (Lucan)	33	C2
The Cres (Grange Manor)	34	D3
The Cres (Tallaght)	44	E4
The Cres (Tallaght)	44	F3
The Cres (Ranelagh)	47	B1
*The Cres (off Donnybrook Road)	47	C1
The Cres (Tallaght)	55	A1
The Cres (Ballyboden)	56	E2
*The Cres (off The Walk Ballinteer)	57	B2
The Cres (Carrickmines)	63	A1
*The Cres (Robswall)	4	D3
The Cres (Moyglare Hall)	17	C1
The Cres (Ongar)	21	A1
The Cres (Park West)	35	C4
The Cres (Kimmage)	46	E3
The Croft	32	D2
The Dale (Dunboyne)	7	B2
The Dale (Manorfields)	21	B1
The Dale (Celbridge)	31	C3
The Dale (Kilnamanagh)	44	F3
The Dale (Belgard)	44	F4
*The Dale (off The Heights Ballinteer)	57	B2
The Dale (Carrickmines)	63	A1
The Dale (Bray)	67	B2
*The Dale (Moyglare Hall)	17	C2
*The Deanery (beside Vanessa Lawns)	31	C3
The Dell	57	A2
The Dingle	35	B2
*The Distillery Apts (Distillery Road)	25	B4
*The Distillery Building Apts (off Distillery Road)	25	B4
The Downs (Dunboyne Castle)	7	A3
The Downs (St. Wolston's Abbey)	32	D4
The Drive (Sadleir Hall)	7	A2
The Drive (Lutterell Hall)	7	B2
The Drive (Dunboyne Castle)	7	B3
The Drive (Mulhuddart Wood)	9	A4
The Drive (Manorfields)	21	B1
The Drive (Oldtown Mill)	31	C3
The Drive (Abbeyfarm)	31	C4
The Drive (Temple Manor)	31	C4
The Drive (Grange Manor)	34	D3
The Drive (Kilnamanagh)	44	F3
The Drive (Tallaght)	55	A1
The Drive (Ballyboden)	56	E1
The Drive (Ballinteer)	57	B2
The Drive (Woodbrook Glen)	67	C1
*The Drive Apts	56	E1
The Dunes	15	A1
The Elm (Rockfield)	57	C1
The Elms (Dunboyne)	7	B2
The Elms (Celbridge)	32	D2
The Elms (Elm Park)	48	E2
*The Elms (opposite Sheelin Drive)	64	E1
The Elms (Crinken Lane)	64	E3
*The Elms (off Northwood Ave)	12	E4
*The Elms (Carrington)	12	E4
*The Elms Apts (adjacent Courtview Apts)	23	C3
The Fairways (Portmarnock)	14	E2
The Fairways (Woodbrook Glen)	67	C1
*The Fairways Apts	8	D3
*The Falls (off Dodder Road Lower Rathfarnham)	46	F3
The Forum	58	E2
The Fosters	48	E3
*The Foundary Apts (Beaver Street)	72	D2
The Gables (Old Cabra Road)	70	D1
The Gables (Grange View Road)	43	B1
The Gables (Rathgar)	47	A2
The Gables (Nutgrove)	57	A1
The Gables (Dundrum)	57	B1
*The Gables (off Torquay Road Foxrock)	59	A3
The Gallan	60	D3
The Gallops	58	E3
The Gardens	63	A1
The Garth (Cookstown)	44	E4
The Garth (Kingswood Heights)	44	F3
The Gasworks	76	F1
The Gate	44	D1
The Gate Lodge	30	E3
The Glade (Palmerstown)	35	B2
The Glade (Oldtown Mill)	31	C3
The Glade (St. Wolston's Abbey)	32	D4
The Glade (Kingswood Heights)	44	F3
The Glade (Ballinteer)	57	B2
The Glebe	34	E2
The Glen (Louisa Valley)	19	C4
The Glen (Raheny)	27	B3
The Glen (Ballyboden)	56	E1
The Glen (Ballinteer)	57	B2
The Glen (Clon Burgh)	58	D3
*The Glen (off Glenageary Road Lower)	60	D1
The Glen (Oldtown Mill)	31	C2
The Glens	63	A1
*The Goulding (adjacent Santry Cross Junction)	12	D4
The Grainhouse	74	E2
*The Granary (Long's Place)	74	E1
The Grange (Malahide)	3	B4
The Grange (Terenure)	46	F2
The Grange (Deans Grange)	59	B1
*The Grange Apts (off Brewery Road)	58	F1
The Green (Malahide)	3	B2
The Green (Lutterell Hall)	7	B2
The Green (Dunboyne Castle)	7	B3
The Green (Mulhuddart Wood)	9	A4
The Green (Larch Hill)	12	F4
The Green (Moyglare Abbey)	17	B2
The Green (Manorfields)	21	B1
The Green (Beaumont)	25	C1
The Green (Celbridge)	31	C3
The Green (Oldtown Mill)	31	C3
The Green (Tallaght)	44	F3
The Green (Templeogue)	46	D3
The Green (Ballyboden)	56	E1
The Green (Ballinteer)	57	B2
The Green (Carrickmines)	63	A1
The Green (Woodbrook Glen)	67	C1
*The Green (Robswall)	3	C3
The Green (Moyglare Hall)	17	C2
The Green Road	60	G2
The Greenlands	46	F4
The Grove (Plunkett Hall)	7	A2
The Grove (Sadleir Hall)	7	A2
The Grove (Dunboyne Castle)	7	A3
The Grove (Lutterell Hall)	7	B2
The Grove (Louisa Valley)	19	C4
The Grove (Whitehall)	25	B3
The Grove (off The Village Raheny)	27	B3
The Grove (Abbeyfarm)	31	C4
The Grove (St. Wolston's Abbey)	32	D4
The Grove (Grange Manor)	34	D3
The Grove (Tallaght)	44	E4
The Grove (Tallaght)	44	F3
The Grove (Tallaght)	55	A1
The Grove (Dundrum)	57	A1
The Grove (Ballinteer)	57	B2
The Grove (Woodbrook Glen)	67	C1
*The Haggard (streets between Tuckett's Lane and Main Street)	30	D2
The Hall	46	F2
*The Hampton (adjacent Santry Cross Junction)	12	D4
*The Hardwick Apts (near Catherine Lane)	70	F3
*The Hardwicke Apts (Church Street Upper)	70	F3
The Haven (Malahide)	3	B2
*The Haven (off St. Mobhi Boithirin)	25	A3
*The Hawthorns (Abberley)	64	E1
*The Hawthorns (off Northwood Ave)	12	E4
*The Hawthorns (Carrington)	12	E4
The Heath (Tallaght)	44	F4
The Heath (Templeogue)	46	D3
The Heath (Ballinteer)	57	B2
The Hedgerows	59	A3
The Heights (Dunboyne Castle)	7	B3
The Heights (Ballinteer)	57	B2
*The Heights (Robswall)	3	C3
*The Hibernian Apts	76	F1
The Hill (Malahide)	3	B3
The Hill (Mulhuddart Wood)	9	A4
The Hill (Monkstown)	49	C4
The Hill (Ballinteer)	57	C2
The Hill (Clon Burgh)	58	D3
The Hill (Stillorgan)	58	F1
The Hole in the Wall Road	14	E4
*The Hollows (adjacent Adamstown Court)	34	D2
The Holly (Rockfield)	57	C1
*The Hops (off Basin Street Lower)	74	D2
*The Innings Apts (off Rathmines Road Lower)	47	A1
The Island	36	E2
*The Ivory Buildings Apts (Hanover Street East)	72	E4
The Killigeen	52	D4
*The Kilmore (adjacent Santry Cross Junction)	12	D4
The Kilns	14	F2
*The Lakelands (off Rathfarnham Wood)	46	F4
*The Landey (adjacent Santry Cross Junction)	12	D4
*The Larches (Abberley)	64	E1
The Laurels (Dollymount)	26	F4
*The Laurels (off Bluebell Ave)	36	E4
The Laurels (Terenure)	46	F2
*The Laurels (off Main Street Rathfarnham)	46	F4
*The Laurels (off Main Street Tallaght)	55	A1
The Laurels (Churchtown)	47	B4
The Laurels (Hazelhatch)	41	B1
The Lawn (Plunkett Hall)	7	A2
The Lawn (Moyglare Abbey)	17	B2
The Lawn (Finglas)	24	E2
The Lawn (Oldtown Mill)	31	C3
The Lawn (Tallaght)	44	E4
The Lawn (Ballyboden)	56	E2
The Lawn (Ballinteer)	57	B2
The Lawn (Woodbrook Glen)	67	C1
The Lawns (Abbeyfarm)	31	C4
The Lawns (Temple Manor)	31	C4
*The Lighthouse (Robswall)	4	D3
The Lime (Rockfield)	57	C1
*The Linden (off Overend Way Dundrum)	57	C1
The Links	14	F2
The Links Apts (Merrion Road)	48	E2
The Little Grove	32	D4
The Lodge (Clontarf)	26	D4
The Lodge (Glenageary)	60	D1
*The Lodge Apts (adjacent Courtview Apts)	23	C3
*The Maieston (adjacent Santry Cross Junction)	12	D4
The Mall (Malahide)	3	B2
The Mall (Baldoyle)	15	A4
The Mall (Leixlip)	33	A1
The Mall (Lucan)	34	D1
*The Mall (off Main Street Ongar)	21	A1
The Malt House	74	E2
The Maltings	67	C2
The Maltings Apts	70	E4
*The Manor (off Kimmage Road West)	46	D2
The Manor (Templelogue)	46	D4
The Maples (Bird Ave)	47	C3
*The Maples (off Monkstown Valley)	49	B4
The Mayne	8	E2
The Meadow	57	B2
The Meadows (Dunboyne)	7	B2
The Meadows (Killester)	26	F3
The Meadows (Oldtown Mill)	31	C3
The Meadows (Newtownpark Ave)	59	A1
The Meadows East	44	F4
The Meadows West	44	E4
The Mews (Hill Street)	71	B2
The Mews (Killester)	26	E3
The Mews (Clontarf)	26	E4
*The Mews (off Clontarf Road)	27	A4
The Mews (Templeogue)	46	E3
*The Mews (off Castleknock Ave)	47	A1
*The Mews (Robswall)	4	D3
The Mews (Ribh Road)	26	F2
*The Mews Apts (adjacent Courtview Apts)	23	C3
The Mill	74	E2
*The Mill Pond Apts (off Nangor Road)	44	D1
The Mills	22	F2
The Moorings (Portobello Harbour)	75	B4
The Moorings (Malahide)	3	C3
The Moorings (Chapelizod)	36	E2
*The Moorings (off Fitzwilliam Quay)	39	A3
The Moorings (Clontarf)	26	F4
The Moorings Apts (off Merrion Road)	76	E3
The New Road	23	B1
The Northumberlands	76	E2
The Nurseries (Swords)	1	C3
The Nurseries (Mulhuddart)	9	B4
*The Nurseries (off Wyattville Road Ballybrack)	60	E4
The Nurseries (Oldcourt)	67	B3
The Oaks (Swords)	1	B3
The Oaks (Hollystown)	9	C1
The Oaks (Dollymount)	27	A4
The Oaks (Celbridge)	32	D3
The Oaks (Belgard)	44	E4
The Oaks (Churchtown)	47	B4
The Oaks (Ballinteer)	57	B2
*The Oaks (off Loughlinstown Drive)	64	D1
*The Oaks (Abberley)	64	E1
The Oaks (Rockfield)	57	C1
*The Oaks (off Northwood Ave)	12	E4
*The Oaks (at The Gallops)	58	E4
*The Oaks (Carrington)	12	E4
*The Oaks Apts	76	F4
*The Oar House Apts (off Portland Street North)	71	C1
*The Observatory (Windmill Lane)	72	D4
*The Old Convent Apts (off Basin Street Lower)	74	D1
*The Old Distillery Apts (off Allingham Street)	74	E2
The Old Forge	34	D3
The Old Golf Links	3	C3
*The Old Presbytery (off Cambridge Park)	39	A3

STREET NAME	PAGE	GRID REF
*The Old Schoolhouse (off Milltown Ave)	47	B2
*The OldeDock Apts (Ship Street Little)	75	A1
The Orchard (Clarehall)	14	D4
The Orchard (Carpenterstown)	22	D3
The Orchard (Killester)	26	E3
The Orchard (Palmerston)	35	B1
The Orchard (Oldtown Mill)	31	C3
*The Orchard (near Primrose Lane)	34	D1
The Orchard (Kimmage)	46	E2
*The Orchard (off Seapoint Ave)	49	B3
The Orchard (Deans Grange)	59	A1
The Orchard (Fassaroe)	67	A2
The Orchard (Lucan)	34	D1
*The Orchard (off Hollybank Ave Upper)	47	B1
The Orchard Apts	35	B3
*The Orchards (Seafield Road)	60	E4
The Oval	35	C2
The Paddock (Moyglare Abbey)	17	B2
The Paddock (Ashtown)	23	C4
The Paddock (Oldtown Mill)	31	C2
The Paddocks (Kilmainham)	73	B2
The Paddocks (Swords)	2	D2
The Paddocks (Dunboyne)	7	B2
*The Paddocks (off Ulverton Road Dalkey)	60	F1
*The Paddocks (Ongar Village)	21	A1
*The Paddock's (off Seaview Ave North Clontarf)	26	E4
The Paddocks Cres	33	C2
The Paddocks Drive	33	C2
The Paddocks Place	33	C2
The Paddocks Rise	33	C2
The Paddocks Road	33	C2
The Paddocks Square	33	C3
The Paddocks View	33	C2
The Paddocks Walk	33	C2
The Paddocks Way	33	C2
The Palms	48	D3
The Park (Plunkett Hall)	7	A2
The Park (Dunboyne Castle)	7	B3
The Park (Larch Hill)	12	F4
The Park (Louisa Valley)	19	C4
The Park (Beaumont)	25	C1
The Park (Celbridge)	31	C3
The Park (Oldtown Mill)	31	C3
The Park (Abbeyfarm)	31	C4
The Park (Grange Manor)	34	D3
The Park (Tallaght)	44	F3
The Park (Templeogue)	46	D3
The Park (Tallaght)	55	A2
The Park (Clon Burgh)	58	D3
The Park (Lutterell Hall)	7	A2
The Park Apts	75	B4
*The Park Lands (off Castleside Drive)	46	F4
*The Pidgeon House Apts	76	F1
The Pines (Castleknock)	23	A3
The Pines (Killester)	26	E3
The Pines (Ballinteer)	57	B2
*The Pines (off Woodley Park Kilmacud)	58	D1
The Pines (Oldcourt)	67	B3
*The Pines Apts	76	F4
The Place (Dunboyne Castle)	7	B3
The Place (Carrickmines)	63	A1
The Place	42	D4
The Plantation	76	D2
*The Plaza (Forster Way Swords)	2	D2
The Plaza Apts	9	B2
*The Poplars (off Monkstown Valley)	49	B4
*The Priory (off St. Margarets Ave Malahide)	03	B2
The Priory (Cabra)	24	D4
The Priory (Grange Road)	56	F1
The Quarry	4	D4
The Ramparts	63	C1
The Rectory (Raheny)	27	A2
The Rectory (Stepaside)	58	D4
*The Red Mill Apts (Brunswick Street North)	70	F3
*The Richmond Apts (Brunswick Street North)	70	F3
The Rise (Malahide)	3	B3
The Rise (Manorfields)	21	B1
The Rise (Glasnevin)	25	A2
The Rise (Newcastle)	42	D4
The Rise (Tallaght)	44	E4
The Rise (Tallaght)	44	F3
The Rise (Mount Merrion)	48	E4

STREET NAME	PAGE	GRID REF
The Rise (Ballyboden)	56	E2
The Rise (Ballinteer)	57	B2
The Rise (Dalkey)	60	E2
The Rise (Carrickmines)	63	A1
The Road (Manorfields)	21	B1
The Rookery	56	D2
The Rose	9	B2
The Rowan (Rockfield)	57	C1
*The Rowans (Abberley)	64	E1
The Sand Holes	22	F4
The Scalp	63	A4
The Slopes	49	C4
The Spinnaker (Robswall)	4	D3
The Spruce	9	B2
The Square (Larch Hill)	12	F4
*The Square (off Main Street Lucan)	34	D1
*The Square (off Irishtown Road)	39	A3
The Square (Greenogue Industrial Estate)	42	E4
The Square (Tallaght)	54	F1
*The Stables (off Hampton Cres)	48	E3
*The Stables Apts (adjacent Courtview Apts)	23	C3
The Steeple (Moyglare Abbey)	17	B2
The Steeples	36	E3
*The Steps Apts (on Kilmainham Lane)	73	B1
The Stiles Road	26	E4
The Summit (Howth)	30	E3
*The Sweepstakes (off Merrion Road)	39	A4
The Sycamore (Rockfield)	57	C1
*The Sycamore (at The Gallops)	58	E4
*The Sycamores (opposite Sheelin Drive)	64	E1
*The Sycamores (off Northwood Ave)	12	E4
The Sycamores (Malahide)	3	C3
*The Sycamores (Carrington)	12	E4
*The Tallow Apts (north of Ashtown Station)	23	C3
*The Tap Apts (King Street North)	70	F3
The Terrace	63	A1
The Thatch Road	25	C2
The Thicket	59	A3
*The Tower (Smithfield)	70	F4
*The Tramyard Apts (off Thomas Davis Street West)	36	F3
*The Turnpike (adjacent Santry Cross Junction)	12	D4
The Vale	35	C1
The View (Dunboyne Castle)	7	A3
The View (Larch Hill)	12	F4
The View (Manorfields)	21	B1
The View (Celbridge)	31	C3
The View (Oldtown Mill)	31	C3
The View (St. Wolston's Abbey)	32	D4
The View (Tallaght)	44	F3
The View (Tallaght)	55	B1
The View (Ballinteer)	57	B2
The View (Carrickmines)	63	A1
*The View (Robswall)	3	C3
The Village (Clonsilla)	21	C3
*The Village (off Drumcondra Road Upper)	25	B3
The Village (Raheny)	27	B3
*The Village Centre (Lucan Village)	34	D1
*The Village Court (Lucan Village)	34	D1
The Village Gate	60	F2
The Walk (Dunboyne Castle)	7	B3
The Walk (Louisa Valley)	19	C4
The Walk (Manorfields)	21	B1
The Walk (Oldtown Mill)	31	C3
The Walk (Templeogue)	46	D3
The Walk (Tallaght)	55	A1
The Walk (Ballinteer)	57	B2
The Walk (Carrickmines)	63	A1
*The Walk (Robswall)	3	C3
The Walk (Moyglare Hall)	17	C2
The Walled Gardens	32	D2
The Walled Orchard	33	B1
*The Warehouse Apts (Clanbrassil Terrace)	74	F2
The Warren	2	F3
*The Watercourse (off Rossmore Road)	46	D4
*The Waterfront (Cian Park)	25	B4
*The Waxworks Apts (north of Ashtown Station)	23	C3

STREET NAME	PAGE	GRID REF
The Way (Dunboyne Castle)	7	B3
*The Weaver Apts (off Meath Place)	74	F1
The Weir	36	E2
*The Wheat Barn Apts (off Portland Street North)	71	C1
The Wicklow Way	61	C4
The Willow	9	B2
The Willow (Rockfield)	57	C1
The Willows (Glasnevin)	24	F3
The Willows (Celbridge)	32	D3
*The Willows (off Claremont Road)	39	A4
*The Willows (off Orwell Road)	47	A3
*The Willows (off Monkstown Valley)	49	B4
*The Willows (Abberley)	64	E1
*The Willows (off Northwood Ave)	12	E4
*The Willows (Carrington)	12	E4
*The Windmill Apts (near Windmill Lane Apts)	72	D4
The Wood (Tallaght)	55	A2
The Wood (Clon Burgh)	58	D3
The Wood (Carrickmines)	63	A1
The Wood (Crinken Lane)	64	E3
*The Wooden Buildings Apts (Exchange Street Upper)	71	A4
The Woodlands (Celbridge)	32	D3
*The Woodlands (off Rathfarnham Wood)	46	F4
*The Woods (off Charlemont)	25	C3
*The Works (Inchicore terrace South)	36	F3
*Theresa House (off Stonepark Court)	46	F4
Third Ave (Seville Place)	72	E3
Third Ave (Tallaght)	44	F4
Thirlestane Terrace	74	F1
Thomas Court	74	E1
*Thomas Court Barn (off Marrowbone Lane)	74	E1
*Thomas Court Bawn (at School Street)	74	E1
*Thomas Davis Court (on Sutton Downs near Bayside Square South)	27	C1
Thomas Davis Street (West)	36	F3
Thomas Davis Street South	74	F1
Thomas Lane	71	B3
*Thomas Moore Court (off Bayside Square South)	27	C1
Thomas Moore Road	45	C1
Thomas Street	74	F1
Thomas Street West	74	E1
*Thomastown Cres (off Sallynoggin Road)	60	D2
Thomastown Road	60	D3
*Thomond (at Eaton Wood Square)	64	E2
Thomond Road	36	E3
Thompson's Cottages	71	C2
Thor Place	70	D3
*Thormanby Grove (south of Church on Main Street Howth)	30	D2
Thormanby Lawns	30	D2
Thormanby Lodge	30	E2
Thormanby Road	30	E2
Thormanby Woods	30	D2
Thorn Wood	48	E3
Thornberry Apts	8	F4
*Thorncastle Court Apts (off Thorncastle Street)	39	A2
Thorncastle Street	39	A2
*Thorncliff (off Dundrum Road)	47	B2
Thorncliffe Park	47	B3
Thorndale Ave	26	D2
*Thorndale Court (off Collinswood)	25	C2
Thorndale Cres	26	D2
Thorndale Drive	26	D3
Thorndale Grove	26	D3
Thorndale Lawns	26	D2
Thorndale Park	26	D2
Thornfield Square	44	E1
Thornhill Court	31	C2
Thornhill Gardens	31	C2
Thornhill Heights	31	C2
Thornhill Lane	27	A4
Thornhill Meadows	31	C2
Thornhill Road (Kilmacud)	48	E4
Thornhill Road (Bray)	67	A2
*Thornhill View (north of Old Connaught Grove)	67	B1
Thornleigh Ave	1	Inset

STREET NAME	PAGE	GRID REF
Thornleigh Close	1	Inset
Thornleigh Court	1	Inset
Thornleigh Green	1	Inset
Thornleigh Grove	1	Inset
Thornleigh Lane	1	Inset
Thornleigh Park	1	Inset
Thornleigh Place	1	Inset
Thornleigh Road	1	Inset
Thornleigh Row	1	Inset
Thornville Ave	27	B1
Thornville Drive	27	B2
Thornville Park	27	C1
Thornville Road	27	B1
*Thornville Terrace (on Thornville Road)	27	B2
*Three Rock Close (off Kipure Ave)	45	B3
Three Rock Grove	57	B3
Three Rock Road	58	E2
Thundercut Alley	70	F3
*Tibradden Close (off Tibradden Drive)	45	B2
Tibradden Drive	45	B2
Tibradden Grove	45	B3
Tibradden Lane	56	F4
Tibradden Road	56	F3
Ticknick	63	B2
Ticknock Ave	57	C3
Ticknock Dale	57	C3
Ticknock Drive	57	C3
Ticknock Grove	57	C3
Ticknock Hill	57	C3
Ticknock Park	57	C3
Ticknock Road	57	B4
Ticknock Way	57	C3
Tiknock	61	B1
Tiknock Bridge	61	B1
Timard	17	A1
Timber Mills Apts	26	E2
*Timberyard (off Brabazon Street)	74	F2
*Time Place Apts (off Corrig Road)	58	E2
Tinkers Hill	21	A4
Tinkler's Path	36	E1
Tinnehinch	66	E4
Tinnehinch Bridge	66	E4
Tivoli Ave	46	F1
Tivoli Close	59	C1
Tivoli Road	49	C4
Tivoli Terrace East	50	D4
Tivoli Terrace North	49	C4
Tivoli Terrace South	49	C4
*Tobernea Terrace (off Seapoint Ave)	49	B3
Tolka Cottages	24	F3
Tolka Estate	24	F2
Tolka Estate Road	24	F3
Tolka Quay	39	A2
Tolka Quay Road	39	A2
Tolka Road	25	B4
Tolka Vale	24	E3
Tolka Valley Road	24	D3
Tolka Valley View	24	D2
Tolka View	22	E2
*Tom Clarke House (off Ballybough Road)	25	B4
Tom Kelly Road	75	B3
Tomar Court 70 D3	70	D3
Tonduff Close	45	B3
*Tonguefield Road (off Blarney Park)	46	E1
Tonlegee Ave	26	F1
Tonlegee Drive	26	F1
Tonlegee Road	27	A1
Tootenhill	52	D2
Tootenhill (Rathcoole)	52	D2
Tor an Rí Close	34	F3
Tor an Rí Court	34	F3
Tor an Rí Lane	34	F3
Tor an Rí Parade	34	F3
Tor an Rí Terrace	34	F3
Tor an Rí Walk	34	F3
Torca Road	60	F2
*Torca View (off Sorrento Road)	60	F2
Torcaill	3	C4
*Torlogh Gardens (off Philipsburgh Ave)	25	C4
*Torlogh Parade (off Griffith Ave)	25	C3
Torquay Road	58	F2
Torquay Wood	58	F2
Tory Square	22	F1
*Tourmakeady Road (off Innishmaan Road)	25	B2

STREET NAME	PAGE	GRID REF
*Tourville Lodge (off Church Lane)	46	F3
Tower Ave	46	F2
Tower Road (Castleknock)	22	F4
Tower Road (Clondalkin)	44	D1
Tower Road	36	D1
Tower Terrace (off Kilmainham Lane)	73	B1
Tower View Cottages	24	F4
*Tower Villas (on Tower Ave)	46	F2
Townsend Street	71	C4
*Townyard House Apts (adjacent Townyard Lane)	3	B2
Townyard Lane	3	B2
Tracy Bonham Lane	70	E4
Traders Wharf	49	C3
*Traders Wharf Apts (Ushers Quay)	70	F4
Trafalgar Lane	49	B4
Trafalgar Terrace (Blackrock)	49	B3
*Trafalgar Terrace (near Meath Place)	67	C2
Tramway Court (Sutton)	29	A1
*Tramway Court (off Old Blessington Road)	55	A1
Tranquility Grove	26	D1
Traverslea Close	60	D1
Traverslea Woods	60	D1
*Traynor Place (O'Reilly Ave)	73	C1
Treepark Ave	45	A3
Treepark Close	45	A3
Treepark Drive	45	A3
Treepark Road	45	A3
Trees Ave	48	E4
Trees Road Lower	48	E4
Trees Road Upper	48	E4
Treesdale	48	F4
Tresilian	59	A3
*Trideat Apts (off Claremont Road)	39	A4
Trim Road	26	D1
Trimbleston Apts	47	C3
Trimleston Ave	48	E2
Trimleston Drive	48	E2
Trimleston Gardens	48	E2
Trimleston Park	48	E2
Trimleston Road	48	E2
Trinity Hall (Rathgar)	47	A2
Trinity Square	72	D1
Trinity Street	71	B4
Trinity Terrace	72	D1
*Tristan House Apts (off Martin's Row Chapelizod)	36	E2
*Tritonville Ave (off Cranfield Place)	39	A3
*Tritonville Close (off Sandymount Road)	39	A3
Tritonville Court	39	A4
*Tritonville Cres (off Tritonville Road)	39	A3
*Tritonville Mews (off Sandymount Road)	39	A3
Tritonville Road	39	A3
*Trosyrafon Terrace (at South Esplanade)	68	D2
*Tuansgate Apts (off Belgard Square East)	54	F1
Tubber Lane Road	33	B2
Tubbermore Ave	60	F2
Tubbermore Road	60	F2
Tuckett's Lane	30	D2
Tudor Court	2	F2
Tudor Lawns	58	F2
Tudor Road	47	B1
Tulip Court	13	C4
Tullyhall	34	D4
Tullyhall Ave	34	D4
Tullyhall Close	34	D4
Tullyhall Court	34	D4
Tullyhall Cres	34	E4
Tullyhall Drive	34	E4
Tullyhall Green	34	D4
Tullyhall Park	34	D4
Tullyhall Rise	34	E4
Tullyhall Way	34	D4
Tullyvale	63	C1
Turnapin Cottages	12	F3
Turnapin Green	12	F3
Turnapin Grove	12	F3
Turnapin Lane	12	F3
Turnberry	28	D1
Turnberry Square	28	D1
Turnpike Lane	44	F2
Turnpike Road	45	A2
Turnstone Apts	48	E3

STREET NAME	PAGE	GRID REF
Turret Road	35	C2
*Turrets Flats (off Summerville Park)	47	A1
Turvey Ave	73	B1
Tuscany Downs	27	A2
Tuscany Park	28	D1
*Twin Cottages (off Yankee Terrace)	49	A4
Tymon Close	55	A2
Tymon Cres	54	F2
Tymon Farm Apts	45	C4
Tymon Grove	55	A2
*Tymon Heights	55	B2
Tymon Lane	45	B4
Tymon Lane	45	C4
Tymon Lawn	55	A2
Tymon Lodge Apts	45	B3
Tymon North	45	B4
Tymon North Ave	45	B4
*Tymon North Court (off Tymon North Road)	45	B4
Tymon North Gardens	45	B4
Tymon North Green	45	B4
Tymon North Grove	45	B4
Tymon North Lawn	45	B4
Tymon North Park	45	B4
*Tymon North Place (off Tymon North Ave)	45	B4
Tymon North Road	45	B4
Tymonville Ave	45	B4
Tymonville Court	45	A4
Tymonville Cres	45	A4
Tymonville Drive	45	A3
Tymonville Grove	45	B3
Tymonville Lawn	45	B4
Tymonville Park	45	B4
Tymonville Road	45	A4
Tynan Hall	44	F3
Tynan Hall Ave	44	F3
Tynan Hall Grove	44	F3
Tynan Hall Park	44	F3
Tyrconnell Park	36	F3
Tyrconnell Road	36	F3
*Tyrconnell Street (off Tyrconnell Road)	36	F3
*Tyrconnell Villas (off Gratten Cres)	36	F3
Tyrrellstown	9	B2
Tyrrellstown Avenue	9	B2
Tyrrellstown Boulevard	9	B2
Tyrrellstown Way	9	B2
Tyrone House	71	C3
Tyrone Place	73	A2
Tyrrell Place	71	C1
*Tyrrel's Lane (off Fitzwilliam Street Ringsend)	39	A3
Tyrrelstown Ave	9	B2

U

STREET NAME	PAGE	GRID REF
UCD Village Belgrove	48	D3
*Ullardmor (off Ardeevin Road)	60	F2
Ulster Street	24	F4
Ulster Terrace (North Strand)	72	D1
*Ulster Terrace (off Stillorgan Grove)	58	F1
*Ulverton Close (off Ulverton Road Dalkey)	60	F1
*Ulverton Court (off Ulverton Road Dalkey)	60	F1
Ulverton Road	60	F1
*Ulysses House Apts (Little Britain Street)	71	A3
University Village Apts	17	C2
Upper Cliff Road	30	D2
Upper Dargle Road	67	A2
Upper Garville Ave	47	A2
Upper Glen Road (Phoenix Park)	36	E1
Upper Kilmacud Road Extension	58	E1
Uppercross	34	F1
*Uppercross Court (off Old Blessington Road)	55	A1
Uppercross Road	73	C2
*Urney Grove (off Killiney Road)	60	E2
Usher Lane	1	A2
Usher Street	70	F4
Ushers Court Apts	70	F4
Usher's Island	70	E4
Usher's Quay	70	F4

V

STREET NAME	PAGE	GRID REF
*Vale Terrace (on lower Dargle Road)	67	B2
*Vale View (Upper Dargle Road)	67	B2
Vale View Ave	59	B3
Vale View Close	59	B3
Vale View Grove	59	B3
Vale View Lawn	59	B3
Valentia House	71	B1
Valentia Parade	71	B1
Valentia Road	25	B3
Valeview Cres	24	D2
Valeview Drive	24	D2
Valeview Gardens (off St. Helena's Road)	24	D2
Valley Close	64	D1
Valley Drive	63	C1
*Valley Park Ave (off Valley Park Road)	23	C2
Valley Park Drive	23	C2
Valley Park Road	23	C2
Valley View	1	B1
Valley View	64	D1
Valley Walk	64	D1
Vallombrosa	67	A2
Vanessa Close	31	C3
Vanessa Lawns	31	C3
Vauxhall Ave	74	D2
Vavasour Square	76	F2
Venetian Hall	26	E3
Ventry Drive	24	D4
Ventry Park	24	E4
Ventry Road	24	E4
Verbena Ave (Kilbarrack)	27	C1
Verbena Ave (Foxrock)	59	A3
Verbena Grove	27	C1
Verbena Lawn	27	C1
Verbena Park	27	C1
Verdemont	22	D2
*Vergemount (off Clonskeagh Road)	47	C1
*Vergemount Hall (off Clonskeagh Road)	47	C1
*Vergemount Park (off Clonskeagh Road)	47	C1
Verney House	62	F3
Vernon Ave	26	F4
Vernon Court (Vernon Ave)	26	F4
*Vernon Court (off Clontarf Road)	39	C1
Vernon Drive	26	F3
Vernon Gardens	26	F4
Vernon Grove (Clontarf)	26	F4
Vernon Grove (Rathgar)	47	A2
Vernon Heath	26	F4
Vernon Park	26	F4
Vernon Rise	26	F3
Vernon Street	75	A2
*Vernon Wood (off Vernon Ave)	39	C1
*Veronica Terrace (off Oliver Plunkett Ave)	39	A3
Verschoyle Ave	53	C2
Verschoyle Close	53	C2
Verschoyle Court	76	D2
Verschoyle Cres	53	C2
Verschoyle Drive	53	C2
Verschoyle Glen	53	C2
Verschoyle Green	53	C2
Verschoyle Heights	53	C2
Verschoyle Mews	76	D2
Verschoyle Park	53	C2
Verschoyle Place (off Lower Mount Street)	76	E2
Verschoyle Rise	53	C2
Verschoyle Vale	53	C2
Verville Court	26	E4
Vesey Mews	49	C4
Vesey Park	34	D2
Vesey Place	49	C4
*Vesey Terrace (off Main Street Lucan)	34	D1
*Vevay Arcade (on Vevay Road)	67	C3
*Vevay Cres (Vevay Road)	67	C2
Vevay Road	67	C3
*Vevay Villas (Vevay Road, Putland Road)	67	C3
Vicar Street	74	F1
Vicars Court	8	F4

STREET NAME	PAGE	GRID REF
Vico Road	60	F3
*Vico Terrace (off Vico Road)	60	F3
Victoria Ave (Donnybrook)	47	C1
Victoria Ave (Bray)	68	D2
*Victoria Cottages (off Bath Street)	39	A3
*Victoria Lane (off Botanic Ave)	25	B4
*Victoria Lane (off South Zion Road)	47	A2
Victoria Quay	70	E4
Victoria Road (Clontarf)	26	E4
Victoria Road (Killiney)	60	E3
Victoria Road (Dalkey)	60	F2
Victoria Road	46	F2
Victoria Street	75	A3
Victoria Terrace (Clontarf)	39	A3
Victoria Terrace (Dundrum)	47	C4
*Victoria Terrace (off Mellifont Ave)	50	D4
*Victoria Terrace (off Dalkey Ave)	60	F2
*Victoria Village (off Rathgar Ave)	46	F2
Victoria Village (Rathgar)	47	A2
Victoria Villas (Clontarf)	26	D4
*Victoria Villas (off Rathgar Ave)	46	F2
Viking Harbour (Ushers Island)	70	E4
Viking Place	70	E3
Viking Road	70	E3
*Villa Bank (Royal Canal Bank)	71	A1
Villa Blanchard	22	F2
*Villa Building Apts (off Harbour Road, opposite west pier)	30	D1
Villa Nova	48	F4
Villa Park Ave	24	D4
Villa Park Drive	24	D4
Villa Park Gardens	24	D4
Villa Park Road	24	D4
*Village Court Apts (off Butterfield Ave)	46	F4
Village Gate Arcade	67	C2
*Village Green (off Main Street Rathfarnham)	46	F3
Village Green (Tallaght)	55	A1
Village Heights	9	A4
*Village House (Reilly's Ave)	74	D3
Village Road (Beside Aiken's Village)	58	D4
Village Square (Tallaght)	55	A1
*Village Weir (off Main Street Lucan)	34	D1
Villarea Park	60	E1
Villiers Road	47	A2
Vintage Court	74	E2
Violet Hill	60	D3
Violet Hill Drive	24	F3
Violet Hill Park	24	F3
Violet Hill Road	24	F3
Virginia Drive	24	D2
*Virginia Hall (off Belgard Square West)	54	F1
Virginia Heights	54	F1
Virginia Park	24	D2
Viscount Ave	12	F4

W

STREET NAME	PAGE	GRID REF
Wadelai Green	25	A2
Wadelai Road	25	A2
Wade's Ave	27	A3
Wainsfort Ave	46	D3
Wainsfort Cres	46	D3
Wainsfort Drive	46	D2
Wainsfort Gardens	46	D3
Wainsfort Grove	46	E3
Wainsfort Manor	46	D3
Wainsfort Manor Cres	46	D3
Wainsfort Manor Drive	46	D3
Wainsfort Manor Green	46	D3
Wainsfort Manor Grove	46	D3
Wainsfort Park	46	E3
Wainsfort Road	46	D3
*Waldemar Terrace (off Dundrum Road)	47	B4
Walker's Cottages	75	B4
Walker's Court	75	B4
Walkinstown	45	B1
Walkinstown Ave	45	B1

STREET NAME	PAGE	GRID REF
Walkinstown Close	45	B1
Walkinstown Cres	45	B1
Walkinstown Cross	45	C2
Walkinstown Drive	45	B1
Walkinstown Green	45	B1
Walkinstown Parade	45	B1
Walkinstown Park	45	B1
Walkinstown Road	45	C1
*Wallace Road		
(off Bunting Road)	45	C1
Walnut Ave (Whitehall)	25	B3
Walnut Ave (Clondalkin)	44	F3
Walnut Close	44	F3
Walnut Court	25	B2
Walnut Drive	44	F3
Walnut Lawn	25	B3
Walnut Park	25	B3
Walnut Rise	25	B3
*Walnut View		
(off Brookwood)	56	E2
Walsh Road	25	A3
Waltersland Road	58	F1
Waltham Terrace	48	F4
Walton Hall (Swords)	1	Inset
Waltrim Grove	67	B4
Walworth Road	75	A3
Walworth Terrace		
(Walworth Road)	75	A4
*Warburton Terrace		
(west side of text Meath)	68	D2
Ward's Hill	74	F2
Warner's Lane	75	C3
Warren Ave	22	E3
Warren Close	22	E3
Warren Court		
(off Warrenhouse Road)	28	D1
Warren Cres	22	E4
Warren Green (Carpenterstown)	22	E3
Warren Green (Sutton)	28	D1
Warren Manor	2	F3
Warren Park	22	E3
Warren Street	75	A3
Warrenhouse Road	28	D1
Warrenmount	74	F2
Warrenmount Place	74	F2
*Warrenpoint		
(off Clontarf Road)	26	E4
Warrenstown	9	B4
Warrenstown Close	9	B4
Warrenstown Court	9	B4
Warrenstown Downs	9	B4
Warrenstown Drive	9	B4
Warrenstown Garth	9	B4
Warrenstown Green	9	B4
Warrenstown Grove	9	B4
Warrenstown Lawn	9	B4
Warrenstown Park	9	B4
Warrenstown Place	9	B4
Warrenstown Rise	9	B4
Warrenstown Row	9	B4
Warrenstown Vale	9	B4
Warrenstown View	9	B4
Warrenstown Walk	9	B4
Warrenstown Way	9	B4
Warrington Lane	76	E2
Warrington Place	76	E2
Warwick Terrace	76	D4
Wasdale Grove	46	F2
*Wasdale House		
(off Wasdale Park)	46	F3
Wasdale Park	46	F3
*Washerwoman Lane		
(off Orwell Road)	47	A2
*Washington Grove		
(off Washington Lane)	46	E4
Washington Grove	46	E4
Washington Lane	46	E4
Washington Park	46	E4
Washington Street	74	F3
Waterfall Ave	25	B4
Waterfall Road	26	F3
Watergate Estate	55	A1
Waterloo Ave	72	E1
Waterloo Lane	76	D4
Waterloo Mews		
(off Shelbourne Road)	76	E3
Waterloo Road	76	D4
Watermeadow Drive	54	F2
Watermeadow Park	55	A2
Watermill	27	B3
Watermill Ave	27	A3
Watermill Close	55	A2
Watermill Drive	27	A3
Watermill Grove	55	A2
Watermill Lawn	27	A3

STREET NAME	PAGE	GRID REF
Watermill Lawn (Tallaght)	55	A2
Watermill Park	27	A3
Watermill Road	27	A3
*Watermint Court		
(at Lockkeeper's Walk)	24	D3
Waterside Apts	76	F1
Waterside Ave	2	E2
Waterside Close	2	E2
Waterside Court	2	E2
Waterside Cres (Swords)	2	E2
Waterside Cres (Portmarnock)	3	C4
Waterside Drive	2	E2
Waterside Green	2	E3
Waterside Grove	2	E2
Waterside King`s Hall	2	E2
Waterside Lawn	2	E2
Waterside Park	2	E2
Waterside Place	2	E3
Waterside Rise	2	E2
Waterside Road	2	E2
Waterside Walk	2	E2
Waterside Way	2	E2
Waterstown	35	C1
Waterstown Ave	35	C1
Waterville Road	22	F1
Waterville Row	22	F1
Waterville Terrace	22	F1
Watery Lane	2	D1
Watery Lane (Swords)	1	C1
Watery Lane (Clondalkin)	44	E1
Watkins Buildings	74	F2
Watling Street	70	E4
Watson Ave	60	D4
Watson Drive	60	D4
Watson Park	60	D4
Watson Road	60	D3
Watson's Estate	60	D3
Waverley Ave	25	C4
*Waverley Terrace		
(off Harold's Cross Road)	46	F1
*Waverley Terrace		
(Adelaide Road)	67	C2
Waynestown	5	C1
Wayside Cottages	62	F2
Weaver Court	35	A2
Weaver Lane	71	A1
Weaver's Close	74	F2
*Weavers Hall		
(at Levmoss Estate)	58	F3
Weavers Row (The Coombe)	74	E2
Weaver's Row (Clonsilla)	21	C2
Weaver's Square	74	F2
Weaver's Street	74	F2
Weaver's Walk	21	C2
*Webster's Cottages		
(off Annaville Ave)	49	A4
Wedgewood Estate	58	D2
*Weir House		
(opposite Convent Ave)	25	B4
Weirview	34	D1
Weirview Drive	58	F1
Weldon's Lane	15	A4
Well Road	2	D2
Wellesley Place	71	C1
*Wellington Cottages		
(off Willington Green)	45	C3
*Wellington Court		
(off Whitehall Road West)	46	D2
*Wellington Court		
(Novara Ave)	67	C2
*Wellington Gardens		
(off Oakley Road)	47	B1
Wellington House		
(off Seafort Ave)	76	E4
Wellington Lane		
(Wellington Road)	76	E4
Wellington Lane (Tallaght Road)	45	C3
*Wellington Lodge		
(off Serpentine Ave)	39	A4
*Wellington Mews		
(Wellington Lane)	76	E4
Wellington Park	46	D3
Wellington Place		
(Leeson Street)	76	E4
Wellington Place North	71	A2
Wellington Quay	71	B4
Wellington Road (Ballsbridge)	76	E4
Wellington Road (Phoenix Park)	69	B4
*Wellington Road (off		
Whitehall Road Templeogue)	46	D3
*Wellington Street (off		
George's Place Dún Laoghaire)	50	D4
Wellington Street Lower	71	A2
Wellington Street Upper	71	A2
Wellmount Ave	24	D2

STREET NAME	PAGE	GRID REF
Wellmount Court	24	D2
Wellmount Cres	24	D2
Wellmount Drive	24	D2
Wellmount Green	24	D2
Wellmount Parade	24	D2
Wellmount Park	24	D2
Wellmount Road	24	D2
Wellpark Ave	25	B3
Wellview Ave	9	A3
Wellview Cres	9	A3
Wellview Green	9	A3
Wellview Grove	9	A3
Wellview Park 9		A3
Wendell Ave	4	D4
Wentworth Apts	76	E1
Werburgh Street	75	A1
Wesbury	58	E1
Wesley Heights	57	C2
Wesley House	76	D4
Wesley Lawns	57	C2
Wesley Place	74	F3
Wesley Road	47	A2
West Park Drive	24	F2
West Pier (Howth)	30	D1
West Pier (Dún Laoghaire)	49	C3
West Road	72	E2
West Terrace	36	F3
Westbourne Ave	43	C1
Westbourne Close	43	C1
Westbourne Court	46	F3
Westbourne Drive	43	C1
Westbourne Green	43	C1
Westbourne Grove	43	C1
Westbourne Lawn	43	C1
Westbourne Lodge	56	D1
Westbourne Park	43	C1
Westbourne Rise	43	C1
Westbourne Road	46	F3
*Westbourne Terrace		
(near Bray Bridge)	67	C2
Westbourne View	43	C1
Westbrook	46	D2
Westbrook Lawns	53	C2
Westbrook Park	33	C2
Westbrook Road	47	B3
Westbury	34	D3
Westbury Ave	34	D3
Westbury Close	34	D3
Westbury Drive	34	D2
Westbury Grove	33	C3
Westbury Park	34	D3
Westcourt	74	D1
*Westend Gate (Castleknock)	22	F3
Westend Gate (Tallagh)	54	F1
Westend Village	22	E2
Western Parkway	35	B2
Western Parkway Motorway	22	E4
Western Road	74	E3
Western Way	71	A2
*Westerton Rise		
(off Ballinteer Road)	57	C1
Westfield Park	68	D3
Westfield Road	46	F1
*Westfield Terrace		
(off Rock Road)	49	A3
*Westgate Apts		
(off St. Augustine Street)	74	F1
*Westhampton Place		
(off Terenure Road North)	46	F2
Westhaven	8	F4
Westland Row	76	D1
*Westland Square Apts		
(Westland Square		
Business Park)	72	D4
Westmanstown	42	D3
*Westminster Court		
(off Brighton Road Foxrock)	59	A3
Westminster Lawns	58	F2
Westminster Park	59	A2
Westminster Road	59	A3
*Westmoreland Park		
(off Sandford Road)	47	B1
Westmoreland Street	71	B4
Weston Ave (Leixlip)	33	B1
Weston Ave	47	B4
Weston Close (Leixlip)	33	B1
Weston Close (Churchtown)	47	B4
Weston Court	33	B2
Weston Cres	33	B1
Weston Drive	33	B1
Weston Green	33	B1
Weston Grove	47	B4
Weston Heights	33	B2
Weston Lane (Leixlip)	33	B1
Weston Lawn	33	B1

STREET NAME	PAGE	GRID REF
Weston Meadow	33	B2
Weston Park (Churchtown)	47	B4
Weston Road	47	B4
*Weston Terrace		
(off Weston Park)	47	B4
Weston Way	33	B2
Westpark (Coolock)	26	F2
Westpark (Rathcoole)	52	F2
Westpark (Tallaght)	55	A1
Westpark Apts	53	F2
*Westview Terrace		
(Adelaide Road)	67	C2
Westway Close	9	C4
Westway Grove	9	C4
Westway Lawns	22	F1
Westway Park	9	C4
Westway Rise	9	C4
Westway View	9	C4
Westwood Ave	23	C2
Westwood Road	23	C2
Wexford Street	75	B2
Wharton Terrace	74	F4
Whately Hall	8	F4
*Whately Road		
(off Upper Kilmacud Road)	58	E1
Wheatfield	67	C2
Wheatfield Grove	4	D4
Wheatfield Road (Portmarnock)	4	D4
Wheatfield Road (Palmerston)	35	C2
Wheatfields Ave	35	B3
Wheatfields Close	35	B3
Wheatfields Court	35	B3
Wheatfields Cres	35	B3
Wheatfields Drive	35	B3
Wheatfields Grove	35	B3
Wheatfields Park	35	B3
*Wheaton Court		
(off Inchicore Terrace South)	36	F3
*Whelan House Flats		
(off Thorncastle Street)	39	A3
*Whelan's Terrace		
(off Temple Road)	49	A3
Whitaker Hall	71	A2
White Gables	64	D2
White Hall (Ballymount Road)	44	F3
White Oak	47	C3
White Oaks	67	B4
Whiteacre Close	25	B1
Whiteacre Court	25	B1
Whiteacre Cres	25	B1
Whiteacre Place	25	B1
Whitebank Road	39	B3
Whitebarn Road	47	A4
Whitebeam Ave	47	C2
Whitebeam Road	47	C2
Whitebeams Road	58	D2
Whitebrook Park	54	E1
Whitechapel Ave	22	D2
Whitechapel Court	22	D2
Whitechapel Cres	22	D2
Whitechapel Green	22	D2
Whitechapel Grove	22	D2
Whitechapel Lawn	22	D2
Whitechapel Park	22	D2
Whitechapel Road	22	D2
*Whitechurch Abbey		
(off Grange Park)	56	F1
Whitechurch Ave	56	F2
Whitechurch Close	56	F2
Whitechurch Court	56	F2
Whitechurch Cres	56	F2
Whitechurch Drive	56	F2
Whitechurch Green	56	F2
Whitechurch Grove	56	F2
Whitechurch Heights	56	F2
Whitechurch Hill	56	F2
Whitechurch Lawn	56	F2
Whitechurch Park	56	F2
Whitechurch Pines	56	F1
Whitechurch Place	56	F2
Whitechurch Road	56	F2
Whitechurch Stream	56	F1
Whitechurch View	56	F2
Whitechurch Walk	56	F2
Whitechurch Way	56	F2
Whitecliff	56	F1
Whitefriar Garden Flats		
(off Whitefriar Street)	75	A1
Whitefriar Place	75	B1
Whitefriar Street	75	A1
Whitehall	25	B2
Whitehall Close	46	D3
Whitehall Gardens	46	D2
Whitehall Mews	59	A2
Whitehall Park	46	D3

STREET NAME	PAGE	GRID REF
Whitehall Road (Kimmage)	46	D2
Whitehall Road (Churchtown)	47	A4
Whitehall Road West	46	D2
Whitehall Square	45	C2
Whites Gate (Phoenix Park)	23	A4
White's Lane North	71	A2
White's Road	23	A4
White's Villas (off Carysfort Road)	60	F1
Whitestown	22	D1
Whitestown Ave	22	D1
Whitestown Cres	22	D1
Whitestown Drive (Blanchardstown)	22	D1
Whitestown Drive (Tallaght)	54	E2
Whitestown Gardens	22	D1
Whitestown Green	22	D1
Whitestown Grove	22	D1
Whitestown Park	22	D1
Whitestown Road	54	F2
Whitestown Walk	22	D1
Whitestown Way	54	F2
Whitethorn	35	B3
Whitethorn Ave	26	D2
Whitethorn Close	26	D2
Whitethorn Cres (Artane)	26	D2
Whitethorn Cres (Coldcut Road)	35	B3
Whitethorn Drive	35	B3
Whitethorn Gardens	35	B3
Whitethorn Grove (Artane)	26	D2
Whitethorn Grove (Celbridge)	32	D3
Whitethorn Park (Artane)	26	D2
Whitethorn Park (Coldcut Road)	35	B3
Whitethorn Rise	26	D2
Whitethorn Road (Artane)	26	D2
Whitethorn Road (Milltown)	47	C2
*Whitethorn Walk (off Pine Ave Foxrock)	59	A2
*Whitethorn Walk (off Carriglea Ave Kill O'The Grange)	59	C2
Whitethorn Way	35	B3
Whitton Road	46	F2
Whitworth Ave	71	C1
*Whitworth Hall Apts (Behind District Court)	70	F3
*Whitworth Parade (off St. Patrick's Road)	25	A4
Whitworth Place (off Binns Bridge)	71	B1
Whitworth Road	25	A4
Whitworth Terrace (off Russell Ave)	71	C1
Wicklow Lane (off Wicklow Street)	75	B1
Wicklow Street	75	B1
Wicklow Way	65	A4
Wigan Road	25	A4
Wikeford Hall (Swords)	1	Inset
Wilderwood Grove	45	C4
*Wilfield (off Sandymount Ave)	39	A4
Wilfield Park	39	A4
Wilfield Road	39	A4
Wilford Court	67	B1
Wilfrid Road	46	F1
*Wilfrid Terrace (off Tivoli Ave)	46	F1
Willans Ave	21	A1
*Willan's Court (Willan's Ave)	21	A1
Willans Drive	21	A1
Willans Green	21	A1
*Willan's Grove (Willan's Ave)	21	A1
*Willan's Lane (Willan's Ave)	21	A1
*Willan's Place (Willan's Ave)	21	A1
Willans Rise	21	A1
Willans Row	21	A1
Willans Way	21	A1
Willbrook	46	F4
Willbrook Downs	56	F1
Willbrook Estate	56	F1
*Willbrook Grove (off Willbrook Street)	46	F4
Willbrook House	75	C4
Willbrook Lawn	46	F4
Willbrook Park	46	F4
Willbrook Road	46	F4
Willbrook Street	46	F4
*Willbrook Villas (Willbrook Street)	46	F4
William Beckett House	76	D3
William Dargan Bridge	47	B4
*William Pallister House (off Stonepark Court)	46	F4
William Street North	72	D1
William Street South	75	B1
William's Lane	71	B3
William's Park	47	A1

STREET NAME	PAGE	GRID REF
Williams Place Lower (Buckingham Street Upper)	71	C1
William's Place South	75	A2
William's Place Upper (off Portland Place)	71	B1
Willie Bermingham Place	73	C1
Willie Nolan Road	15	A4
Willington Ave	45	C3
Willington Court	45	C3
Willington Cres	45	C3
Willington Drive	45	C3
Willington Green	45	C3
Willington Grove	45	C3
*Willington Lawn (off Willington Grove)	45	C3
Willington Park	45	C3
Willow Ave	32	E4
Willow Ave (Clondalkin)	44	D2
Willow Ave (Loughlinstown)	64	D1
Willow Bank	49	C4
Willow Bank Drive	56	E1
Willow Bank Park	56	E1
Willow Brook	32	E4
Willow Court (Clondalkin)	44	D2
Willow Court (Loughlinstown)	64	D1
Willow Cove	32	E4
Willow Cres	32	E4
Willow Cres	64	D1
Willow Drive	32	E4
Willow Drive	44	D2
Willow Gate	57	B1
Willow Green	32	E4
Willow Grove (Clondalkin)	44	D2
Willow Grove (Cornelscourt)	59	B3
*Willow Grove (off Carriglea Ave)	59	C1
Willow House	76	D3
Willow Lawn	32	E4
Willow Lodge	23	A4
Willow Mews	48	E1
Willow Park (Dunboyne)	7	B2
*Willow Park (off Pine Ave Foxrock)	59	A2
Willow Park (Loughlinstown)	64	D1
Willow Park Ave	24	F1
Willow Park Close	24	F1
Willow Park Cres	24	F1
Willow Park Drive	25	A1
Willow Park Grove	24	F1
Willow Park Lawn	24	F1
Willow Park Road	24	F1
Willow Place (Booterstown)	48	F3
Willow Place (Loughlinstown)	64	D1
Willow Rise	32	E4
Willow Road (Fox and Geese)	45	A1
Willow Road (Dundrum)	57	B1
Willow Terrace	48	F2
Willow Vale	60	D4
Willow View	32	E4
Willow Wood Close	21	C2
Willow Wood Downs (off Willow Wood Grove)	21	C2
Willow Wood Green	21	C2
Willow Wood Grove	21	C2
Willow Wood Lawn	21	C2
Willow Wood Park	21	C1
Willow Wood Rise	21	C1
Willow Wood View	21	C2
Willow Wood Walk	21	C1
Willowbank	57	C1
Willowbrook Grove	31	C3
Willowbrook Lawns	31	C3
Willowbrook Lodge	31	C3
Willowbrook Park	31	C3
Willowfield	39	B4
Willowfield Ave	47	C4
Willowfield Park	47	C4
*Willowmount (off Willow Place)	48	F3
Willows (opposite Knockmaroon Gate)	36	D1
Willows Court	21	C2
Willows Drive	21	C2
Willows Green	21	C2
Willows Road	21	C2
*Willsbrook Apts (on Clonshaugh Road)	13	A4
Willsbrook Ave	34	E2
Willsbrook Cres	34	F1
Willsbrook Drive	34	E2
Willsbrook Gardens	34	E1
Willsbrook Green	34	E2
Willsbrook Grove	34	E1
Willsbrook Park	34	E1
Willsbrook Place	34	E1

STREET NAME	PAGE	GRID REF
Willsbrook Road	34	E2
Willsbrook View	34	E2
Willsbrook Way	34	E1
*Wilmont Ave (off Glasthule Road)	60	E1
Wilson Cres	48	D4
Wilson Road	48	E4
Wilson's Place	76	D1
Wilson's Terrace	74	F1
Wilton Court	76	D3
Wilton Place	76	D3
Wilton Terrace	76	D3
*Windele Road (off Joyce Road)	25	A3
Windermere	21	B2
*Windermere (off Gilford Road)	39	B4
Windgate Rise	30	D3
Windgate Road	30	D3
Windmill Ave (Swords)	1	C2
Windmill Ave (Crumlin)	46	D1
Windmill Cres (Swords)	1	A2
*Windmill Cres (off Windmill Road Crumlin)	46	D1
Windmill Lands	1	C2
Windmill Lane	72	D4
Windmill Lane Apts	72	D4
*Windmill Lodge (Windmill Road)	46	D1
Windmill Park	22	D3
Windmill Park	46	D1
Windmill Rise	1	C2
Windmill Road	73	B4
Windmill Square	22	D3
Windmill Terrace	22	D3
Windmillhill	51	C3
*Windrush (north of Church)	64	E2
Windsor Ave	25	C4
*Windsor Court (off Stradbrook Road)	59	B1
Windsor Drive	59	B1
*Windsor Mews (off St. Margarets Ave Malahide)	03	B2
Windsor Park	59	B1
Windsor Place	75	C2
*Windsor Place (off Lanesville)	59	B1
Windsor Road	47	B1
Windsor Terrace (Ranelagh)	75	A4
Windsor Terrace (Malahide)	3	B3
Windsor Terrace (Dún Laoghaire)	50	D4
*Windsor Villas (off Philipsburgh Ave)	25	C4
Windy Arbour	47	C3
Windy Ridge	64	D4
Winetavern Street	71	A4
Wingfield	62	E1
*Winston Ville (off Charlemont Road Clontarf)	26	D4
Winter Garden Apts	72	E4
Winton Ave	47	A2
*Winton Grove (off Terenure Road North)	46	F2
Winton Road	76	D4
Wogansfield	33	A1
*Wolfe Tone Ave (off Cross Ave)	50	D4
Wolfe Tone Close	71	A3
Wolfe Tone Quay	70	D4
Wolfe Tone Square East	67	C3
Wolfe Tone Square Middle	67	C3
Wolfe Tone Square North	67	C3
Wolfe Tone Square South	67	C3
Wolfe Tone Square West	67	C3
Wolfe Tone Street	71	A3
Wolseley Street	74	F3
Wolstan Haven Ave	31	C3
Wolverton Glen	60	E2
Wood Avens	35	A3
Wood Dale Close	55	B2
Wood Dale Cres	55	B2
Wood Dale Drive	55	B2
Wood Dale Green	55	B2
Wood Dale Green	55	C2
Wood Dale Grove	55	C2
*Wood Dale Oak (Wood Dale Green)	55	C2
Wood Dale View	55	C2
Wood Lane	70	E4
Wood Quay	71	A4
Wood Street	75	A1
Woodbank Ave	23	C2
Woodbank Drive	23	C2
Woodberry (Carpenterstown)	22	D3
Woodberry (Lucan)	34	D3
Woodbine Ave	48	E2
Woodbine Close	27	A1
Woodbine Drive	27	A1

STREET NAME	PAGE	GRID REF
*Woodbine House (off Woodbine Road)	48	E2
Woodbine Park (Raheny)	27	A1
Woodbine Park (Booterstown)	48	E2
Woodbine Road (Raheny)	27	A1
Woodbine Road (Booterstown)	48	E2
*Woodbine Terrace (off Dundrum Road)	47	C4
Woodbrook Court	22	D3
Woodbrook Cres	22	D3
Woodbrook Downs	64	E4
Woodbrook Glen	67	C1
Woodbrook Hall	22	D3
Woodbrook Lawn	67	C3
Woodbrook Park (Carpenterstown)	22	D3
Woodbrook Park (Templelogue)	46	D3
Woodbrook Square	22	D3
*Woodchester House (Golden Lane)	75	A1
Woodcliff Heights	30	E2
*Woodfarm Ave	35	C2
*Woodfarm Cottages (off Lucan Road Palmerston)	35	C1
Woodfarm Drive	35	C2
Woodfield	56	D2
*Woodfield Cottages (off Sarsfield Road)	36	F3
*Woodfield Place (off Sarsfield Road)	36	F3
*Woodfield Terrace (Blank Tony)	36	F3
Woodford	58	E2
Woodford Ave	44	F1
Woodford Close	44	F1
*Woodford Court (off Leinster Road West)	46	F1
Woodford Cres	44	E1
Woodford Downs	44	F1
Woodford Drive	44	E1
Woodford Garth	44	E1
Woodford Green	44	F1
Woodford Grove	44	F1
Woodford Heights	44	F1
Woodford Hill	44	F1
Woodford Lawn	44	F1
Woodford Meadows	44	E1
Woodford Parade	44	E1
Woodford Park	44	F1
Woodford Park Road	44	E1
Woodford Rise	44	F1
Woodford Road	44	E1
Woodford Terrace	44	F1
Woodford View	44	F1
Woodford Villas	44	E1
Woodford Walk	44	F1
Woodford Way	44	F1
*Woodhaven (off Milltown Bridge Road)	47	C2
Woodhazel Close	25	A1
Woodhazel Terrace	25	A1
Woodlands (Malahide)	14	F1
Woodlands (Maynooth)	17	B3
Woodlands	22	D1
*Woodlands (off Orwell Road Rathgar)	47	A2
Woodlands Ave (Stillorgan)	48	E4
Woodlands Ave (Cornelscourt)	59	C3
Woodlands Court	15	A1
Woodlands Drive (Stillorgan)	48	E4
Woodlands Drive (Johnstown Road)	59	C3
Woodlands Park (Mount Merrion)	48	F4
Woodlands Park (Johnstown Road)	59	C3
Woodlands Road	59	C3
Woodlawn	12	F4
Woodlawn Ave	12	F4
Woodlawn Close	12	F4
Woodlawn Court	12	F4
Woodlawn Cres (Coolock Lane)	12	F4
Woodlawn Cres (Churchtown)	47	B4
Woodlawn Drive	12	F4
Woodlawn Green	12	F4
Woodlawn Grove (Coolock Lane)	12	F4
*Woodlawn Grove (off Churchtown Road Lower)	47	B4
Woodlawn Park (Coolock Lane)	12	F4
Woodlawn Park (Churchtown)	47	B4
Woodlawn Park (Tallaght)	55	C2
*Woodlawn Park (off Mountown Lower)	59	C1
Woodlawn Park Ave	55	B1

STREET NAME	PAGE	GRID REF
Woodlawn Park Drive (Firhouse)	55	B1
Woodlawn Park Grove	55	C2
Woodlawn Rise	12	F4
*Woodlawn Terrace		
(off Churchtown Road)	47	B4
Woodlawn View	12	F4
*Woodlawn Villas		
(off Mounttown Road Lower)	59	C1
Woodlawn Walk	12	F4
Woodlawn Way	12	F4
*Woodleigh		
(off Rathmines Road Upper)	47	A2
*Woodley Court		
(off Woodley Park Kilmacud)	58	D1
Woodley Park	58	D1
Woodley Road	60	D3
Woodpark (Blanchardstown)	22	F2
*Woodpark (off The Rise)	25	A3
Woodpark (Ballinteer)	57	B2
Woods End	22	F2
Woodscape	34	D3
Woodside (Leixlip)	19	C4
Woodside (Clontarf)	26	F4
Woodside (Howth)	30	D2
Woodside (Rathfarnham)	47	A3
Woodside Drive	47	A3
Woodside Grove	47	A3
Woodside Hall	57	C3
Woodside Road	57	C3
*Woodstock Court		
(off Sandford Road)	47	B1
*Woodstock Gardens		
(off Sandford Road)	47	B1
*Woodstock Hill	55	C2
Woodstock Park	56	D1
Woodstown	55	C2
Woodstown Abbey	56	D2
Woodstown Abbey	55	C2
Woodstown Ave	55	C2
Woodstown Close	55	C2
*Woodstown Court		
(Woodstown Ave)	55	C2
Woodstown Cres	55	C2
Woodstown Dale	55	C2
Woodstown Drive	55	C2
Woodstown Gardens	55	C2
Woodstown Green	55	C2
Woodstown Heath	55	C2

STREET NAME	PAGE	GRID REF
Woodstown Height	55	C2
Woodstown Hill	55	C2
*Woodstown House		
(off Stonepark Court)	46	F4
Woodstown Lane	56	D2
Woodstown Lawn	55	C2
Woodstown Meadow	55	C2
Woodstown Parade	55	C2
Woodstown Park	55	C2
Woodstown Place	55	C2
Woodstown Rise	55	C2
Woodstown Road	55	C2
Woodstown Vale	55	C2
Woodstown Walk	55	C2
Woodstown Way	55	C3
*Woodthorpe		
(off Coolnevaun Kilmacud)	58	E1
Woodtown Way	56	D3
Woodvale Ave	21	C1
Woodvale Cres	21	C1
Woodvale Drive	21	C1
Woodvale Garth	21	C1
Woodvale Green	21	C1
Woodvale Grove	21	C1
Woodvale Park	21	C1
Woodvale Way	21	C1
Woodview (Celbridge)	32	D2
Woodview (Lucan)	33	C2
*Woodview		
(on Commons Road)	64	E2
Woodview (Mount Merrion Ave)	48	F3
Woodview Close	27	A1
*Woodview Cottages		
(off Church Lane)	46	F3
Woodview Court (Dunboyne)	7	B3
*Woodview Court		
(off Ard Lorcain Stillorgan)	58	F1
Woodview Court Apts	33	C2
*Woodview Drive		
(on Boghall Road)	67	C3
Woodview Grove	22	E2
Woodview Heights (Dunboyne)	7	B3
Woodview Heights (Lucan)	33	C2
Woodview House	48	F3
Woodview Park (Castleknock)	23	A3
Woodview Park (Ardara Ave)	27	A1
Woodville Ave	34	E1
Woodville Close	34	E1

STREET NAME	PAGE	GRID REF
Woodville Court	26	E1
Woodville Green	34	E1
Woodville Grove	34	E1
*Woodville House		
(off Kilmore Road)	26	D1
Woodville Lawn	34	E1
*Woodville Road		
(off Botanic Ave)	25	A4
Woodville Walk	34	E1
Wormwood Gate		
(off Bridge Street Lower)	70	F4
Wyattville	64	D1
Wyattville Close	64	D1
Wyattville Hill	64	D1
Wyattville Link Road	63	C2
Wyattville Park	64	D1
Wyattville Road	64	D1
*Wyckham Ave		
(off Wyckham Place)	57	C1
Wyckham Grove	57	C1
Wyckham Park Road	57	B1
Wyckham Place	57	C1
*Wyckham Point Apts.		
(Gort Muire)	57	C1
Wyckham Way	57	C1
Wynberg Park	49	B4
*Wyndham Court		
(Chancery Lane)	75	A1
Wyndham Park	67	C2
*Wynnefield Park		
(off Charleville Road)	47	A1
Wynnefield Road	47	A1
Wynnsward Drive	47	C2
Wynnsward Park	47	C2
Wyteleaf Grove	14	D4
Wyvern Estate	60	E3

X

STREET NAME	PAGE	GRID REF
Xavier Ave	72	E1
*Xavier Court		
(Sherrard Street Upper)	71	B1

Y

STREET NAME	PAGE	GRID REF
Yale	48	D3
Yankee Terrace	49	A4
Yarnhall Street	71	A3
Yeates Hall	59	B4
Yeates Way	35	C4
*Yeats Court		
(off Sandymount Ave)	39	A4
Yellow Meadows Ave	44	F1
Yellow Meadows Drive	44	E1
Yellow Meadows Estate	44	E1
Yellow Meadows Grove	44	E1
Yellow Meadows Lawn	44	E1
Yellow Meadows Park	44	E1
Yellow Meadows Vale	44	E1
Yellow Road	25	C2
Yellow Walls	3	A2
Yellow Walls Road	3	A2
Yellownook Ave	59	C3
Yewlands Terrace	46	F2
York Ave	47	A1
York Road (Ringsend)	39	A2
York Road (Rathmines)	47	A1
York Road (Dún Laoghaire)	49	C4
York Street	75	B2
*York Terrace		
(off York Road Dún Laoghaire)	49	C4

Z

STREET NAME	PAGE	GRID REF
Zardoz Court		
(off Claremont Road)	76	F4
Zion Road	47	A2
Zoo Road (Phoenix Park)	69	B3
Zuma Terrace		
(on Mount Drummond Ave)	74	F4